Web-Based Learning
Design, Implementation, and Evaluation

Gayle V. Davidson-Shivers
University of South Alabama

Karen L. Rasmussen
University of West Florida

PEARSON

Merrill
Prentice Hall

Upper Saddle River, New Jersey
Columbus, Ohio

Library of Congress Cataloging in Publication Data
Davidson-Shivers, Gayle V.
    Web-based learning : design, implementation, and evaluation / by Gayle V.
Davidson-Shivers and Karen L. Rasmussen.
    p. cm.
Includes bibliographical references and index.
ISBN 0-13-081425-3
    1. Education—Computer network resources. 2. Teaching—Computer network resources.
3. Internet in education. 4. Web-based instruction. I. Rasmussen, Karen L. II. Title.
LB1044.87.D38 2006
371.33′44678—dc22
2005041538

Vice President and Executive Publisher: Jeffery W. Johnston
Executive Editor: Debra A. Stollenwerk
Assistant Development Editor: Elisa Rogers
Editorial Assistant: Mary Morrill
Production Editor: Alexandrina Benedicto Wolf
Production Coordinator: Carlisle Publishers Services
Design Coordinator: Diane C. Lorenzo
Cover Designer: Ali Mohrman
Cover Image: Corbis
Production Manager: Pamela D. Bennett
Senior Marketing Manager: Darcy Betts Prybella
Marketing Coordinator: Brian Mounts

This book was set in Times Roman by Carlisle Communications, Ltd. It was printed and bound by Courier Stoughton, Inc. The cover was printed by Courier Stoughton, Inc.

Pearson Education Ltd.
Pearson Education Singapore Pte. Ltd.
Pearson Education Canada, Ltd.
Pearson Education—Japan

Pearson Education Australia Pty. Limited
Pearson Education North Asia Ltd.
Pearson Educación de Mexico, S.A. de C.V.
Pearson Education Malaysia Pte. Ltd.

10 9 8 7 6 5 4 3 2 1
ISBN 0-13-081425-3

In loving memory of my parents, Gunnar V. and Laila M. (Kallio) Davidson, and my sister, Judith R. Bonnell, who supported my love of learning and my educational pursuits in many ways.

Gayle V. Davidson-Shivers

To my family and friends, who "hung in there" with me, and in loving memory of my father, Homer D. Rasmussen.

Karen L. Rasmussen

Preface

The Internet and the World Wide Web have changed how we obtain and share information. The rapid expansion of and access to the Web have created a powerful alternative to traditional instructional delivery. By understanding the effective ways to design and deliver Web-based instruction (WBI), instructional designers and other professionals are able to harness the Web for education.

In this text, we provide comprehensive coverage of developing online instruction for a variety of educational and training settings. We discuss research and theory in combination with practice to present a practical approach to WBI design and delivery. Our purposes in writing this book are to enable professionals to (1) gain a conceptual framework for WBI design and delivery, and (2) use the Web-Based Instructional Design (WBID) Model for designing instruction.

Our Approach

About five years ago, we began conceptualizing what we believed would be an effective and efficient (not "the best") approach to WBI design. This approach reflects our instructional design (ID) backgrounds and experiences, our teaching philosophies, and the realities that exist in Web-based environments. After much discussion and argument (the philosophical kind), we developed and implemented our plan for the book. Although we subscribe to an ID approach and philosophy, we have modified the main stages found in the generic Analyze, Design, Develop, Implement, Evaluate (ADDIE) model and in traditional ID models.

As the Web environment stabilized to some degree and learning management systems (LMS) became more commonplace, our Web-Based Instructional Design (WBID) Model continued to evolve. We expanded the ID principles to Web-based learning environments when we discuss the WBID model. The focus of the text is on the designer's preparation and execution of procedures no matter which stage is being discussed. In this book, we have incorporated ID principles based on research, theory, and practice; presented examples that exemplify those principles; and presented evidence to support our approach.

Target Audience

The primary audience for this book is instructors and students in instructional design and technology courses who are developing Web-based learning environments. It can also serve as a reference tool for ID practitioners using the Web for creating and delivering online instruction.

v

Teachers in PK–12 school systems and other higher education instructors will find the book a useful resource for developing online instruction for their own classroom situations.

Instructors or designers within unique situations (e.g., continuing education or in nontraditional educational environments such as museums, health care settings, nonprofit organizations, and so on) may also find this book useful. We hope that this book helps anyone who is trying to harness online environments for teaching and learning.

Overview

This book contains 10 chapters in 3 main parts, and 2 appendices. The first 2 chapters provide an overview and background on WBI environments. The organization of the remaining 8 chapters changes as the discussion moves through the stages of Web-Based Instructional Design. A glossary, reference list, and index follow the appendices. The book's Companion Website (http://www.prenhall.com/davidson-shivers) provides additional information not contained in the text.

Part 1 (Chapters 1–2): Introduction to Web-Based Learning, Communities, and Instructional Design

Chapter 1 presents an overview of the Web-based environment and Web-based learning communities. We define WBI and review the first foundation area of the WBID Model, distance education. This chapter presents a discussion of the advantages and disadvantages of WBI to help readers determine whether WBI is right for them and whether they are right for WBI design and delivery. This realistic approach examines aspects of the Web-based environment, its learning community, and the various roles and responsibilities involved in designing and implementing WBI.

Chapter 2 introduces the four remaining foundational bases for the WBID Model—learning theories, general systems theory, communication theories, and instructional design models—and identifies how each area relates to Web-based design. Chapter 2 also provides an overview of the WBID Model. In the last section, we briefly describe the case example, *GardenScapes,* which is incorporated into the remaining chapters, and introduce four supplementary case studies, which appear at the end of the remaining chapters.

Part 2 (Chapters 3–8): The WBID Model for Creating a Web-Based Community of Learners

Chapter 3 presents the two parts of the analysis stage: problem analysis and instructional component analysis. Problem analysis involves identifying the nature of the problem and appropriate solutions. We discuss procedures for conducting problem analysis and how to determine whether WBI is the appropriate solution for the problem. We then describe the analysis of the components found within an instructional situation for three of the four instructional components—the goal, context, and learners.

Chapter 4 completes the analysis stage of WBID by describing the last instructional component, the content. We explain the procedures for developing a learning task map based on the instructional content, and introduce the Task-Objective-Assessment Item

Blueprint (TOAB) in relation to the items found on the learning task map. The chapter ends with a discussion on finalizing the instructional goal statement and identifying implications for WBI design and delivery based on the results of the instructional component analyses.

Because evaluating instruction is critical to its success, we chose to split the evaluation stage and placed the first part of evaluation, the evaluation planning stage, after the analysis chapter. Chapter 5 provides procedures for detailed planning of formative evaluation, preliminary planning of summative evaluation, and documenting and reporting formative evaluation. The other parts of the evaluation stage, conducting formative evaluation, which appears within the concurrent design stage (in the remainder of Part 2), and conducting summative evaluation, which appears in Part 3. (Please note that in this text we use *evaluation* to refer to determining the effectiveness of the instruction program itself, and *assessment* to refer to determining how well learners in the program have achieved the learning targets.)

Another difference found in the WBID Model is its emphasis on the concurrent design stage, introduced in Chapter 2. The next three chapters discuss the steps involved in this stage. Chapter 6 explains that design and development along with formative evaluation are often accomplished in concert with each other. The emphasis in this chapter is on preplanning design activities and the essential design tasks. The TOAB tool presented in Chapter 4 is brought back with the discussion of the objectives and assessment. The chapter ends with a discussion of clustering the objectives into instructional sets.

Chapter 7 focuses on designing instructional and motivational strategies for WBI. We introduce the WBI Strategy Worksheet as a tool to identify the four main categories of instructional strategies—Orientation to Learning, Instruction on the Content, Measurement of Learning, and Summary and Close. Two motivational design theories, Keller's Attention, Relevance, Confidence, Satisfaction (ARCS) model and Wlodkowski and Ginsberg's Motivational Framework for Culturally Responsive Teaching, are discussed as ways to approach motivational strategies. This chapter ends with a discussion of other factors to consider in WBI design, including media selection.

Chapter 8 is focused on the Web interface, and on message and visual design. Flowcharting and storyboarding provide examples of the first WBI prototypes. Creating Web pages and websites moves the WBI design plans into development activities, and we discuss some of the technical issues involved. This chapter ends with a discussion of using the first implementation as a continuation of WBI prototype development and formative evaluation.

Part 3 (Chapters 9–10): Implementation and Evaluation of Web-Based Instruction

Somewhat unique to the WBID Model is the discussion of implementation. Chapter 9 presents a discussion of two major aspects of implementation: facilitation and management. Although intertwined, these two aspects are presented as separate entities for clarity. *Facilitation* relates to online teaching and learning processes from implementation preplanning to early startup events to developing a sense of community within the learning environment. We discuss *management* in terms of administrative infrastructure operations and systems maintenance and as it relates to the management roles of various participants.

Chapter 10 presents the final details of planning and conducting summative evaluation and research. This chapter also provides information on reporting and displaying the results of this type of evaluation.

Pedagogical Features

In this book, several features help readers learn about and apply the WBID model. They include providing advance organizers, chunking instructional content, presenting a main example, and discussion questions and additional case studies. Two appendices and the text's Companion Website enhance the text.

Advance Organizers

All chapters begin with an advance organizer in the form of a chapter overview, followed by the chapter's objectives, sequenced in order of discussion. A graphic organizer at the beginning of Chapters 3 through 10 presents the WBID Model stage discussed in that chapter.

Chunking the Instructional Content

Each chapter is presented in appropriately sized "chunks" that are followed by an opportunity for the reader to apply the content through "On Your Own" activities. The activities are designed around the premise that each reader will undertake a course-long WBI project of his or her own choosing under the instructor's direction. This process is iterative until all of the chapter content has been presented and practiced and the project is complete. For example, in Chapter 1, we provide guidelines on how to select an appropriate project in the "On Your Own" following the section, "Is WBI Right for You? Advantages and Disadvantages of WBI" (p. 15). Instructors are, of course, at liberty to specify their own guidelines for student projects. The "On Your Own" activities can be used by instructors as assignments or to help guide students through the WBID Model.

In Chapters 3 through 10, the case example, *GardenScapes,* appears between the chunked information and the practice exercises to further illustrate the progression in WBI design. All chapters end with a brief summary followed by additional opportunities for extending the discussion and practice.

Case Example: *GardenScapes*

One of the main features of the text is the case example, *GardenScapes,* introduced in Chapter 2. It is used to expand the principles and procedures discussed. This case example, which runs throughout the book, details a WBI project on developing a garden planning course for adults in a continuing education setting within a two-year college. The instructor (who does not have an ID background) works with an ID intern (a master's student) in a design team approach to design, implement, and evaluate the WBI.

We deliberately chose not to create or use an example from traditional ID settings for several reasons. First, most ID students will choose their course project from one of these settings. We did not want to add undue emphasis on one setting over another and consequently leveled the playing field, so to speak, by using a nontraditional setting. Second, we believe that the content of garden planning is interesting and that most readers will have a basic understanding of the general concepts. Third, using a nontraditional scenario to exemplify WBID means that other professionals who do not have an ID background will be able to use our textbook (and the ID principles within) for their own WBI projects. Finally, and probably most important, we used this novel situation to discuss and debate the WBID Model's processes as we wrote; we were able to think and rethink the ID principles to see what worked and what didn't. In other words, it helped us to think creatively as we built the course example, developed the WBID Model, and wrote this text.

Expanding Your Expertise: End-of-Chapter Discussion Questions

Discussion questions at the end of each chapter relate to the concepts and procedures presented. The questions go beyond recall of the information by asking the reader to delve into trends and issues related to WBI design and delivery. Instructors may use them as discussion starters or as additional course assignments; students may use them as study guides for a comprehensive understanding of WBI design.

Extending Your Skills: Additional Case Studies

This section, which appears at the end of Chapters 2 through 10, provides additional case studies from four different workplace settings—K–12 education, business and industry, military, and higher education. By reading closely the *GardenScapes* case example and following these four case studies from one chapter to the next, the instructor and students can examine and discuss how WBI design may vary from one setting to another. In developing these cases, we varied them by the instructional purposes, audience, context, and of course, content. They also vary by type of online instruction (i.e., Web-based, Web-supported, and Web-enhanced). These cases are intentionally not developed in detail to allow instructors and students to work through or discuss as WBI projects. The lack of details allow readers to come up with their own ideas or adapt the case to their own situation.

Appendices

The Appendices contain additional information that readers may need to complete their WBI projects. Appendix A, "Methods and Tools for Gathering Data and Information," presents information on various ways to conduct an analysis or evaluation. Appendix B, "Further Design Considerations for WBI," contains additional information related to designing and implementing WBI. They are linked to relevant locations in the chapters by the following icon and instructional line:

See Appendix A [or B] for additional information.

Companion Website

Information not found in the text is included in the accompanying website. For instance, complete design documentation appears for the *GardenScapes* case example. We include links to other Web resources that pertain to the contents of the text, as well as a bibliography of references used to develop the case example and case studies. We link the Companion Website to its relevant text locations by the following icon and instructional line:

See this textbook's Companion Website at http://www.prenhall.com/davidson-shivers for additional information, templates, or examples.

Acknowledgments

Many people have helped us along the way in writing this book; we certainly could not have written it without them.

We would like to thank Debra Stollenwerk, executive editor at Merrill/Prentice Hall, for her invaluable guidance and encouragement with this endeavor. We appreciate Developmental Editor Elisa Rogers and Production Editor Alex Wolf as well as the editorial staff at Merrill/Prentice Hall for their skills and efforts in producing this book. We also would like to thank Robert L. Marcum, the copyeditor, for his careful shaping of our text material, and thank, too, Becky Barnhart and Carlisle Publishers Services. This work would not have been possible without their support.

We would also like to thank the reviewers for their conscientious reviews, insightful advice, and ideas that improved the drafts to the final product: J. Michael Blocher, Northern Arizona University; Vance A. Durrington, Mississippi State University; Scott Fredrickson, University of Nebraska, Kearney; Janette Hill, University of Georgia; Lorana A. Jinkerson, Northern Michigan University; S. Kim MacGregor, Louisiana State University; Martha Mann, Arizona State University; Sara McNeil, University of Houston; Kay Persichitte, University of Northern Colorado; and David VanEsselstyn, Columbia.

Thanks, too, to George Houtman for supplying many of the garden photographs we used for the website. Special thanks go to Mike Barrington, Holly Ellis, Chotika Kalyanamitra, Teresa Weldy, and other ID graduate students who helped us develop and review the case studies. We appreciate the students in our WBI design courses for their willingness to use the working drafts. They, along with other students, gave us valuable feedback and encouraging words.

Finally, we would like to thank our families and friends. For me, Gayle Davidson-Shivers, I would like to thank my family, friends, and colleagues across the country who gave us advice and support. In particular, I extend my heartfelt gratitude to my husband, Joe, for his loving friendship and support. I would like to thank and acknowledge my coauthor, for her friendship and her invaluable contributions to this major undertaking.

For me, Karen Rasmussen, I would like to thank my family, friends, students, and colleagues, especially Dorothy, Nancy, Megan, John, Donna, Sharon, Pam, Russell, and Dave, who collaboratively have forgiven my preoccupations and permitted me the luxury of time to focus on the ultimate goal of completion. They have lived through every page of this textbook—and we are all grateful that it is, at last, completed. Since we have begun this task, many events have taken place that could have easily pulled us off track. I, too, thank my coauthor, who worked tirelessly on this project and kept us focused. This journey has been made all the easier with her friendship and support.

Gayle V. Davidson-Shivers

Karen L. Rasmussen

About the Authors

Gayle V. Davidson-Shivers   Gayle Davidson-Shivers is a full professor in the Instructional Design and Development program at the University of South Alabama. Being the first in her program to teach an online course, she continues to design and teach both online and on-campus courses. She currently teaches graduate courses on designing online instruction, psychology of learning, instructional models, and trends and issues of the IDT field. She has a master's degree and a doctorate in Curricular and Instructional Systems from the University of Minnesota; her undergraduate degree was in education from Western Oregon University.

As part of her faculty work, she conducts research, presents, and publishes in the areas of online instruction and learning, faculty development, and instructional and learning strategies in relation to various delivery systems. Currently, her research focuses on gender and communication patterns in online discussions. She serves on review boards of several major journals. Some of her service work includes past president of the SIG-Instructional Technology of AERA, past board member of the AECT Research and Theory Division, and faculty advisor to the IDD Student Group.

She has worked as an instructional systems specialist for a major lending institution and has taught in the public schools in both Oregon and Minnesota. She conducts workshops on teaching and learning styles, advising, teaching/learning and assessment tools, among other topics. She consults with businesses, industry, governmental agencies, and schools on a regular basis.

Karen L. Rasmussen   Karen Rasmussen is an associate professor and the chair of the Division of Engineering and Computer Technology and the Department of Instructional and Performance Technology at the University of West Florida. She teaches in the Division of Graduate Studies, Department of Instructional and Performance Technology. She has a doctorate in Instructional Design and Development from the University of South Alabama.

Dr. Rasmussen has worked with teachers in the area of accountability and reform for over 10 years. She has been involved with helping teachers plan for integrating standards into their classrooms, with a particular interest in integrating technology into the classroom. Recently she has been working to create a standards-based science curriculum as part of the QuickScience project.

She has worked extensively in the area of teacher professional development, delivering a variety of workshops, and designing and developing online professional development workshops: *The Making of a Technology-Rich Classroom; Reading in the Content Areas; Closing the Loop; Charting the Course for Inclusive Education;* and *Putting the Pieces Together.*

Dr. Rasmussen's research interests focus on the integration of emerging technologies that support learners through a variety of methodologies, including online virtual expeditions and field trips and online professional development. She has written in the areas of mentoring, online program development, and online learning. She was codeveloper of UWF's first online program, a master's degree in Instructional Technology. She works with many groups, including teachers, military trainers, instructional designers, and business and industry professionals.

Brief Contents

Contents

Chapter 2
Foundations of Web-Based Instructional Design   38

Chapter 4
Analysis: Considering Instructional Content for Web-Based Instruction   105

Chapter 5
Planning the Evaluation of Web-Based Instruction   127

Chapter 6
Concurrent Design: WBI Preplanning and Design Tasks   169

Chapter 8
Concurrent Design: Putting Design Plans into Development Action 244

Appendix B: Further Design Considerations for WBI   361

Glossary   378

References   383

Index   398

Overview of Web-Based Instruction, Web-Based Learning Environments, and Web-Based Learning Communities

Web-based instruction (WBI) is used by a variety of organizations, including PK–12 schools, business and industry, military, and higher education, to provide learners with educational and training opportunities. Web-based learning environments are comprised of individuals, technology, instruction, and organizational support structures. There is a continuum of these types of learning communities. The Web-based learning community can be comprised of independent instruction, in which learners complete the instruction with no interaction with an instructor or with other learners. At the other end of the continuum, learners and instructors form learning environments that are highly interactive and participatory, with a strong sense of community.

This chapter begins with a description of current uses of the Internet and the World Wide Web. Web-based instruction and distance education are defined, followed by a brief overview of distance education and the advantages and disadvantages of WBI. A description of three types of online instruction and a discussion on the current, emerging, and merging technologies used in WBI follows. We then discuss the framework for a Web-based learning environment and learning community, after which we explore stakeholder roles, responsibilities, and challenges.

Objectives

At the end of this chapter, you should be able to do the following:

- Define *Web-based instruction.*
- Define *distance education.*
- Explain how distance education is fundamental to WBI.
- Discuss advantages and disadvantages of WBI.
- Define three types of online instruction.
- Describe technological tools used in WBI.
- Describe Web-based environments and learning communities.
- Describe the roles, responsibilities, and challenges of the stakeholders involved in WBI.

Introduction

There are literally millions of websites on the Internet and World Wide Web that provide a wealth of information. One billion people use the Internet and Web, with the global market estimated at $300 billion. It is estimated that by 2006, 60 percent of all U.S. households will have broadband access to the Internet and Web and that the fastest-growing segment using broadband is the 50+ age group (Nix, 2003). Coincidentally, it is estimated that average adults will spend about two years of their life online (Dempsey, 2002), with most of the time being spent communicating through electronic mail (email) and accessing information and resources for news, sports, weather, entertainment, and so on.

Many of these types of resources are contained in portals for easy access. According to the website Whatis?com (2005), a **portal** (also called a *gateway*) is a specialized website "that is or proposes to be a major starting site for users when they get connected to the Web or that users tend to visit as an anchor site. There are general portals and specialized or niche portals. . . . Typical services offered by portal sites include a directory of Web sites, a facility to search for other sites, news, weather information, e-mail, stock quotes, phone and map information, and sometimes a community forum." Figure 1.1 shows a portal that provides a variety of links related to weather.

Other portals are directed toward children and adolescents. The portal displayed in Figure 1.2 was created by the Commonwealth of Virginia. Of course, parental guidance or adult supervision is advisable when children and young adults are allowed to "surf the Net" for information.

Additionally, the **Internet** and the **World Wide Web (WWW)** (referred to as simply the **Web** in this text) are used by vendors to market merchandise and services and by private individuals to buy and sell items. The U.S. Department of Commerce (2003) reports that e-commerce sales for the first quarter of 2001 comprised 1.5 percent of total sales and increased approximately 25 percent from the first quarter of 2000. For instance,

Figure 1.1 An example of a portal: Coast Weather Research Center (http://www.southalabama.edu/cwrc/stfbill.html). Reprinted by permission.

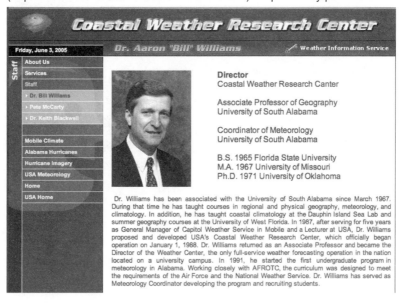

Figure 1.2 An example of a portal: Commonwealth of Virginia Kids Commonwealth (http://www.kidscommonwealth.virginia.gov/home). Reprinted by permission.

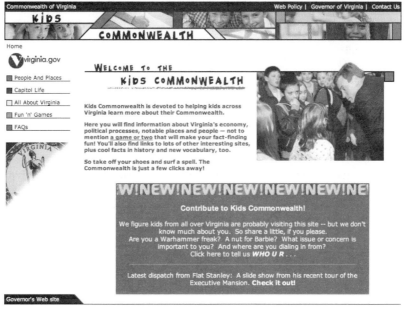

Figure 1.3   eBay (http://www.ebay.com). These materials have been reproduced by permission of eBay Inc. Copyright © eBay Inc. All Rights Reserved.

eBay (Figure 1.3) had more than 1.4 billion listings on its auction pages in 2003, and its members conducted $34.2 billion in annualized gross merchandise sales (eBay Inc., 2005). In the second quarter of 2003, Amazon.com posted shipping revenues of $94 million, increasing 20 percent from the previous year's fourth-quarter report (Amazon.com, 2004).

Another way that commercial entities share information is by integrating portal structures into their websites. An example is the Creativity Portal (Figure 1.4). These types of portals combine products and free information. Many websites also contain articles and ways to communicate with other interested parties.

Figure 1.4   Creativity Portal (http://www.creativity-portal.com/). These materials have been reproduced by permission of © 2004 Chris Dunmire, Creativity Portal (www.creativity-portal.com).

This icon indicates that the textbook's Companion Website contains additional information on this topic. See the website (http://www.prenhall.com/davidson-shivers) for links to these and other examples of portals.

Education and Training Delivered on the Web

Since the early 1990s, there has been a steady rise in the use of the Web by the military, business and industry, and educational institutions for training and education. The U.S. military has intensified efforts to provide Web-based training for worldwide personnel (Andrews, Moses, & Duke, 2002; Barrington & Kimani, 2003; OTT/HPC Spider, 2003). The U.S. Navy is building an online portal, *Navy Knowledge Online* (NKO), that makes courses and references available to sailors and officers to enhance individual growth and development and to provide direction for their military careers (Flynn, 2003; Harvard Business School, 2003). Other initiatives, such as eArmyU and Navy College, provide military personnel with opportunities for expanding their expertise through distance learning via the Web (U.S. Army, 2003; U.S. Navy, 2003) and other delivery systems (U.S. Coast Guard Institute, 2003).

With the globalization of markets, business and industry are turning to the Web to customize their training for specific cultures and nationalities (Parks, 2001; Richey & Morrison, 2002). Schank (2002) reports that businesses are eager to use the Web for teaching and learning and that it may be used as a lure for attracting high-performing talent; for example, the A. G. Edwards company trains newly hired financial consultants by having them attend Web-based training rather than their traditional classroom seminars. Using the Web, new brokers train on an "as needed" basis while continuing their work with clients. This type of Web training is an attractive incentive for these new hires in their competitive workplace.

Higher education has seen the same phenomenal increase in the use of the Web (Davidson-Shivers, 2002). Dempsey (2002) indicates that the number of Web-based courses in the year 2000 was about 18,000; only a few hundred existed six years prior. The U.S. Department of Education (cited in Dempsey, 2002) reported the market for postsecondary Web-based learning was $1.2 billion in 2001 and was expected to increase to $11.4 billion by 2003.

Universities across the United States and in other nations are creating virtual campuses and programs for the students in hopes of attracting new students to their campuses in a declining student market base (Barker, 1999; Davidson-Shivers, 2002; University of Illinois, n.d.). Yet, Bourdeau and Bates (1997) claim that these Web-based programs tend to attract participants from the local area rather than attracting new students at a distance.

See this textbook's Companion Website (http://www.prenhall.com/davidson-shivers) for other examples of education and training websites.

ON YOUR OWN

How do you use the Web? Estimate the amount of time spent on those activities. Consider how your online activities have influenced your personal or professional life and mark the accompanying chart accordingly.

Use of the Web	Check Those That Apply	Time Spent on Activity
Email		
Gather Information on		
News/Current events		
Sports		
Weather		
Entertainment, music, etc.		
Finances, stocks, etc.		
Travel		
Home & garden		
Hobbies		
Other		
Buying or Selling		
Homes		
Vehicles, boats, etc.		
Antiques and collectibles		
Furniture		
Clothing		
Other		
Professional Development		
Education or training		
Job searches		
Career opportunities		
Web workshops		
Organizations		
Other		
Work-related activities		
Teaching		
Research		
Library services		
Net conferencing		
Other		
Other		

See this textbook's Companion Website (http://www.prenhall.com/davidson-shivers) for a printable version of this On Your Own activity.

Defining Web-Based Instruction

The terms *e-learning* (electronic learning) and *online learning* have been used synonymously with *Web-based instruction (WBI)*. The term *e-learning* is typically found in business and industry training literature (Schank, 2002; Stockley, 2003; Wagner, 2001) or in international education and training information (Joint Information Systems Committee [JISC], 2003). In international settings, a clear distinction is made between e-learning and WBI, where **e-learning** refers to the use of any electronic applications and processes for instruction, including CBT (computer-based training), WBI, CDs (compact discs), and so on, whereas *WBI* is defined as instruction via the Internet, Intranet, and Web only (JISC; Stockley; Department for Education and Skills, 2002). In the United States, the concepts of WBI and **online learning** (or online instruction) are situations where "learners are at a distance from the instructor but all are connected via the Internet and Web" (Center for Technology in Education at Johns Hopkins University [CTE], 2003, n.p.). For purposes of this discussion, *WBI* and *online learning* (or *instruction*) will be considered synonymous. Following the international convention, *e-learning* will encompass a variety of electronic applications, including WBI, CBT, and other multimedia that can be distributed via the Web or on CD or DVD.

Distance education and WBI are sometimes thought to be the same (CTE, 2003; Stockley, 2003). Simonson, Smaldino, Albright, and Zvacek (2000) define *distance education* as "institution-based, formal education where the learning group is separated geographically, and where interactive telecommunication systems are used to connect learners, resources, and instructors" (p. 7). By contrast, CTE refers to distance education as "quite simply . . . any type of instruction wherein students are enrolled at a distance from the faculty" (n.p.), and WBI is one type of distance education. Although both CTE and Simonson et al. explain that WBI is a form of distance education, CTE's definition tends to be very general whereas Simonson et al. emphasize the use of telecommunications and distance in terms of different geographic locations.

When describing a distance environment, the factor of time may be used as well. **Distance education** can, then, be defined as instruction that exists where instructors and learners are separated by time and/or location (Davidson-Shivers & Rasmussen, 1999). Figure 1.5 provides a schematic for time and location factors as distance education situations are identified.

The most evident setting of distance education occurs when both time and location are different. An example would be WBI with student and instructor residing in different parts of the country and interacting via email at times convenient for each. Distance education also occurs when interaction happens at the same time (**synchronous**), but at different locations, such as a Web-based course using a chat room with an instructor at one site and learners at others. A third type of distance education occurs when instruction is offered at different times (**asynchronous**). In asynchronous instruction, learners and instructors are not online at the same time.

Figure 1.5   Distance education occurs when there is a difference in either time or location or both.

		LOCATION	
		Same	**Different**
T I M E	**Same**	Not Distance Education	Distance Education
	Different	Distance Education	Distance Education

Distinctions Between Distance Education and Distributed Education

One term often interchanged with distance education is that of **distributed learning.** Definitions of distance education and distributed learning (or education) are often confused with each other (Bowman, 1999; Hawkins, 1999; Oblinger, Barone, & Hawkins, 2001; Teaching and Learning in an Information Environment [TLITE], 2004). There is no standard definition for either term, although several attempts in recent years have been made to develop such a definition. For instance, the CSU Center for Distributed Learning (2004) states that "distributed learning means using a wide range of computing and communication technology to provide learning opportunities beyond time and place constraints of traditional classrooms" (n.p.). TLITE discusses distributed learning concepts in a similar vein. Yet, when emphasis is placed on the concept of participants interacting at differing times and places, the two terms can be interchanged. Likewise, emphasis on using technology adds to the confusion and helps blur definitional lines.

Nevertheless, Oblinger et al. (2001), among others, maintain that distributed learning (or education) is the broader, overarching term of the two, and that distance education and online learning are subsets of it. The authors agree that the commonalities between distance and distributed learning include the use of technology and participant interactivity. However, they maintain that the distinction is that "distance learning refers to individuals separated by time or place [whereas] distributed learning can take place on or off campus" (p. 1). Similarly, Bowman (1999) suggests that the distributed learning models can be used in combination with traditional ones on campus classrooms, in distance learning courses, or they can be used for a totally virtual classroom (i.e., online), which again suggests that participants need not be distanced by time and/or location.

Whether the terms *distance* and *distributed* are distinct from each other or refer to the same thing will not be resolved within this discussion nor is it a focus of this textbook. Whether distributed or distance learning is the broader, overarching term is not the point of this discussion as well. However, it is important to note that there are no common, standard definitions of the terms. Consequently, we have used our own definitions based on our literature search and other considerations. In sidestepping these issues, we will use *distance education* as the overarching term; it then serves as one of the foundational areas for WBI.

Overview of Distance Education

The expansion of distance education in recent years has been, at least in part, due to the rapid growth of the Internet and increased availability of WBI. Whenever there is rapid increase in the use of an innovation, the past may become lost or seen as irrelevant (Pittman & Moore, cited in Bunker, 2003). To use instructional design processes for effective WBI development, there needs to be a solid understanding of this form of design's historical roots (Richey, 1986; Smith & Ragan, 2005). Bunker would concur: "Looking historically at global distance education will give us an appreciation of the present and a perspective on the future" (p. 63).

Distance Education Delivery Systems

One way to provide a historical overview of distance education is by examining its delivery systems. A **delivery system** (sometimes known as the *delivery medium*) is the means by which instruction is brought to and from learners (Figure 1.6). Peters (2003) uses the term *carrier media* to indicate how distance education is delivered.

Correspondence Courses.   One of the earliest forms of distance education, the correspondence course, has been available to learners since the 1800s, when postal services and railways were used for course delivery (Cyrs, 1997; Dede, 1990; Willis, 1994). The early print-based format included text and, sometimes, illustrations. Today, these packaged courses contain audio and video (e.g., DVDs, CDs, and CBT) as well as print materials (Peters, 2003; Pittman, 2003; Verduin, 1991). In addition, the most recent versions integrate electronic technologies such as online bulletin boards and email to supplement the other media used (Correspondence Courses and Schools, 2003). Web searches for "correspondence schools" find institutions such as the University of Phoenix, Kaplan, Walden, Jacksonville University, St. Leo University, and American College of Computer and Information Sciences.

Broadcast Systems.   Broadcast systems for distance education began with the use of radio during the 1920s and continued with television in the 1930s. Early radio offerings enabled learners to hear lessons and course requirements that they then responded to through mail systems. A 1952 decision by the Federal Communications Commission established hundreds of TV channels for education. This decision, along with the advent of satellite technology in the 1960s, facilitated the rapid development and use of instructional television (Reiser, 2002; Simonson et al., 2000). With the emergence of television, video merged with audio to deliver instruction over the airwaves. Yet, supplemental materials and learner work continued to be delivered through postal services. Although television quickly caused

Figure 1.6   Types of distance education systems.

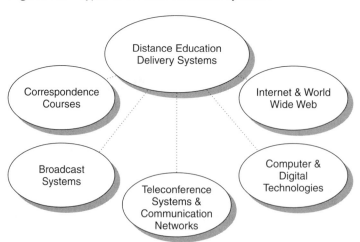

radio to fade as an educational tool in the United States, radio is still used as a mainstay for communication and education in remote regions of the world. A variety of distance education programs continue to be available through broadcast systems. For example, networks affiliated with Cable in the Classroom, such as the Discovery Channel and the History Channel, offer hundreds of hours of commercial-free programming per month, providing teachers and learners with extensive resources (Cable in the Classroom [CIC], 2002).

Teleconferencing Systems and Communication Networks. Teleconferencing systems range from simple telephone-to-telephone audio systems to desktop video conferencing between two (or more) computers to complex comprehensive interactive environments using compressed video (Darbyshire, 2000; Hill & Chidambaram, 2000). Teleconferencing systems permit learners to participate in synchronous instructional activities. Community college, university, business, and military networks use teleconferencing systems to link groups together to save travel and personnel costs. In a university network, branch campuses may be linked so that classes and meetings can be transmitted from one campus to another. Businesses can connect their national and international corporate offices through telecommunication networks. Teleconferencing is used in Prekindergarten through 12th grade (PK–12) schools as well: In New Zealand, up to 200 schools are connected through a telecommunications network to share curriculum and facilitate interaction among schools (Ministry of Education, 2003).

Computers and Digital Technologies. Although computers came into existence during the 1940s, it wasn't until the 1980s that computers became commonplace tools for educators (Davidson, 1992; Reiser, 2002). Reiser indicates that the use of computers, even as late as the mid 1990s, was not widespread within schools nor was it a major part of distance education for universities in the United States. By contrast, business and industry organizations and the military used computers extensively for training; training developed on CDs, disks, and so on was then distributed via postal services.

With advances in computer-mediated communications and digital technologies, a major change in distance education occurred (Reiser, 2002; Simonson et al., 2000). The development of interconnected networks permitted synchronous interaction among participants in distance educational experiences.

Interconnected networks include **local area networks (LANs)** and **wide area networks (WANs).** LANs are usually found in a single organization and serve as an internetworking communication system, whereas WANs connect computers and smaller networks into a large-scale communication network typically within a state, geographical region, or country (Smaldino, Russell, Heinich, & Molenda, 2005; Ryder & Hughes, 1998). For example, the State of Florida uses the Florida Information Resource Network (FIRN) to link schools together through a series of site-based LANs (Florida Information Resource Network [FIRN], 2003). Individual PK–12 school districts, community colleges, and universities access FIRN to obtain educational materials and communicate with each other. Such advances in technology led the way to using the Internet and the World Wide Web for distance education.

Internet and World Wide Web. The Internet and the Web have become major forms of delivery for distance education since the early 1990s. The U.S. Department of Defense

(DOD) in 1969 created the Internet to link four institutions under DOD contract for research purposes: the University of California at Los Angeles, SRI (in Stanford University), the University of California at Santa Barbara, and the University of Utah. These early uses of the Internet required knowledge of UNIX, a complex operating system (Ryder & Hughes, 1998). Later, the Internet was used to link military sites and other universities. The Internet became more widely available in the early 1980s with the system known as *Gopher.* *Gopher,* developed at the University of Minnesota, enabled users to locate information on the Internet in a text-based format.

Today, the Web is not generally thought of as being a separate entity from the Internet, but it is in actuality a subset of the Internet. While the Internet allows text-based material to be transmitted, the Web allows a graphical environment to be displayed (Crumlish, 1998; Smaldino et al., 2005). The Web allows users to find information, communicate, and use software. However, these capabilities didn't happen without the aid of search engines, portals, and browsers.

Search Engines, Portals, and Web Browsers. Initially, it was very difficult to find information or resources on the Internet using text-based search engines such as *Gopher,* *Archie,* and *Veronica.* Users of these early search engines accessed information with *BITNET* (*B*ecause *I*t's *T*ime *NET*work) to communicate through electronic mail and text-based document transfer (Simonson et al., 2000).

Search engines are software programs that assist users in connecting to databases of Web addresses (uniform resource locators, or URLs) and that help users locate information on the Web and the Internet. As Crumlish (1998) explains, these databases are "compiled by computer programs (called webcrawlers, spiders, or robots) that explore the Web, catalog the pages found, and send references back to the main database" (pp. 92–93). Search engines, therefore, can in turn provide large numbers of pages (called *hits*) in response to a single search in both text and graphical formats.

As noted previously, *portals* are specialized websites that organize information and resources for easy user access. They are designed to provide access to different Web services much the same as search engines do, but provide a wealth of other services, including expanded search capabilities (Smaldino et al., 2005).

To use any search engine or portal, an individual must have access to the Web. The most common form of entry, a **browser** (or **Web browser**), must be installed on the user's computer and the computer connected to the Internet. Currently, the most popular browsers are Microsoft *Internet Explorer,* Netscape *Navigator* (Crumlish, 1998), and Apple *Safari.* Other browsers include *Amaya, Internet in a Box, Emissary, Lynx* [text browser], *OmniWeb, Firefox, Mosaic, Mozilla, NeoPlanet, Opera, I-View, I-Comm, UdiWWW,* and *SlipKnot* (Jupitermedia Corp., 2003; Opera Software, 2003; Ryder & Hughes, 1998; Zillman, 2003).

Browsers, search engines, and portals have permitted easy acceptance and widespread integration of the Web into our daily lives for resources and services. Without them, it would be difficult to consider the Web as a delivery system for distance education.

See this textbook's Companion Website (http://www.prenhall.com/davidson-shivers) for links to other examples of delivery systems.

Growth of Web Delivery for Distance Education

The tremendous growth in the use of the Web for distance education delivery has been partly fueled by the availability of technology in homes, schools, work, and public libraries. This increased interest also may be due to ever-improving technology that allows computer users, even those with low technical skills, to easily access Web-based learning environments (Wagner, 2001). Relatively affordable technologies, low-cost connections to networks, and easily used software applications and utilities have helped a large percentage of the U.S. population to access the Internet and Web; these individuals have the potential to become online learners. Wagner adds that with the growing use of learning objects and knowledge management for workplace performance improvement, Web-based instruction provides employees with individualized, personalized learning when compared to traditional classroom settings.

This revolution of technology, in combination with a revolution of information, has forced workers of the twenty-first century to continue their own development and learning to become part of the global economy (Secretary's Commission on Achieving Necessary Skills [SCANS], 1999). Although formal educational institutions (i.e., PK–12 schools, community and technical colleges, and universities) prepare individuals to enter the workforce, they do not provide all the knowledge individuals require to maintain their skills throughout their entire careers or occupations. It is estimated that individuals change their careers three times over a lifetime (American Association of Retired Persons [AARP], 2002; Robinson, 2000). Web-based instruction offers individuals the flexibility of pursuing training while they continue in their day-to-day activities. From this perspective, graduation is not an end of schooling, but rather the beginning of the next stage in an individual's lifelong learning.

ON YOUR OWN

How would you define Web-based instruction and distance education? What factors influence or extend your definitions of these terms? Are there other terms that could be interchanged for WBI?

Have you participated in distance education courses other than online learning? If so, describe the situation and the type of delivery used. Of the various delivery types of distance education, do you prefer one to the other(s)? Why?

Web delivery has experienced phenomenal growth in a short period of time. Are there other explanations than the ones described in this textbook for its growth? If so, what are they? How has this growth influenced your use of the Web?

Is WBI Right for You? Advantages and Disadvantages of WBI

Web-based instruction (WBI) is not appropriate for everyone, every content area, or every situation. Detailing the advantages and disadvantages of WBI helps to focus attention on being sure that an intervention using WBI is an appropriate one for the stated problem. Table 1.1 outlines the advantages and disadvantages of WBI.

Table 1.1 Advantages and Disadvantages of WBI

Advantages	Disadvantages

For Institutions or Organizations:
• Potential to reach large numbers of learners
• Potential for cost efficiency (over life-span of the WBI)
• Effectiveness
• Repurposing current instruction for Web delivery
	For Institutions or Organizations:
	• Initial costs
	  • Development
	  • Infrastructure
	• Maintenance costs
	• Learner support systems
	• Instructor support systems

For Instructors: • Convenience • Flexibility • Potential to develop professional relationships with students in different locations, cultures, etc.	For Instructors: • Overload of students • Lack of technical expertise • Lack of instructional strategies for WBI • Loss of intellectual property rights • Time-intensive teaching

For Learners:
• Convenience
• Flexibility
• One on one with instructor
• Access: Anywhere, anytime
• Potential for continued development of knowledge, skills, and abilities
• Type of feedback received
	For Learners:
	• Isolation
	• Technology roadblocks
	  • Challenges or problems
	  • Weak resources
	  • Illiteracy
	• Computer anxiety
	• Confusion about topics and assignments

Source: Table data are from Alagumalai, Toh, & Wong (2000), Berge, Collins, & Fitzsimmons (2001), Brooks (1997), Collins & Berge (1996), Davidson-Shivers (2002), Hawkridge (2002), Khan (1997), Kubin (2002), Reddick & King (1996), Schank (2002), University of Illinois (n.d.).

Advantages: What's the Attraction to WBI?

Hawkridge (2002) and Schank (2002) suggest that using Web-based delivery of instruction is attractive because of the belief that it can deliver training at a faster and cheaper rate than other delivery forms. Schank states that the savings occur "not through putting a training manual on a web page, but by creating training once and then continually delivering" (p. xv). However, Schank later suggests that another feature of Web-based learning is that it is easy to update. The idea of packaging a course that does not change is not appropriate in most situations, online or face to face; instead, most courses need updating to remain current with the content.

An equally strong incentive for universities and PK–12 schools to use Web delivery is the rising cost of on-campus education. Hawkridge (2002) reports that "the cost for 3,500 U.S. colleges to serve 14 million students is at an annual rate of $175 billion" (p. 270) and is steadily rising. He further notes that "even though there is a lower cost per an elementary or a secondary level student, there is a similar rising expenditure to that of higher education" (p. 270). Institutional advantages focus on quality and cost effectiveness and efficient use of institutional resources. Instructor advantages are related to flexibility and convenience in teaching and the potential to work with students across campus and across the world. Specific advantages for learners include flexibility, convenience, and easy access to instruction.

An additional incentive for using the Web for educational and training purposes may be the large number of individuals who want to expand their professional opportunities or career options. WBI can be an effective vehicle for such learning and continued development of knowledge, skills, and abilities (Hall, Watkins, & Ercal, 2000). Furthermore, WBI offers these individuals and others the flexibility of pursuing training while they continue other day-to-day activities.

Disadvantages: What's Not So Great About WBI?

There have been hundreds of uses of WBI, but not all implementations have been successful, nor even seen as desirable. Although online instruction has been championed as being both more cost effective and cheaper than on-campus instruction, it may not be true. A report by the University of Illinois (n.d.) states that "the scenario of hundreds or thousands of students enrolling in a well developed, essentially instructor-free online course does not appear realistic" (secs. 3, 5). Institutional or organizational up-front costs for creating an infrastructure for developing and delivering WBI may be incurred. In addition, there are costs for maintaining and upgrading Web-based courses. For instance, Western Governors University spent millions of dollars and years of preparation in its online operation, which netted only limited student enrollment when it was implemented (Nobles, 1999, cited in University of Illinois, n.d.).

Administrators may not find the means to motivate instructors to teach online. Nobles in 1999 (cited in University of Illinois, n.d.) reported that fewer than 30 percent of the UCLA faculty complied with a mandate for all arts and science courses to have websites. He further reported that 900 University of Washington faculty opposed movement to digital initiatives. While some instructors may have the desire to embrace a digital presence, current incentive systems within most university settings do not reward faculty members for developing instruction or innovative teaching methods (Davidson-Shivers, 2002). General movement toward using the Web will no doubt increase as issues of training and intellectual property are addressed and resolved.

Instructors may not have the necessary skills (instructional or technical) to teach online, let alone develop instruction (Davidson-Shivers, 2002). The University of Illinois (n.d.) indicates that although new ways of teaching may be introduced, effective and high-quality experiences may not be had. An organization must commit institutional resources for support systems for both instructors and learners, which again may add to already overextended budgets and resources.

Instructor disadvantages relate to online workload and intellectual property issues. Kubin (2002) finds that the time demand of teaching an online course is two or three times that of teaching a face-to-face class. Similarly, the University of Illinois (n.d.) reports that successful online courses are those consisting of low learner–instructor ratios, another indication that WBI may not be an inexpensive or expedient way to deliver instruction to large groups of students. Additionally, without clear policy, the issue of faculty members retaining their intellectual property rights in online materials could also be in question. According to the University of Illinois (n.d.),

> in-depth involvement of an expert professor is needed in order to ensure high quality of online teaching. The issue of course ownership is directly related to this principle: the highest quality of online materials is usually assured when faculty members are in control of the material. There may be legitimate circumstances under which . . . the University has some share in copyright. (n.p.)

Finally, learners may not view WBI as an attractive alternative to traditional learning environments. Learners may feel isolated from the instructor and other class members (Sriwongkol, 2002). This isolation may lead to frustration and ultimately to attrition from the course of study (Brooks, 1997; Sherry, 1996; White & Weight, 2000). Learners may experience irritating roadblocks when using Web technology, ranging from a lack of computer and other technology skills to actual technical problems with their own computer or the learning management systems. Learners may also not have time-management skills needed to be successful distance learners.

Although some of these disadvantages are certainly important, there may be ways to learn from them to change them into advantages or at the very least, minimize their negative effects.

 ## ON YOUR OWN

What do you see as the main advantages and disadvantages of WBI? How do advantages and disadvantages differ based on the varying perspectives (institution, instructor, or learner)? Do the varying perspectives conflict with each other? How may conflicts be resolved?

Although it may seem early, begin formalizing your thoughts about the advantages and disadvantages for using the Web as the delivery system for your project.

Begin brainstorming topics that you might pursue as a WBI design project. Start with a subject or content area that you find interesting and with which you have some expertise. Use the following criteria to help you select an appropriate topic.

- *Make sure the problem can be solved appropriately with WBI.*
  For the purposes of this course, we will assume that instruction and learning is the most appropriate solution for the problem. Your project should be a problem that can be remedied through WBI.
- *Identify the purpose of your WBI.*
  Make sure that the instructional purpose (or goal) is *not trivial.* It should be meaningful and have practical importance. Using Gagné's (1985) Categories of Learning, the instructional purpose should be at the outcome level of concepts, rules, or problem-solving task. If familiar with Bloom's Taxonomy, then the instructional purpose should be at the comprehension level or higher. (The outcome levels of verbal information [Gagné] and knowledge [Bloom, Engelhart, Furst, Hill, & Krathwohl, 1956] are too low for an end-of-course goal.) (See Chapter 3 for a discussion of this topic.)

- *Choose a content area in which you have expertise and that is of interest to you.*
  Pick a topic for which you are a subject matter expert (SME). You do *not* have the time to learn both a new content area and a new process for designing and evaluating WBI (cognitive demand or overload may occur!). Because you will be working with this topic all semester, make sure that your chosen topic is both interesting and relevant to you.
- *Select a topic for which participants will be available.*
  During the latter part of the course, you may need members from your targeted learner group to help you implement and evaluate your WBI. Make sure that they will be ready to learn (i.e., have the necessary prior knowledge and skills) at the time of this trial implementation.

  Although the final WBI might be delivered over a period of several days or weeks (depending on age level, topic, etc.), trial implementation (& evaluation) may take about two hours to complete. Consider the learner characteristics when implementing and evaluating your WBI project.
- *Select a topic for which you have technology available to develop and implement.*
  Make sure that you and your participants will have the technology and/or access capabilities necessary for developing and implementing your WBI project when conducting your trial implementation.

See this textbook's Companion Website (http://www.prenhall.com/davidson-shivers) for a printable set of design and project checklists and other information related to selecting your WBI project.

Web-Based Learning Environment and Community

Web-based instruction is part of an overarching system that makes up the learning environment and its associated learning community. For WBI to be successful, the environment and community must be defined. Web-based learning environments are open systems, accepting inputs from several elements.

Web-Based Learning Environments

Learning environments are comprised of interrelated and integrated components that interact with each other (Banathy, 1987) and that are focused on meeting needs of individuals within that entire system or organization. Learning environments include any subsystems that are part of their overarching organization (Figure 1.7). In Web-based learning environments, major systems are a combination of individuals and technologies that help to create the environment.

Figure 1.7   Web-based learning environment and community.

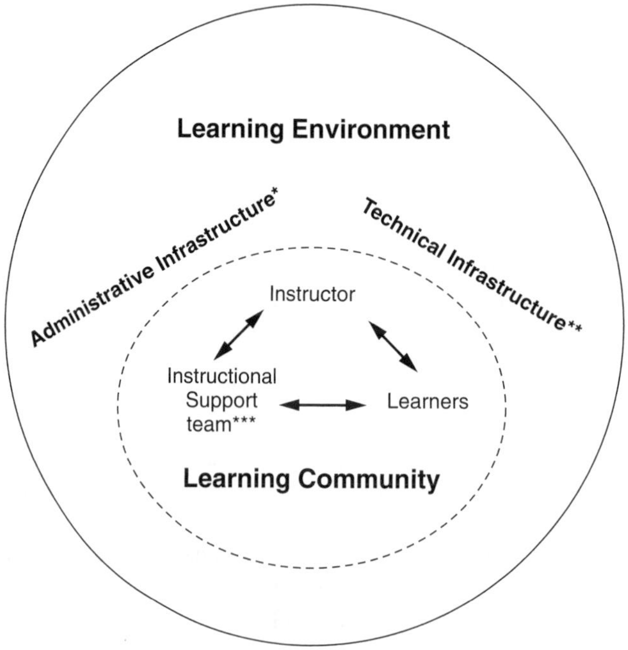

*   includes administrators & administrative support staff

**   includes technical support staff

*** includes instructional designer, mentors, etc.

Individuals who help create the environment include those in the organization's administrative infrastructure, those who work for the organization but are not a part of the organization (i.e., consultants), and the participants in the learning community. The administrative infrastructure staff may include managers and those individuals who are a part of the organization's day-to-day functions, such as accounting and bookkeeping support, library support, and so on (Dean, 1999; Greer, 1999).

The technology infrastructure includes technology support teams and work groups (webmasters, network technical support, etc.) and the software, hardware, servers, learning management systems, and so on, that support the WBI and its environment. This infrastructure also is accessed by other individuals in the learning community (instructor, learners, and instructional support team) and the **instructional designer,** the key person who establishes the Web-based instruction and its associated environment. For instance, the instructional support team (the instructional designers, mentors, and others involved in designing or implementing the WBI) will have access to servers and server files to support and maintain the site. Instructors and learners, generally for security purposes, will have "read only" access to the WBI and will be unable to alter the environment.

How much direct or indirect access a designer has to either the administrative or technology infrastructure depends on the situation, whether the designer is a part of the organization, and the designer's own skills and abilities. For instance, individual designers, who build not only the WBI but also the website, will be able to access to the server on which the website resides. However, designers who work with a team that includes technical support staff may not directly access the server or other aspects of the Web environment. Instead, they may direct others on website requirements and administrative needs; but even without direct access, designers will have influence on the Web environment and community.

The major component of the Web learning environment is the **learning community.** The system elements of the learning community are instructors, learners, the instructional support team, and the instruction itself.

Learning Communities

Shapiro and Levine (1999) propose that the notion of learning community is not new. Instead, it is considered one of the oldest educational models in existence, with a continual debate as to how it is defined. The early academic models of learning communities imply that they were place based, i.e., on a college or university campus (Palloff & Pratt, 1999). However, Palloff and Pratt maintain that this implication no longer holds true because of the expansion of education and training into nonacademic settings. Currently, such collective memberships may be found in business, industrial, military, or lifelong learning settings, as well as in academe.

Seufert, Lechner, and Stanoevska (2002) characterize a learning community as a group of agents who have a common language and value system who have similar interests. Similarly, Palloff and Pratt (1999) suggest that learning communities are based on differentiation and membership in that "people [who] seek commonality and shared interests formed groups and communities to pursue the interests that distinguished them from other groups" (p. 21) and, consequently, indicate that membership is maintained by adhering to the norms of the group. Merriam and Caffarella (1999) add that a learning community provides its members with tools and processes required to develop each individual member's potential.

Web-Based Learning Communities

Seufert et al. (2002) include electronic media as a distinguishing feature of online experiences, extending the concept of learning communities to Web-based environments. They define such a community as "the ensembles of agents who share a common language, world, values in terms of pedagogical approach and knowledge to be acquired. They pursue a common learning goal by communicating and cooperating through electronic media in the learning process" (p. 47).

Web-based learning communities provide a social structure in which instructors and learners work collaboratively to achieve goals and participate in a distributed experience (MacKnight, 2001; Palloff & Pratt, 1999). Learners bring different interests and experiences to the instructional setting. Taking advantage of these interests and experiences provides opportunities for learners to follow different paths as they reflect on their own needs and interact with instructors and peers. This kind of approach to WBI brings a shared responsibility for facilitating learning (Driscoll, 2004).

Similarly, Palloff and Pratt (1999) suggest that a Web-based learning community is based on developing relationships among and between instructor and learners, but that these relationships depend very much on the role the instructor plays. Although instructors and learners may have a shared responsibility for building the community, the main responsibility is the instructor's, who guides and facilitates interaction and provides feedback, encouraging learners to become community members.

In essence, a **Web-based learning community** can be described as a Web-based group of individuals who share common goals, interests, and experiences. The opportunity for all members to integrate concepts, acquire deep learning, and develop their potential exists through the group's communication and **interaction,** where a sense of responsibility for relationship building is shared. The community can vary from one with minimal interaction among the learners and the instructor to one that is highly collaborative. Interacting with the instructor and learners are the instructional support team, who work together to define, support, and maintain the community. Defining the scope and function of the Web-based learning community is essential to establishing the framework of the WBI.

A Continuum of Web-Based Learning Communities

Three main types of interaction predominate in WBI: student-to-instruction (or content), student-to-student, and student-to-instructor. Student-to-instruction interaction occurs when the participant is connecting to information and activities contained in the WBI (Davidson-Shivers & Rasmussen, 1999; Moore, 1989; Sherry, 1996). Student-to-student interactions are experienced when participants interact with each other individually, in small groups, or as a whole class. Such interactions may facilitate affiliations among learners. In student-to-instructor interaction participants and instructor directly communicate with each other. Mentors, teaching assistants, or others involved with the WBI are included in this type of interaction and may, at times, substitute for the instructor. These interactions occur through emails, feedback on assignments, or general communiqués and, again, may be on an individual or group basis. Northrup (2002), among others, suggests a fourth type of interaction, student-to-learning management system. Such systems permit learners to keep track of their progress, grades, and turned-in assignments and allow the instructor to automate some instructional duties.

For the most appropriate learning community to be created, the level of interaction must be defined. Such differences in interaction help form a continuum for Web-based learning communities. At one end, individual learners participate in independent, self-paced learning and interact with the content, but have minimal to no direct interaction with other learners, the instructor, or other participants (e.g., mentors, technical support staff, etc.). By contrast, at the other end of the continuum, participants are highly interactive with each other and the instructor and are motivated to build a sense of community (Figure 1.8).

The midpoint of the continuum is a Web-based learning community that combines activities involving group member interaction and collaboration with independent participant activities. Variations in the amount of interactive and independent work place the community's interaction level more toward one end of the continuum or the other. For in-

Figure 1.8 Continuum of Web-based learning communities.

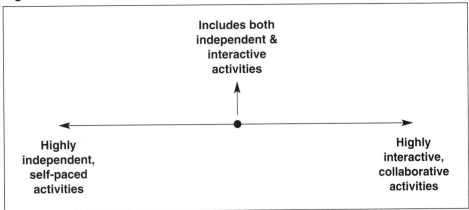

stance, as learner activities move toward more group participation, collaboration, and community building, then the community moves closer to the highly interactive end of the continuum. If learner activities require some interaction among members but are mostly independent exercises, then the community moves closer to the other end. The two end points should not be viewed as "good" or "bad"; rather, placement on the continuum should be viewed as an instructional element that is determined by what will best serve the WBI purposes.

Somewhat surprisingly, the vast majority of current online learning is independent, self-paced WBI. According to Clark and Mayer (2003), 77 percent of Web-based training is individualized. For most independent WBI, participants interact with the materials but have minimal interactions with the instructor and other learners.

One of the unique features of using the Web for instruction is the capability of interaction among its participants. Gabelnick, MacGregor, Matthews, and Smith (cited in Shapiro & Levine, 1999) suggest that learning communities not only provide opportunities for deep understanding and integration of content, but also provide a chance for the instructor and other learners to interact. Gunawardena, Plass, and Salisbury (2001) propose that community building is especially important for diverse or novice learners who need to develop a comfort level to fully engage in learning; community building may not be required for all learners or for all types of WBI.

Resurgent Use of Learning Communities

There has been a strong resurgence of the use of learning communities on college and university campuses. This resurgence may be due, in part, to demands for improved undergraduate education from students, their parents, and the business sector (Palloff & Pratt, 1999; Shapiro & Levine, 1999). It may also be due to the demand for virtual programs and campuses by nontraditional learners in graduate and undergraduate programs and the increased availability of and access to Web-based technology.

ON YOUR OWN

How do Web-based learning communities relate to Web-based learning environments? Describe situations that fit high, medium, and low levels of participant interactivity based on the continuum of types of learning communities. How are those situations appropriate for the type of learning community selected?

Begin formalizing your thoughts about your learning environment and community for your planned WBI project. What kinds of administrative and technology infrastructure will you have access to? Consider the elements of your own Web-based learning environment. Where do you think your WBI project will be on the learning community continuum? Why?

See this textbook's Companion Website (http://www.prenhall.com/davidson-shivers) for more information on Web-based learning environments.

Types of Online Instruction

Online instruction has three forms: Web based, Web enhanced, and Web supported. They vary by the amount of instruction delivered online and how that delivery is organized (Davidson-Shivers, 1998). Table 1.2 provides examples of these forms of online instruction.

Web-Based Instruction

Web-based instruction (WBI) is a form of distance education whereby the instruction is delivered entirely online. In WBI, the learners and instructor do *not* have face-to-face interactions or meetings; all of the instructional materials and assignments are delivered through the Web.

Web-Enhanced Instruction

To be considered **Web-enhanced instruction (WEI),** a course must have some class sessions or lessons delivered entirely on the Web and others delivered face-to-face. The key distinction from WBI is that some class sessions require that the learners and instructor meet in person, whereas others do not. Some universities or schools make distinctions between WBI and WEI by using specific percentages of when sessions are held online versus on campus. For instance, at the University of South Alabama a Web-enhanced course must have less than 50 percent of the entire course delivered via the Web. The term *Web-blended instruction* has been used interchangeably with WEI (Stockley, 2003), as well as with the third type of online instruction, Web-supported instruction.

Web-Supported Instruction

Web-supported instruction (WSI) occurs when learners regularly attend classes (i.e., with face-to-face meetings), but are assigned Web assignments and activities to support classroom activities. These assignments may include group work such as extended dis-

Table 1.2 Types of Online Instruction

Type	Definition	Example
Web-based Instruction	All of the instruction, communication, and assignments are delivered completely through the Web. (Assessment of students may be at a proctored location, however.)	Psychology of Learning course is delivered to students using *WebCT*. All lectures, assignments, and discussions occur through the Internet and Web. Students work both together and independently through online means and are not required to come to campus. The instructor interacts with students through emails, drop boxes, document sharing, threaded discussions, and chats. All support materials can be delivered through online services, such as obtaining reserved readings via the college's online library.
Web-enhanced Instruction	Some class sessions are delivered completely online and others are delivered completely through face-to-face, on-campus meetings.	A course on designing online learning environments is delivered through both online and on-campus forums. In the beginning of the course, a number of class sessions require on-campus meetings; later sessions allow students to work together and independently entirely on the Web.
Web-supported Instruction	Instruction is delivered through traditional and regular face-to-face classroom meetings with additional Web assignments or activities.	The fourth-grade teacher requires that her students complete an online assignment in their unit on the Louisiana Purchase and the Oregon Trail. The instruction transpires in the classroom, which includes reading the textbook, holding class discussions on various topics, and other in-class activities and assignments. However, a specific assignment requires that they use the Web to research a historical person or event related to this unit. The teacher develops a series of questions to help guide students, and they are allowed to go to the computer lab for online research. Once completed, the students report their findings with in-class presentations.

Source: Table data are from Davidson-Shivers (1998).

cussions, collaborative projects, or communicating with other learners through emails. Other types of assignments may be independent projects or activities, such as locating Web resources, conducting online library searches, or emailing information or assignments to the instructor.

ON YOUR OWN

Have you participated in Web-based, Web-enhanced, or Web-supported instruction? If so, which did you prefer? Why? If not, reflect on the differences and consider how you might view each type.

Begin thinking about the type of online instruction that you may create for your own project. Explain why it would be an appropriate choice for you.

See this textbook's Companion Website (http://www.prenhall.com/davidson-shivers) for more information on the different types of Web-based instruction.

Current, Emerging, and Merging Technology for WBI

WBI by its nature is highly dependent on technology. Designers who are able to manipulate available technologies can take full advantage of technology innovations.

Current and Emerging Technological Tools

Current and emerging technological tools allow designers to create innovative WBI. The term *emerging* is applied when the tool is either new on the market or has been repurposed for educational or training use. Because most technological tools continue to evolve, some will be replaced with newer versions and others will become obsolete with new innovations; an example is replacing hardwired computer networks with wireless networks. Most technologies improve in terms of increased speed, capacity, and ease of use with each new version or innovation. At the same time, innovations seem to decrease in physical size; for example, while new versions of the laptop computer have increased power, their physical size continues to become smaller and smaller. Table 1.3 presents technological tools and potential WBI activities that may incorporate them.

Merging Technological Tools

Another advance in technology can be seen in the merging, or blending, of technology tools. Beginning in the late twentieth century, an explosion of multimedia was seen in the merging of animation, audio, video, and text. As technology progresses, multimedia will become even more robust. Broadcast and teleconferencing systems may expand their current focus and merge with the Web to provide increased access to education and training. The range of new tools in this new century will afford designers new capabilities to improve WBI design and delivery.

However exciting it is to use any of these innovations, it is critical to remember that they are merely *tools* to help designers design, teachers teach, and learners learn. It is the designer's skills and creativity that have the greatest impact on the quality of the WBI being produced.

Table 1.3   Current and Emerging Technologies for WBI

Technological Tool	Definition	Potential WBI Activity
Cell Phone	Wireless telecommunications device can integrate text, voice, and images and access the Internet. Instant messaging (IM) can occur.	Communication
Chatrooms, or Chats Internet Relay Chats Instant Messaging Systems	A real-time, text-based, conversation among groups of individuals.	Group discussion Question and answer sessions
Desktop Video Conferencing	Video and audio interaction combination.	Small-group discussion Instructor and participant presentations
Listservs	A system that allows people to send email to one central location, where their message is distributed to other subscribers of the list.	Threaded discussion groups Course instruction Instructor–student communication
Newsgroups/ USENET	A worldwide system of discussion groups, similar to a distributed bulletin board system decentralized information utility.	Discussion groups Debates Course instruction
Multi-user Domain, Dungeon, or Dimension (MUDs) Multi-user Object Oriented (MOOs) Multi-user Shared Hallucination (MUSHs)	A multi-user simulated environment (usually text-based) that permits users to create things that stay after they leave and others can use in their absence, thus allowing a world to be built gradually and collectively.	Scenarios for role playing Games Group projects
Personal Digital Assistants (PDAs)	Handheld computers that can be connected to desktop computers for sharing of information.	Download data from computer for field experiments Schedule learning experiences Communicate with other learners and instructors via email
Plug-ins	Software that adds new features to a commercial application.	Music and audio Videos Animated presentations
Web or Discussion Boards	A discussion group or forum accessed via the Web.	Threaded discussion groups Instructor-led presentation of materials Student interaction
Web Cams	Video camera connected to a computer that permits the most recent image to be requested via a Web page.	Viewing of real-time pictures from one of a thousand or more sites or site-to-site video imaging

Source: Table data are from Aggarwal (2000), Khan (1997), Reddick & King (1996), Whatis.com (2001), Zillman (2003).

Learning Management Systems

The **Learning management system (LMS)** has emerged as a technology that supports planning, designing, developing, implementing, and administering online learning experiences (Brennan, Funke, & Anderson, 2001). Its function is to provide an organized environment for WBI delivery (Metagroup, 2003; Wagner, 2001), as well as to structure WBI design and development. An LMS is a software tool that schedules, registers, and tracks learner progress and performance (Brennan et al.; R. H. Hall, 2001; B. Hall, 2002). LMSs also permit decision makers to track data related to online learning. For instance, LMSs such as *Angel, Blackboard, Desire2Learn, ecollege, TopClass,* and *WebCT* are used in university settings. Each LMS tends to have similar features, but may be structured differently; all have tools and systems available for design, student enrollment, accounting, and so on. All have associated usage fees, which may be determined in a variety of ways, including by the number of user accounts (whether it is an institution or an individual), amount of use, and types of tools and systems included. Some LMSs, such as those available from Nicenet.org, are commercial free (Nicenet, 2003) and free to individuals on a limited basis. These free tools have similar features but are not as comprehensive and complex as a commercial LMS.

Some LMS functions are used to promote instructional strategies in WBI. Typically these functions contain chat rooms, discussion boards, forums or threads, student lists with email addresses, electronic drop boxes (assignments to be sent to instructor for grading), and assessment (quizzes and grading) tools (Brennan et al., 2001). LMSs permit designers to take advantage of tools that support learning environments and learning communities without having to individually create software support systems. An LMS supports automating processes such as interaction, enrollment, registration, and assessment (B. Hall, 2002; Haugen, 2003).

Designers who have access to an LMS should analyze its characteristics carefully to select appropriate functions for their own WBI. For example, if learners will interact with peers, email, chat rooms, or discussion forums should be active. When assignments are incorporated into the WBI, a drop box can be used to submit electronic products (projects, papers, etc.). For WBI that contains content assessments, quizzing or testing functions should be available.

Not all LMS features or functions may be applicable to the WBI, and, consequently, not desired or used by the designer. Some systems will permit deactivating unused features. In other cases, the LMS will display the feature regardless of its use, which potentially can confuse users, who may try to access all functions. In this case, designers should consider whether the LMS is actually an appropriate tool for use with the WBI.

A **learning content management system (LCMS)** is a software tool that focuses on content development and management. Although similar in name, the LMS and LCMS have different strengths and functions (Brennan et al., 2001); the LMS organizes the learning environment and the LCMS manages and tracks content.

On Your Own

If you have participated in or observed WBI, what technological tools were used? Were they used effectively? How would you have improved the teaching and learning experiences?

Think about the type of technological tools you will be able to use in your WBI project. Describe the tools you would choose and explain why they would meet the needs of your instructor (or you as the instructor) and of learners.

See this textbook's Companion Website (http://www.prenhall.com/davidson-shivers) for more information on learning management systems.

Are You Right for WBI? Examining Stakeholder Roles, Responsibilities, and Challenges

All of the individuals involved in WBI must work together to facilitate learner success in achieving the instructional goal, and all may be considered stakeholders. The term **stakeholder** is all-inclusive and often refers to the client or manager, who approves, supports, funds, and supplies necessary resources to a project and is usually considered the primary decision maker (Dean, 1999; Greer, 1999). However, developing WBI can be a complex process that involves others and, they too may be decision makers. Delegating the client (or manager/administrator) as the only stakeholder does not fit well in the WBI situation. Dean (1999) and Greer (1999) state that *stakeholders* are any individuals or groups who are actively involved in the WBI project or significantly affected by it from the organizational perspective, other than those who are the target of the instruction (learners, employees, etc.). They suggest that any of the following individuals may be considered a stakeholder:

- Clients (owner, customer, project sponsor, etc.)
- Employees (staff, training participants, students, etc.)
- Shareholders, administrative boards, advisory committees, etc.
- Suppliers, distributors, vendors, etc.
- Professionals (designers, evaluators, etc.) and other specialists (SMEs, webmasters, computer technicians, graphic and media artists, etc.)
- Project managers
- Governmental and accrediting agencies and the public

The Joint Committee on Standards for Educational Evaluation (1994) divides this group into *primary stakeholders*—individuals that are directly involved or have direct decision-making power—and *secondary stakeholders*—individuals that are indirectly involved or have limited decision-making power or that are affected by decisions made. Hence, all individuals who have some role and responsibility in developing or delivering the WBI may be considered stakeholders.

These roles and responsibilities associated with WBI stakeholders are categorized into three general areas: administrative, technological, and learning community. The administrative area includes managers, accountants and bookkeepers, and librarians, and may also include clients, shareholders, suppliers, and accrediting agencies. Other administrative stakeholders provide support to the functionality of the system, or Web learning environment. In the technology area, the stakeholders include individuals who work with the technical infrastructure such as webmasters, networking staff, and technicians. The learning community includes the instructors, learners, and the members of the instructional support team, such as mentors and others. Each stakeholder holds varying degrees of responsibility for creating, facilitating, and/or participating in the Web-based instruction, the Web-based environment, and its associated learning community. Each of these individuals will face a set of challenges.

Not every WBI project will include each type of stakeholder. In some cases, the entire Web environment is far smaller, made up of only one or two individuals with multiple roles and responsibilities within all three stakeholder areas. For example, a lone designer/instructor may take on the various roles and responsibilities in the design and development of a WBI and its website entirely. Other situations may involve a team, in which the designer makes decisions about the WBI and its website, and then delegates the activity or assigned task for others to carry out.

No matter how the various scenarios that could be envisioned are played out, by examining these roles and responsibilities individuals can determine whether they are "right" for participating in WBI design and delivery.

Administrative Stakeholders

There are two roles within the category of administrative stakeholders: (1) administrators themselves and (2) the administrative support staff.

Administrator Roles.   From a systems perspective, administrators focus on issues that pertain to and support the entire Web-based learning environment. Depending on their position in the organization (e.g., manager, vice president, principal, technology director, superintendent, chair, dean, etc.), these individuals can be the main decision makers who set project priorities, provide approval for the project, and fund and allocate resources needed to develop and deliver the instruction (Dean, 1999; Greer, 1999). Based on the organization's size and structure and the WBI requirements, administrator stakeholders either may have day-to-day interactions with the WBI designer or may rely on the designer to make decisions and only provide periodic progress reports.

Administrator Responsibilities.   The primary responsibility of administrators, in addition to setting priorities and approving projects, is allocating necessary resources such as personnel, equipment, and materials (Greer, 1999) to others involved in the WBI design and delivery. These individuals ensure that others in the work team, such as the project manager, designer, instructor, and so on, have the appropriate levels of authority to make decisions about the use of the resources. For example, administrator stakeholders would provide resources to support WBI instructors in adapting good teaching skills to an online environment (Palloff & Pratt, 1999; Salmon, 2000). Again, depending on the organization, these stakeholders may have the authority over WBI dissemination throughout the organization and may determine issues related to WBI implementation and evaluation.

Administrator Challenges.   Administrators may lack expertise and resources to develop appropriate conclusions about using WBI as a training intervention; they may need to rely on others for accurate and timely information to make appropriate decisions about WBI and the Web environment. Another challenge may be to justify costs associated with

WBI projects to higher-level managers or administrative boards (Berge et al., 2001; Hannum, 2001; Kinshuk & Patel, 2001).

Administrative Support Staff Roles. An administrative support staff or team is another administrative stakeholder group. These individuals act in several capacities to facilitate access to organizational processes and systems. Their functions include enrolling learners into courses and billing them for tuition and fees. Administrative staff may help in the assessment functions, such as proctoring, or with posting grades in a registrar's office. Administrative personnel may distribute offline materials (e.g., CDs, workbooks, evaluations) to instructors and learners and process the paperwork involved in hiring instructors and mentors.

Administrative Support Staff Responsibilities. Administrative staff/team members maintain records and handle accounting processes associated with assessing tuition or fees for the WBI. They also process costs associated with the WBI design (payment of instructors, mentors, SMEs, contractors, etc.). Administrative staff is responsible for ensuring that requirements of the organization's policies and procedures are met.

Administrative Support Staff Challenges. For the administrative support staff, the challenge is to update records accurately and in a timely manner. When problems arise associated with enrollments, fee assessments, and student records, time is of the essence in resolving them. As the number of instructors and learners increases, administrative support teams must be able to upwardly scale their activities.

Technology Stakeholders

The stakeholders in the technology category are the technical support staff or team. Webmasters, networking specialists, and computer programmers are in this category. Their roles are usually involved with other divisions of the organization, such as management information systems, computer service centers, and so on. For WBI projects, these professionals and specialists are often considered secondary stakeholders because their technical support for WBI may not be their main role within the organization and they may be only indirectly involved in the WBI decision making.

Technical Support Staff Roles. Technical support staff members are often asked to carry out the decisions already made and to work with the WBI participants to solve technical problems. The role of the team is to assist designers with the technology tools used in the WBI. They work to solve problems that designers, instructors, and learners may have with hardware and software systems, ranging from network servers and desktop computers to software used in the LMS. They may also be asked to develop Web pages or multimedia products. Webmasters may be part of the technical support team and work with designers to move instructional websites to networks so participants can access them.

The technical team might host a help desk system for designers, instructors, and learners. They may work with the LMS or other technology, including servers and network infrastructure (Darbyshire, 2000; de Boer & Collis, 2001). The team may continue to work with stakeholders through WBI implementation. They may also assist during evaluation of the WBI.

Technical Support Staff Responsibilities.   The responsibilities of this support staff may vary by whom they support (i.e., the designer, instructor, learners, or perhaps each other). They may be asked to troubleshoot instructor and learner technology problems, upgrade technology resources, and back up technology systems. These responsibilities may change depending on when and what services are needed.

Technical Support Staff Challenges.   One challenge that faces all support teams is troubleshooting problems in a timely and efficient manner, and this is no less true for the technical staff. Normal pressures experienced in support services increase when problems arise; these pressures increase at the startup of Web-based courses and programs. It is the technician who must maintain a professional, calm approach while working with distraught and potentially demanding WBI participants. Building relationships with instructors and learners may keep communication lines open when everyone is under pressure.

Another challenge the technical staff faces is the need to continually upgrade knowledge and skills so that members have expertise in the software and hardware and are able to troubleshoot technical problems. A third challenge is to determine when to upgrade to newer versions of hardware and software; this challenge involves both the expense of upgrading and determining when it will cause the least disruption to WBI participants.

Overall, technical support team members must be able to communicate with the other WBI stakeholders. Regardless of the issue, technical support individuals must ascertain the problem and generate a solution; they must be able to talk with the designer, instructor, or learner through the problem situation to its resolution. This communication becomes even more challenging when working with novice technology users.

Learning Community Stakeholders

The learning community stakeholders are those people actively involved in participating in or supporting the WBI's functions as it is being designed and conducted. These stakeholders include instructors, learners, and mentors. The instructional designer is also part of the learning community; we discuss the roles, responsibilities, and challenges of the instructional designer in the following section. These stakeholders work together to form the foundations for a learning community or the WBI learning community itself.

Instructor Roles.   Titles such as *online trainers, facilitators,* or *moderators* are sometimes associated or used interchangeably with the term **instructor.** The online instructor is the principal contact for the learners and is the primary person responsible for WBI implementation.

Instructors may have a role in WBI development, but their most critical role is as facilitators of learner success (Fisher, 2000). In essence, they are in charge of establishing the Web-based learning community and setting the tone, or climate, for that community. Instructors may assume roles of advisor, performance evaluator, and feedback provider; they may even troubleshoot technology problems (Hannum, 2001; Kinshuk & Patel, 2001; Spector & de la Teja, 2001).

Instructor Responsibilities.   The primary responsibility of the Web-based instructor is to lead teaching and learning. Good teaching requires that the purposes of the instruction, course policies and requirements, and so on be explained in a manner that learners understand. Good teaching traits include empathy, excellence in instructional strategies (or methods), expertise in content, and ability to structure the instructional events for learning to take place.

Such good teaching practices usually transcend the instructional delivery form and a good instructor in a face-to-face teaching environment can usually transfer or adapt these traits to an online situation. For instructors to adapt such traits to online teaching, they will need support (Palloff & Pratt, 1999; Salmon, 2000), which administrator stakeholders should provide. However, Spector and de la Teja (2001) maintain that online teaching requires additional competencies to those skills required of the classroom instructor. These additional skills are due in part to technology demands and requirements placed on them as they moderate online discussions (Davidson-Shivers & Rasmussen, in press).

Online instructors may need to describe technical requirements for learners. They must be accessible to learners and must establish appropriate communication channels and online office hours (Berge et al., 2000). Communicating and assisting learners occur online and this interaction is mainly text based (emails, threaded discussions, etc.) rather than verbal (Berge et al., 2000; Fisher, 2000; Hannum, 2001; Romiszowski & Chang, 2001).

Instructor Challenges.   WBI differs from classroom teaching in terms of the interactions between instructor and learners (Palloff & Pratt, 1999), with one major difference being the perceived immediacy of interactions. Learners, who contact the instructor at all hours of the day, may expect an instant response and such expectations pose a challenge for online instructors. Such expectations are far above what is standard in traditional classroom settings; in those environments students generally have to wait to speak to an instructor after the class has ended or have a meeting during scheduled office hours.

The sheer volume of learner contacts (emails, written responses, etc.) can be challenging as well. Romiszowski and Chang (2001) report that instructors spend twice the amount of time with online instruction as in traditional on-campus courses; WBI with large enrollments or highly collaborative communities may require that the instructor's time commitment be even greater. Other factors that affect an instructor's time demands include the complexity of content, type and quantity of instructional activities, and availability of instructor support (e.g., mentors, help desks, etc.).

Another challenge for online instructors is the requirement that they keep abreast of the pervasive and ever-changing technologies required for WBI. New versions of or upgrades to software applications can require that the WBI and its associated website be modified. Web resources must be verified to ensure that they are functioning; new URLs must be located when URLs go bad. Other changes related to updating the WBI include personalizing the content and modifying the instructional strategies.

Adapting the WBI to these changes can be quite daunting, especially for novice online instructors (Berge et al., 2001; Brooks, 1997). Such changes continue throughout the WBI's life cycle and require that the online instructor have technology skills and a foundational experience in implementing instructional strategies (Hannum, 2001).

Learner Roles.   Learners are the second stakeholders in the learning community category. They are the individuals who participate as students or trainees in the WBI. Typically, individuals who participate in online learning require convenience, flexibility, and access to education and training from a distance (Davidson-Shivers, Muilenberg, & Tanner, 2001; Northrup, 2002). These individuals may be traditional learners, training participants, or lifelong learners outside a traditional educational setting.

Learners' roles in the Web-based learning community are to participate in instructional events, complete course assignments, and communicate with the instructor and other students as required. They may also help establish WBI goals (depending on how strongly the learning community is based on constructivist learning principles), share their prior knowledge and experiences, and build a sense of shared community (Driscoll, 2004; MacKnight, 2001; Palloff & Pratt, 1999). Likewise, they contribute to building a sense of community by their involvement in the activities and events within the WBI and their interactions with each other.

Learner Responsibilities. Online learning requires that individual learners have working knowledge of computers, the Web, and software applications. However, and more importantly, to be an effective online learner, an individual should be an autonomous learner—a self-starter who "takes the initiative and seeks out needed resources" (Peal & Wilson, 2001, p. 152). WBI requires that individuals display self-motivation and good study skills including those of time management and organization (Berge et al., 2000; Carr-Chellman, 2001; Northrup, 2002; Peal & Wilson).

Learner Challenges. Challenges abound with any new experience. In online learning, individuals may face feelings of isolation and increased anxiety from unfamiliarity in the WBI (Hannum, 2001). This isolation may negatively influence student motivation (Berge et al., 2000).

A second challenge that might be faced, especially by new WBI participants, relates to how they handle metacognitive issues, including information overload and evaluation of their own learning experiences. Becoming a self-regulated learner (Berge et al., 2000; Kinshuk & Patel, 2001) and possessing skills such as comprehension monitoring, decision making, self-evaluation, and good questioning techniques, reduce these challenges.

Instructional Support Team Roles. The third set of learning community stakeholders is the instructional support team. It is made up of staff members that support the learning environment; these individuals work with instructors and learners as the learning community is designed or formed. A common instructional support staff member is the **mentor,** an individual who assists the online instructor (Davidson-Shivers & Rasmussen, 1998, 1999; Rasmussen, 2002; Salmon, 2000). Sometimes known as a **tutor,** this individual performs a variety of tasks, depending on the needs of the instructor and learners. Mentors may help to resolve learner technical difficulties, work with learners on content questions, lead discussions, track student progress, or act as a learner coach or encourager.

Instructional Support Team Responsibilities. The instructional support team assists instructors and learners in building the learning community and making sure that the WBI experience is successful. Responsibilities of the instructional support team depend primarily on the needs of instructors and learners during the WBI, but may include resolving participant technical problems, making contact with learners, and tracking learner progress.

Instructional Support Team Challenges.   The challenge for the instructional support staff is to balance their workload so that they can support instructors and learners. Simultaneously, they must not overstep professional bounds and take on responsibilities that they are not prepared for nor have the authority over.

Instructional Designer Stakeholder

Although instructional designers may appear in all three stakeholder categories (as previously mentioned), they are mainly associated with the learning community and could be considered as part of the instructional support staff for it. The two main roles an instructional designer can assume are (1) the designer working with a WBI design team and (2) the lone WBI designer/instructor.

Instructional Designer Roles.   The instructional designer may serve as the main decision maker in a WBI project, depending on the structure of the organization and how responsibility has been allocated. The instructional designer is usually the primary architect of the WBI or is the project manager, who manages the design team and oversees the WBI design and delivery. Designers are sometimes known as *instructional developers* and are often involved in creating the actual Web pages and websites.

Typically, designers have several potential roles in a WBI project. They may serve, of course, as the project designer. They may take on the roles as analyst, evaluator, and developer of the WBI and website or, as stated, project manager (Greer, 1999). They may be seen as primary communicators who supply others involved in the project with information to make timely decisions and/or move the WBI to completion and who report progress to the administrator stakeholders. Their other major role is that of developer; in this capacity, designers put the design plan into action. In a coordinated effort with other team members, the designer ensures that the WBI design plan is followed closely.

Instructional Designer Responsibilities.   Instructional designers analyze situations and problems to recommend to administrative stakeholders whether WBI is the appropriate training solution. They may be responsible for monitoring the WBI design and delivery as well as be the individual who actually creates it. Overall, the designer's primary responsibility is to meet the needs of the instructor and learners (Carr-Chellman, 2001; Hedberg, Brown, Larkin, & Agostinho, 2001). The designer must communicate with other project team members and any other stakeholder to keep the WBI progressing.

Instructional designers work with software systems to create the instructional materials. Guided by the design plan, they create Web pages and multimedia products, and use an LMS to structure the learning community.

Instructional Designer Challenges.   Creating effective WBI is a challenging task in and of itself. Balancing adherence to quality standards and expectations (and those of other stakeholders) with the constraints of limited resources, funding, and time is a common set of issues. The design endeavor becomes further complicated when the WBI involves complex content and instructional strategies or novice team members (e.g., support staff, instructors, learners, etc.), who do not understand all aspects of the ID process (Carr-Chellman, 2001; Hannum, 2001; Milheim & Bannan-Ritland, 2000; Romiszowski & Chang, 2001).

Instructional designers' challenges are further exacerbated when working with other stakeholders who are naïve or passively involved in the project, or who make unrealistic demands. Being an adept communicator may alleviate part of this challenge. According to Shrock and Geis (1999), the challenge is to keep other stakeholders informed; they claim that "nothing is to be gained by surprising the [other] stakeholders" (p. 204). It is crucial that the WBI design information be shared in a timely fashion. Designers face an additional challenge of ever-changing software systems for which they must continue to update their knowledge and skills.

Lone WBI Designer/Instructor Role.   Although roles may be carried out by a number of individuals or teams, there are situations in which a designer/instructor carries out all of the roles in a WBI project, often creating the WBI on their own. Horton (2000) suggests that although some instructors can complete such a task by themselves, most require some assistance and support. She stresses that it is a good idea to assess how much support is available before venturing into Web-based design and delivery.

Lone WBI Designer/Instructor Responsibilities.   In the role of lone designer, the instructor then takes on the task of being her own administrative, technical, and instructional support team. The instructor may use an LMS (e.g., *Angel, Blackboard, Desire2Learn, eCollege, TopClass,* or *WebCT*) to assist in meeting multiple roles and responsibilities. Due to these varied and multiple roles, the instructor may also become a learner in the online learning environment.

Lone WBI Designer/Instructor Challenges.   Rasmussen, Northrup, and Lombardo (2002) maintain that it is impractical to expect instructors [or designers] to be their own support staff in online instruction, even when using an LMS. It is difficult enough for a faculty member to stay abreast of his own content specialty area; having to keep up with technological innovations as well as being the technical troubleshooter places extraordinary demands on a faculty member's time. These demands are especially heavy if the designer/instructor is designing a new course or repurposing content into online instruction for the first time.

Lone designer/instructors need to develop a support system (either formal or informal) of their own to help offset expected challenges. The degree of support system involvement varies throughout the design and delivery of WBI depending on organization resources. A strong support staff facilitates WBI design and provides support services to the WBI stakeholders that is fundamental to the success of the WBI.

ON YOUR OWN

Are you right for WBI? Will you be the lone designer/instructor for your own WBI project or will you have access to a design team? Describe your situation in terms of roles, responsibilities, and challenges that you may face. Who are the other stakeholders that may be involved in your WBI project? Identify the other stakeholders by their stakeholder category and explain their roles and responsibilities.

See this textbook's Companion Website (http://www.prenhall.com/davidson-shivers) for more information on stakeholders.

Wrapping Up

The Web (or Internet and World Wide Web) has seen phenomenal expansion since the early 1990s. At the same time, there has been a rapid increase in the use of the Web for distance education and training by PK–12 schools, business and industry, military, and higher education institutions. Distance education has shown wide variation in its delivery systems over the centuries, with the Web being one of its latest. The three types of online instruction—Web-based, Web-enhanced, and Web-supported—offer instructors and organizations a variety of ways to incorporate the Web into their own teaching and learning settings. There are several advantages and disadvantages in using WBI for an institution, for an instructor, and for learners; these advantages and disadvantages may help instructional designers determine whether WBI is an appropriate solution to a given problem. Further exploration into current, emerging, and merging technologies may also reveal WBI's appropriateness for a particular situation. Understanding the various roles, responsibilities, and challenges facing WBI stakeholders facilitates the decision to pursue WBI as an instructional solution.

Expanding Your Expertise

1. The Internet and the Web have been used for a variety of purposes. In forecasting the future of the Web, what do you think will be the next areas of expansion?
2. Discuss the types of distance education delivery systems. Are all of them still needed? Justify your thoughts.
3. Define *WBI* in your own terms. What other terms might be used to describe the concept of WBI? What term(s) do you prefer to use? Why?
4. What WBI technology tools are available to you at your organization? Are there restrictions placed on their use? How might you use those technologies in your own WBI project?
5. What do you think will be the next innovation(s) or enhancement(s) in the technology tools used for WBI design, development, and implementation? How might these innovations influence the quality of WBI?
6. What are advantages and disadvantages of being involved in a highly interactive Web-based learning community? What would be advantages and disadvantages of being an independent online participant? Which do you prefer? Why?
7. How do the challenges differ for the lone instructor from the instructor who has multiple design team members involved developing WBI? How would using a learning management system affect these challenges?
8. What are the advantages and disadvantages of being the lone instructor in a Web-based learning environment? What are the advantages and disadvantages of being an instructional designer in a design team? Explain which you would prefer and why.

Chapter **2**

Foundations of Web-Based Instructional Design

The remaining four foundational areas of the Web-Based Instructional Design (WBID) Model are learning theories, systems theories, communication theories, and instructional design (ID) models. Principles within each of the learning paradigms provide the theoretical basis for the integrated, multitheoretical approach to learning used in the WBID Model. Systems theories identify aspects of systematic and systemic processes that underlie most ID models. Communication theories provide general principles related to message and visual design. Traditional and nontraditional ID models are fundamental to the stages within the WBID Model, providing a foundation for designing and developing Web-based instruction (WBI).

Chapter 2 begins with a brief description of each of these four foundational areas, followed by an overview of the WBID Model that highlights its interrelated stages. The case example, *GardenScapes,* which is used throughout the book, is introduced in a section entitled Meet the Players. Chapter 2 ends with a new section, Extending Your Skills, which contains four other case studies that we will develop throughout the remaining chapters.

Objectives

At the end of this chapter, you should be able to do the following:

- Explain the importance of the foundational areas (learning, systems, and communication theories, and instructional design models) of the WBID Model.
- Describe the integrated, multitheoretical approach to learning.
- Explain your own theoretical approach to learning.
- Identify the common stages of ID models found in the WBID Model.
- State the sequence of stages in the WBID Model.
- Describe the purpose of each stage of the WBID Model.

Introduction

Learners must be actively engaged for learning to occur; this active engagement depends on careful planning and good instructional design. Planning and designing activities are equally important to Web-based instruction. According to Smith and Ragan (2005), a strong theoretical foundation is necessary for effective use of instructional design (ID) models and for developing effective instructional products. In addition to distance education (discussed in Chapter 1), other theory bases for WBI design are the theories of learning, systems, and communication, and ID models (Figure 2.1).

Figure 2.1   Foundational areas of the WBID Model.

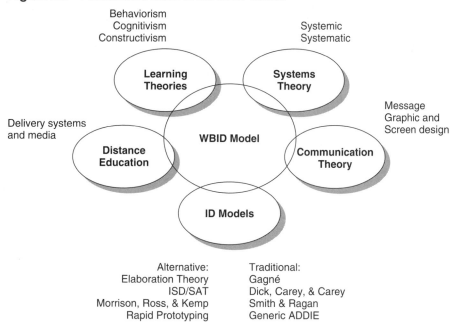

An Overview of Learning Theories

An instructional designer's perspective on learning theories (Figure 2.2) affects how instruction is created and implemented. The three main theoretical bases of learning are behaviorism, cognitivism, and constructivism (Figure 2.3). In addition to providing explanations of the phenomenon of learning, these theories provide descriptions and prescriptions of how to use principles for instruction and, ultimately, how to apply them in instructional design.

Behavioral Learning Theories

From a **behavioral** perspective, learning is considered to be an action and is studied through observable measures of overt behaviors. The mind (often termed the *black box*) was generally not researched or discussed in behaviorist literature because, although its existence

Figure 2.2   Learning theories in the WBID Model.

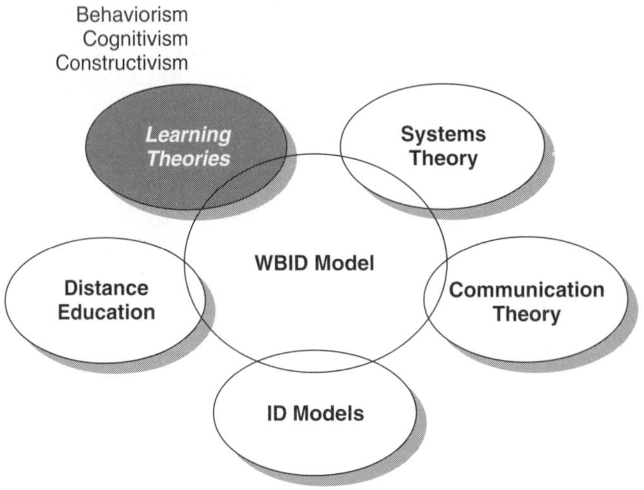

Behaviorism
Cognitivism
Constructivism

Learning Theories

Systems Theory

WBID Model

Distance Education

Communication Theory

ID Models

Figure 2.3   Principles within learning theory bases.

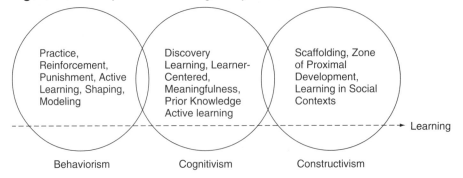

Practice, Reinforcement, Punishment, Active Learning, Shaping, Modeling

Discovery Learning, Learner-Centered, Meaningfulness, Prior Knowledge Active learning

Scaffolding, Zone of Proximal Development, Learning in Social Contexts

Learning

Behaviorism   Cognitivism   Constructivism was not in doubt, its inner workings could not be directly observed. The study of behavioral learning psychology gained prominence during the 1950s and 1960s, although behavioral research began in the nineteenth century (Lefrançois, 2000). Early behaviorists conducted experiments on animals; later behaviorists shifted their research to the study of humans and maintained an emphasis on the need to study observable behaviors (Driscoll, 2004; Lefrançois, 2000; Ormrod, 2004).

Two major behavioral theories are those of classical conditioning and operant conditioning. With *classical conditioning,* the focus is on the stimulus (the external conditions) and the response (the resulting overt behavior) and how the stimulus affected a change in response. This relationship, according to Ormrod (2004), is associated with S–R (stimulus–response) psychology. James, Wundt, Watson, Guthrie, and, of course, Pavlov are a few of the early behaviorists associated with classical conditioning. Although often viewed from a historical perspective of learning theory, classical conditioning still has relevance today (Lefrançois, 2000; Ormrod). Basic training in any of the U.S. military branches, for example, is a prime example of classical conditioning. When a drill instructor commands newly enlisted recruits to "fall in" (stimulus), these recruits had better "fall into formation" (or "form up") and stand at attention immediately (response). Such conditioning is conducted so that when an order is given, an immediate, involuntary, ingrained response occurs. For example, one of our friends recently attended a graduation ceremony on a U.S. Naval base. When the commanding officer entered the room and the command "attention on deck" was given, his reflexes started to take over and he almost stood at attention—even though he had not been in the Navy for some 20 years.

As behavioral theories continued to evolve, the focus gradually shifted to look at the antecedents of a response. Behaviorists associated with examining consequences of responses or actions include Thorndike, Hull, and Skinner (Lefrançois, 2000; Ormrod, 2004). Of these researchers, Skinner is best known for radical behaviorism and operant conditioning theory. Skinner maintained that there were two types of responses: "those elicited by a stimulus were termed respondents and those simply emitted by an organism were operants" (Lefrançois, p. 96).

One of the main principles of *operant conditioning* emphasizes the consequence of a response, not the stimulus, focusing on the implications of **reinforcement** and punishment (Lefrançois, 2000; Ormrod, 2004). *Positive* reinforcers are used to maintain and strengthen desirable behaviors and are those things considered to be pleasant that are presented after the desired response has occurred, such as praising a student for good work. *Negative* reinforcers are those things considered unpleasant that are removed after the desired behavior has occurred. A classic example of a negative reinforcer is the loud beeping that stops once a seatbelt is fastened.

Two types of punishment can be used to diminish or extinguish undesirable behaviors. Punishment 1 is the presence of something aversive to stop an undesired behavior. For example, to decrease a child's misbehaving, a parent may scold the child. Punishment 2 is the removal of something pleasant to stop undesired behavior. An example would be a teenager's loss of privileges for misbehaving. Both forms of punishment are used after the undesired response has occurred; consequently, punishment is seen as a consequence of a response.

There are several important principles from behaviorism that can be applied to WBI design: practice, reinforcement, active learning, shaping, and modeling. Behavioral research results have shown that repetition through practice strengthens learning. For instance, including instructional strategies or activities, such as sequenced practice after content presentation throughout a course, would allow learners to strengthen a target skill by providing an opportunity for practice.

Reinforcement is another important application of behaviorist themes. Behavioral researchers propose that learners would learn, or exhibit desired behaviors, when provided with positive and negative reinforcers. For positive reinforcers to be effective the learner must view them as pleasant; negative reinforcers must be viewed as unpleasant. For example, to reinforce promptness in submitting assignments and perhaps reduce student anxiety, the WBI instructor can email the students acknowledging receipt of their work (positive reinforcement). In turn, by *not* responding to extraneous emails (negative reinforcement), the WBI instructor may reduce the number of student emails to those that are germane or meaningful for class. Specific examples of positive reinforcers that may be used within emails are identified in Figure 2.4. Because reinforcers are subjective, the WBI designer needs to select potential reinforcers carefully by considering the intended learners' interests, aspirations, backgrounds, and so on.

Undesirable behaviors can be reduced or extinguished by punishment. When administering punishment (due to safety or the requirement of an immediate response), only Punishment 1 type should be used. When continued inappropriate online behavior—such as *spamming* (sending unsolicited or unwanted email [Whatis?com, 2005]) or flaming ("giving someone a verbal lashing in public" [Whatis?com, 2005])—keeps occurring in discussions, the instructor may bar guilty individuals from participating with the group. However, adverse side effects may occur if punishment is used too often or inappropriately (Lefrançois, 2000; Ormrod, 2004). Individuals may display avoidance behaviors (try to avoid learning situations associated with the punishment) or if placed in the situation, learners may try to escape. For example, PK–12 school teachers or coaches should use caution when punishing students by assigning extra assignments (reading, writing, extra laps in swimming, etc.). The unintended result may be that the individual never reads for pleasure or does not participate in sports when such opportunities arise. Because it is doubtful that

Figure 2.4   Positive reinforcers via email.

Positive Reinforcement via email

If you look at Grades, you will see feedback on your matrices. There is an attached file for each of you with my notes and actual scores. **(Knowledge of results with explanation)**

Scores ranged from 73–100. **(Knowledge of results)**

Several of you did not identify the categories of characteristics that you used to compare the models. For those of you who did not include names of characteristics, you may resubmit the matrix to let me take another look at it. **(Corrective feedback)**

Please remember to put your name on your files—when I grade, I generally print the files and take them with me! **(Reminder to encourage appropriate class behaviors)**

any form of punishment would be very successful within a WBI situation, it is best to apply positive reinforcers and avoid negative consequences.

A third principle of behaviorism relevant to WBI is the need for learners to be active rather than passive when responding to an instructional stimulus for learning to occur (Lefrançois, 2000; Ormrod, 2004). Requiring learners to participate in chats or threaded discussions allows the instructor to observe how they are shaping their views on a given subject and whether they are interpreting materials correctly. When mandating such participation, the WBI designer or instructor should both ensure that discussion is essential for student learning and select topics that are not trivial. An example of requiring active behavior through document sharing (uploading information for WBI participants to review) is shown in Figure 2.5.

The principles of shaping and modeling used in instruction also come from behavioral learning theories. *Modeling* is demonstrating a desired goal or response so learners may imitate it to learn a novel response. *Shaping* occurs when reinforcement is provided to individuals' responses as they perform progressively closer approximations to the desired goal (Lefrançois, 2000). Providing exemplary work of past students is one form of modeling. Allowing students to resubmit revised work based on feedback is an example of shaping that could be used (within limits) in WBI. Although such feedback may be essential, it may also be extremely time consuming, even with the use of voice-activated text conversions or change-tracking utilities.

In summary, from behavioral learning theories WBI most often will use practice, reinforcement, and being active responders. Principles used in WBI and underlying the WBID Model from the behavioral perspective include practice, feedback, shaping, and modeling. Together these constructs support appropriate design elements in individual instances of WBI.

See this textbook's Companion Website (http://www.prenhall.com/davidson-shivers) for links to behavioral learning theory sites.

Figure 2.5   Sample requirements for active participation within a threaded discussion.

Directions for threaded discussions

Use the discussion areas for your group to share ideas about evaluation questions.

Task #1: Based on the scenario that you have identified, develop an evaluation goal and post your goal to the discussion area.

Task #2: Brainstorm at least 4 evaluation questions that can be used with your scenario and goal. List your questions on the Evaluation Planning Matrix. For each question, "evaluate" it, based on the ranking or selecting evaluation questions proposed by Fitzpatrick, Sanders, and Worthen (2004). Share your scenario, goal, and evaluation questions with your group.

Have questions about models? Want to share information about models? Visit the Discussion Link about Models. Use this topic to help you with your Model Comparison Matrix.

Cognitive Learning Theories

Cognitive theories emphasize information processing activities within the learner's mind (Ormrod, 2004); *information processing* refers to the mental operations that individuals go through as they apply knowledge, skills, and abilities (Gagné, Briggs, & Wager, 1992). Consequently, the research within this theory base was primarily conducted using humans (Lefrançois, 2000; Ormrod; Richey, 1986).

Even with advances in brain and neuropsychology research, it is often difficult, if not impossible, to observe the actual mental operations an individual performs. For this reason, educational researchers infer how an individual processes information by measuring or observing resulting actions, or responses. For instance, while behaviorists may observe the written answers of a student calculating a mathematical formula to determine whether a behavior is learned, cognitivists use the answers to infer how the learner processed the information when learning and if learning took place. For cognitivists, it becomes not only a matter of what learners do to answer the question but also how they explain (or demonstrate) how they arrived at the answers.

Cognitive learning theories have had a major influence on teaching and learning (and on instructional design) since the mid to late 1970s (Saettler, 1990), and they are still relevant today. The actual beginnings of cognitive research date from the early 1900s with the work of Gestalt theorists such as Wertheimer, Koffka, and Kohler (Sprinthall, Sprinthall, & Oja, 1994). These theorists placed an importance on perception, learning, and the principle that learners were predisposed to organize information in particular ways.

Two noted cognitive theorists are Jean Piaget and Jerome Bruner (Mayer, 2003; Ormrod, 2004). Piaget's theories on development gained popularity in the United States during the 1960s and are still used today. He proposed that humans are active processors of information, more than just being the active responders as suggested by behavioral learning theories. Rather than just responding to a stimulus, Piaget believed that humans are actively involved in their learning and that their perceptions, prior knowledge, skills, and experiences help influence learning. In WBI, learners can be directed to reflect on the lesson at hand, bringing their prior knowledge and skills to the forefront of their attention.

A combination of external stimulus and internal processing facilitates an individual's learning. Additionally, Piaget suggested that as individuals mature, they move through four stages of cognitive development—sensorimotor, preoperational, concrete operations, and formal operations (Driscoll, 2004; Ormrod, 2004; Sprinthall et al., 1994). However, some later research findings do not support all features of his stages in that "it appears that infants and young children are cognitively more sophisticated than Piaget's description of the sensorimotor and preoperational stages would indicate" (Ormrod, p. 167). Ormrod suggests that Piaget (along with Tolman and the Gestalt psychologists) held the idea that an individual's knowledge changes in terms of its structure and organization. Piaget's idea that individuals must assimilate new knowledge into their preexisting knowledge was "groundbreaking research" and is considered current. For designers of WBI, realization that content and activities may have to be tailored to the level of cognitive development might entail heavy use of graphics for concrete learners and use of textual explanations for mature learners.

Bruner's proposals for theories of cognitive development were first made in the late 1950s and implemented during the 1960s and 1970s. One of his notable contributions to instruction and learning was the concept of discovery teaching and learning (Driscoll, 2004;

Lefrançois, 2000; Mayer, 2003; Ormrod, 2004). Bruner did not believe that the lecture method was always the best way to teach (as did B. F. Skinner [1986], by the way); he considered activity the key to successful learning. Bruner proposed that hands-on learning—e.g., discovery teaching and learning—was the best solution to facilitate learning. Discovery learning, which allows students to actively experience learning by manipulating objects, is an important cognitive principle, and may be facilitated in WBI by permitting learners to find their own paths. Providing learners with questions and letting them explore for answers allows instructors to implement a discovery strategy.

Another key principle of cognitivism, learner-centered instruction, emphasizes learners as individuals and central to the creation of effective instruction. The criticalness of hands-on learning and learner-centeredness to cognitive learning theory are reinforced by Mayer, who suggests, "it is not what is done to the learner, but how the learner interprets what happens, that is, on the learner's personal experience" (2003, p. 5). Learner-centeredness is exemplified by the recognition that students are individuals and the main instructional task is to assist each in becoming a successful learner. WBI can be both hands on and learner centered. Simulations can be used to challenge learners and involve them in learning activities.

Related to learner-centeredness is the cognitive principle that all learners have their own perspectives, experiences, and prior knowledge, which influence their learning. Cognitivists maintain that learning must be meaningful and relevant to the individual for learning to take place. When creating WBI, links can be made to prior knowledge and learners can be directed to share experiences and perspectives.

In general, the main cognitive principles that apply to successful WBI include that learning must be meaningful, considering learners' prior knowledge, and centering instruction on the learner. To establish learner meaning or relevance, the designer should structure WBI activities to learners' interests, prior knowledge, and so on. For example, the designer might develop examples that relate to the backgrounds and/or interests of the intended audience. Learners may persist even when they experience feelings of isolation if they perceive that the WBI is meaningful and relevant. To subscribe to the principle of learner-centeredness, designers and instructors recognize that students are individuals and, more importantly, instill an atmosphere that promotes learner success. The instructor may enhance this with personalized, professional responses to student email, to questions, and to learners' work.

See this textbook's Companion Website (http://www.prenhall.com/davidson-shivers) for links to cognitive learning theory sites.

Constructivist Learning Theories

Constructivism derives from the idea that learners construct meaning based on their own experiences and through a social negotiation of that meaning during learning. In the constructivist view, learners interact and contribute to building their own knowledge and skills (Duffy & Jonassen, 1992). Learners are seen as active contributors to their learning and should be involved in their own goal setting.

Constructivism is a relatively new learning theory that came into its own during the 1990s, but not without controversy. This theory has been considered by some to be at one end of the cognitive theory continuum, as a philosophical explanation about the nature of knowledge or as an approach to teaching and learning (Scheurman, 2000). Others contend that it is an emerging set of learning theories that permits extended use of exploration activities for instructional purposes (Airasian & Walsh, 2000; Brooks & Brooks, 1999; Duffy & Jonassen, 1992). Some cognitive principles, such as self-regulated learning, active learning, and schema theory, are found in constructivist learning theories as well. Cognitive theorists (such as Piaget and Bruner) appear as founding theorists for constructivism. Activities in WBI that promote socialization in the learning environment include individual and group interaction, working with experts, mentors, and instructors. The interaction that learners have with other learners helps to build social contacts that help build a learning community.

Other theorists' work, such as Vygotsky's theories on social construction and interaction, are considered fundamental to constructivism. Lev Vygotsky conducted his research in the 1920s to the mid 1930s. Banned in the U.S.S.R. for several decades after his death in 1934, Vygotsky did not gain much influence in Western countries until his writings were translated from Russian into English in the 1960s (Driscoll, 2004; Ormrod, 2004). Two of Vygotsky's main tenets are "complex mental processes begin as social activities as children develop, they gradually internalize these processes and can use them independently from those around them" (Ormrod, p. 169), and "with complex tasks, children benefit from assistance of people who are more advanced and competent than themselves" (Ormrod, p. 170). Competent individuals guide novice learners through scaffolding and their zone of proximal development, providing structured guidance so that learners can perform the tasks (Driscoll, 2004; Ormrod).

Driscoll (2004) suggests that one difference between constructivism and cognitivism lies in the idea that constructivism explores new approaches to theories of cognition and information processing. She postulates that the focus is on adaptation and management of learning and of the environment. This processing occurs when learners construct knowledge from information received rather than just absorb it directly from external sources. Ormrod (2004) maintains that "[some] theorists refer to their perspective as constructivist rather than information processing theory" (p. 180). Another main difference between the two theories is that cognitivism focuses on the learner as an individual whereas constructivism views learners within social settings or contexts (Bigge & Shermis, 2000; Santrock, 2001).

Constructivist principles can be used in WBI in a number of ways. Learners can help generate goals as a class activity. From this perspective, learners participate in directing the learning environment as they build relationships with others in the class and work with an expert (the instructor or mentor) to create a learning experience. For example, Task 1 in Figure 2.5 could have a constructivist orientation by making it a shared group activity; students mutually agree on a scenario and then on a common goal.

A constructivist activity can be made up of authentic tasks that mirror an actual work setting or experience. For example, WebQuests frame activities that learners can complete collaboratively (Dodge, 1997). WebQuests typically pose an issue or problem, then provide a framework with team member roles and activities that help learners resolve the problem (Figure 2.6). The path to the solution is left open to the interpretation of the team members. Dodge recommends that WebQuests be structured around five elements: introduction, tasks, process, evaluation, and conclusion. WebQuests and similar types of Web searches can promote constructivist environments depending on how they are designed and implemented.

Figure 2.6   WebQuest example from QuickScience (http://quickscience.uwf.edu).

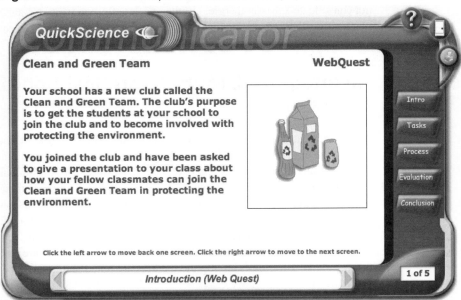

See this textbook's Companion Website (http://www.prenhall.com/davidson-shivers) for links to constructivist learning theory sites.

Foundational Definitions of Learning

Using these perspectives of learning, a definition that frames a view of learning can be established. *Learning* has been commonly defined as permanent changes in behavior due to experiences other than maturation, fatigue, hunger, and so on (Lefrançois, 2000). Mayer (2003) suggests that change that is only physiological is not learning and that learning is a long-term change—any change that disappears in a few hours is not learning. Posttests that occur immediately after a lesson may not be assessing whether learning has occurred; instead, they may be testing only short-term memory.

Ormrod (2004) acknowledges both behavioral and cognitive perspectives in her definition of learning by stating that it is either a permanent change in behavior or a permanent change in mental associations (cognitive processes). In contrast to Ormrod's and Lefrançois's definitions, Mayer (2003) acknowledges that learning is a combination of cognitive and behavioral changes. He considers learning as "lasting changes in the learner's knowledge where such changes are due to experience [and that] learning involves a cognitive change that is reflected in a behavioral change" (p. 5). From a constructive approach, *learning* is defined as acquired knowledge that learners have constructed to make sense of their environment and shared experiences with others (Driscoll, 2004; Duffy & Jonassen, 1992).

With the exceptions of Mayer's (2003) and Ormond's (2004), the other definitions do not consolidate learning theories. Rather, each definition is unique and related to a particular learning theory base. However, for purposes of this discussion, learning is defined from a multitheoretical perspective.

An Integrated, Multitheoretical Approach to Learning

A common practice among psychologists and educators was to subscribe to only one theoretical base or theorist, as when psychologists consider themselves Freudian, Jungian, etc. Some educators maintain this practice today. The American Educational Research Association continues to have special interest groups related to a single theorist or theoretical paradigm, such as the John Dewey Society, Foucault and Education, and Constructivist Theory, Research, and Practice (American Educational Research Association, 2005). Others integrate principles from different theoretical bases. Integrating learning theories does not mean that the principles from each are blended and blurred so that there are no distinctions among them. Instead, differences among the theories are noted and maintained, but used in a cohesive manner.

The **integrated, multitheoretical approach to learning** uses specific principles from a given learning theory for an identified goal, audience, content, or context. It combines as needed elements of behaviorist, cognitive, and constructivist learning theories, suggesting that learning is a permanent change in an individual's cognitive processes, skills, and behaviors. Ertmer and Newby (1993) make distinctions for use of behavioral, cognitive, and constructivist learning theories based somewhat on the outcome level of the intended goal/objective (e.g., use behavioral principles for verbal information or basic knowledge, cognitive for application-type objectives, and constructivism for problem-solving outcomes). Although their approach provides a simple way to extract differences among the three theory bases, it limits the extent to which these theories can explain, describe, or predict learning phenomena. A multitheoretical perspective allows for these robust theories to describe and prescribe teaching and learning processes for various situations. Figure 2.7 represents the integrated, multitheoretical approach to learning.

The integrated, multitheoretical approach employs the three learning theories and their corresponding principles in an eclectic yet pragmatic manner to develop appropriate learning environments. For example, when the learning task requires practice and repetition, it may be best to incorporate principles from behavioral theories. Modeling and shaping can be applied to complex tasks when it is important to have the individual(s) work in small steps while achieving close approximations, moving toward the instructional goal. Use of feedback and positive reinforcement would strengthen the success of each small step during shaping (Ormrod, 2004).

Traditional tutorials might be viewed as presenting stimulus (instructional information) and response (active responding during practice exercises). For example, content on various types of mammals could be presented as the stimulus, followed by practice that requires learners to correctly identify the mammal being shown or described. Corrective feedback follows to shape learners' responses. Presentation of material and practice activities followed by feedback continues until the entire lesson is completed.

Figure 2.7   Integrated, multitheoretical approach to learning.

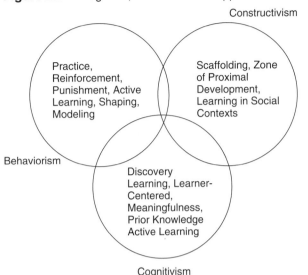

Another example of using behavioral concepts is drill and practice. For instance, students may know the multiplication tables, but instructors will use various speed drills to increase the speed and accuracy of their responses. Another drill and practice example is improving accuracy and speed in appropriate keyboarding (i.e., typing) through timed trials.

By contrast, a cognitive approach to a course would teach individuals to use metacognitive strategies, such as comprehension and affective monitoring, imagery, and schema building, while developing and refining their knowledge. Using encoding processes of selection, acquisition, construction, and integration (Weinstein & Mayer, 1986), the individual would replace inaccurate knowledge with accurate knowledge, which further refines learning. For example, in refining their concepts of birds, learners would include penguins and ostriches, even though they do not have the attribute of "being able to fly" typically associated with birds. Further refinement could extend to categorizing birds into various general classifications (raptors, waterfowl, etc.) and to identifying them by genus and species.

Determining which approach (behavioral or cognitive) to use depends on the characteristics of the individual learners, such as age and prior experiences, and on the context and complexity of the content.

Other examples of strategies that integrate learning theories include using behavioral principles to learn the alphabet, to speak Spanish, or to identify chemical element symbols. With each, the stimulus (the alphabet letters, the actual sounds of Spanish words, or the chemical elements) could be shown, modeled, or displayed in some manner, followed by learners actively responding to the stimulus. Instructors may offer feedback as to whether a learner's response is correct, along with an appropriate positve reinforcer (a token, a smile, or praise).

Cognitive learning principles might be used for instructional purposes related to conceptualizing or applying rules. Learners would classify schemes and determine whether instances fit into categories. The cognitive approach would help learners use schema theory to develop concepts, identify common characteristics of those concepts, and integrate them with preexisting knowledge. Such knowledge integration occurs so that the concepts (or rules) do not become fragmented, isolated bits of information; rather, they are combined and organized to become complete and comprehensive. Such integration also is required of the rules thus learned (Driscoll, 2004; Merrill, Tennyson, & Posey, 1992; Ormrod, 2004).

Consider as examples the processes of learning to calculate algebraic formulas, demonstrate appropriate safety rules, or explain how the three branches of the U.S. government function and interrelate. The relevant cognitive principles would connect new learning to prior knowledge, skills, or experiences to promote meaningful learning. Students may use elaboration strategies for storage and retrieval and practice for automaticity to support their learning.

When problem-based learning is the intended instructional purpose, either constructive or cognitive principles may be most appropriate. (However, behaviorists would argue that principles from behavioral learning theories could be prescribed for effective problem solving.) Which type of learning theory approach to employ depends in part on whether the focus is on the individuals within a learning group or on the group as a whole and on the structure of the content. Cognitivist principles related to problem-solving situations facilitate transferring learning from one situation to a new situation or problem by allowing retrieval of prior knowledge, learning in context (i.e., situated learning) and a thorough learning of the background information and use of heuristics (Driscoll, 2004; Ormrod, 2004). Examples of applying constructivist principles to problem-solving situations include establishing connectivity to learning information (Driscoll, 2004) and allowing for learning in social settings wherein multiple perspectives stimulate multiple solutions. Once the group identifies multiple solutions, they may negotiate to determine the best solution.

An integrated, multitheoretical approach selectively uses the learning principles that are appropriate for particular context, goals, and learners as well as for the content. To fully integrate principles from the learning theories when developing WBI, designers must more thoroughly understand the various learning theories than this brief overview provides. However, this introduction to the philosophical underpinnings should help designers begin to explore the possibilities of an integrated approach.

Defining Learning with the Integrated, Multitheoretical Approach

Based on this integrated approach, **learning** is defined as permanent changes in an individual's cognitive processes, skills, and behaviors brought about by active, meaningful engagement with the knowledge- or skill-based information and with the environment, and by purposeful interaction with others. See Figure 2.7 for the presented learning theories and common strategies associated with those theories.

ON YOUR OWN

What is your theory of learning? How do you define the term? To which theory base(s) do you subscribe? Subscribing to a learning theory or a set of learning theories is a personal choice. How will your views on learning influence the design, delivery, and implementation of your WBI project? Define learning and explain your personal theory. Provide examples of your learning theory in action.

An Overview of Systems Theory

Another foundational area for designing and developing WBI is systems theory (Figure 2.8). The idea of a model, in and of itself, is an example of how systems theory underscores the nature of the ID field (Seels & Richey, 1994). Under general systems theory, interrelated parts of a model work together to build a product in a complete, logical manner (Andrews & Goodson, 1980). There are generally two types of systems, open and closed. **Closed systems** are those entities that are self-reliant and excluded from external elements, including the environment. Conversely, in **open systems,** the environment, in addition to the parts of the entity, influences the processes, inputs, and outputs involved in the system (Rothwell & Kazanas, 2004). In turn, feedback is received from the environment that can be used to improve, worsen, or in some other manner affect the system. Thus, an open system may be considered as always evolving and adapting to inputs via feedback (Banathy, 1987).

Most educational and training systems are open environments. The "within system" factors for educational systems include elements such as administrators, faculty, staff, and learners; buildings and other facilities; and organizational policies and procedures. External, environmental factors include legislatures and taxpayers (if a public school or higher education institution), parents, accrediting agencies, and so on.

For training systems, internal factors would include the various levels of personnel, facilities, policies, and so on; external factors could be the marketplace, the national and/or global economy, world events, and so on. Because development of training is influenced by factors from inside and outside the system, it is considered an open system.

Figure 2.8 Systems theory in the WBID Model.

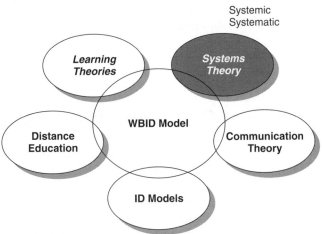

As instruction is defined, designed, and developed, a systematic approach ensures that the factors from the various inputs, processes, and outputs are considered. The systematic development of instruction enables a logical plan that facilitates the design and development of effective instruction. Using a model for instructional design embodies the systematic view of the instructional design process itself.

Systematic and Systemic

Two terms that are often bandied about in the instructional design field are systematic and systemic. **Systematic** refers to an organized approach to developing instructional innovation (product or process). **Systemic** relates to the idea that the innovation, whether it is a product, policy, or process, is disseminated and diffused throughout the organization (Reigeluth & Garfinkle, 1994). In other words, *systemic* refers to the impact of the innovation and how it is experienced by the entire organization.

Just because a systematic approach is used does not mean that design is a linear or lock-step process (i.e., one step is completed before another begins); instead *systematic* means that the approach is methodical, orderly, and logical. Most ID models are organized so that a designer does *not* have to perform steps in a predetermined and specified manner. Although the schematics of a model may suggest a linear pathway, most include loops back through the steps, which indicate complex procedures (Gustafson & Branch, 2003). For instance, a designer may choose to start with analyzing the learner audience before instructional content, or may complete both tasks simultaneously.

The very nature of instructional design makes its procedures iterative. This iterative aspect is especially seen when formative evaluation is incorporated early into design and development procedures. Early results through these reviews and tryouts allow for the designer to change the instruction as needed. For instance, during design and development, WBI may go through various iterations (initial drafts, graphics added, etc.) prior to its implementation. These iterations are based on the formative evaluation results.

The greatest influence from systems theory on the WBID Model is shown in how ID procedures systematically allow for the WBI to progress through various iterations as the product is readied for implementation. A systemic influence occurs when WBI becomes integrated into the organization and has shown an effect on the entire organization's mission, or goal.

See this textbook's Companion Website (http://www.prenhall.com/davidson-shivers) for links to general systems theory websites.

An Overview of Communication Theory

The fields of communication, psychology, and education are closely associated with each other in that they focus on how individuals perceive, attend to, and retain instructional content (Fleming, 1987; Grabowski, 1995; Lohr, 2003; Seels & Richey, 1994). From this perspective, communication theory is another foundational area for WBI design (Figure 2.9). Richey (1986) states that "communication theory explains the process of transmitting information, the form and structure of the information and the functions and effects of the information" (p. 43).

Figure 2.9   Communication theory in the WBID Model.

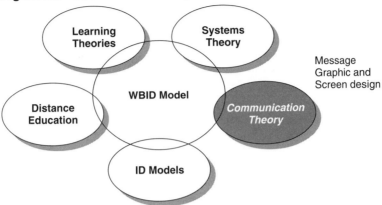

Figure 2.10   Simple model of communication between sender and receiver.

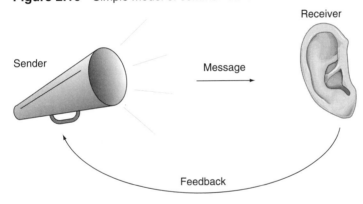

Communication influences how messages are created and distributed to and from learners, among learners, and between learner and instructor, and influences the instruction itself. In the basic communication model, a sender creates a message and sends it to a receiver through a delivery system. On receiving the message, the receiver processes and interprets it and then provides feedback to the sender. Messages may be unclear for a variety of reasons, referred to as *noise* in a traditional communication model (Grabowski, 1995; Lohr, 2003; Ormrod, 2004). **Noise** is anything that prevents the sender from correctly sending the message or the receiver from correctly receiving or interpreting a message. Figure 2.10 illustrates a simple model of communication.

Noise in a Web-based environment may range from faulty message composition to poor page design to the stability of the learning management system (e.g., technical problems due to equipment malfunction or access problems). Such noise can keep learners from interacting with the instruction, the instructor, and each other.

The main communication theory principles used in WBI design are associated with message design. Grabowski (1995) states that

> message design is one step in the instructional development process which carries out the specifications of the ID blueprint in greater detail. Like blueprints for a house which do not specify the finishing touches of color, furniture, placement, etc., instructional blueprints do not always specify the "form" the message should take. (p. 225)

Message design encompasses the visual features of text and graphics and their placement on the page. In a Web-based environment, proper message design allows designers to create appealing and suitable layouts for Web pages and websites. Additionally, communication principles facilitate smooth navigation within these virtual environments by using buttons, icons, or hypermedia links and through text and media (e.g., audio, video, and multimedia). Ideas based on message design help designers facilitate effective dialogue and exchange of information.

See this textbook's Companion Website (http://www.prenhall.com/davidson-shivers) for links to communication theory sites.

On Your Own

How do systems theory and communications theory relate to the design and delivery of WBI? What key concepts in systems and communication theory will you consider when designing your WBI? How do systems and communication theory concepts influence your use of learning theories in the design of WBI?

Instructional Design Models

The final foundational base of the WBID Model is the use of instructional design (ID) models (Figure 2.11). Andrews and Goodson (1980) conducted an analysis of the basic models and delineated attributes of over 40 instructional design models. Of those 40 and more recently developed ID models, only a few are commonly used within ID programs.

Traditional ID Models

Most ID models follow the generic ADDIE model: analysis, design, development, implementation, and evaluation. The most commonly used ID models are associated with Gagné's (1985) conditions of learning, such as the Gagné, Briggs, and Wager (1992) model, the Dick, Carey, and Carey (2005) model, and the Smith and Ragan (2005) model. These models are known as either condition-based models (Ragan & Smith, 2004) or product-development models (Gustafson & Branch, 2003) and prescribe designing and developing instruction at the micro level. **Micro-level design** focuses on planning and de-

Figure 2.11 Instructional design models in the WBID Model.

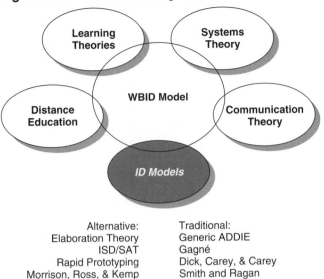

Alternative:
Elaboration Theory
ISD/SAT
Rapid Prototyping
Morrison, Ross, & Kemp

Traditional:
Generic ADDIE
Gagné
Dick, Carey, & Carey
Smith and Ragan

veloping at the lesson, unit, or course level, using any form of delivery (print-based, multimedia, etc.). Commonly used ID textbooks discuss design in terms of self-paced, independent learning, although instructional materials may be adapted to facilitator-led classroom approaches.

These models have common core elements that include determining learner needs, identifying instructional goals and objectives, developing assessment tools, planning for instructional strategies and media, and conducting field tests (formative evaluation) (Andrews & Goodson, 1980; Richey, 1986; Seels & Glasgow, 1990, 1998). Summative evaluation is described as occurring after initial instructional implementation. However, when teaching ID models, the last stages, implementation and summative evaluation, do not receive much attention due to lack of time and availability of target audiences; implementation procedures may not be planned and summative evaluation may be planned but not conducted. In professional ID practice, both stages are typically left for others to carry out and may not receive much designer input.

Alternative ID Models and Processes

In addition to traditional ID models, other models, known as *alternative models,* have been proposed. Elaboration Theory is a model associated with the development instruction at the macro level (Reigeluth, 1987, 1999). **Macro-level design** involves entire training or educational programs or curricula rather than course or lesson design (Reigeluth). Following a macro-level design for WBI, the organization's curriculum or programs are taken into consideration.

Other alternative models are geared toward particular settings. The Department of Defense (DOD) has a model called the Instructional Systems Design/Systems Approach to Training (ISD/SAT) that replaces the formerly used IPISD model (Barrington & Kimani, 2003). The ISD/SAT model has been developed for use within branches of the U.S. military and has three main parts—the inner part is instructional design, the middle part relates to management, and the outer part relates to quality improvement. Other models, such as those proposed by Morrison, Ross, and Kemp (2004) or Reiser and Dick (1996), are particularly applicable for teachers in PK–12 school environments. These classroom ID models often incorporate a stage that requires the teacher/designer to locate and supply instructional materials rather than to actually develop them.

Another alternative ID model is, in actuality, a process known as rapid prototyping. The purpose of rapid prototyping is to show that the instructional product will work and gain approval prior to full-scale development (Gustafson, 2002; Reiser, 2002; Seels & Glasgow, 1998; Tripp & Bicklemyer, 1990). The guiding principle behind rapid prototyping is to expeditiously develop prototypic instructional materials. In other words, designers quickly build a working (but perhaps not fully functioning) model in the early stages of the project and its development continues through a set of tryouts accompanied with product revisions until an acceptable version is completed (Gustafson).

According to Richey and Morrison (2002, p. 203), "rapid prototyping is thought to decrease the design time" and a cost savings occurs due to this shortened timeframe. However, the use of rapid prototyping within instructional design is not without controversy. Gustafson (2002) warns that there may be risks associated. Clients or the design team may not have a clear understanding of the process, complexity may add to the management of the project, and endless revisions may be conducted. When such risks occur, the potential cost savings in time, resources, and effort may vanish. With some caution, rapid prototyping procedures have gained acceptance within the ID field, especially related to business and industry and the military.

Boling and Frick (1997) suggest using holistic rapid prototyping in Web-based design to test usability early in development. They advocate that the designer begin with a paper prototype, test and revise accordingly, and then build the website. They state that this process allows "for efficient Website development that avoids the most errors possible and offers the most of what your users want" (p. 320).

The traditional ID procedures of designing and then developing a prototype, followed by a series of formative evaluation tryouts, may not be realistic or practical in most situations. Nichols (1997, p. 379) suggests that traditional ID formative evaluation procedures are usually conducted in a "close personalized manner" and to perform such with WBI evaluation may be more expensive in that the evaluator and the tryout members will have to be brought together, which could be cost prohibitive if they must travel great distances. However, he does suggest that formative tryouts, although different from the traditional, may be conducted at a distance through electronic means, such as emails and conferencing systems.

WBI usually requires revision after implementation and, again, changes the conventional ID process. Such revisions are necessary to account for the influx of new information, changes with website links, and new innovations found in the learning management system, computer hardware, or software applications and utilities.

See this textbook's Companion Website (http://www.prenhall.com/davidson-shivers) for links to instructional design model websites.

ON YOUR OWN

Why is it important to understand both traditional and alternative ID models in relation to WBI design? How do such ID models provide a foundational base for your own WBI design?

An Overview of the Web-Based Instructional Design (WBID) Model

The Web-Based Instructional Design (WBID) Model includes the basic stages of analysis, design and development, implementation, and evaluation that are common to traditional ID models, but applied in a different order. Figure 2.12 illustrates the WBID Model stages. The WBID Model approaches design as an iterative process, which allows for the WBI to evolve throughout its design stages. This process begins in the early conceptualization of a WBI project and culminates with summative evaluation after full implementation. The concurrency of design, development, and formative evaluation (Davidson-Shivers & Rasmussen, 1999) is illustrated by the overlapping circles in the figure.

The WBID Model begins with the analysis stage and moves to evaluation planning. Preliminary planning of formative and summative evaluation occurs at the same time. Concurrent design, development, and the conducting of formative evaluation follow the evaluation planning stage. Initial WBI implementation occurs next. In this system, evaluation becomes an integral part of WBID. Summative evaluation is conducted after full implementation occurs. Determining the time frame for summative evaluation depends on the life cycle of the WBI.

Each stage of the WBID Model contains or culminates in decision points, action plans, and products. The shift from one stage to another is seamless in nature. This seamlessness is especially observed in WBI design and development where prototypes are designed and tested before moving into full implementation. A short description of each of the stages appears next; subsequent chapters present full explanations and examples of the stages.

Analysis Stage

The analysis stage is the initial stage in the WBID Model and contains two phases: problem analysis and instructional component analysis. Documentation of the WBID process begins in the analysis stage. This written documentation is part of a larger report, commonly known as a **Design Document.** Designers use Design Documents to describe the procedures used, state decisions made, and report results. Included in a Design Document are rationales and justifications as to why decisions were made and by whom. (The analysis stage is the subject of Chapters 3 and 4.)

Figure 2.12   Interrelationship of the WBID Model stages. The "Concurrent Design" circle indicates an iterative process among the stages within the circle. Solid arrows are direct connections. Dashed arrows connect results of one stage to another. For example, evaluation planning is connected to conducting both formative and summative evaluations. Final planning of and conducting summative evaluation occurs after full WBI implementation.

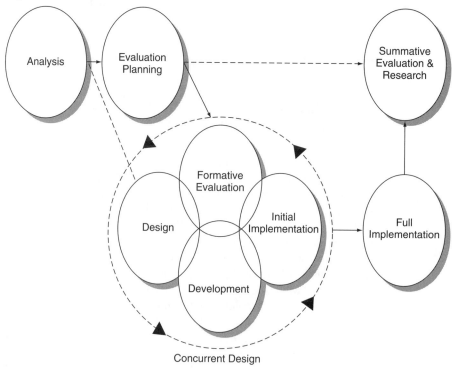

Concurrent Design

Problem Analysis.   The purposes of this first phase of the analysis stage are to investigate performance problems and identify appropriate solutions. Several steps are involved in examining any gap between the desired performance and the actual performance. The gap, or problem, may be based on lack of skills, knowledge, or motivation (Rossett, 1987, 1999; Rothwell & Kazanas, 2004; Stolovitch & Keeps, 1999). In some cases, instruction is not the best solution and designers need to examine performance technology alternatives such as policy revisions, job aids, and personnel issues (Jonassen, Hannum, & Tessmer, 1989; Rossett, 1987, 1999, 2002b; Van Tiem, Moseley, & Dessinger, 2001; Zemke & Kramlinger, 1982). If instruction is selected as the appropriate solution, the designer determines the appropriate delivery system. One influential factor to consider when determining the feasibility of WBI is to evaluate the WBI tools and options and support available in an institution. WBI may be created by developing Web pages using an authoring tool or learning management system, which have specific facilities for designing online instruction (Horton, 2000). Designers must have access to software and hardware tools to design and develop WBI.

Instructional Component Analyses. The second phase of analysis requires the designer to analyze the four components of the instructional situation. This analysis is conducted only when instruction has been determined as the best solution to the problem and when WBI is a viable form of delivery. The four main components of the instructional component analyses are goals(s), context, learners, and instructional content. The following questions can be used to frame this analysis (Davidson, 1990; Davidson-Shivers, 1998):

- What should be the goals, or purposes, of the WBI?
- What is the WBI context?
- Who are the learners?
- What is the instructional content?

Instructional Goal Analysis. The second phase begins with instructional goal identification. An *instructional goal* is a general statement of what learners or participants will be able to do after the WBI is completed. The outcome level for the instructional goal is determined here.

Instructional Context Analysis. As a matter of our personal preference, the context, or environmental, analysis of the instructional situation occurs next in the WBID Model. The two main purposes of context analysis are to (1) describe the environment in which WBI is designed and delivered and (2) examine the organizational infrastructure, the competency of its personnel, learners' access to technology, and capacity of support systems in the virtual environment.

Learner Analysis. The purpose of learner analysis is to identify learner interests, needs, and abilities, as well as learners' prior knowledge, skills, and experiences (Davidson-Shivers & Rasmussen, 1999; Dick et al., 2005; Smith & Ragan, 2005). For instance, determining interests of the intended learner group is necessary to create appropriate instructional examples and relevant practice exercises. Learner analysis involves determining reading and computer skills because of the text-intensive nature of WBI in its current state. However, the need for such skills may be reduced as WBI technological tools evolve to allow nonreaders and novice computer users to become involved in online learning. The *Americans with Disabilities Act* (ADA), which was signed into law in 1990 (U.S. Department of Justice, 1990), and the Web Accessibility Initiative (World Wide Web Consortium [W3C], 2001) mandate that Web-based instruction be designed to accommodate individuals with disabilities.

Instructional Content Analysis. The last component for analysis is the instructional content. The designer determines the structure and sequence of major steps and subskills that will be presented within the WBI. This analysis takes the learner analysis into account to identify where the WBI should begin and what entry skills are needed for learners to participate successfully.

The findings from this second analysis phase provide implications for how the WBI will come to fruition. Findings have a direct impact on the remaining WBID stages.

Evaluation Planning Stage

The evaluation planning stage specifically directs the designer to plan for formative and summative evaluation of the instructional product. (Formative evaluation is the subject of Chapter 5.) The formative evaluation plan addresses the following:

- Who are the stakeholders?
- What is being evaluated?
- Who are the evaluators and reviewers?
- What are the evaluation methods?
- When and how should this evaluation take place?
- What types of decisions need to be made as the WBI design plans and prototypes are developed?

As design and development occurs, other experts may be asked to review the WBI prototype for accuracy, completeness, clarity, instructional soundness, and appeal. The WBID Model uses both ID experts and subject matter experts (SMEs) in this process to improve the WBI as it evolves. Additionally, learners and instructors (if not a part of the design team) review WBI, but that review may occur during later stages.

The final part of formative evaluation planning is the tryouts with end users, another point of departure of the WBID Model when compared to traditional ID models. The initial implementation is used for the field trial of the WBI prototype. Whereas traditional ID models generally include one-to-one, small-group, and field trials at the end of development, WBI is often developed and implemented without the advantage of using such groups. Field testing may not occur because the instructor developing WBI does not have an ID background, the organization does not provide support for it, or such tryouts are impractical. Even with an ID background or organizational support, it may not be feasible for the designer to locate sample groups to try out the WBI prior to initial implementation since one object of WBI is to provide access to individuals who are at a distance from the sponsoring organization.

The second part of the evaluation planning stage is developing preliminary plans for summative evaluation. This preliminary planning is an important feature of the WBID Model. Often, data about instructional products or practices currently in use are *not* collected before a new innovation is introduced (Solomon & Gardner, 1986) and then valuable information is lost. Losing such data makes comparing new and old interventions or innovations difficult, if not impossible, and discussion of the new innovation's effectiveness becomes somewhat limited. The purpose of preliminary planning of summative evaluation is to ensure that necessary data collection happens related to the instruction currently in place.

Concurrent Design Stage

Based on the findings of the analysis stage and the formative evaluation plans, the concurrent design stage incorporates the processes of design, development, and evaluation. (This stage is the subject of chapters 6–8.)

Preplanning Activities.   The concurrent design stage actually begins with preplanning activities prior to the start of design processes, related to establishing a budget and allocating resources. The instructional designer or project manager assigns design team members to identified project tasks. A timeline for the WBI project is developed.

Design Processes.   Design processes include specifying objectives and drafting assessments (Gagné et al., 1992), which are displayed on the Task-Objective-Assessment Item Blueprint (TOAB) (Davidson-Shivers, 1998; Northrup, 2001). The TOAB is a matrix containing identified learning tasks (of the instructional content), WBI objectives (with outcome levels), and sample assessment items, and provides a way to align task, objective, and assessment. Instructional and motivational strategies are also planned, and are documented on the WBI Strategy Worksheet. This worksheet becomes the second blueprint for the WBI product and its development and includes four sections—Orientation to Learning, Instruction on the Content, Measurement of Learning, and Summary and Close (Davidson-Shivers, 1998; Rasmussen, 2002).

Development Processes.   As the strategies for each section are planned, iterative design and development begins: development does not wait until the design for the entire WBI is completed. For instance, once the Orientation to Learning section of the WBI is planned (i.e., designed), then its development may begin simultaneously with the design of the next section, Instruction on the Content; this occurs until all sections are designed and developed. For complex WBI projects, it may be that one segment (i.e., unit, lesson, module, etc.) of the WBI is designed and moves into development, followed by another segment, until all are completed. Concurrent design allows for seamless and simultaneous design and development. Formative evaluation is involved in the cyclical process as each prototype becomes an improved iteration of the former one. Concurrent design helps designers plan and create either the instructional events within a simple WBI project or multiple lessons or units within a complex WBI project.

Implementation Stage

The implementation stage occurs when the WBI is ready to be used by learners. It is discussed in terms of initial and full implementation. (Implementation is the subject of Chapter 9.)

Initial Implementation.   The initial implementation is included as a part of concurrent design. It is part of formative evaluation because it may be the first opportunity to field test the WBI with an actual audience in its intended setting. This inclusion in the concurrent design stage is a distinction between the WBID Model and other ID models.

Full Implementation.   With full implementation, the interrelated aspects of facilitation and management are emphasized. Full implementation occurs when any major revisions have been completed and the WBI has been disseminated to a large portion of its intended audience (Gagné et al., 1992). Within either implementation (initial or full), the two main aspects are facilitation and management.

   Facilitation.   **Facilitation** is the execution of the WBI and establishment of the learning community by the implementation team. The implementation team may include the instructor, learners, technical and administrative support, administrators, and mentors.

Management.   **Management** refers to the operations of maintaining the Web-based learning environment throughout the WBI's life span. It includes routinely updating the website, repairing any inactive links, and upgrading the software and utilities.

Summative Evaluation and Research Stage

The final stage of the WBID Model is summative evaluation that occurs at a designated point during the WBI life cycle, when the WBI has been fully implemented for a specified time. The purpose of summative evaluation is similar to that in other ID models: determining whether the WBI is still needed and still effective. Summative evaluation procedures are based on the preliminary plan proposed by the designer during evaluation planning. With WBI, summative evaluation often becomes a plan for conducting research, and a report of the process, results, and recommendations is prepared for stakeholders to help them make decisions about the future use of the WBI. (Summative evaluation is the subject of Chapter 10.)

Summary of the WBID Model

The WBID Model is an integrated approach that ensures that WBI design, development, and implementation meet the instructional goal(s) as well as the needs of the learners and the organization. Although each stage will be discussed separately in the following chapters, it is important to realize that some stages need to be carried out in tandem. The stages and phases within the stages are conjoined rather than being isolated. This concurrency makes the WBID Model unique and complex, yet practical when designing WBI.

The remaining chapters further delineate the stages of the WBID Model. We will discuss some aspects of the stages separately for the purposes of simplification and clarity; however, the reality is that most are intertwined during WBI design. We will note when such aspects should be used in concert.

 ## On Your Own

Compare the WBID Model to other ID models with which you are familiar. Evaluate the specific stages of the WBID Model. What are the advantages and disadvantages of using the WBID Model when creating WBI as opposed to using other models?

Meet the Players

To facilitate the discussion of the WBID Model stages, we provide one case example of a WBI project being designed and developed by a small design team and will refer to it throughout the remaining chapters. Four additional case studies, introduced at the end of this chapter, provide alternative scenarios to the primary example in order to enhance your instructional design skills. They appear at the end of each subsequent chapter in a section titled Extending Your Skills. The introduction to the primary case example, *GardenScapes,* follows.

GardenScapes

GardenScapes features Kally Le Rue, a junior college continuing education instructor who is interested in the possibilities of creating a Web-based course. She teaches in the landscaping and gardening division of the college. Her introductory course, *Garden Basics: Just Another Day at the Plant,* earned high interest and increasing enrollment over the last few years. Begun as a homeowner's guide to lawns and gardens, its main purpose was to identify the soil type, temporal zone, and types of plants that would do well in the learners' locations, and introduce basic garden tools.

Because of the growing interest in gardening and landscaping, she would like to create a new, second course that would allow amateur gardeners and landscapers to add garden features to their yards. Her current conception of this proposed course is that it would help participants design a garden and develop it to create a new home garden feature.

Clatskanie Junior College (CJC) is located in Westport, Somewhere, U.S.A. CJC administrators have shown a recent interest in expanding their campus and reaching new students through online courses. They have always had distance education programs available, but until recently did not use online delivery. A relatively new institutional commitment to online courses has expanded the duties of the director of the Teaching and Learning Development Center (TLDC), Carlos Duartes. The TLDC also houses the technical support system for CJC in addition to providing faculty development services.

Kalantha (Kally) Le Rue, the instructor of *Garden Basics,* has been given approval to create a second course with the expressed administrative goal of reaching a larger audience and generating funding for continued enhancement and growth of distance delivered courses. Ms. Le Rue has had general experiences in using the Web, but none in course delivery. However, she is committed to using Web-based delivery for this project. Ms. Le Rue is not an instructional designer, nor has she developed any instruction other than her face-to-face courses. She will be the instructor and one member of the project's design team.

ON YOUR OWN

From the information you have gathered about your proposed WBI project, describe its general scenario. Describe the educational or other organization you are producing the project for. Briefly identify your primary WBID team members, and list their strengths and weaknesses as they relate to the project.

Wrapping Up

The purpose of this chapter was to establish the framework for the WBID Model, which is based on the theories of learning, systems, and communication, and on instructional design models. Another foundational area, distance education, was discussed in Chapter 1. In this discussion, various principles associated with the theoretical bases were explained and incorporated into the WBID Model.

This chapter provided an overview of the WBID Model and its stages. The initial stage, analysis, has two phases, problem analysis and instructional component analysis, which in turn, includes analyses of the instructional goal, context, learner, and content. The findings from the analysis stage provide information for the next two stages: evaluation planning and concurrent design. The evaluation planning stage has the designer developing two plans: one for formative evaluation and a preliminary plan for summative evaluation. Based on the plans for formative evaluation, evaluation procedures are incorporated into the concurrent design stage. Once development of the WBI and its website are completed, its implementation may begin.

The implementation stage has two interrelated aspects: facilitation and management. However, during the initial implementation, formative evaluation may continue in terms of a field trial with a tryout group (or the participants in the initial course offering). Full implementation occurs once major revisions have occurred and the majority of its intended audience is using the WBI.

After a predetermined number of the WBI runs or specified time period, a final plan for summative evaluation is created and then conducted. The purpose of summative evaluation is to determine whether the WBI in its present state should be continued.

The WBID Model provides for an integrated approach to design, drawing on theory and practice. This model is a naturalistic way for instructional designers to develop WBI. The WBID Model identifies guidelines and considerations for delivering instruction through the Web. By facilitating a seamless flow of information, products, and processes between and among its stages, the model allows for flexibility. The WBID Model is robust and works well with other types of instructional and learning environments, not just WBI.

A final section in this chapter, Meet the Players, introduced the case example, *GardenScapes,* that will be used throughout the book to showcase the stages of the WBID model.

Expanding Your Expertise

1. What is the main learning theory of your organization? Does it align with your personal theory of learning?
2. Conduct an online library search on a particular learning theorist or learning theory or paradigm to increase your knowledge on the subject. How does the information that you acquire change your view of learning?

3. Conduct a Web search on general systems and/or communication theories as related to WBI design. What other principles from these theoretical bases can be applied to WBI design? As you review, how do you evaluate the found websites for reliability and trustworthiness?

4. How does general systems theory relate to designing online instruction?

5. Do you have a personal theory for effective communication? Explain it and how it relates to designing online instruction.

6. Which ID models have you used for other instructional design projects? How do those models fit into your personal theory of learning? How do those models compare to the WBID Model?

7. What are stages of the WBID Model? Why is the sequence of the stages not the same as the ordering of most traditional ID models? Do you think that this modification is (or will be) a good ID practice? If so, why? If not, why not?

8. How could the WBID Model be adapted for other instructional design situations that do not involve Web-based delivery? Should it be adapted for other ID uses? Why or why not?

Extending Your Skills

The following four case studies are used throughout this book to provide additional scenarios of Web-based instruction design. They can be used as a focus of class discussions and as an extension of each chapter's instructional content. The cases are designed for practicing and enhancing instructional design skills. Purposefully, we have *not* completely detailed all possible elements of each case. This lack of full detail allows for interpretation of events and permits adding or inferring further information.

Case Study 1   ## PK–12 Schools

Megan Bifford works at the central office of the Westport District Schools. She has completed her master's degree in Instructional Design and Technology at Myers University while teaching elementary school. Certified in elementary and science education, Megan was hired to fill a new county technology coordinator/curriculum development position. One of her major responsibilities is to promote technology integration in the elementary schools in her district. Although her charge is to facilitate changes in elementary grade levels, kindergarten through fifth grade, she wants to make sure that the changes that she initiates are successful. Megan wants to start out with a pilot program that she can implement throughout the schools focusing on the successful integration and use of technology. She would like to use WBI as a delivery system.

The new superintendent has been in his position for six months. He is particularly interested in how the Internet can be incorporated into the classroom to excite and motivate students. He just returned from a conference where reports were presented of student performance improving when technology was integrated into the curriculum. He is also concerned about safety and making sure children only access appropriate sites. To help with this concern, the district has a firewall system that governs access. In addition, district policy states that students do not access the Internet without adult supervision. In a new position, with an excited superintendent, who is demanding change and improved performance, Megan is feeling pressure to succeed.

Megan realizes that it is impossible for her convert all of the curricula to technology-rich environments. Instead, she decides to look at this problem systematically. With the help of Cassie Angus, the school district's science education coordinator, Megan decides to start with the science curriculum for fifth grade, based on the results from the statewide, standardized tests from the last two years, which found that the fifth-grade students scored well below the norm in the area of science. On top of that, for the first time, science scores will be included in the overall school assessment grade in the next academic year. With the national, state, and district emphasis on science, especially in developing inquiry-based skills, as mandated by National Science Standards and federal legislation, the pressure is on.

One of the strategies that Megan is considering is a series of WebQuests where students will solve real-world problems using scientific methods and actual data. The WebQuests will be designed to let students explore topics in a constructivist framework as they practice inquiry learning. The WebQuests will be comprised of online and offline activities using an authentic learning environment. Students will work independently and in cooperative groups.

Megan attends school improvement and PTA meetings at one of the elementary schools and talks with several parents about the new planned curriculum enhancements. Some parents express concern about their children having access to the Web. Other constraints such as severe cuts in the school budget and personnel may impede the technology integration. Not all of the news is bad, however; the district was awarded a technology grant, and there are other resources for enhancing technical support. As she considers whether a WebQuest is an appropriate solution for improving performance, she will further investigate how technology and the Internet can be used in the classroom.

Case Study 2   Business and Industry

Homer Spotswood is responsible for designing, developing, and facilitating training for the Milton Manufacturing (M2) Company, Inc., an international manufacturing company. The CEO of M2, Ira "Bud" Cattrell, has mandated that the new training initiatives must focus on safety issues to comply with ISO standards and new OSHA regulations. He has also required that the training occur with minimal disruption to plant operations. Because the plant operates on a 24/7 schedule, training will have to be available around the clock. The administrative team expects that WBI will allow for employees to clock in and out of their normal duties to virtually "attend" the safety training.

To meet governmental requirements, a portion of the proposed WBI requires that teams of plant employees complete the instruction at the same time to develop collaborative and cooperative safety skills, requiring a moderate amount of physical, face-to-face interaction. At the same time, some team members will still be required to remain at their job site for safety and security reasons.

Plant operations have been computerized, with systems located throughout the plant; in addition, there are a number of computers in one of the training rooms. Each employee break room has at least one computer available for communication and training purposes.

M2 does not have the facilities or necessary support for complex Internet applications. Following company policy, advanced computer systems are housed and administered externally. Outsourcing will permit the use of a learning management system, if deemed to be appropriate for the instruction, to schedule and record employee progress as they complete the safety training. It is anticipated, based on administrative directives, that WBI, along with face-to-face activities, will be the preferred solution. One of the main considerations that Bud Cattrell has stressed is that whatever system is used, it must be able to show who has successfully completed the training and when, and what level of performance each employee has attained.

A new focus on performance at M2 has required that the training department show a positive return on investment (ROI). In addition, easily accessible reports are necessary should any OSHA inspectors request them. Additionally, these computer systems will help the M2 Company comply with EPA, ISO and OSHA standards. With these requirements in mind, Homer plans to use a behavioral framework to develop the instructional materials, since personal performance is the key to an employee's success and M2's compliance.

Case Study 3   Military

Commander Rebekah Feinstein returns to her office after a meeting with the commanding officer, Captain Cameron Prentiss. As the academic operations officer of a U.S. Navy Training Support Center, she and her staff of military and civilian education and training professionals are responsible for the development and delivery of curricula for the Combat Systems and Engineering Systems "A" schools.

Commander Feinstein has learned that Naval Education and Training Command has begun a comprehensive program to transform how Navy training is conducted. The "Revolution in Training" capitalizes on the efficiencies afforded by human performance technology and a government/industry initiative called Advanced Distributed Learning (ADL).

A redesign and repurposing development effort is currently underway. In the Support Center, there are subject matter experts (SMEs), graphic artists, animators, information technologists, and instructional designers available to participate in the project. Photographic, videographic, and narration support will be available as required. The redesign will take a cognitivist perspective of the learning environment.

Case Study 4   Higher Education

Dr. Joe Shawn is an associate professor in the Business College at Myers University. In addition to teaching on-campus courses in the Management Department, he has created his own online courses for the last eight years and is considered the guru of online learning by the department chair and other faculty. He has already decided that his next project will be the revamping of his undergraduate course, *Introduction to Management,* to Web delivery. The objectives outlined in the course syllabus are a variety of skills, ranging from foundational to analysis and evaluation.

Although Dr. Shawn has found that undergraduates are usually very proficient Web users, he has observed that they are not necessarily motivated to take online courses. He considers that the best approach might be to use Web-enhanced format (WEI) rather than fully online WBI. As he reviews the present course topics, content, and assignments, he will outline the advantages and disadvantages of the different ways that the Web can be used in the college classroom. He believes that WEI would enhance the content and assignments.

Additionally, after five years as an associate professor, he is beginning to think about promotion to full professor. He knows the requirements for that promotion and wonders if spending time producing another WBI will help in meeting this goal. The administration at Myers University considers technology integration and course development to be part of a faculty member's workload; however, Dr. Shawn is not sure whether the University's promotion and tenure system accepts such creative activities as evidence of creative endeavors or teaching excellence when considering promotion to full professor. He has scheduled meetings to discuss these concerns with his department chair, Dr. Amber Wolfgang. As he waits to meet with her, he begins work on repurposing the course for Web-enhanced delivery.

PART 2

THE WBID MODEL FOR CREATING A WEB-BASED COMMUNITY OF LEARNERS

Analysis: Considering Outcomes, Context, and Learners

Analysis is the initial stage of the WBID Model. At the beginning of this stage, problems are investigated and potential solutions are identified. If a Web-based instructional solution is considered to be the most viable approach to the problem, the second phase is to analyze the four main instructional components within the situation: the instructional goal, instructional context, learners, and instructional content. The findings from these analyses provide the foundation for how the WBI will come to fruition.

Chapter 3 begins with discussion of the first analysis phase, problem analysis. Included in this discussion is determining the causes, symptoms, and solutions and identifying the procedures for gap analysis. We next address the first three components of the instructional situation, examining their purposes, methods for gathering data, and procedures for documenting the findings. We devote Chapter 4 to a thorough discussion of the remaining analysis component, instructional content analysis, and the associated implications of the anaylsis process.

Objectives

At the end of this chapter, you should be able to do the following:
- Define terminology associated with the analysis stage.
- State the purpose of the analysis stage.
- Identify two phases of the analysis stage.
- Distinguish among problems, causes, symptoms, and solutions.
- Determine when a problem, or gap, analysis should be conducted.
- Decide the type of solution required.
- Identify the four main components of the instructional situation.
- Classify the instructional goal by the Categories of Learning or other taxonomy.
- Write a preliminary instructional goal statement.
- Describe important aspects of the context.
- Describe pertinent attributes of the learners.

Introduction

The first stage of the WBID Model is analysis (Figure 3.1), as is true for most ID models. Hannum and Hanson (1989) consider analysis one of the most complex instructional design stages, and this is no less true for Web-based instruction (WBI). They further state that analysis is considered one of the most time-consuming stages. Beliefs that analysis is time consuming and, therefore, expensive often lead to this stage being short changed in projects. However, through expedient planning and careful execution, analysis can be both efficient and cost effective. Carefully planned and expedited analysis has the potential to save resources by increasing the likelihood that only appropriate solutions are identified, designed, and implemented. The adage "an ounce of prevention is worth a pound of cure" is often true when conducting an analysis.

Purposes of Analysis

Analysis involves examining a performance problem as well as investigating the various components that affect how a solution is designed and delivered. This stage is sometimes called *front-end analysis* (Romiszowski, 1981) or *instructional analysis* (Smith & Ragan, 2005). Other terms associated with the analysis stage are *problem identification* (Dick et al., 2005), *problem, or gap, analysis* (Hannum & Hansen, 1989; Seels & Glasgow, 1998), and *needs assessment* (Rothwell & Kazanas, 2004).

The main purpose of analysis is to obtain sufficient information to identify performance or instructional problems within an organization, suggest alternative solutions, and select and justify the most appropriate solution (Hannum & Hansen, 1989; Rothwell & Kazanas, 2004; Smith & Ragan, 2005). If it is determined that the best solution is an instructional

Figure 3.1   Analysis stage of the WBID Model.

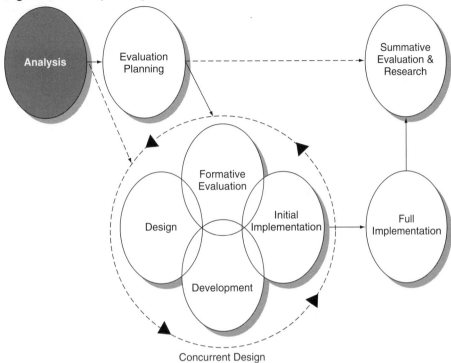

Concurrent Design

one, then a second purpose of this stage is to analyze the components associated with the instruction, that of the instructional goal, context, learners, and content. In the WBID Model, the analysis stage has two major phases: problem analysis and analysis of the components in the instructional situation.

Problem Analysis

In problem analysis, problems are investigated and appropriate solutions are identified. Instructional design and performance systems models discuss defining a problem as determining the **actuals** (identifying the current conditions and happenings within an organization) and the **optimals** (identifying the desired conditions of what should be occurring within an organization) as well as determining the **gap,** the difference between the actuals and optimals (Hannum & Hansen, 1989; Rossett, 1987, 1999; Rothwell & Kazanas, 2004; Seels & Glasgow, 1998). Problem analysis, also called **gap analysis,** involves two primary steps:

1. Determine the nature of the problem, or the gap between actual and optimal.
2. Determine if and how the problem can be resolved.

Table 3.1   Problem Analysis Methods and Tools for Gathering Data

Method	Tools or Materials
Retrieve extant data	Data on or from absenteeism, hirings, terminations, safety reports, recall of products, customer complaints, etc.
Observation	Site visits
	Videotapes
Interviews	Individual(s)
	Small or focused group(s)
	Telephone
Surveys	Paper-based or online questionnaire(s)
	Telephone-based questions with given response choices
	Open-ended questions

Source: Table data are from Rossett (1987, 1999), Rothwell & Kazanas (2004).

The designer asks questions to gain multiple perspectives about the problem (Rothwell & Kazanas, 2004; Stolovitch & Keeps, 1999):

- How many people are affected?
- When did the problem become evident?
- How did the problem become evident?
- What is happening at the present?
- How do you know there is a problem? (e.g., What are the requirements? What is being accomplished? What is being accomplished? Are there deficiencies? Is there urgency to the problem?)
- Where is the problem? (e.g., are some locations more affected than others?)

Through such questions the designer identifies the causes of the problem and ultimately its potential solutions. Rossett (1987, 1999), and others (see, e.g., Rothwell & Kazanas, 2004) suggest a variety of methods and tools for gathering data. Table 3.1 presents several problem analysis methods and their corresponding tools.

 See Appendix A for information on other data collection methods and tools for analysis. Note that these analysis tools also may be used when evaluating WBI.

Determining the Nature of the Problem

Determining the nature of the problem involves identifying the needs in an organization, which come from a variety of sources. Problem analysis is conducted when an expressed problem occurs due to anything from changes in content or technology to changes in policy and procedures (Rothwell & Kazanas, 2004; Smith & Ragan, 2005). Table 3.2 presents sample changes that may occur within any organization that would signal the need for a problem analysis.

Table 3.2　When to Conduct Problem Analysis

Changes	Example
Expressed problem in performance	A company sees poor performance on the job and subscribes to knowledge management as a way to distribute tacit knowledge to the workers and improve their performance.
New or changing population of students, employees, or volunteers	Universities eye distance education, or virtual campuses, as a way to attract new students to their institution. In addition, nontraditional students (older, fully employed) may need the flexibility of distance education programs to obtain their degrees.
New or changing content	State education departments require that new curriculum be added to schools. Lacking content-certified teachers, small or rural school districts seek outside resources for professional development or instruction for certification via distance education. Through the Web, schools can provide courses that had been taught with correspondence courses.
Self-study or accreditation review	Without available resources, universities often use these reviews by accreditation units to identify problems within their organization.
New law or mandate coming into effect	In order to react quickly to new laws or ISO standards, changes to procedures within a company may need to occur.
Change in technology or equipment	Implementation of an EPSS to provide just-in-time, just enough assistance.
Change in philosophy	To save resources and react quickly to their market, a business may go through changes in mission or philosophy such as de-leveling (reducing the layers of management) or cross-training (employees trained to do each other's jobs).

Source: Table data are from Hannum & Hanson (1989), Rossett (2002b), Rothwell & Kazanas (2004), Smith & Ragan (2005), Wager & McKay (2002).

Problems, Causes, and Symptoms.　Rothwell and Kazanas (1998) examine the gap between what is happening and what should be happening in terms of causes and symptoms. As they define the terms, "**causes,** [which] relate to why a problem exists" (p. 34) and "**symptoms** [are] the effects of the problem" (p. 36). They suggest that designers and managers often may simply react to symptoms rather than get to the rudimentary causes and that "managers [often] confuse a symptom with a problem . . . leaving the root causes untouched" (p. 36).

Rothwell and Kazanas (2004) suggest that managers, eager to use a new technology for delivery or any new instruction or training innovation, may create problems that do not, in reality, exist. In other words, they consider the lack of an innovation *as* the problem. It is, rather, a symptom in search of a problem, and is not in itself the root cause of a problem. This situation occurs for school or university administrators, instructors, instructional designers, and personnel in other sectors, not just those in business and industry. For example, administrators and teachers in a PK–12 school may observe that students' standardized test scores are below the national average. However, low test scores are not the problem, nor are they a cause of the problem. Rather these scores are a *symptom,* the consequences of an existing problem. According to Rothwell and Kazanas (2004), it is essential that the cause of the problem be identified to alleviate it. In this example, the PK–12 school officials would need to ask questions:

- Why do low test scores exist?
- In what schools (grade levels, curriculum areas) do these low test scores occur?
- Are test scores similar throughout the district?
- What are the conditions in which low test scores occur?

By addressing these and other questions, the school administrators and teachers may discover the *actual* problem and its cause(s). Only then will any proposed solutions prove effective.

Solutions Mistaken for Problems.   From time to time, solutions have also been mistakenly identified as problems. For example, university administrators and faculty may determine a need for courses delivered through the Web. However, not having online courses to offer to students is not a problem in and of itself, but a *solution* in search of a problem. The university officials need to examine how having access to the Internet and Web for course delivery would impact the university's mission by asking questions:

- Why do we need to offer courses through the Web?
- How can the Web improve student [or faculty or staff] learning and/or performance?
- How can the Web allow us to perform [tasks] more effectively than at present?
- Will these technologies make routines easier, less cumbersome, less complex, etc.?
- Will these innovations provide faster or better quality instruction, service, etc.?
- Will these innovations reduce training costs or time?
- What kind of administrative improvements might be seen?

By investigating how venturing into using the Web for course delivery relates to the university's mission, faculty, staff, and student body, they may identify a true problem for which online courses may be the solution.

The Causes of Problems.   Causes of performance problems have been widely discussed in the literature, with three of the most common lists developed by Rothwell and Kazanas (2004), Stolovitch and Keeps (1999), and Rossett (1987, 1999). Rothwell and

Kazanas' list is the most comprehensive of the three. They categorize performance problem factors into three major levels—organization, work groups, and individuals—identifying and explaining within each level specific factors that affect performance. Finally, they determine questions for each specific factor, to identify how that factor may affect performance and to pinpoint the underlying cause of performance problems.

Stolovitch and Keeps (1999) organize their list by three main environmental factors: skills and knowledge, emotional, and political. They suggest that such factors may be generally or specifically related to a performance problem. Environmental factors may be external or internal to the organization; emotional and political factors are related to incentives and motivation. Rather than listing skills and knowledge separately, Stolovitch and Keeps combine them.

Rossett (1987, 1999) considers four factors focusing on the individual as the main causes of performance problems. Her most current list relates to human performance needs while her 1987 list identified similar factors but limited their scope to training needs only. In the 1999 list, she describes each factor in terms of anything lacking within the individual in terms of skills, knowledge, or motivation, or flaws in the workplace that would make it difficult for the employee to perform well or at all. Her list contains examples of such flaws.

Determining If and How the Problem Can Be Resolved

The second step in the problem analysis is the determination of whether the problem can be resolved and, if so, whether it can be solved by instruction or by some other means. Not all problems are resolved by training or instruction. Hannum and Hansen (1989) state that in many organizations, "training is often offered as a solution, if not *the* solution" (p. 67, emphasis added). They maintain that training or education is often recommended, not because it is the correct solution, but because it is the most convenient one. Too often managers or administrators suggest implementing training or education even though some other factor has created the poor performance. In many cases, managers tend to ignore or not examine the symptoms and causes to determine whether training or instruction is an appropriate solution. For example, the evening shift at Company Z falls behind in their paper towel productions; yet the day and night crews often exceed the specified output. Company Z production manager has required that all personnel attend training on maintaining quotas. However, it may be more expedient to find out the cause of the evening crew's reduced production; for instance, it may be due to equipment malfunctions when the maintenance team is on call rather than being onsite, due to absenteeism, and so on.

Generally, causes for which instruction is the solution relate to lack of skills or knowledge. Although problems related to lack of motivation could be resolved through instruction, other interventions may be more effective.

When motivation and other factors are the causes of performance problems, noninstructional solutions may be applied, such as updating job aids, adding resources, streamlining work logistics, changing or providing additional incentives, restructuring departments, disciplining an individual, and so on (Rossett, 1999; Stolovitch & Keeps, 1999; Van Tiem, Moseley, & Dessinger, 2001). As the focus of this book is Web-based instruction (WBI), we only mention these other performance problem solutions here.

Determining If WBI Is Appropriate

As a matter of purpose, it may be an inherent assumption that Web-based instruction is an appropriate solution to any instructional problem. This is not true. WBI must be used appropriately to be effective; sometimes in the zeal for using a new innovation, its actual viability is often overlooked and the success of the WBI project suffers.

Determining an appropriate solution to a problem requires considering the instructional strategies, or methods, and the available delivery systems (Dick et al., 2005). Although sometimes viewed as separate entities, the two concepts are often intertwined, partially because of when decisions of strategy and delivery systems are made.

Decisions related to strategies and delivery systems occur at two main decision points during instructional design. At the first point, delivery strategy decisions may be made prior to selecting the instructional strategy, and perhaps even prior to the start of the WBI project. When a delivery strategy is selected this early, Dick et al. (2005) suggest that it becomes an assumption made by the designer, administrator, manager, or client. Smith and Ragan (2005) agree and add that early selection of a delivery system may occur because of the type of ID model used (e.g., rapid prototyping) or because the selected delivery system requires a large and early investment in resources for media, support staff, and so on.

As an example, in some large organizations, strategic decisions about online instruction are made early on. For instance, a specific learning management system (LMS) is often mandated because of price and compatible technology and human resources. Such mandates affect the designer's choice of instructional strategies and how they are designed and implemented. LMSs include chats, threaded discussions, Web links, and so on. How these functions are incorporated into the LMS affects what instuctional strategies will be appropriate for the learning environment.

When the instructional delivery decision occurs early, the designer is able to (in fact, must) consider capabilities and limitations of the delivery system when selecting instructional strategies; in this situation the technology may drive the instructional methods. Some types of instructional goals or content for Web-based delivery may be precluded because of delivery system limitations. When the delivery strategy decision is made early, designers should ask questions such as the following:

- What are the goals of using Web-based delivery?
- Do proposed instructional strategies fit Web-based delivery?
- Do the proposed tasks fit with Web-based delivery?

Alternatively, the delivery system is identified after determining the instructional strategy; this situation is desired most often by designers (Dick et al., 2005; Smith & Ragan, 2005). Smith and Ragan (2005) suggest that choosing an instructional strategy before choosing a delivery system allows designers to be flexible in recommending the best solution for the situation. The delivery strategy does not drive the instructional project as an early decision might. Smith and Ragan (1999) also contend that this later decision point is "critical to those designers who have the capability, budgets, and time to produce elaborate instructional materials" (p. 286). For example, designers, who identify the instructional strategies prior to deciding how to deliver the online instruction may find that an LMS is not necessary and that email, listservs, and an instructor-developed Web page comprise the most appropriate options.

Designers who can choose instructional strategies prior to delivery systems also may factor in problem analysis findings and implications. Choice of instructional strategies then drives delivery system decisions. Designers in this situation should ask questions such as the following:

- Do the capabilities of the Web (delivery system) fit the purposes of the instruction based on the findings from the problem analysis?
- Do the capabilities of the Web (delivery system) fit the subject matter area?
- Do the capabilities of the Web (delivery system) fit the organization's policies and procedures?

Determining the appropriateness of WBI isn't always a clear-cut decision; other considerations are involved, as well. Using the Web for instructional delivery often involves allocating or reallocating resources involving LMSs, computers, Internet and Web access, software applications, and support staff. Consequently, designers need to identify available systems and support as they build the instruction.

Because WBI may be created by developing Web pages with a website authoring tool or through an LMS, designers also need to consider the specific tools available (Horton, 2000). Each tool varies by its features (e.g., bulletin boards, chat rooms, threaded discussions, etc.), its robustness (e.g., availability and ease of use of the development tools), assessment and grading tools, registration, accounting systems, and the fees associated with its usage. Designers also should consider the following:

- Is time available to design and develop the WBI?
- Are resources (budget, personnel, and tools) available for WBI design and development?
- Is content available or is a subject matter expert (SME) available for consultation?
- Are learners available to take the course?
- Is there an instructor who is able to teach the online course?

In addition to those points discussed, it is important to note that WBI is more appropriate for some types of instructional content than for others. Some outcomes within the psychomotor and affective domains may not be suited for Web-based delivery, especially those involving performance and/or that require careful observation and precise feedback. Examples include serving a volleyball, guarding the goal in hockey, or holding the correct *fouetté* (a ballet position). These and like outcomes would not be appropriate for WBI at present. However, WBI is perfectly appropriate for teaching basic concepts and fundamentals of various sports and games (e.g., the purpose of the game, rules, number of players needed, basic scoring procedures, etc.). Additionally, the Web may be an excellent delivery medium for instructor/learner discussions on issues and concerns related to physical fitness, such as best types of exercises to reduce stress, good sportsmanship, and whether college athletes should be paid.

Instructional outcomes within the affective domain may require instructional strategies using face-to-face interactions (e.g., role playing) and observations and feedback on verbal and nonverbal language and other nuances of the situation that may not be appropriate for Web delivery. For instance, online instruction on empathetic counseling, applying anger management techniques, demonstrating negotiating skills, or assertiveness training could be difficult. Other topics, such as theories of counseling and psychotherapy, may be applicable for WBI.

The distinction should be clear. It is often more appropriate to use WBI to teach verbal information, concepts, and rule-using application types of outcomes than to use it to teach performance-related outcomes (when instruction targets the affective or motor-skills domain).

ON YOUR OWN

What instructional projects are *not* appropriate for Web-based delivery? What other factors could you address when determining WBI's appropriateness as an instructional solution?

What is the subject of your WBI project? What makes your project appropriate for Web-based delivery?

Do you need help in selecting a topic for your WBI project? See this textbook's Companion Website (http://www.prenhall.com/davidson-shivers) for assistance on WBI project selection.

Documenting and Reporting Problem Analysis

Written documentation begins as problem analysis is completed and becomes part of a larger report, known as the **Design Document.** Designers use Design Documents as written records, supplemented with tables and figures, of what has occurred within any part of the WBID stages.

Design Documents become increasingly valuable when WBI projects are complex and if, at various times, team members work independently of each other on separate aspects of the project. The Design Document becomes the means for coordinating such efforts so that an integrated and cohesive outcome prevails, that is, a well-designed WBI is achieved. Because human memory often fails and perceptions are often inaccurate, a Design Document keeps the lines of communication open among team members and stakeholders. It is also an important tool for maintaining accurate records available to all involved in the WBI project.

The Design Document records the procedures for data collection and analyses and findings for the problem analysis phase. The designer identifies the problem(s) and proposes and explains an instructional solution and alternative solutions. This part of the Design Document also includes who is involved in the analysis, what materials were analyzed, and the methods used to gather data. Samples of the instruments used often appear in an appendix. Charts and tables may be used to illuminate the text. The Design Document usually begins with an executive summary, or abstract; the body of the report contains the complete details.

Designers are tasked either simply to identify potential solutions for decision makers, or to recommend a best solution from those identified. The Design Document must, therefore, contain sufficient information on all solutions so that decision-makers can either confidently choose a solution or see clearly the rationale and justification for the designer's recommendation.

GardenScapes

Originally, there was a single course on home gardening and landscaping in the Department of Continuing and Distance Education (CDE) at Clatskanie Junior College (CJC) in Westport, a small town in the USA. *Garden Basics: Just Another Day at the Plant* earned high interest and has experienced growing enrollments over the last five years. The goal of *Garden Basics* is to teach basic gardening concepts such as soil types and climate zones, and to distinguish among plants that are used in the area. In addition, the course covers the care and use of basic tools for lawn and garden work.

The course instructor, Ms. Kalantha (Kally) Le Rue, is interested in developing a second course, teaching amateur gardeners to design sophisticated gardens and yards and how to incorporate focal points and other landscape features. She gathers ideas for course elements from several sources: previous evaluations; followup interviews with former learners, and data on unsolicited phone calls to CDE requesting additional gardening courses.

A CDE staff member assists Kally in a literature search documenting that interest in home and garden and do-it-yourself home projects has grown phenomenally in the last five years. Trend analysts have noted the expansion of home and garden stores and superstores, book and magazine coverage, and new home and garden television reports, programs, and networks.

Based on the literature review and data from her previous course, Kally, with help from CDE staff members, writes a proposal for this second course and submits it through CJC's curriculum approval process.

In the Design Document, both actual and optimal performances are used to identify the problem (the gap). The following chart is included.

Actuals	Problem (Gap)	Optimals
Individuals with basic gardening skills.	Lack of skills between basic and advanced gardening.	Skills in creating a themed garden design.
Declining student enrollments.	Add new students and maintain current population base.	Increase student enrollments.

The problem statement reads as follows:

Increasing numbers of homeowners are spending additional time in their own yards and gardens. Many of these individuals do not have the knowledge and skills needed to landscape their properties. They need information beyond basic knowledge of garden tools, plant types, and climate zones.

The new course, *GardenScapes,* will cover advanced gardening skills. The course will help participants develop a garden design that will improve features of their home landscapes.

Kally knows of the college administrators' interest in online instruction. The CJC administration is highly interested in attracting new students. They commissioned a study on distance education several years ago to investigate the possibility of using the Web for delivering programs and courses. Although the findings of this study were mixed, the administrators believe that using the Web has potential for increasing enrollment and also for reducing costs associated with building and renovating new classrooms and office spaces; it also may help reduce rising costs in other ways.

Complementing this administrator interest, Kally and the CDE staff conclude that the Web is an appropriate delivery system for the course and may have the potential to expand the college's market share. Kally provides this information about Web delivery in her report for course approval:

With the course developed as WBI, the following purposes can be served:

1. *The audience can work from their homes rather than coming into campus on a specified night and time, providing students and instructor with flexibility and convenience.*
2. *Garden and landscaping websites can be incorporated into the course to add to learners' knowledge and skills.*
3. *The course could attract new learners from distant locations.*

Consequently, the new course is approved. Kally's report becomes a part of the Design Document.

The college hires Elliott Kangas, on instructional design intern, to help Kally design and develop this Web-based course. Carlos Duartes, director of the Teaching and Learning Development Center (TLDC) at CJC, will supervise him in coordination with his advisor, Dr. Judith Chauncy, professor at Myers University.

See this textbook's Companion Website (http://www.prenhall.com/davidson-shivers) for the *GardenScapes* Design Document.

ON YOUR OWN

Start planning your own WBI project by beginning your problem analysis:

- What problems are you trying to address?
- What are the symptoms of the problem?
- What is the root cause of the problem?
- Is instruction an appropriate solution for the problem?
- Is WBI an appropriate instructional solution?

Identify the actuals, optimals, and problem (gap) in the given situation. Explain how you would (or did) gather data and then report the findings as part of your Design Document. Use a chart similar to the following to organize your findings.

(For illustrations of how other designers tackled these same issues, review the case studies appearing in the Extending Your Skills section at the end of this chapter.)

Write a problem statement, documenting your procedures and findings. Provide a rationale justifying why this problem can be corrected by instruction. Explain why the most appropriate solution for the problem is WBI.

 See this textbook's Companion Website (http://www.prenhall.com/davidson-shivers) for printable templates for your Design Document.

After completing the problem analysis, the focus shifts to the second phase, analyzing the four components of the instructional situation. This phase occurs only if the problem analysis has determined that instruction is the best solution.

Analyzing Components of the Instructional Situation

The second phase of analysis examines the four components that make up the instructional situation: instructional goal, instructional context, learners, and instructional content. Identifying the preliminary *instructional goal* and its *outcome level* sets the stage for the rest of the analysis. *Instructional context* analysis examines the environment in which instruction occurs (Figure 3.2). *Learner* analysis looks at pertinent characteristics of the intended participants. The elements of the instructional content are decomposed into main steps and subskills during the *instructional content* analysis. Based on the findings from these analyses, designers arrive at the final goal statement. These analyses also reveal issues and implications for the remaining WBID stages (Davidson, 1988; Davidson-Shivers, 1998). For the remainder of this chapter we will discuss analyzing the first three components. Chapter 4 is devoted to the fourth component, instructional content analysis, and the implications of each component analysis.

Figure 3.2   Instructional component analyses.

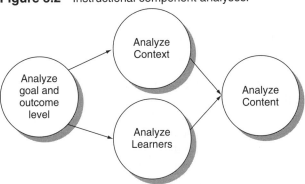

Typically, designers first gather and analyze information about the instructional goal and outcome level. The sequence varies for addressing the remaining three components, and is usually left to the discretion of the designer, who bases the choice on project tasks, personal preferences, professional experience, and educational background. In our experience, it makes sense to analyze the context and learners prior to the instructional content. Other designers prefer to begin by analyzing instructional content. Choosing which sequence to follow is a matter of preference and training.

What Is the Instructional Goal?

Goal identification refines the problem statement into one or two sentences that focus the instruction. An *instructional goal* is a general statement of what learners will be able to do after the instruction is completed; the type of learning outcome for the goal is then identified (Davidson, 1988). Such goals must be able to be achieved through instruction rather than through some other means (e.g., job aids, changes in incentives, etc.). According to Dick et al. (2005), an instructional goal provides the designer with a clear statement of learner outcomes and is related to the identified problems and instructional setting.

Determining the Type of Learning Outcome.   An important part of defining the instructional goal is to identify its learning outcome level. A *learning outcome,* also termed a *domain of learning* (Dick et al., 2005), refers to a specific type of learning associated with the goal and is based on the findings from the problem analysis. There are several classification systems for identifying types of learning outcomes.

Two commonly used classification systems for learning outcomes are Gagné's (1985, 1987) Categories of Learning and the Taxonomy of Objectives for the Cognitive Domain (Bloom et al., 1956), commonly known as Bloom's Taxonomy. The Categories of Learning provide outcomes of attitudes, motor skills, cognitive strategies, verbal information, and intellectual skills (Gagné, 1985; Gagné, Wager, Golas, & Keller, 2005). The category of intellectual skills is further subdivided into five types, for a total of nine outcomes. With each category Gagné designates a specific action verb, known as a *learned capability verb* (LCV), that is associated with each of the nine outcomes. Bloom's Taxonomy classifies cognitive domain objectives into five subcategories.

While instructional designers know the Categories of Learning, Bloom's Taxonomy tends to be better known by classroom teachers. Both classification schemes have stood the test of time, with only a recent suggestion for revision to Bloom's. In 2002, Krathwohl suggested several changes to Bloom's Taxonomy, including adding "metacognitive knowledge" to the knowledge dimension. This addition is similar to Gagné's category of cognitive strategy.

Other taxonomies have been developed, including the Taxonomy of Objectives for Affective Domain (Krathwohl, Bloom, & Masia, 1964), the Taxonomy of Objectives for Psychomotor Skills (Simpson, 1972), and the Learning of Motor Skills (Singer, 1982). Instructional designers and classroom teachers are not as familiar with these last three taxonomies. They are more often used by those professionals associated with affective outcome (school counselors, counselor educators, etc.) and motor skill instruction (physical education instructors, coaches, etc.). Table 3.3 presents Gagné's Categories of Learning, together with their LCVs, explanations, examples, and comparisons with the other listed taxonomies.

Table 3.3 Categories of Learning Descriptions

Gagné's Category of Learning	Learned Capability Verb	Explanation	Example	Similar to
Verbal Information				
	State	Declarative knowledge; knowing *what;* learning to list, label, state, etc.	State the chemical elements.	**Bloom's Knowledge** with other verbs: (list, recite, name, match, tell, etc.)
Intellectual Skills *Taxonomy of 5 skills listed in ascending order as follows*	(See following)	Procedural knowledge; knowing *how;* learning to apply declarative knowledge		
Discrimination	Discriminate	Comparing items as similar or different by tangible attributes	Discriminate between two sounds as same or different.	
Concrete concepts	Identify	Identifying and labeling tangible ideas, objects, or events	Identify plants as examples or nonexamples of perennials.	**Bloom's Comprehension** (describe, discuss, explain, summarize, interpret, etc.)
Defined concepts	Classify	Classifying and labeling intangible or abstract ideas, events, or objects by defined meanings	Classify instances of democratic governments correctly.	**Bloom's Comprehension**
Rule-using or application	Apply	Applying lower-order procedural knowledge; demonstrating relationships among concepts in various situations	Apply correct theorem to various geometry problems.	**Bloom's Application** (perform, predict, transfer, calculate, compute, interview, etc.)
Higher-order rules or problem solving	Generate	Assessing problem situations, determining applicable concepts and rules, applying 2 or more rules in combination	Generate environmentally sound development plan for residential district.	**Bloom's Analysis, Synthesis, or Judgment** (analyze, differentiate, create, design, compose, evaluate, judge, prove, etc.)

(continued)

Table 3.3   Categories of Learning Descriptions *(Continued)*

Gagné's Category of Learning	Learned Capability Verb	Explanation	Example	Similar to
Cognitive Strategies				
	Adopt	Learning to control and monitor one's own information or cognitive processes	Adopt self-talk strategy to monitor own cognitive processing.	**Metacognitive Knowledge**— suggested change to Bloom's taxonomy (Krathwohl, 2002)
Attitudes				
	Choose	Learning of a personal action of choice to exhibit	Choose to refuse illegal drugs when offered.	**Krathwohl's** taxonomy of objectives for the affective domain further divides attitudes
Motor Skills				
	Execute	Learning physical movement skills that are coordinated and precise	Execute a back flip.	**Simpson's** taxonomy of objectives or **Singer's** classifications for the psychomotor domain further divides into subskills

Source: Table data are from Bloom et al. (1956), Davidson–Shivers (1998), Gagné (1985), Gagné et al. (1992), Krathwohl (2002), Krathwohl, et al. (1964), Simpson (1972), Singer (1982).

The various types of learning outcomes associated with the cognitive domain are commonly taught in PK–12 schools, colleges, and universities. Gagné, et al. (2005) suggest that designers begin with cognitive domain (i.e., intellectual skills) goal(s) before incorporating goals from the affective or motor skills domains. Instructional goals that are easiest to deliver via the Web may be those of the cognitive domain; and include the following types:

- Facts, labels, basic information (relate to Gagné's learning category of verbal information)
- Ideas, concepts, application, and problem-solving outcomes (relate to Gagné's higher-order rules within the intellectual skills category)
- Learning strategies and study skills (relate to Gagné's category of cognitive strategies)

Matching the instructional goal to a learning outcome is the basis for establishing congruence with the remaining tasks in designing WBI. It allows for common understanding and consistency in communication about the project among the WBI team members.

Gathering Data on the Instructional Goal. To supplement the problem analysis, designers can gather data by surveying or interviewing subject matter experts (SMEs) and end users and by reviewing extant data. *SMEs* are individuals with expertise in the content, learner audiences, context, and so on, and may be course instructors, trainers, content authorities, and other experienced practitioners. *End users* are those individuals who have been targeted as potential course participants. They may be learners or trainees who are going to participate in the WBI or have already participated in similar instruction. Existing learner data, such as course evaluations, grades or test scores, and absenteeism and withdrawals provide information about learner opinions and success rates.

When surveying participants or examining extant data, designers should review the organization's data collection and reporting policies. The use of human participants in collecting data may require permission from the organization and, perhaps from the individuals themselves. Access and use of extant data also requires permission from the organization and, in some cases, individuals. Results of the data should be presented in aggregate form so as to maintain individual anonymity.

See Appendix A for additional information on data-gathering methods.

Writing a Preliminary Goal Statement. Having gathered data about the anticipated instructional goal and its learning outcome, the designer writes a preliminary goal statement. This is a draft of the final version and will change as additional information is gathered.

An instructional goal should be written as an overarching statement that subsumes the steps of the entire learning process. While being stated broadly, the goal should *not* be vague or fuzzy (Smith & Ragan, 2005); it should be written with enough clarity to guide the designer through the WBI design.

An instructional goal statement focuses on what the learner will be able to do after the instruction is completed. Generally speaking, the goal is directed toward the performance of an individual learner rather than a group of learners (Smith & Ragan, 2005). If constructivist learning approaches are used, then the instructional goal may focus on performances beyond what is expected of an individual learner (Driscoll, 2005). The goal statement is written in measurable terms so that evaluators may ascertain the learner's precise level of achievement.

Goal statements are learner-centered rather than teacher-centered; the focus is not on activities that a teacher performs (the teacher will explain the Bill of Rights, or the instructor will demonstrate dance steps), but on what learners are to know or do (*learners* will describe the Bill of Rights, or *learners* will demonstrate dance steps). The goal statement does *not* include lesson activities (participants will read the manual on data entry, students will complete exercises 1 through 3 in their calculus text, or learners will complete the language arts worksheet); rather, goals focus on the purposes for completing such activities. Goal statements are *not* about the assessment (learners will take a quiz or achieve a passing score on the exam) because such tools (tests, projects, products, etc.) are used to evaluate, or measure, mastery of the goal. Table 3.4 provides examples and nonexamples of goal statements.

Documenting the Instructional Goal Statement. The procedures, data collected, findings, and the preliminary goal statement are included in the Design Document. The designer then continues to analyze the other three components (context, learners, content) of

Table 3.4 Examples and Nonexamples of Goal Statements

Examples	Nonexamples
At the end of the WBI, the [learner, participant, or student] will be able to describe five conflict management techniques.	At the end of the WBI, the [learner, participant, or student] will be familiar with ways to resolve conflict management. *(Vague goal that can't be easily measured)*
At the end of the WBI, the [learner, participant, or student] will be able to explain basic differences and similarities among constructivist, behavioral, and cognitive learning theories.	The basic differences and similarities among the learning theories of constructivist, behavioral, and cognitive learning theories will be explained. *(Teacher or instructional activity)*
At the end of the WBI, the [learner, participant, or student] will identify 10 reasons to implement technology in classrooms.	Upon completion of instruction, the student will take a 20-item multiple-choice exam. *(Assessment that measures whether a student has achieved a goal)*
At the end of the WBI, the [learner, participant, or student] will be able to establish employee performance guidelines.	Students will read the chapter on how to establish and communicate with employees about performance standards. *(Activity within the instruction)*

the instructional situation, and may revise the preliminary goal statement based on the findings of these analyses. Changes in wording, outcome level, or conditions for mastery could, and are expected to, occur before a final version is written.

GardenScapes

Elliott and Kally study the problem analysis findings and the problem statement to create their preliminary instructional goal statement. The course will cover advanced gardening skills that will help adults develop a garden for improving their home landscapes. As a result, they write the following preliminary goal statement:

> *At the end of the instruction, the participant will be able to develop a garden that follows his or her GardenScapes plan, which is based on a garden theme of his or her choice and follows basic gardening guidelines and procedures.*

Elliott and Kally decide that learners will have to identify and apply basic concepts and guidelines (in gardening and landscaping) to develop and carry out a garden plan. Consequently, the outcome level for the WBI goal falls at the application level of Bloom's Taxonomy or within the intellectual skill of rule using in Gagné's Categories of Learning.

See this textbook's Companion Website (http://www.prenhall.com/davidson-shivers) for the *GardenScapes* Design Document

ON YOUR OWN

Write your preliminary instructional goal statement, identify its learning outcome, and include it in your Design Document. Make sure that your problem analysis findings are the basis for your instructional goal. Write your goal using only one or two sentences. Be sure that the goal statement is learner centered. Focus on what the learner will be able to do at the end of the instruction. Make sure that the instructional goal is appropriate for Web-based delivery. Use Gagné's Categories of Learning or one of the other taxonomies to identify the learning outcome level for your goal.

(For illustrations of how other designers tackled these same issues, review the case studies appearing in the Extending Your Skills section at the end of this chapter.)

What Is the Instructional Context?

As important as it is for designers to determine the instructional goal, it is equally important to analyze the context, or environment, in which that goal will be achieved. Context analysis is the next step in the WBID Model. The two purposes of context analysis are to describe the environmental situation in which WBI is delivered and to determine the capacity of elements within that setting (Table 3.5). Under scrutiny in WBI context analysis are the organizational infrastructure, the competency of its personnel, and the learners' technology.

Organizational Infrastructure.   *Organizational infrastructure* refers not only to an organization's physical makeup, but also to its management and operation (Davidson-Shivers, 2002). The four main areas that affect WBI design are resources (facilities and equipment), management support, organizational culture, and WBI ownership.

Table 3.5 Main Elements in Contextual Analysis for WBI

Main Elements	Aspects
Organizational infrastructure	• Resources (e.g., available facilities, technology resources, information services and servers) • Management functions • Organizational culture • Ownership of WBI materials
Allocation and competencies of personnel	• Technical, instructional design, and content knowledge of instructor • Instructional design support personnel • Technical support staff • Administrative support staff
Learner location and technology	• Location of participants (local, regional, widely disbursed in country or world) • Locations, urban or rural • General technological requirements (speed and memory capacity of hardware; operating system) • Required utilities and software applications

One crucial task in this part of the analysis is to determine the capacity of technical resources available for Web-based instruction, including items such as computer systems and servers that will be used to design, develop, and house the WBI. The designer must consider what computer systems the organization has, whether a learning management system is available, and what types of support systems (e.g., help desks, registration, instructor assistance, tutorials, etc.) are available. The type and adequacy of software, email systems, Internet browsers, and so on and their compatibility with the computer hardware must be determined.

Management and operations of the organization is another aspect to consider during this phase. Management, according to Schermerhorn (1999), has four main functions: planning, organizing, leading, and controlling. How decentralized and flattened an organization's structure is, often indicates its management style and the manner in which these four functions are conducted. Determining who makes decisions and how, may directly affect WBI design.

Another consideration relates to organizational culture. Hellreigel, Slocum, and Woodman (cited in Mosley, Pietri, & Megginson, 1996) define *organizational culture* as "the shared philosophies, values, beliefs and behavior patterns that form the organization's core identity" (p. 95). Mosley et al. further suggest that in addition to the way things happen in an organization, *culture* relates to employee and management characteristics, reward and promotion systems, and how processes and decisions are influenced and made.

As a part of organizational culture, the administration, or management, support for WBI development should be reviewed for breadth and depth. In doing so, the designer should consider aspects such as support of top, middle, and line-level management, as well as incentive systems, professional development and training practices, and access to the organization's resources.

It is important that designers consider organizational policies of ownership and fair use and define those policies for WBI design and delivery. Policies on copyright and ownership of course materials (intellectual property rights of university faculty with corresponding fair use rights of the university, and proprietary use and ownership by business, nonprofit, and for-profit organizations) should be examined. Ownership issues revolve around contracts and/or policies in place at the time of employment, compensation for the work (e.g., work-for-hire practices and policies), and policies comparable to those applied to other types of instruction and instructional materials used within the organization (Richey & Morrison, 2002; Throne, 2001).

Allocation and Competencies of Personnel.   As a part of context analysis, the designer must ascertain the skills and abilities of those individuals involved with the WBI development and delivery. The designer gathers information and data related to the expertise of the online instructors (trainers or teachers) in relation to the instructional content, Web technology, instructional design, and online teaching, and also collects information on skills and abilities of other personnel involved. Designers should consider the following questions:

- What type of instructional design and/or technical assistance is available for instructors and designers? Will there be a team of designers, technical support staff, and instructors for Web delivery? Or, will a lone instructor be the designer and the technical support person, as well?
- What type of administrative support staff is available for assistance to the designer and/or instructor?

- When would assistance be available during the WBI's design, development, and implementation?
- Who would assist and support the instructor? The instructional designer? The learners?
- If available, how is access to support allocated—on apportionment, a first-come, first-served basis, or other standards?
- What policies or procedures must designers follow when seeking assistance?

Learner Location and Technology.   Context analysis also involves determining the location of distance learners and the current status of their technology. Distance in space (location) and time (response delay) may affect designers' choices of which WBI instructional strategies to employ. For example, it may be feasible to ask students within the local area to come to the campus for face-to-face meetings. However, if other students are located in many parts of the world, on-campus meetings may be impossible, and it may also prove difficult to set up synchronous chats. Other aspects of location, such as whether students live in urban or rural areas, may indicate that both types of settings be considered when developing authentic examples, practice exercises, and so on.

Context analysis discovers the general technology requirements for learners, especially if they must have their own computers and access to the Internet and Web. Within PK–12 schools and universities, learners may have access to a computer and the Web on campus. Universities may require that their students have off-campus access, as well (University of Florida, 2002). Other organizations (business or military) provide their employees or officers and enlisted personnel with access to computers and the Web for training as deemed necessary.

Designers must identify technology specifications of speed, memory, and operating system, and note any required utilities and software applications, such as PDF readers, sound and video recorders and players, and so on. Such requirements may be known at the outset; however, if not predetermined, these decisions can be made during design and development. Exact technology requirements for learners must be finalized prior to pilot testing and well before final implementation. During early context analysis, a preliminary outline of technology needs will suffice, as long as the finer points are detailed later.

Gathering Data on the Instructional Context.   Extant data such as blueprints, organizational charts, policy manuals, newsletters, and annual reports provide information about facilities, physical environments, and management styles. Observing the actual site may also provide helpful information about the physical layout of the organization. Interviewing or surveying faculty, trainers, technical and administrative support personnel, and representatives from the LMS can provide additional information about the context.

See Appendix A for additional information on data gathering.

Documenting and Reporting the Context Analysis.   Designers must document findings of the context analysis and report methods undertaken in gathering information, and must describe important features about the instructional context that will have implications for the remaining design procedures and for the WBI itself.

GardenScapes

Kally and Elliott begin gathering information related to their proposed course, using surveys, interviews, and field trips to various locales on the CJC campus. The following is the context analysis portion of their Design Document.

The Infrastructure of Clatskanie Junior College

The TLDC within CJC has a comprehensive system of faculty and learner support. The system involves initial training of faculty and students in all aspects of distance and distributed learning environments, ranging from designing and developing Web-based instruction to implementing online programs. Support staff consists of personnel who provide assistance to faculty and learners, with student laboratory assistants available to help individual faculty.

The TLDC has three faculty development laboratories. Each laboratory contains equipment to accommodate up to 10 individuals at one time. In each laboratory, the following technology equipment and materials are maintained and updated on a three-year cycle:

- *10 state-of-the-art multimedia computers with appropriate disk space, memory, and Internet and Web connectivity*
- *3 digital cameras and 1 digital video camera*
- *Variety of software, including productivity software, website editors, digital media editors, and graphics programs*
- *Access to a shared development server as well as a production server when materials are ready for implementation*
- *Access to a library of instructional strategies, WBI templates, and other training and support materials*

The laboratories are designed to provide faculty with individualized support and small-group training opportunities.

Full-time CJC faculty members have state-of-the-art computers in their offices, with Internet connections, email, and the necessary software needed to conduct their faculty work. Extensive software is available for development, including HTML editors, graphics packages, and productivity software. CJC supports include a learning management system, which offers a chat system, organized threaded discussion facility, electronic drop box for student assignments, and a gradebook. Part-time faculty, including Kally, share offices that contain a single computer.

Full-time faculty are given release time from one course in order to develop a Web-based course; however, they are not given additional release time when they teach the course, unless they are developing and teaching at the same time.

The CJC administrators and faculty have established, as part of promotion and tenure policy, that WBI development is defined as a creative work product. Pending final review and approval by CJC faculty, WBI development and delivery will be considered under the standard campus intellectual property policy: the course instructor who developed the materials will have the intellectual property rights and CJC will have rights to fair use of those materials.

Technical Support Staff

Online instructors and learners will be supported through the TLDC through a help desk, which is focused on solving technical problems for individuals participating in distance and distributed classes. Support is available online, in person, and via telephone and desktop conferencing. The support team also has a training classroom where they can assist learners face to face in accessing classes and troubleshooting specific problems. Staff will work with faculty development teams to test Web-based instruction and programs for quality control before they are delivered.

Personnel Support Staff

Faculty members are supported through the TLDC by facilities and personnel; they have access to the TLDC technology laboratories. TLDC personnel include instructional designers, computer programmers, graphic designers, and Web developers who train faculty and provide assistance in developing strategies for distance delivery systems.

Teaching assistants from the Instructional Design and Technology (IDT) master's program at Myers University work at the TLDC as interns. Interns who are not working with a specific faculty member are assigned to work in the development laboratories.

Allocated Personnel for the GardenScapes WBI Project

The allocated personnel and their competencies for the WBI on GardenScapes are as follows:

The instructor, Kalantha (Kally) Le Rue, is a master gardener who works as a volunteer at the Golden Valley Botanical Gardens of Westport. Kally created the original course, Garden Basics, approximately five years ago and has taught it since its inception. She has an undergraduate degree in sociology and her vocation is social work. She earned the title of master gardener seven years ago through a program developed by the state's agricultural extension services in conjunction with the Botanical Gardens in Westport.

Although she has taught the original course for five years, she has neither formal training in education nor any formal training in instructional design. She will be relying on the TLDC staff for assistance in this area.

The instructional designer, Elliott Kangas, is an IDT master's student at Myers University, located in Westport. He has completed the required courses and a majority of his electives in his program of study. He has accepted the internship position under the supervision of Carlos Duartes, director of TLDC at CJC. The primary purpose of his internship is to help develop Web-based and multimedia instruction for courses in the CDE. As his first internship project, Carlos has assigned Elliott to assist Kally to design GardenScapes.

Other TLDC technical support staff will be identified as they become involved in the development of this WBI project on an "as needed" basis.

Learner Location and Technology

It is anticipated that learners, for the most part, will be located within the regional service area of CJC for at least the first few offerings of GardenScapes. Westport is a relatively small city with surrounding suburbs, with more rural areas to the north and south. However, its participant base may expand to other regions within the state, country and, possibly, other parts of the world in later course offerings, which will affect how the course is implemented.

To participate in the course, learners must be able to access and use computers and the Web, ideally from home or work; if unable to do so, the computer labs at CJC are available to them. Specific access requirements will be developed during the design stage when the technology requirements will be detailed.

ON YOUR OWN

Analyze the context surrounding your WBI project. Explore available resources. Using Table 3.5 as your template, identify and describe the infrastructure of the organization and the availability and capacity of resources and administration support. Name and identify the personnel available for and assigned to the project; describe their competencies in the areas of content, technology, and/or instructional design. Develop a general outline of technology requirements for learners who will be taking the course.

Write this information up as a formal part of your Design Document. Include resources and personnel allocated to your WBI project, as well.

Begin thinking about how the findings from your context analysis have implications for the design, development, and implementation of your WBI project. You will be adding these implications to your Design Document later.

(For illustrations of how other designers tackled these same issues, review the case studies appearing in the Extending Your Skills section at the end of this chapter.)

See this textbook's Companion Website (http://www.prenhall.com/davidson-shivers) for the *GardenScapes* Design Document.

Who Are the Learners?

The purpose of learner analysis is to determine who will be the WBI participants. The instructional design literature usually discusses this type of analysis as identifying learner characteristics or individual differences and similarities (Cornell & Martin, 1997; Davidson, 1988a; Dick et al., 2005; Smith & Ragan, 2005). Identifying learner characteristics is important so that the designer can make the WBI interesting and relevant to the intended audience.

Part of learner analysis is to determine the diversity of the targeted audience, and, if wide variations occur, infer how such diversity may affect WBI design, development and implementation. Learner characteristics that might be investigated include general characteristics, motivation, prior knowledge, communication skills, technical skills, and abilities and disabilities (Table 3.6).

Table 3.6   Main Elements for Consideration in WBI Learner Analysis

Main Elements in Learner Analysis	Aspects
General characteristics	• Gender • Ethnicity • Age • General ability • Education level • Work experience • Reading level
Motivations	• Interest • Curiosity • Attributions • Aspirations • Persistence/Conation
Prior knowledge	• Content familiarity
Communication skills	• Written communication ability
Technical skills	• Keyboarding skills • Comfort level • Familiarity with file types (e.g., documents, PDF, SWF, JPEG, etc.) • Skill with emails, threaded discussions, chats, etc. • Skill and comfort levels with the Internet and the Web • Navigation and search skills
Abilities and disabilities	• Physical impairments • Mobility impairments • Visual impairments • Learning disabilities • Hearing disabilities • Speech impairments • Seizure disorders
Other learner characteristics	• Personality traits • Learning styles • Anxiety traits

General Characteristics.   General characteristics pertain to factors such as gender, ethnicity, age, general ability, education level, work experience, and reading level (Davidson, 1988; Dick et al., 2005; Smith & Ragan, 2005). Determining general characteristics allows the designer to discover commonalties and distinctions among the target audience members. Smith and Ragan (2005) make an important point regarding gathering information on the factors of gender and ethnicity (we add *age* to their list). They state that they "consider the differences not because members of one gender or racial group process information differently, but because . . . members of a gender, ethnic, or racial [or age] group tend to have common experiences because of their group membership that may be quite different from those had by members of other groups" (p. 64).

Examining general characteristics to identify unique and relevant differences and similarities among the target audience provides data on how the WBI should be designed and delivered so that learners succeed. For instance, the types of examples developed for the WBI should be relevant and interesting to audience members. When learners are diverse (in terms of ethnicity, gender, age, etc.), examples need to be diverse as well.

Motivation. Cornell and Martin (1997) view *motivation* as an overarching term in which interest, curiosity, attribution, and aspiration are included. They suggest that motivation is a particularly challenging individual difference to consider when designing WBI. It is estimated that the dropout rate for distance education courses is between 30 and 50 percent (Moore & Kearsley, 1996) and identifying learners' levels of curiosity and interest are especially important to help them persist and finish the course.

Prior Knowledge. Prior knowledge of content is probably the strongest factor for predicting success in learning (Driscoll, 2004; Ormrod, 2004; Smith & Ragan, 2005). Prior knowledge helps to determine familiarity with new content and facilitates retention. Information about learners' prior knowledge helps designers determine what skills or knowledge the learners "bring" to the learning environment (Smith & Ragan). Instructional designers use this information, along with the content or learning task analysis, to determine the point at which the instruction begins. This point is simply called "above and below the line," a phrase meant both literally and figuratively; we discuss it further in Chapter 4.

Communication Skills. With any instruction, having learners communicate well is a desirable attribute; it is a critical attribute for WBI participants. Because learners and instructor are meeting at a distance, without face-to-face contact, each learner's ability to write and be understood is an important skill. Designers need to find ways to assess students' levels of communication.

Technical Skills. Key to a learner's success in online learning is having a basic level of technical skills, including being able to keyboard because so much of the communication is in written form. Identifying skills such as students' familiarity with various types of files (e.g., HTM, HTML, JPEG, GIF, PDF, etc.), email procedures, threaded discussion applications, uploading and downloading files, chatting, and so on helps designers structure any initial training and orientation. The range of skills and comfort levels in being able to troubleshoot technical difficulties should also be determined.

Prior experience in using technology may influence a learner's performance in a Web-based environment. Abbey (2000) suggests that learners' navigation skills are important to successful performance in WBI, as are perceptual, search, and information processing skills and cognitive strategies. These attributes may affect how learners browse and comprehend information and interact among participants and WBI materials.

Abilities and Disabilities. The Americans with Disabilities Act (ADA), signed in 1990, and the Web Accessibility Initiative (W3C, 2001) require electronic accessibility for everyone. Not only are there U.S. mandates for equal access, there are international policies and legislation mandates (French & Valdes, 2002). WBI designers must provide access for people with a range of disabilities, including mobility impairments, visual impairments, learning disabilities, hearing disabilities, speech impairments, and seizure disorders (Burgstahler,

2002; Joint ADL Co-Laboratory, 2001; W3C, 1999, 2000, 2001). It is also relevant to consider other physical limitations, such as color blindness. Identifying disabilities among potential learners becomes imperative so that their access to the WBI is not denied.

Other Learner Characteristics.   Depending on the instructional context, content, and goal, other learner characteristics may need to be analyzed, including personality traits, learning styles, anxiety traits, and so on. Learner analysis, if all learner characteristics were considered, could last forever. Instructional designers must be pragmatic in selecting those learner characteristics that potentially have a direct bearing on WBI design and delivery.

Designers determine the impact of these findings on their design, development, and implementation of instructional strategies (such as the types of questions asked, examples and nonexamples presented, interaction strategies employed, etc.). Identified learner characteristics also affect the "look" or visual design of the WBI, the level of vocabulary used, and the instructional tone of the information.

Gathering Data on Learners.   Data on learners may be obtained using sources such as grades, applications, assessments or instruments (such as anxiety scales, learning style inventories, etc.), and surveys of the participants (past or present) themselves. Instructors or trainers of the target population are another valuable source of information.

See Appendix A for additional information on methods of and tools for gathering data on learners.

Documenting and Reporting Learner Analysis Findings.   A written report on pertinent characteristics of the targeted audience is part of the Design Document. It is important to describe the procedures and instruments used to gather and analyze data, and all findings and their implications in relation to the WBI design, delivery, and implementation.

GardenScapes

Kally provides Elliott with information (evaluations, etc.) about the learners who were in her most recent offering of the *Garden Basics* course. Elliott surveys a sample of past participants, requesting their responses to a 14-item questionnaire that covers basic demographics, gardening skills and interest in gardening, attitude towards technology, and computer skills. He decides to use a Likert-type response sheet for ease of response and data interpretation, and allows space for the respondents to add open-ended comments. His data collection and analysis yields the following results.

The audience for *GardenScapes* will be adults of various ages and economic backgrounds. Some work as professionals while others are in service-oriented positions or in technical and trade industries. Their education varies from those with high school and technical schooling to some with college degrees and a few with graduate degrees.

A common bond among this diverse group is that they are all homeowners who have or are developing an interest in gardening and would like to enhance their own yards. Some may be interested in performing the work themselves; others may hire the work out.

All of the individuals want to increase their understanding of how to design a healthy and beautiful garden, using appropriate plants and landscape features. The designer and instructor recognize, however, that these potential participants are a "voluntary audience." The course is *not* required; because participants choose to take the course, interest and motivation should be high.

Elliott and Kally recognize that this will be the first time for many of the learners (as well as Kally) to be involved in a Web-based course. Regarding prior skills of technology, the data indicate a variety of experience and skill levels with computers and the Web. Kally is gaining experience with using the Web as she works with Elliott on the design and has been able to observe a Web-based course being offered in the IDT program at Myers University.

Because most of the targeted audience have taken the first course, *Garden Basics,* they should have the prerequisite content skills for the new, advanced course. Others who have not taken *Garden Basics* also may be interested. Based on the topics of the first course, they propose the following entry skills:

1. *Explain differences in annuals, biennials, and perennials.*
2. *State differences between shrubs and trees.*
3. *State the temporal/climate zone of their location.*
4. *Determine if the area of interest in their home landscape is considered full sun, partial sun, partial shade, or full shade.*
5. *Demonstrate that they can, if necessary, amend the soil based on its condition.*
6. *Identify the basic garden tools necessary for gardening.*
7. *Name the basic requirements for maintaining plants.*

For learners who may not meet all of the entry skills, websites and tutorials will be available to help them reach minimum skill levels.

In the survey, Elliott asks respondents if they have any disabilities that need to be considered when designing the Web-based course. No one responds to that question and, due to privacy restrictions, Elliott and Kally are unable to obtain information about any specific disabilities. However, they plan to ask the TLDC support staff to provide them with means to accommodate for various disabilities as needed.

They are unable to assess communication skills of past learners from the survey results. Kally recalls that learners participated in lively face-to-face class discussions and activities. She is unaware of their writing skills because of the hands-on nature of the *Garden Basics* course; however, the education-level data lets her assume basic reading and writing competence.

See this textbook's Companion Website (http://www.prenhall.com/davidson-shivers) for Elliott's survey the *GardenScapes* Design Document.

ON YOUR OWN

Identify your target audience and explain their relevant learner characteristics in your Design Document by addressing the question, Who are your learners? Use Table 3.6 as your template for organizing this information.

Include an explanation of their prior skills, knowledge, or experience; the knowledge or skills that they are lacking; and their technical expertise with computers, email, the Web, and so on. Address as needed learners' comfort level with these technologies and their anxiety about being in a virtual learning environment. What commonalties and distinctions have you found among the target audience?

Additionally, would learners take the course voluntarily or is it part of a job, degree, or certification? How does this status impact the way you would design the WBI? How would you assess motivation levels?

What methods and tools will you develop and/or use to obtain such pertinent information about your learners? In your Design Document, describe the instruments and provide samples. You may purchase an instrument or modify someone else's questionnaire, rather than developing your own; in this case, you must obtain permission to use and provide a reference citation for these resources.

Begin thinking about how the information gathered about your target audience will impact the design, development, and delivery of the WBI. You will be writing these implications in your Design Document later.

(For illustrations of how other designers tackled these same issues, review the case studies appearing in the Extending Your Skills section at the end of this chapter.)

Wrapping Up

Discovering the problem in performance and its cause is a major part of the analysis stage. Determining the most appropriate solution for the problem is essential to producing changes that affect the learner or employee as well as the organization. The designer identifies the problems and solutions, then gathers information on goals, context, and learners. This information allows the designer to articulate the instructional goal and its outcome level, explain the important aspects of the instructional context, and describe the pertinent learner characteristics of the target audience for the WBI. These descriptions, explanations, and findings are reported in the Design Document. The findings of the instructional component analyses have implications for WBI that affect the remaining stages of the design process and the WBI project.

Expanding Your Expertise

1. Explain why problem analysis is important to WBI design.
2. Would there ever be a time when a problem analysis is considered unnecessary? Why?

3. If you were designing *GardenScapes,* would your approach to the analysis stage be different from Elliott and Kally's approach? Describe and justify the process you would follow.

4. What other information would you have liked to know about the *GardenScapes* components? How would you go about getting this data if you were Elliott or Kally?

5. Why is the first draft of the goal statement considered preliminary? What could alter or cause changes to this initial statement? How might these changes influence WBI design and development?

6. Describe the purposes of context and learner analyses. Why are these two components so important in WBI design? What might happen if you didn't conduct such fact finding?

7. Suppose you were on an instructional design team for developing Web-enhanced materials on how to write a check with the instructional goal being, "Learners will be able to write a check and record it in the register accurately." This WEI would cover parts of a check, the check register, and signing the check. What would you want to know about the instructional need, the learning context, and the learners? How would you go about finding answers to your questions?

Extending Your Skills

Case Study 1   ## PK–12 Schools

Ms. Megan Bifford has chosen to start her project using the science curriculum at three of the elementary schools in the Westport School District. The decision to focus on science was based on analysis of student performance data on recent accountability tests and on the fact that science "counts" in school grading for the first time in the next academic year. With the mandates to enhance technology integration from the district office, she plans on using a framework that will use the Internet and the Web to support the project.

Student performance on science standards is below the norm, based on standardized test score results for the last two years. Many deficiency areas relate to applying scientific methods to situations, specifically in the area of inquiry learning. Students exhibit a combination of lack of content knowledge and deficits in being able to apply the scientific method to analysis. The root cause is a lack of knowledge. After examining the current science textbook and other materials she determines that the content focuses on knowledge and comprehension and does not integrate higher-level thinking skills very well. To help teachers help students make the leap to the next level, Megan is considering using WebQuests to develop those inquiry-based skills. Megan creates a preliminary goal statement:

The students will be able to apply scientific methods to real-world problems.

The fifth-grade teachers are enthusiastic about working with distance education and online resources. Their current textbook lists some websites as instructional resources, which they want to access in hopes of motivating their students. Although they have not used Web resources previously, this year each fifth-grade class has access to the Web, either in the classroom, in the media center, or in a nearby computer lab. Students have practiced key-boarding skills since third grade and have learned how to use CD-ROMs to locate information. Teachers participated in extensive workshops over the summer and are ready to try out their new skills. There is a small, working science lab adjacent to the fifth-grade wing of the school.

Each class consists of approximately 20 to 25 students between ages 10 and 11, with a fairly even split between genders. Fifty percent of the students read on grade level. The others range from one to three levels below grade. Most of the students play video games and have those games at their home; however, most students report that they do not have access to a computer at home. The student population is ethnically diverse and some students come from a highly economically disadvantaged area. Fifty-five percent of the students receive free and reduced school lunches.

Computers are used in language arts classes for reading and writing. The language arts teachers also use an Integrated Learning System (ILS) for assessing student reading and writing performance. The district science coordinator is investigating adding a module on science to the ILS to enhance basic science knowledge. Students have some experience with using computers in science labs. They are interested in things that are typical to that age group. Girls are starting to show less interest in science than boys. About 10 percent of the school population has been diagnosed with either a physical or learning disability.

Data in hand, Megan is ready to start working on her Design Document.

Case Study 2   Business and Industry

Homer Spotswood meets with his CEO, Ira "Bud" Cattrell, to clarify the full scope of new safety training to be delivered via the plant's Intranet. As a preface to his meeting, Homer collects initial data:

- Plant safety records for the past three years, organized by department
- Government (state and federal) guidelines for safety
- Current training outlines, handouts, and course evaluations
- Personnel rosters organized by departments
- Current inventory of technology, including computers with Intranet access

Based on Homer's interpretation of the available data, he needs clarification on several issues. He asks Bud Cattrell the following questions:

- What are the priorities for the safety training initiative?
- Will technology be accessible by all plant employees?
- What is the technology plan for access to that technology?
- What will be the role of the company trainers in the project?
- What additional support will be available for the initiative?
- What time frame does the initiative need to meet?

Bud clarifies Homer's major issues by stating the following:

- Plant fire safety is the first priority.
- Access to the plant's technology will be available through all departments.
- The training will be a combination of in-house training and modules presented via the Web. The in-house training will be performance based, practicing skills that are outlined in the Web-based part of the project.
- Company trainers will facilitate both online and face-to-face training sessions.
- Employees will be able to dial up from their homes to access the instruction. Incentives will be provided for employees who are willing to participate in the online portion of the training on their own time. Human Resources will acquire 10 laptops for employees who want to check them out so that they can complete the training on their own time.
- All employees need to complete the training within six months.

Homer returns to his office to complete his analysis. In addition to the materials he's already collected and reviewed, he will observe tapes of previous trainings and observe plant safety operations. Based on his meeting with Mr. Cattrell, Homer's analysis must progress quickly so that the training can begin.

Home develops a preliminary goal statement to help guide him through his analysis:

At the end of the training, employees will be able to close their plant area and evacuate within three minutes.

Case Study 3   Military

Commander Rebekkah Feinstein has established a committee to conduct an analysis of the upcoming project. The committee includes educational specialists from the Curriculum and Instructional Standards division, the New Technologies division, and instructors/SMEs from the Electrical Core and Advanced Electronic Technical Core courses. Lieutenant Rex Danielson, a seasoned Limited Duty Officer and the New Technologies division officer, will be her principal point of contact.

Commander Feinstein provides the entire committee with the final report of an extensive review of Revolution in Training and a generalized profile of Navy learners. A work group, led by Lieutenant Sandra Cole, has focused on analyzing the curricula of each of the Training Support Center's four "A" schools to what elements of the instruction are common across the four schools.

Cole's team has gathered data on the resident student population of the past five years and has surveyed Fleet commands regarding existing resources and opportunities for supporting WBI. After a month of meetings, surveys, and analysis, Lieutenant Cole presents to Commander Feinstein her team's findings and recommendations. The team determines that their initial conversion efforts should focus on the fundamentals of electricity, in a course to be named *Electricity and Electronic Common Core* (E^2C^2). They formulate a preliminary instructional goal statement:

This course will provide foundational instruction in the concepts, processes, and principles of alternating- and direct-current electrical power to sailors throughout the Fleet and Training establishment by means of the Navy e-Learning learning management system.

While E^2C^2 will be accessible to anyone eligible to take courses through Navy e-Learning, the committee describes its target population as junior enlisted personnel (Seaman Recruit through Petty Officer Third Class, E-1 through E-4) who are or soon will be engaged in the electrician's mate or electronic technician's "A" schools.

The committee's analysis includes some issues about the infrastructure required to support this WBI. Enlistees entering the "A" school directly from recruit training will have access to the Training Support Center's computer labs. The lab servers offer high-speed, broadband access to the Web. However, Fleet (afloat versus dockside), shore-based, and individual home-based delivery of this series of lessons presents a complicated mix for consideration. While afloat (deployed) Fleet ships will have limited communication bandwidth available for nonoperational purposes (email, online learning, etc.). Finally, a recent survey shows that only 30 percent of home computer users have broadband connectivity; others rely on much slower 56K dial-up connections.

Case Study 4   Higher Education

Dr. Joe Shawn, an associate professor in the Management Department at Myers University, is re-analyzing data he has collected about his students and their performance. His next project, repurposing of the undergraduate course, *Introduction to Management,* has begun and he plans to implement it as a Web-enhanced course. He is scheduled to teach the class in the upcoming term.

The course goal is to have students apply the essentials of management practices to the dynamic work settings within organizations. Using a WEI format will improve his teaching of the management functions (planning, organizing, leading, controlling, etc.) and will allow better access to information on organizational performance. Course objectives range from knowledge level to evaluation, using Bloom's Taxonomy.

Although undergraduates are usually proficient Web users, Dr. Shawn has found that they are not necessarily motivated to take online courses. His management course has a course limit of 35 students per section. The students range in age from 18 to 25, with most being around 20 years old. There are slightly more males than females. Most students have some work experience, but limited management experience. The majority of students are in college full time, taking between 12 and 15 semester hours.

Dr. Amber Wolfgang, his department chair, supports teaching innovations through available resources. Dr. Shawn has a computer in his department office and one at home; both have high-speed Internet connections. The Management Department has a dedicated computer lab available for its students. The lab has 25 computers and a teaching station. All computers are connected both to the campus Intranet and to the Internet. There is also a university laboratory with 24/7 access.

He has been assigned a teaching assistant, Brian Cody, who is a relatively new graduate student in the MBA program at the college. Dr. Shawn recently found out that Brian has an interest in e-commerce and has a basic understanding of the Web. However, he does not have much teaching experience. Dr. Shawn will send Brian to the technology training offered by the university so that he will be able to use available technology resources.

The following applies to all case studies. Consider how you, as the designer, might act or respond in each case study.

- Would you do things differently? If so, how would they be different? If not, why not?
- What other information would you like to have had or known?
- How would you go about gathering that information?
- What direction are the instructional goals taking? Are they appropriate for the scenario?
- How could the information presented impact the remaining stages in the WBID Model and the actual Web-based learning project? How would the implications differ for each case? What would the differences be among the implications?

Chapter 4

Analysis: Considering Instructional Content for Web-Based Instruction

Instructional content is the last part of the second phase of analysis. During instructional content analysis, the designer delineates the major steps and subordinate skills (subskills) that learners perform to reach the instructional goal. These steps and subskills are illustrated in a learning task map (LTM) containing a line that divides the new learning from required entry skills. The LTM facilitates ordering and sequencing steps and skills. Task items and their identified outcome levels are entered into a table called the Task-Objective-Assessment Item Blueprint (TOAB). Later in the WBID Model, the TOAB is used as a tool to match objectives and assessment items with task items. The preliminary goal statement is then reviewed and changed as needed to create a final instructional goal. Findings from the entire analysis stage provide implications for WBI design, implementation, and evaluation.

Chapter 4 describes instructional content analysis. We explain the types of learning task maps and the numbering system used, and provide directions for beginning the TOAB. We then discuss reviewing the findings for all four of the instructional components and finalizing the instructional goal statement. The chapter closes with an examination of the implications of the analysis findings on WBI design and delivery.

Objectives

At the end of this chapter, you should be able to do the following:

- Define terminology associated with instructional content analysis.
- State the purpose of instructional content analysis.
- Develop a learning task map (LTM) for a content area.
- Convert task items and their learning outcomes for inclusion in a Task-Objective-Assessment Item Blueprint (TOAB).
- Generate a final instructional goal statement.
- Determine implications for the remaining WBID stages.

Introduction

Instructional content analysis is the final phase of the analysis stage of the WBID Model (Figure 4.1). In the ID literature, this analysis is also known as *instructional analysis* (Dick et al., 2005), *instructional task analysis* (Gagné et al., 1992; Gagné et al., 2005), and

Figure 4.1   Analysis stage of the WBID Model continues.

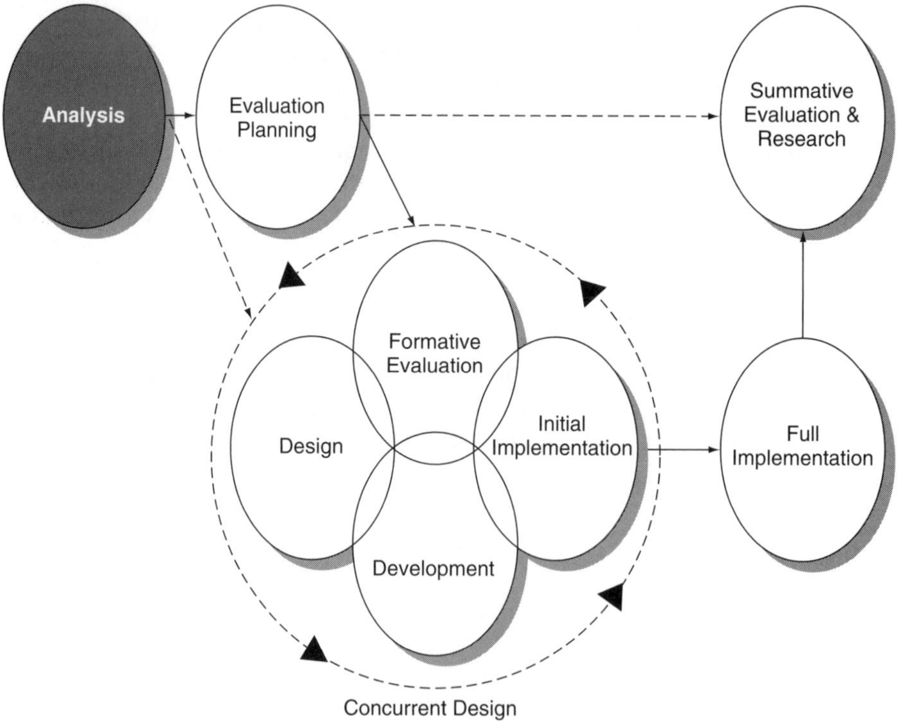

learning task analysis (Smith & Ragan, 2005). Instructional design approaches offer specific procedures to identify the sequence and number of steps required to meet the desired instructional goal. Smith and Ragan (2005) maintain that using such an approach eliminates "deadwood" in the content. Furthermore, they suggest that

> decomposing goals into prerequisites does not mean that these prerequisites have to be taught in a piecemeal fashion. In fact, we suggest that you seriously consider strategies that integrate the instruction of these prerequisites in meaningful ways. The analysis of goals for prerequisites is conducted solely to identify what cognitions [mental processes] make up the higher-order goals. This information will be used to design instruction that in some way considers these prerequisites so that learners will not be challenged beyond their "zone of proximal development." (p. 93)

Instructional content analysis in the WBID Model is based on similar assumptions.

The main purpose of this analysis is to identify the skills learners must perform to achieve the instructional goal. A second purpose is to develop a learning task map (LTM) to illustrate relationships among the major steps and subskills to begin identifying the best sequence for learning the skills and tasks specified by the goal.

The *major steps* are the main tasks to be performed by the learner and are considered to be the prerequisite skills needed to achieve the instructional goal (Gagné et al., 2005). Smith and Ragan (2005) offer the rule of thumb to keep the number of major steps between 3 and 12; Dick et al. (2005) offer a similar suggestion of no less than 5 and no more than 15 steps. Although these authors differ in the number of steps, they do agree that identifying too many or too few can be problematic. Smith and Ragan (2005) suggest that fewer than 3 major steps may mean that the designer is working with two separate goals and more than 12 may mean that the major steps are being mixed with subordinate skills.

In the WBID Model, the term *subskill*(s) is used for what is typically known as *subordinate* or *prerequisite* skills in traditional instructional design models. Subskills are those mental processes that learners must perform to achieve each of the identified steps and are, therefore, considered as prerequisite skills (Dick et al., 2005; Gagné et al., 1992; Smith & Ragan, 2005). The designer needs to ask the following questions when breaking down a goal into major steps and when breaking down these steps into subskills:

- What must the [learner] already know or do to accomplish the task?
- What are the subskills?
- What is the outcome level for this skill?
- What are the relationships of these particular prerequisite skills to each other?
- What is the skill order and sequencing?

The answers to the questions are stated in short phrases that include an action verb and the object of the action. That action verb then becomes a part of the learning task and later serves as the basis for the objectives and assessment items (to be discussed in

Figure 4.2 Examples of learning task items from various LTMs stated in a phrase with their identified outcome level underneath.

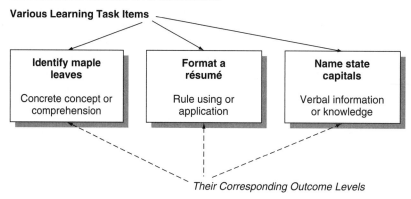

Chapter 6). Examples of learning task items are *identify maple leaves, format a résumé,* and *name state capitals.* Identifying the corresponding outcome level for each task item completes the learning task analysis.

The Categories of Learning (Gagné, 1985) or Bloom's Taxonomy (Bloom et al., 1956) are used to identify outcome levels of each learning task item, just as in identifying the outcome level of the Web-based instructional goal (see Chapter 3). Using these categories assists in linking the instructional goal, steps, and subskills to specific outcome levels within an LTM. The outcome levels for the previously identified examples would be *concrete concept* for identify maple leaves, *rule using* for format a résumé, and *verbal information* for name state capitals. If using Bloom's Taxonomy, the outcome levels would be comprehension, application, and knowledge (Figure 4.2).

Developing a Learning Task Map

During the instructional content analysis the designer organizes the Web-based instructional goal, major steps, and subskills into the learning task map (LTM), sometimes called a *flowchart* (Morrison et al., 2004; Seels & Glasgow, 1998) or *instructional curriculum map (ICM)* (Gagné et al., 2005). The LTM is a graphical representation that illustrates the relationships among the goal, steps, and subskills and in its final form becomes a part of the Design Document. Various instructional design models (Dick et al., 2005; Morrison et al., 2004; Smith & Ragan, 2005) suggest a three-step procedure for developing the learning task map, identifying each of the following in sequence:

1. Major steps needed to achieve the goal
2. Subskills needed to achieve each step
3. Entry skills needed to begin the instruction

When building an LTM, designers work with the major steps and subskills to develop the correct relationships and sequencing. Breaking down subskills continues until entry skills are identified. *Entry skills* are the prior knowledge or skills that learners must already possess to effectively engage in the new learning.

A dotted line on the LTM indicates the instructional line that separates the to-be-learned skills from the entry skills. The "above the line" steps (and subskills) lead to the instructional goal and are the instructional content that will be included in the WBI. Entry skills are "below the line" and are not developed as part of the WBI. It is important to analyze the instructional content in relation to the learner analysis to determine where to begin instruction.

It usually takes several attempts to identify all of the appropriate steps and subskills; it will take several as well to arrange (and rearrange) them so that the LTM reflects the most appropriate sequence for the WBI. Even the most experienced designers create several drafts before arriving at a workable LTM; some use a "top down" approach (working from the goal and major steps down to the subskills), others work from a "bottom up" approach, which obviously goes in the other direction. There are times when a designer will employ a combination of these two approaches.

LTM Formatting

Most LTMs are formatted with boxes and diamonds, with arrows as connections. There is no reason that other geometric shapes can't be used to identify steps and subskills (Seels & Glasgow, 1998). These boxes contain the short phrases for each learning task item and its corresponding outcome level (see Figure 4.2). These formats need not be symmetrical; in other words, it is not necessary that there be equal numbers of subskills for each identified major step. The instructional goal is contained in a box, centered above the major steps; however, it is usually not attached to the last step. It is assumed that when the last step has been achieved, the instructional goal has been mastered.

LTM Numbering System

The LTM uses a numbering system to show relationships. The system uses integers and decimal numbers and is placed in the task item box. Figure 4.3 presents an example of possible number placement.

With the LTM numbering system, 1.0, 2.0, and so on indicate the major steps toward reaching the WBI goal, and 1.1, 1.2, 2.1, 2.2 . . . *n* indicate the immediate subskill level below a major step. Each additional sublevel adds a decimal point and number. For instance, the numbers 2.1.1, 2.1.2, 2.1.3 would relate to and be placed below subskill 2.1. This numbering system both presupposes and imposes an ordering of the steps and subskills of the WBI. Although various instructional design models continue this type of numbering for entry skills, zeros (0.1, 0.2, 0.3, etc.) are used in the WBID Model to distinguish the entry skills from the learning task steps and subskills (Davidson, 1990; Davidson-Shivers, 1998).

Figure 4.3   Examples of the numbering for learning task items from various LTMs. The *5.0* indicates that this learning task item is a major step, the others are subskills.

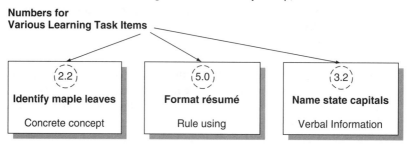

Three Types of Analysis and LTM Formats

Generally speaking, the LTM will show a procedural progression of the major steps toward the instructional goal. However, with the subskills, the LTM may use hierarchical or procedural strategies, or a combination of the two (Dick et al., 2005; Gagné et al., 2005; Morrison et al., 2004; Seels & Glasgow, 1998; Smith & Ragan, 2005).

Hierarchical Analysis and LTM Format.   The hierarchical analysis and LTM format indicate a specified order of steps and subskills based on superordinate and subordinate levels. A hierarchical analysis presumes that the skills at a subordinate level must be learned before ascending to the next higher level. Subskills at the same level may be learned in any order. For instance, if intellectual skills are the outcome levels associated with an instructional goal, steps, and subskills, then participants should be presented with concepts before rules, rules before problem solving, and so on. (Recall that Gagné's Intellectual Skills category contains five skills; these skills follow a specified ascending order from discrimination to problem solving.) Intellectual skills require that learners master all of the subskills at one level prior to proceeding to the next level, but when these subskills are at the same level on the LTM, they may be learned in any order.

In Figure 4.4, the WBI goal and major steps appear at the top of the LTM with horizontal arrows leading from one major step to another. The subskills are in boxes attached to the major steps with arrows indicating an *upward* flow of the to-be-learned skills toward the goal. The numbers indicate an identified step and its related subskill(s). Each level of subskills must be performed (in any order) before moving to the next level. For instance, in the example with the WBI goal of identifying trees of North America (see Figure 4.4), the subskills of 2.2.1, 2.2.2, and 2.2.3 are at the same subskill level and can be learned in any order; however, they all must be learned before moving up to the next subskill level, that of 2.2.

Procedural Analysis and LTM Format.   A procedural analysis implies that a step-by-step process is undertaken when achieving the instructional goal. This LTM is one of the easiest to construct since the analysis of the instructional goal follows an orderly succession of major steps and subskills. With the procedural ordering of subskills, sometimes a step will repeat one or more previous steps. If so, it will be indicated by a line pointing back to the intended step. Figure 4.5 illustrates a procedural format in an LTM, which identifies outcomes based on Bloom's Taxonomy. In this example, subskill 3.1 must be learned be-

Figure 4.4   Hierarchical analysis and LTM format. The dotted line separates the start of the instruction (learning task items) from entry-level skills.

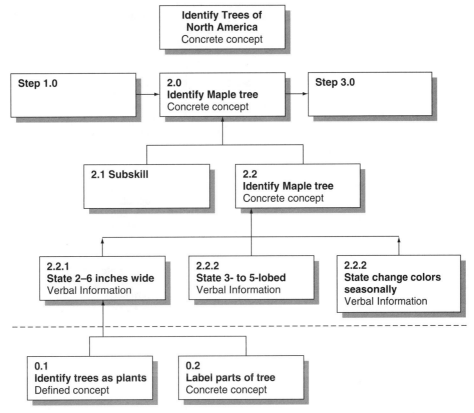

fore subskill 3.2, and both subskills must be learned to achieve the 3.0 major step of identifying northern states and capitals.

Combination Analysis and LTM Format.   Sometimes the instructional goal, major steps, and subskills require a combination of both hierarchical and procedural analysis and ordering. Figure 4.6 illustrates an LTM that uses a combination analysis. In this example with the WBI goal, "Prepare effective résumé for job search," one major step is "5.0—format offline résumé." It has two procedural subskills, 5.1 and 5.2 (5.1 must be learned before proceeding to 5.2). In addition, two hierarchical subkills of 5.1.1 and 5.1.2 appear; these two can be learned in any order, but prior to achieving the 5.1 subskill.

Gathering Data on the Instructional Content

It is not uncommon for instructional designers to work with unfamiliar content and this situation is true in WBI, as well. There are several ways to gain expertise in particular subject matter (Morrison et al., 2004). Designers may work with subject matter experts (SMEs), which may be the best way to gain familiarity. Observing SMEs teaching or observing the

Figure 4.5   Procedural analysis and LTM format. The arrows indicate the specified order for learning task items.

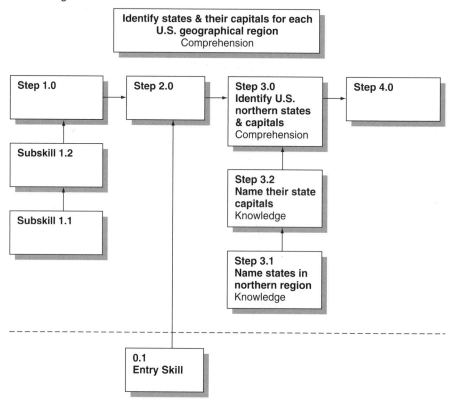

task being completed provides valuable information, especially if the skill is a job-related task. Former learners or participants also may identify missing, deleted, or changed information based on their experience. Acquiring and reading reference materials (books, journals, websites, etc.) or taking a course may help designers acquire insight into the content.

Reviewing the Instructional Content Analysis and LTM

With any of these analysis and LTM formats, the designer notes any divergent points in the learning path; these points indicate alternative directions or other steps. It is best to choose the most common, easiest path as the primary sequence for WBI (Seels & Glasgow, 1998; Smith, 1990; Smith & Ragan, 2005). This choice is especially important if the content is difficult, the participants are novice learners, and the environment has time constraints or other limitations. Alternate steps or pathways can be addressed later as a means to enhance learning retention and transfer.

Once the designer is satisfied with the analysis and has a workable LTM, the sequence of steps and subskills should be confirmed for accuracy and completeness. Designers who

Figure 4.6 Combination analysis and LTM format. Both procedural and hierarchical analysis are used.

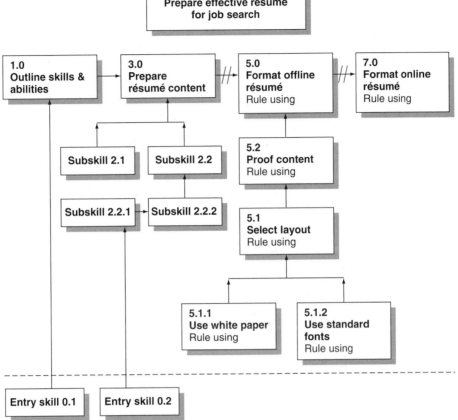

are working alone may locate other experts to review the LTM. Generally, instructional designers work in teams and, for confirmation, other team members or SMEs will review the LTM.

GardenScapes

Elliott conducts the instructional content analysis and creates the LTM for the advanced course, *GardenScapes*. Because Elliott is unfamiliar with landscaping and gardening content, he relies on Kally for the content information to draw out the major steps and subskills. After a series of drafts and review meetings, he arrives at a workable LTM that he places in the Design Document. This LTM appears here. (Note that, due to lack of space, the outcome levels are omitted here. They appear in the TOAB, discussed later in this chapter.)

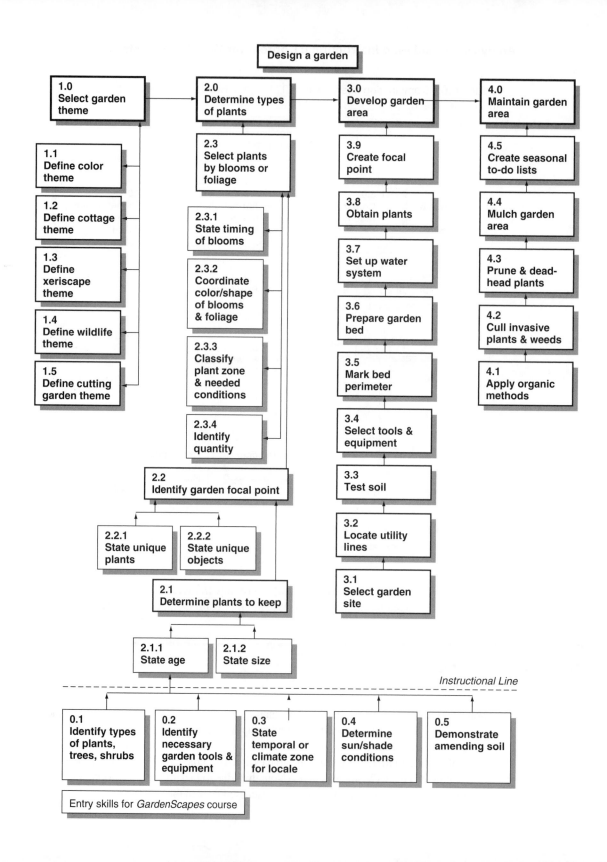

Elliott uses a combination analysis for his *GardenScapes* LTM. Entry skills are based on the instructional goal and main objectives for the introductory course, *Garden Basics*. Elliott uses a dotted line to indicate the instructional line and a 0.X numbering system to indicate required entry skills.

See this textbook's Companion Website (http://www.prenhall.com/davidson-shivers) for Elliott's GardenScapes LTM.

ON YOUR OWN

Conduct an instructional content analysis on your instructional goal. Decide which type of analysis and LTM format you will use. To break down the goal, ask yourself, "What do learners need to know or do to reach the goal?" Repeat this question for each of the major steps to determine the subskills. You should have between 3 and 12 major steps.

As you conduct your analysis, begin working on your LTM. Write the WBI goal in a box above your major steps. Determine the major steps to reach this goal and then break each step into subskills. Use short phrases for the learning task items within the boxes. Set the instructional line between the to-be-learned and entry skills using information from your learner analysis.

Use a technology tool, such as *Inspiration*® (Inspiration Software, Inc., 2005) or the draw portion of Microsoft *PowerPoint* or *Word* (or other word processor program), to develop your LTM. Novice LTM builders may find it helpful to begin their LTM by first using a "sticky notepad," rearranging each "sticky note" until they find an optimum sequence. These notes can then be drawn using a technology tool.

Identify the outcome level for each major step and subskills using the Categories of Learning or some other domain taxonomy. Once you are satisfied with your analysis and have a workable LTM, ask an ID expert and an SME to review your LTM. Place your LTM in your Design Document.

(For illustrations of how other designers tackled these same issues, review the case studies appearing in the Extending Your Skills section at the end of this chapter.)

When Is Instructional Content Analysis Finished?

Instructional content analysis is *not* an exact science. Instructional designers become adept at analysis through experience and practice. However, it bears repeating that it takes a number of attempts to identify the major steps and subskills, as well as their relationships to each other and their connection to the WBI goal.

There is no one correct way of conducting an instructional content analysis or of creating an LTM; there may be many versions of the "right" LTM. The LTM is "finished" when the designer and, if appropriate, the client, are satisfied with its content and format. Of course, modifications may still occur as the project continues. Ultimate satisfaction occurs when the design efforts are completed and the WBI itself is implemented successfully.

Table 4.1   Overview of the Contents of the TOAB

Learning Task Item and Number	Objective	Outcome Level	Assessment Item
Instructional Goal Statement	End-of-instruction objective (Use 3- or 5-component objectives)	Identify outcome level by Gagné's Categories or Taxonomy by Bloom, Krathwohl, Singer, or Simpson	Explain authentic assessment tool and/or provide sample test items or questions
Step 1.0	Major objective		
Subskill 1.1	Subordinate objective		
Subskill 1.2			
Step 2.0		Problem solving	
Subskill 2.1			
Subskill 2.1.1			
Subskill 2.1.2			
Subskill 2.2			
Steps and subskills continued			
Entry Skill			
Entry Skill			

Task-Objective-Assessment Item Blueprint (TOAB)

When the LTM is more or less finished, one last aspect remains: creating the Task-Objective-Assessment Item Blueprint (TOAB) (Davidson-Shivers, 1998; Northrup, 2001). The LTM provides an illustration, or schematic, of the sequencing of the major steps and subskills. The TOAB shows the direct linkage of the identified learning tasks to the outcome levels (Table 4.1). The designer can use the TOAB to illustrate congruence among all items (i.e., learning task, objective, outcome level, and assessment item), starting by placing the major steps and subskills of the LTM in the first column. The associated outcome level for each task item is placed in the third column. Later, the designer uses the TOAB to align the WBI objectives and assessment items with the learning task items and outcome levels (we will discuss WBI objectives and assessment in Chapter 6).

GardenScapes

Although Elliott could use other taxonomies for objectives and outcomes, he prefers to use Gagné's Categories of Learning, noting them in the third column. He places the TOAB in the *GardenScapes* Design Document.

Elliott's Draft TOAB for *GardenScapes*

Learning Task Item and Number	Objective	Outcome Level	Assessment Item
Develop a Garden. *(Derived from goal statement)*		Intellectual skill: Rules	
1.0 Select garden theme.		Intellectual skill: Rules	
1.1 Define color theme.		Defined concept	
1.2 Define cottage theme.		Defined concept	
1.3 Define xeriscape theme.		Defined concept	
1.4 Define wildlife theme.		Defined concept	
1.5 Define cutting garden theme.		Defined concept	
2.0 Determine types of plants.		Intellectual skill: Rule	
2.1 Determine plants to keep.		Intellectual skill: Concrete concept	
2.1.1 State age.		Verbal information	
2.1.2 State size.		Verbal information	
2.2 Identify garden focal point.		Intellectual skill: Concrete concept	
2.2.1 State unique plants.		Verbal information	
2.2.2 State unique objects.		Verbal information	
2.3 Select plants by blooms or foliage.		Intellectual skill: Concrete concept	
2.3.1 State timing of blooms.		Verbal information	
2.3.2 Coordinate color/shape of blooms and foliage.		Intellectual skill: Defined concepts	
2.3.3 Classify plant zone and needed conditions.		Intellectual skill: Defined concept	
3.0 Develop garden area.		Intellectual skill: Rule & Motor skill	
3.1 Select garden site.		Intellectual skill: Concrete concept	
3.2 Locate utility lines.		Intellectual skill: Rule	

(continued)

Learning Task Item and Number	Objective	Outcome Level	Assessment Item
3.3 Test soil conditions.		Intellectual skill: Rule	
3.4 Select tools and equipment.		Intellectual skill: Concrete concept	
3.5 Mark bed perimeter.		Motor skill	
3.6 Prepare garden bed.		Motor skill	
3.7 Set up water system.		Intellectual skill: Concrete concept & Motor skill	
3.8 Obtain plants.		Motor skill	
3.9 Create focal point.		Intellectual skill: Rule & Motor skill	
4.0 Maintain garden area.		**Intellectual skills: Rule**	
4.1 Apply organic methods.		Intellectual skill: Defined concepts & Motor skill	
4.2 Cull invasive plants and weeds.		Intellectual skill: Concrete concept & Motor skill	
4.3 Prune and deadhead plants.		Intellectual skill: Concrete concept & Motor skill	
4.4 Mulch garden area.		Intellectual skill: Concrete concept & Motor skill	
4.5 Create seasonal to-do lists.		Intellectual skill: Rules	
Entry Skills			
0.1 Identify types of plants, trees, and shrubs.		Intellectual skill: Concrete concepts	
0.2 Identify necessary garden tools and equipment.		Intellectual skill: Concrete concepts	
0.3 State temporal or climate zone of locale.		Intellectual skill: Verbal information	
0.4 Determine sun/ shade conditions of locale.		Intellectual skill: Rule using	
0.5 Demonstrate amending soil.		Intellectual skill: Rule using	

See this textbook's Companion Website (http://www.prenhall.com/davidson-shivers) for the *GardenScapes* Design Document.

ON YOUR OWN

Begin a TOAB for your WBI project. Use this tool to align your learning task items to corresponding outcome levels. Place the instructional goal at the top of the table. List all of the major steps with their corresponding subskills in a sequential order, preserving the task numbering system established in your LTM. Add the entry skills last. List the outcome level of each major step and subskill. Use the overview in Table 4.1 as your template. Include your TOAB in the Design Document for your WBI project.

See this textbook's Companion Website (http://www.prenhall.com/davidson-shivers) for a printable TOAB template.

Finalizing the Instructional Goal Statement

The analysis stage of the WBID Model contains one more procedure, reviewing the instructional goal statement for accuracy. WBID is a fluid process and new information may have been discovered during the various instructional component analyses; hence, the designer verifies that the original (or preliminary) goal statement is still congruent with the content, learners, and context (refer to Chapter 3 and to the Design Document for your WBI project).

Furthermore, the designer checks whether this goal statement simply and clearly reflects the appropriate outcome level. There are four indicators that may suggest that the goal needs some adjustment. The first indicator is the inclusion of imprecise verbs, such as "is familiar with," "knows," or "is aware of." These types of verbs indicate that the instructional goal is "fuzzy." A second indicator that a goal needs revision is imprecision in the general statement. In other words, it is difficult to ascertain whether a learner has achieved because the WBI goal is worded imprecisely. Examples of such imprecise goal statements are, "feels a sense of pride in one's work" and "understands math computations." The third indicator is that the goal is written in terms of lesson activities or assessment events rather than in terms of achieving an outcome. An example is, "the student will pass the unit exam." The fourth indicator is that the goal statement is not centered or oriented on the learners; instead, it is written in terms of what the teacher will do when conducting the lesson. An example of this fourth type is "the teacher will demonstrate long division" (Smith, 1990; Smith & Ragan, 2005).

To correct imprecise goal statements, designers must use action verbs that state the desired learning performance, linking the verbs to a specific outcome level. Further, designers must state clearly the object of the action. To remove any vagueness from the preliminary WBI goal statement, Smith (1990) suggests the following procedure:

1. Write down the things that learners would do to demonstrate that they had achieved the goal in an assessment situation. *What are the indicators that mastery has been achieved?*
2. Incorporate each of those indicators from step 1 into a statement that tells how well, or to what extent, learners will be able to do the performance.

3. Review the new WBI goal statement. Ask the question: *If learners achieve or demonstrate each performance(s), will they have achieved the goal?*
4. Review the new WBI goal statement. Ask the question: *Does the goal describe what learners achieve at the END of instruction rather than during instruction, not worded in terms of assessment?*
5. Review the new WBI goal statement. Ask the question: *Is the goal **learner**-centered rather than **teacher**-centered?*
6. If so, the designer can ask additional evaluative questions:
   - Can the goal be achieved through instruction, rather than another solution?
   - Is the goal related to an identified problem or based on the results of the analyses?

GardenScapes

Kally and Elliott review the instructional goal statement as originally written:

> *At the end of the instruction, the participant will be **able to develop a garden** that follows his or her garden plan that is based on a garden theme of his or her choice and follows basic gardening guidelines and appropriate procedures.*

The designated outcome level for the WBI goal is the intellectual skill of rule using (Gagné) or application (Bloom).

Although Elliott and Kally are satisfied with the stated outcome level, they are uncomfortable with part of the goal statement (shown in boldface). Instead of focusing on developing an actual garden site, they would rather that the participants create a *garden plan* and identify the sequence of necessary steps to complete their garden projects. In that way, the instructional goal is achievable for all participants within the timeframe of the course, regardless of location and seasonal conditions that may be occurring at the time the course is offered. Their final instructional goal statement now reads as follows:

> *At the end of the instruction, the participant will develop a **garden plan** that is based on a garden theme of their choice. The participant will be able to describe the appropriate steps to bring the garden project to fruition.*

The outcome level remains rule using (or application).

Elliott, with Kally's approval, changes some of the learning tasks and outcome levels listed on the original TOAB as well. (These changes are noted in Chapter 6 as the work on their TOAB continues.) Elliott includes the changes and provides a rationale for them in his Design Document for *GardenScapes*.

 See this textbook's Companion Website (http://www.prenhall.com/davidson-shivers) for the *GardenScapes* Design Document.

ON YOUR OWN

Review your preliminary instructional goal statement and its outcome level. Check for fuzziness with the goal by going through the procedures as outlined in this text. Modify any imprecise elements of the goal to arrive at a final goal statement. Be sure that the outcome level is still set at the correct level. If the goal statement or its outcome level is changed, be sure that the LTM and TOAB reflect similar adjustments. Identify your changes to the goal, LTM, and TOAB in your Design Document and explain why you made them.

(For illustrations of how other designers tackled these same issues, review the case studies appearing in the Extending Your Skills section at the end of this chapter.)

Implications for the Design and Delivery of WBI

According to Smith and Ragan (2005), "consideration of the general characteristics of the target audience [and goal and outcome level, context, and content] may be what elevates a mundane segment of instruction into compelling, imaginative, and memorable instruction" (p. 70). The findings from all four parts of the instructional component analyses (chapters 3 and 4) provide the designer with implications for the remaining WBID stages and enable her to identify the capabilities and limitations of the WBI project itself.

Determining such implications is the one of the most important aspects of the analysis stage. Yet, this task is sometimes minimized or performed in haste. A designer may rush through it to move the WBI project forward. Alternatively, while skilled at analysis, a designer may *not* be skilled in drawing conclusions. In other words, he or she may not be able to point out how the results may affect the design or implementation of the WBI. Furthermore, some designers may view the analysis stage as merely routine tasks simply performed to satisfy a project requirement. However, asking the critical question, "And so, what does this mean for . . . ?" is important. Or, more pointedly, asking, "How does this information further the effective design and delivery of the WBI?" may prevent inappropriate, inadequate, or inferior WBI being created.

Influencing the Remaining Stages of the WBID Model

Designers must consider not only what can be discovered about WBI context, learners, and content during analysis, but how that information will be used in the other stages. For example, the final instructional goal statement and its outcome levels have direct bearing on the types of instructional strategies identified and developed in concurrent design (the stage in which design, development, and formative evaluation tasks are conducted simultaneously; it was introduced in Chapter 2, and is the subject of chapters 6–8). As illustration of this point, when an instructional goal is established at an application outcome level, the employed instructional strategies should provide detailed procedures for that application, provide examples of how the process is and is *not* applied, and allow participants to demonstrate performance of that application. By contrast, when an instructional goal is at a verbal information level, the instructional strategies should illustrate and describe specific facts, figures, and so on and allow for types of practice that promote retention and recall.

The results of the instructional context analysis impact the design as well and this is especially true for WBI projects. With WBI, it is common practice that the website used during design becomes the actual environment of the implemented WBI. Designers must be cognizant of the existing features of the websites or LMSs that are used. Although some systems place few restrictions, other websites may have limited resources that constrain the design and delivery of the WBI project. For instance, some free websites and LMSs used for WBI development may contain restrictions that affect the actual appearance of the website, how the participants interact with each other, and the amount and types of information that can be loaded to the site or the manner in which it is uploaded or downloaded. These and other environmental features affect how the designer will structure the WBI pathways that are used for learner navigation.

Learner characteristics have a great deal of impact on the WBI instructional and motivational strategies. For example, general characteristics such as age, general ability, reading level, and so on will affect the size of the instructional "chunks" that are presented, as well as how many chunks are needed for the participants to meet the goal and the level of detail that must be provided. These characteristics, along with cultural, ethnic, gender, and other identifiers influence the types of examples, the amount and types of practice, and the type of feedback that can be used. For instance, learners familiar with the content will not need as much practice as will novice learners.

Additionally, understanding the types of humor that are and are *not* appropriate for any type of instruction (Bork, 2000) is important, but this understanding is especially true for Web-based instruction. Because most WBI participant interactions do *not* contain verbal language (tone of voice and voice inflection), intended humorous messages sent and received can often be misinterpreted. Consequently, the designer/instructor must have a clear conceptualization of how participants' backgrounds (culture, ethnicity, age, gender, etc.) will affect their response to any attempt at humor. Additionally, ensuring that a message is *not* taken seriously is highly dependent on a skilled instructor's use of **netiquette** (guidelines for courteous communication) (Albion.com, 1999) and **emoticons** (facial expressions made with various keystrokes) (ComputerUser.com, Inc., 2000).

Instructional content analysis results serve as the basis for creating the WBI objectives and assessment items, a part of the concurrent design stage. They help direct the instructional strategies that will be designed in terms of sequencing the information.

Although most of this discussion to this point has been about the impact of analysis on design and delivery, findings also affect the evaluation of the WBI project (the subject of Chapter 5). Overall, the data-gathering methods, type of information gathered, and accuracy of the findings affect how future evaluations are planned and conducted, and the evaluator's ability to use various evaluation methodologies and tools. In other words, if performance data are the preferred source for the answer to a question, gathering attitude data will not be appropriate.

As the remaining stages of the WBID Model are completed, a periodic review of the analysis findings is in order. These reviews help designers do the following:

1. Discover other important findings that will impact the WBI.
2. Make certain that WBI design is on target and consistent with the findings.

GardenScapes

The TLDC has obtained excellent hardware and software for WBI development, and has a knowledgeable staff to provide assistance and support. Elliott wants to take advantage of those resources. However, Kally wants to ensure that the WBI doesn't become too sophisticated so that she (because of her lack of technical abilities) and her targeted participants don't become overwhelmed.

Elliott estimates the amount of additional support, such as tutorials on hardware and software, that learners might need. As part of the course overview, Elliott may need to develop information on how to get started in the course, how learners are to interact with each other, and how to send messages to the instructor to raise the comfort level of the participants. Establishing these processes may help Kally improve her technological abilities as an instructor and alleviate some of her concerns.

Based on the instructional content analysis and the LTM, the information presentation will be chunked into four major sections. Two additional sessions, one for course overview and another for course wrapup, will be added. In total, *GardenScapes* will be presented in six sessions for 1.2 CEUs (continuing education units).

Visual examples and nonexamples that feature good and poor garden plans will be incorporated into the WBI to showcase best practices and add motivational appeal. Kally used fun titles in the *Garden Basics* course that made these adult participants relax about "being back in school"; she thought they went over well and wants to use them in this course. Although somewhat skeptical about how much *fun* they are, Elliott acknowledges that they may help create a relaxed, informal tone to the WBI and agrees to include her ideas. He notes that this strategy will be one to ask participants about during the formative evaluation. Because their findings indicate that the audience is highly motivated to learn, presenting the information must be kept interesting *and* relevant to the learners.

Kally and Elliott realize that all of the participants may not be from the local area, and that the content (examples) will need to show typical plants and garden plans appropriate to other U.S. regions and, perhaps, to other parts of the world.

As they begin to work on the evaluation and concurrent design plans, Elliott refers to their analysis findings to make sure that all of the WBI elements and features will align. Both he and Kally want to be certain that they haven't missed other important information that could impact this WBI project.

See this textbook's Companion Website (http://www.prenhall.com/davidson-shivers) for the *GardenScapes* Design Document.

ON YOUR OWN

Consider the findings of your analyses in terms of their implications for the remaining WBID stages. In other words, now that you have gathered this information, how will you use it? What do the findings mean in relation to the instructional effectiveness of the WBI, its visual appeal, and so on? What kinds of examples will you use? What types of questions will you ask? What types of practice exercises will you include? Overall, how do the findings affect your choices of instructional and motivational strategies?

In your Design Document, identify and describe the key factors in relation to their effect on your design, implementation, and evaluation stages as well as on the WBI itself.

(For illustrations of how other designers tackled these same issues, review the case studies appearing in the Extending Your Skills section at the end of this chapter.)

Wrapping Up

Instructional content analysis is the last part of instructional component analysis, and is where the major steps and subskills of the WBI goal are determined and an LTM is created. Based on the LTM, the TOAB is begun with each learning task item and outcome level listed.

In the final phases of the analysis stage, the preliminary goal statement is reexamined for consistency and clarity. Based on the analysis findings, changes to the preliminary goal statement may be made. The final goal statement will need to accurately identify and state the instructional purpose of the WBI.

Once the analysis stage is completed, the designer will be able to articulate the instructional goal and its outcome level, and describe critical learner characteristics and pertinent contextual features. Additionally, the designer will be able to illustrate the relationship of the major steps and subskills of the instructional content to the instructional goal using the LTM and the TOAB. Based on the results of the analysis stage, two WBI plans are begun: one for evaluation and another for the concurrent design; we explore these plans in the next four chapters.

Expanding Your Expertise

1. Describe the purposes of instructional content analysis. What might happen if you didn't conduct such fact finding? Are there any reasons for *not* conducting an instructional content analysis or developing an LTM? Explain your answers.
2. What is meant by "above and below the line" in terms of the learning task map (LTM)? What could cause an item's placement on the LTM to change? Explain your answers.
3. Complete an instructional content analysis and an LTM for the following instructional goal statement:

   At the end of the instruction, the learner will be able to bake cookies.

   Identify the major steps and subskills for the instructional goal. It may help to identify a specific age group and contextual setting to determine the instructional line. For instance, will your audience be a Boy or Girl Scout troop on a campout? High school sophomores in a *Contemporary Life Skills* course? Adults with special needs? A basic cooking 101 for beginning chefs at a fancy culinary arts school? Choose your target audience and environment.
4. How detailed should the LTM be in terms of illustrating the majors steps and subskills? When is the detail too much or not enough?

5. Is developing a TOAB necessary? Why or why not? Explain your answer.

6. What is the relevance of determining outcome levels for each of the task items within the LTM or TOAB?

7. Is it really necessary to review the preliminary instructional goal statement? Explain and support your position.

8. What is the difference between task analysis and instructional content analysis? For discussion purposes, you may wish to review the literature.

Extending Your Skills

Case Study 1 ## PK–12 Schools

Ms. Megan Bifford begins the instructional analysis of the fifth-grade science curriculum, using state and national standards, as well as the county's curriculum frameworks. At the same time, she begins analyzing the content from district-approved textbooks. She requests lesson planning books from the teachers to see how they organize their science classrooms and content.

After gathering and reviewing the curricula, Megan creates an initial list of skills for discussion with her subject matter experts. She meets with two of the district's teachers, Rhoda Cameron and Buzz Garrison, and the district science coordinator, Cassie Angus. They use Megan's brainstormed list as a beginning for specific skills that students need to acquire to improve their performance on the spring high-stakes tests.

Using findings from the instructional component analysis, she revises her instructional goal to reflect a more accurate statement for the project. It now states:

At the end of the instruction, the fifth-grade students will be able to apply inquiry techniques, using scientific methods to resolve real-world problems.

Incorporating all of the suggestions, Megan develops a draft LTM and aligns each skill to Bloom's Taxonomy as she begins to develop the TOAB. After drafting these items, she sends the files to Cassie, Rhoda, and Buzz for additional review. Once she receives their feedback, she will be ready to begin to think about project evaluation.

Case Study 2 ## Business and Industry

Homer Spotswood has collected all of the safety manuals and OSHA rules related to plant safety. He starts his instructional content analysis by listing all of the knowledge, skills, and abilities that individuals must display to meet safety requirements. As he works he considers how the items he is identifying will influence his use of instructional strategies in the final project.

After his list is completed, he begins developing his LTM to sequence the content. As a check on his work, he meets with the plant safety officer, Greta Dottman, to confirm his LTM. As an additional check, he reviews similar training initiatives that are sponsored by the federal government. Once the LTM is approved, he begins the TOAB.

Based on the analysis, he revises the training goal as follows:

> At the end of the training experience, employees will secure
> their work area and evacuate within two minutes.

Case Study 3   Military

During his briefing of Commander Rebekkah Feinstein, Lieutenant Rex Danielson introduces EMSC (Electricians Mate, Senior Chief) Gus Mancuso, the senior instructor at the Electricians Mate "A" school. E^2C^2 is an introductory survey course, requiring little prior knowledge of the field of electricity. E^2C^2 will contain three major topics:

- Introduction to matter, energy, and direct current
- Introduction to alternating current and transformers
- Introduction to generators and motors

Based on the content analysis, Lieutenant Danielson's team finalizes their goal statement to submit to Commander Feinstein and develops a set of implications for her to review.

The commander and Lieutenant Danielson are scheduled to provide a progress report to Captain Cameron Prentiss soon. If the captain finds their analysis sound and their vision of the project's approach reasonable, they can begin to create the course LTM and TOAB.

Case Study 4   Higher Education

Joe Shawn is not only the course instructor, but also the subject matter expert for the *Introduction to Management* course. As the SME, he identifies and sequences the required content to meet the stated objectives (as outlined in the department's approved course syllabus) and then builds the course topic outline. He asks Brain Cody, his teaching assistant, to conduct Web and library searches to locate websites and journal articles relevant to management practices and organizational operations to use as resources.

Joe meets with other faculty who teach the *Introduction to Management* course to ensure that his topics are consistent with their syllabi. They offer suggestions and he finalizes the instructional goal as follows:

> Students will apply management techniques to real-world situations.

Joe documents the meetings and materials. These documents will be useful resources when preparing for reaccreditation. One of the accrediting agencies for the College of Business is the American Association of Collegiate Schools of Business (AACSG). All of the proposed changes must meet established AACSG criteria.

The following applies to all case studies. Consider how you, as the designer, might act or respond to each case study:

- What information is *not* presented that you would like to have had? How would you go about gathering that data?
- How do the analysis procedures presented in chapters 3 and 4 influence the design and development of WBI? How do these procedures differ for each case?
- What you would do differently from each of the principals in the case studies?

Chapter 5

Planning the Evaluation
of Web-Based Instruction

There are two types of evaluation plans, formative and summative. At this stage of the WBID Model, formative evaluation plans are fully developed and summative evaluation plans are developed to a preliminary state. The formative evaluation plan facilitates the revision of the WBI prototype and its website as they are developed. This evaluation is enacted once the concurrent design stage begins and is then carried into the initial implementation of the WBI, which would be considered a field trial. The second part of planning, the preliminary planning for summative evaluation, is an important feature of the WBID Model. It allows for data about the instructional situation to be collected prior to the WBI being implemented. Often, valuable information is lost when data on the state of instructional products or practices is *not* collected before a new innovation is introduced (Solomon & Gardner, 1986). The final planning for and conducting of summative evaluation occur after full implementation.

Chapter 5 begins with an overview of the main purposes of evaluation and five general evaluation orientations, followed by a discussion of the evaluation methods and tools. We then discuss how to develop each plan and ways to communicate and report formative evaluation findings. The chapter closes with a discussion of preliminary planning for summative evaluation (Chapter 10 is devoted to the final planning and conducting of summative evaluation and research.)

Objectives

At the end of this chapter, you should be able to do the following:
- Explain the general purposes of evaluation.
- Name the five general evaluation orientations.
- Compare and contrast *formative* and *summative* evaluation.
- Describe procedures for planning formative evaluation.
- Explain the advantages and disadvantages of internal and external evaluators.
- Write a formative evaluation plan.
- Develop a communication plan for reporting the formative evaluation process and results.
- Write a preliminary plan for a summative evaluation.

Introduction

Evaluation is another critical stage in WBI design (Figure 5.1). **Evaluation** is the means for determining the value, or worth, of an instructional product or program (Fitzpatrick, Sanders, & Worthen, 2004). In addition, it is the process of gathering information to decide whether the WBI needs revision or whether it should be continued as is. We distinguish it here from **assessment,** which is gathering information used to measure learners' progress toward achieving instructional goals.

WBI's value is often communicated to its stakeholders in terms of its instructional effectiveness, efficiency, and appeal. All three criteria help determine the ultimate success of WBI, or how well the learners met the goals and objectives. Table 5.1 presents brief definitions of these criteria. Because all WBI situations differ, the use of these evaluation criteria will vary. In some situations, all three may be applied; others may require only one or two. For some situations, such as those involving vital safety issues, effectiveness will be more important than appeal to an instructor or organization.

Effectiveness

Effectiveness of WBI is measured by determining whether learners achieved the instructional goals (McLellan, 1997). Success is primarily based on the standards stated in the WBI goal or objectives. For example, consider the following fire safety goal statement:

> *In case of fire, the hospital orderly will apply the correct five-step procedure for patient care according to the mandated hospital safety policy manual.*

Because it is critical that orderlies attain this goal, effectiveness would be the primary criterion for judging the WBI's value. When discussing WBI evaluation, Khan and Vega (1997) focus heavily on the criteria of effectiveness. In this example, the orderlies demonstrating the five steps with precision would indicate that the WBI was effective.

Figure 5.1   The WBID Model.

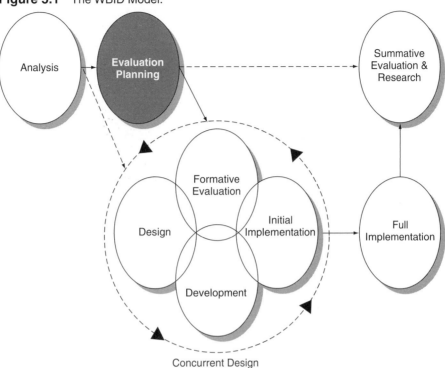

Concurrent Design

Table 5.1   General Overview of Evaluation Criteria

Evaluation Criteria	Explanation	Data Sources
Effectiveness: mastery of goals and success of WBI	Determine whether essential learning has occurred with WBI	Expert opinion Performance assessments Practice items
Efficiency: delivered in a timely or cost-saving manner	Determine whether time and other resources for WBI were used expediently	Baseline data comparison Design and delivery cost factors Time factors
Appeal: gain and maintain learner attention and interest; usability (i.e., ease of access and use)	Determine whether attention-getting and interest elements were appropriately used in WBI; determine ease of use and navigation	Instructor and participant opinions Expert reviews

Source: Table data are from Dick et al. (2005), Khan & Vega (1997), McLellan (1997), Smith & Ragan (2005).

Efficiency

Even though we know that training and instruction should be effective, there are situations when time, monies, or other resources are in short supply. In these situations, placing emphasis on **efficiency** focuses the evaluation on determining whether there was a savings (in time, money, or other resources) as a result of the WBI intervention. Stakeholders may view the WBI as being able to deliver essential information "just-in-time."

Delivering just-in-time learning experiences through WBI or other interventions, such as electronic performance support systems (EPSS) (Northrup, Rasmussen, & Dawson, 2004), systems that use reusable learning objects (RLOs) (Shepard, 2000), or systems that use a sharable content object reference model (SCORM) (Advanced Distributed Learning, 2003), may minimize downtime on the job and reduce associated training costs. When the focus is on reducing costs, saving time, or increasing personnel proficiency, WBI evaluation may emphasize efficiency over effectiveness and appeal (Reiser, 2002; Rosenberg, 2001; Van Tiem et al., 2001; Wager & McKay, 2002).

When efficiency is of greater importance than effectiveness, it is important that the evaluator realize that the WBI may not provide all-inclusive content, but only the specific information pertinent to complete a particular task. Furthermore, a heavy reliance may be placed on both the learner and instructor in diagnosing the type of information needed and determining when it is best to supply it. Just-in-time learning requires that learners' weaknesses are known and that only relevant, appropriate materials are included in the product. Consequently, all of these elements are taken into consideration when evaluating WBI that emphasizes efficiency.

Appeal

Although not always considered by evaluators, appeal is another important criterion in WBI (Smith & Ragan, 2005). **Appeal** involves gaining and maintaining learners' attention on and interest in the instructional task. Appeal usually focuses on the motivational aspects of instructional content and WBI features (activities, message design, etc.).

Trainers and educators sometimes assume or hope that participants are self-motivated with regard to their training and that students are motivated to learn; teachers, trainers, and designers in fact find that the opposite is more often the case. Slavin (1991) asserts that people are motivated; it is just that their motivations may *not* be directed toward the instruction. He argues that it is the trainer's and educator's task to redirect learners' attention from something else (e.g., lunch, the big game on Friday, unopened mail, television, etc.) back to the instruction.

Evaluating WBI in terms of appeal as the main focus occurs when participant support is needed for a new policy, procedure, technology, or other change to be implemented in an organization. Appeal may be a concern for evaluators when determining whether participants will persist in WBI that involves complex or difficult tasks. An evaluator should consider whether the WBI appeals to learners and encourages persistence in the learning tasks.

Determining appeal is subjective. What might be considered appealing to children may not be appealing to adults; appeal may vary for individuals due to their gender, culture, or other characteristics (Ormrod, 2004; Slavin, 1991; Weiner, 1992). For these reasons, findings from the learner analysis (see Chapter 3) should be used in conjunction with any evaluation planning.

Usability. Another factor of appeal for WBI is usability. **Usability** refers to the ease of use and access to the instruction, and how easy and intuitive it is to navigate through the website. Usability is an important factor in WBI evaluation. Some Web management tools are easier to navigate (for both instructor and learners) than are others. The ease of navigation may be compounded when noncommercial or instructor-built websites are used for WBI.

With some WBI evaluations, it may be necessary to limit the focus to one or two value criteria; in-depth evaluation uses all three criteria. The designer evaluates the WBI and shares these results with and makes recommendations to the stakeholders, who will then determine its fate.

GardenScapes

Kally and Elliott are primarily concerned with the effectiveness and appeal of *GardenScapes*. It is important that learners meet the course goal, which is to develop a garden plan based on a garden theme, and they want to find out whether the participants enjoyed both the course and its Web-based delivery. Finally, they want to know the time intensiveness for both instructor (Kally) and participants. Consequently, they emphasize the evaluation criteria of effectiveness and appeal with a secondary interest in the course's efficiency, identifying the criteria in order of importance in the following table.

Evaluation Criteria	Explanation	Data Sources
Effectiveness: Mastery of WBI goals	Determine if participants are able to create a garden plan	Participant's final garden plan Pre- and posttest on concepts and procedures Practice exercises in WBI
Appeal: Gain and maintain learner attention and interest Ease of use (usability)	Review graphics, videos, text, etc. for interest Review content for interest Review technology for ease of use and intuitiveness in navigation	Participants' opinions about course content, activities, message design, and delivery system Instructor opinions about ease of course materials and delivery system Expert review of motivational factors Ask instructor and learners about ease of use
Efficiency: Instruction delivered in a timely manner	Investigate time required in using the Web delivery	Document instructor's time in preparation, facilitation, and scoring/feedback Document participants' time on WBI activities

See this textbook's Companion Website (http://www.prenhall.com/davidson-shivers) for *GardenScapes* Design Document—Evaluation Planning.

On Your Own

Decide what evaluation criteria are appropriate for your WBI project, address general areas of inquiry, and identify specific potential data sources. Organize your overview using Table 5.1 as your guide.

(For illustrations of how other designers tackled these same issues, review the case studies appearing in the Extending Your Skills section at the end of this chapter.)

General Evaluation Orientations

WBI may be evaluated from a number of orientations. Fitzpatrick et al. (2004) characterize five orientations to, or models of, evaluation:

1. *Objective*—How well WBI achieves project objectives
2. *Management*—How well WBI meets external decision makers' requirements
3. *Consumer*—How well WBI serves general consumers' needs
4. *Expertise*—How well independent experts judge that WBI has achieved its objectives
5. *Participant*—How well WBI serves specific participants' needs

It is beyond the scope of this book to examine these five evaluation models in detail. Designers unfamiliar with these models should consult evaluation resources to determine the best model for their instructional situation. Regardless of the model selected, using one guides the scope and direction of both formative and summative evaluation.

GardenScapes

Elliott decides to use a combination of objectives-oriented and management-oriented evaluation models, as described by Fitzpatrick et al. (2004). From the perspective of objective orientation, it is very important that learners meet the objectives of the course. Another requirement is to evaluate the value-added elements of the course for the CJC and the overall viability of using the Web for instruction with the student population and the instructor.

See this textbook's Companion Website (http://www.prenhall.com/davidson-shivers) for *GardenScapes* Design Document—Evaluation Planning.

On Your Own

Which general evaluation model appears most appropriate for you to follow for your project?

As part of your Design Document, identify and explain the main purposes for your evaluation and your orientation. Justify your choices.

(For illustrations of how other designers tackled these same issues, review the case studies appearing in the Extending Your Skills section at the end of this chapter.)

Two Basic Types of Evaluation Used in WBI

Two basic types of evaluation occur in the design and development of instruction, and, consequently, in the design of WBI—formative and summative. The processes associated with each strongly influence the choices WBI designers make.

Formative Evaluation

Formative evaluation is the process of evaluating the instructional product during its design and development. The purpose of formative evaluation is to review the instruction for weaknesses and make the necessary revisions to correct errors and enhance effectiveness before implementation (Gagné et al., 1992). Gagné et al. state that "this stage in materials development is probably one of the most frequently overlooked because it comes late in the design process and represents a significant effort in planning and execution" (p. 30). They consider that any instructional design process is incomplete if formative evaluation does *not* occur. Typically, formative evaluation involves expert reviews and tryouts with a representative sample of the intended target audience (Table 5.2).

Summative Evaluation

Summative evaluation is the study of the effects of the instruction that provides information to the stakeholders on how well it has worked within the organization. The stakeholders use the information to determine the overall value, or worth, of the WBI after it has been produced and disseminated to its intended audience (Dick et al., 2005; Gagné et al., 2005; Smith & Ragan, 2005). Summative evaluation may be conducted to determine whether value was added as a result of implementing WBI: "Was value added because the instruction was implemented?" The term **value added** means that something positive happened that would not have otherwise been accomplished without the intervention. An example of value-added criteria is when individuals at different geographical locations are able to take a course because it is now being distributed through the Web. Questions that determine if

Table 5.2   Comparison of Formative and Summative Evaluation

	Formative Evaluation	Summative Evaluation
Timeframe	Conducted during design and development	Conducted after formative stages when no revisions are being made
Purpose	To review WBI for weaknesses and make revisions	To determine overall value of WBI
Evaluators	Expert reviewers and sample of target audience	Large number of target audience

value has been added include, "What might have happened if the WBI had not been implemented?" and "Was the performance enhanced because of the WBI itself?"

Based on the summative evaluation findings, stakeholders make decisions as to whether the WBI should be continued as is, modified, or discontinued. Not all instruction is meant to last forever. Stakeholders must consider whether the WBI has served its purpose and no longer has utility; if it does not have utility, then it should stop being offered. However, if it is still found to be useful, then stakeholders must decide whether to leave it as is or modify it.

Typically, summative evaluation is used within a cyclical maintenance schedule during the life of the WBI. Summative evaluation is conducted after the instruction has passed through its formative stages, is no longer undergoing revision, and after a large number has used the instruction, and may occur after the first year or as late as five years, depending on the WBI's life cycle (Gagné et al., 1992).

Developing WBI requires the use of both formative and summative evaluation. The purposes of WBI formative and summative evaluations do not differ from those of traditional ID models, but three main differences exist with the WBID Model.

Differences Between the WBID Model and Traditional ID Models

One difference between evaluation in the WBID Model and in traditional ID models is in the timing of the formative evaluation planning. When providing an overview of their formative evaluation stage, Smith and Ragan (2005) advocate that these procedures be planned early in the design process and conducted as soon as instructional goals have been stated, to facilitate revising the design prior to its actual development. As with other traditional models (e.g., Dick et al., 2005; Gagné et al., 2005), Smith and Ragan place such discussions toward the end of the presentation of their model rather than at the beginning. With the WBID Model, such planning occurs immediately after the analysis stage, before the design process gets underway. The early timing of the evaluation discussion allows the designer to implement a plan for reviewing and revising the WBI as it is designed and developed; early planning facilitates integrating evaluation into both the design and development stages rather than at development only. Such formative evaluation planning may allow for time saving and cost effectiveness because corrections can be made during design, which usually has less costly prototypes (although this point has not been proven). Ultimately, early planning and implementation will help ensure that formative evaluation is no longer an overlooked ID process. Table 5.3 contrasts traditional ID models with the WBID Model.

As WBI design and development gains momentum, so does the emphasis on formative evaluation. Figure 5.2 illustrates this fluidity among the design and development tasks and the formative evaluation tasks. The arrows indicate the integration of formative evaluation with design and development activities during the concurrent design stage (discussed in chapters 6–8).

A second difference between the WBID Model and traditional ID models is in the use of tryout groups during formative evaluation (see Table 5.3). ID models (e.g., Dick et al., 2005; Gagné et al., 2005) advocate the use of tryout groups (one-to-one, small-group, and field trial) at the end of the development stage. The WBID Model, however, not only includes such tryout group activities but also systematically integrates opportunities for ex-

Table 5.3 Comparison of Evaluation in Traditional ID Models and WBID Model

	Evaluation in Traditional ID Models	Evaluation in WBID Model
Timing of formative evaluation planning	Planning occurs after the design stage but before development	Planning occurs after the analysis stage, before design begins
Tryout groups	Tryout groups evaluate instruction at the end of the development stage	Tryout groups have opportunities to review from the beginning of the design stage
Planning of summative evaluation	Planning occurs after implementation and use by a large number of users	Preliminary planning occurs early in the process

Figure 5.2 Integration of formative evaluation with WBI design and development.

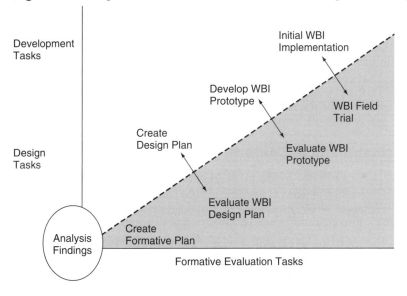

perts and learners to review the instruction at the beginning of and throughout design. For example, after the objectives and assessment items have been designed, an ID expert or subject matter expert (SME) may review them for clarity and congruence. Another example of this integration would be review of instructional strategies by experts, potential instructors, and learners. These early reviews provide designers with information from a variety of viewpoints so that they may revise the WBI accordingly and enhance it immediately.

The third difference is in the early, preliminary planning of summative evaluation found in the WBID Model as compared to other ID models (see Table 5.3), although detailed planning (and conducting) of summative evaluation occurs after the WBI has been used by a large number of learners, which is similar to processes in traditional ID models. The main purpose of this early preliminary planning is to ensure that data on the existing instructional situation can be obtained prior to the WBI being adopted and implemented (Boultmetis &

Dutwin, 2000; Sherry, 2003; Solomon & Gardner, 1986). Such data can be easily retrieved for comparison once the WBI has been implemented, if it has been organized and archived in a central location.

Formative Evaluation Plan: Detailing Its Purposes

Based on the analyses' findings and after selecting a general evaluation model, the designer plans for formative evaluation. This early planning allows the designer to review the WBI products of design (objectives, assessment, instructional strategies, etc.) and development (storyboards, prototypes, websites, etc.) for their strengths and weaknesses and revise them accordingly. The four main areas for review are instructional goals, instructional content, technology, and message design. The designer uses these categories for further detailing of the criteria (i.e., efficiency, effectiveness, and appeal) and the purposes of the formative evaluation.

Instructional Goals

The instructional goals and objectives are reviewed for accuracy, clarity, and completeness as well as congruence with other parts of the WBI. **Congruence** is the degree to which instructional goals and objectives, content, instructional activities, and learning assessment are consistently matched, or aligned, to each other.

Instructional Content

The instructional content is evaluated for accuracy and appropriate sequence. Supporting information in terms of practice exercises and their directions are checked for completeness and clarity; the content must be congruent to other parts of the WBI. The amount of detail provided should be sufficient for learners to achieve the instructional goal. Evaluation of content relates to the educational soundness of the WBI (its effectiveness and efficiency). The content also is evaluated on its appeal to the learners (relevant examples provided, satisfying exercises, etc.) (Cross, 1981; Keller, 1987; Knowles, Holton, & Swanson, 1998; Weiner, 1992; Wlodkowski, 1999).

Technology

Technology is evaluated for functional errors such as typographical, spelling, grammar, punctuation, and word usage. Errors should be immediately corrected when found. As development tasks become predominant, technology applications, such as links to other sites and access to discussion forums, are evaluated for appropriate insertion into the WBI. Part of the evaluation is to make sure that everything within the website functions properly. For instance, chat rooms are established and tested to see if they function as expected; learner and instructor access to document sharing and assignment drop boxes are investigated. The availability of support and assistance (e.g., help desks, mentors, online help, or frequently asked questions [FAQs]) to overcome technical troubles would be another element to evaluate (Khan & Vega, 1997; Nichols, 1997; Tweedle, Avis,

Wright, & Waller, 1998). The overall structure of the website is examined for its technical soundness, specifically its effectiveness and efficiency.

Message Design

Message design is evaluated in terms of whether the media are aesthetically pleasing and integral to the instructional message. The *message,* how the materials are presented graphically and textually, is reviewed in terms of direction clarity, instructional sequence and organization, minimization of distractions, and use of elements such as humor, language, and tone (Lohr, 2003). Graphical, visual (animated or static), and audio elements are examined to ascertain whether they support and enhance the instruction and help learners achieve the instructional goal. Graphical devices, such as icons, links, and so on are evaluated for their relevance to the Web-based learning, navigation, and purpose.

Using the three evaluation criteria and the four preceding categories, a number of questions can be identified for the formative evaluation (Table 5.4). The designer selects questions that directly relate to the particular online instructional situation, rather than attempting to answer all of the listed questions.

Table 5.4   Evaluation Matrix: Sample Formative Evaluation Questions

Evaluation Criteria and Categories	SAMPLE QUESTIONS
Effectiveness	
Goals	Is the goal accurate? Are the goals and objectives clear? Are goals and objectives achievable? Are the goals and content appropriate for the method of delivery?
Content	Is the information complete, covering the content properly? Is there a match among content, objectives, activities, and assessment tools? Are reference citations provided? Do the instructional activities promote thoughtful and reflective responses or discussions? Do the activities promote learning?
Technology	Do the technology applications function properly? Were materials easy to access by students? Are copyright and intellectual property *not* violated?
Message Design	Are messages an integrated whole? Do supporting graphics and features enhance the learning without distracting? Is the appropriate voice used in expressing the content to the learners? Was humor used appropriately? Are directions clear? Was the time frame of the course appropriate? Does the text stand alone if graphics are unavailable?

(continued)

Table 5.4 Evaluation Matrix: Sample Formative Evaluation Questions *(Continued)*

Evaluation Criteria and Categories	SAMPLE QUESTIONS
Efficiency	
Goals	Are the goals stated clearly and concisely?
	Is the purpose stated clearly and concisely?
	Is there congruence between the instructional goals and content?
Content	Is the content information clearly and concisely presented?
	Is it appropriate to the discipline?
	Is it timely, up to date?
Technology	Is access to the instructor or other learners provided?
	Is the website structured appropriately?
	Do the technology applications function easily and efficiently?
Message Design	Is the organization and structure of the message coherent?
	Are the titles and subtitles used to organize the content?
	Are there asynchronous and synchronous types of activities for students and instructor?
Appeal	
Goals	Are goals relevant to learners?
Content	Is the content interesting? Challenging?
Technology	Are typographical, spelling, grammar, punctuation errors distracting?
	Are there any coding errors?
	Is the code written in a user-friendly protocol?
	Is navigation easy?
Message Design	Are the message and the media pleasing?
	Is the vocabulary level and tone appropriate for the content and audience?
	Are the screens uncluttered and with plenty of white space?
	Is the color, typeface, emphasis used appropriately and to enhance learning?
	Do supporting graphics and features enhance learning without distracting?
	Do the graphic devices function properly?
	Are the graphics, animations, or sound clear?
	Does it have good navigational design? Are the icons easy to use and clear as to their meaning?
	Are the screen layouts appropriate to the content and goals?

Source: Table data are from Davidson-Shivers (1998), Khan & Vega (1997), Nichols (1997), Tweedle et al. (1998).

As the design and development (and formative evaluation) process begins, the designer may find it necessary to make adjustments by deleting some questions and adding others. If necessary, the designer provides a rationale for the selected questions and may need to describe the process used to specify the questions; this additional information is necessary only with large, complex WBI projects or when upper-level management or administration requires such documentation.

With their own set of questions, designers can develop an evaluation matrix for the specified questions. Later, the methods and tools for data collection will be added to complete this matrix, which will then be incorporated into the Formative Evaluation Plan, a part of the WBI Design Document.

GardenScapes

After consultation with Kally, Elliott develops a list of questions that they plan to address during formative evaluation; they are based on the evaluation criteria already identified and use the four main categories. Elliott organizes their questions into an evaluation matrix. As part of his rationale, he explains that he reordered the criteria in terms of their importance to the *GardenScapes* project.

GardenScapes Evaluation Matrix: Formative Evaluation Questions

Evaluation Criteria and Categories	Specific Questions
Effectiveness	
Goals	Is the information accurate?
	Are the goals and objectives clear and achievable?
	Are the goals and content appropriate for Web delivery?
Content	Is the information complete and accurate, covering the content properly?
	Are objectives, instructional activities, and final garden project congruent?
	Do the activities promote learning?
	Does the information reflect the current views in landscape and garden plan?
Technology	Is there access to the instructor or other learners?
	Is the overall website appropriate for the content and learners?
	Are copyright and intellectual property *not* violated?
Message Design	Is the appropriate voice used in expressing the content?
	Is humor used appropriately? Are the icons appropriate for adult learners?
	Are directions clearly stated?
	Does the text stand alone if graphics are unavailable?

(continued)

GardenScapes Evaluation Matrix: Formative Evaluation Questions *(Continued)*

Evaluation Criteria and Categories	Specific Questions
Appeal	
Goals	Are goals relevant to participants?
Content	Is the content interesting? Enjoyable?
Technology	Are there errors in typography, spelling, grammar, punctuation, etc.?
	Is navigation easy? Intuitive? Are materials easy to access by students? To modify by the instructor?
Message Design	Are the message and the media pleasing?
	Is the language level and tone suitable for adults?
	Are the screens uncluttered with good use of white space?
	Are color, typeface, emphasis, etc. aptly used?
	Do supporting graphics and features enhance the WBI?
	Are screen layouts appropriate to the garden content?
Efficiency	
Goals	Is the purpose concisely stated?
	Are goals and lesson objectives congruent with each other and the content?
Content	Is the information clearly, concisely presented?
Technology	Is Web-based delivery efficient? Do the technology applications function properly?
	Do the graphic devices function properly?
Message Design	Is the organization and structure of the message coherent? Do titles and subtitles help organize the content?
	Are there asynchronous and synchronous activities for students and instructor?
	Is the time frame for the WBI appropriate?

Note: Elliott reordered the criteria according to the evaluation purposes.

See this textbook's Companion Website (http://www.prenhall.com/davidson-shivers) for *GardenScapes* Design Document—Evaluation Planning.

On Your Own

Based on the analyses of your WBI situation, develop specific questions that detail the purposes of your formative evaluation. Use the evaluation matrix in Table 5.4 as a template to list your specific questions; later, you will add the data collection methods and tools to this matrix. The complete matrix will become a part of your Formative Evaluation Plan. Explain the process used to identify the specific questions and provide any necessary rationale. The Formative Evaluation Plan, when finished, will be a part of your WBI Design Document.

(For illustrations of how other designers tackled these same issues, review the case studies appearing in the Extending Your Skills section at the end of this chapter.)

See this textbook's Companion Website (http://www.prenhall.com/davidson-shivers) for a printable template of the complete evaluation matrix.

Formative Evaluation Plan: Detailing the Main Steps

The main steps in planning for WBI formative evaluation are similar to any evaluative process: identifying people, materials, and resources; gathering data; processing information; and reporting results back to the stakeholders.

Six questions provide a structure for developing and organizing the Formative Evaluation Plan (Table 5.5). For the question, *What are the evaluation methods?* part of the information has already been identified in the analysis phase and can be used in the plan.

- Who are the stakeholders?
- What is being evaluated?
- Who are the evaluators and reviewers?
- What are the evaluation methods?
- When and how should this evaluation take place?
- What decisions need to be made as the WBI design plans and prototypes are developed and revised?

Table 5.5 Formative Evaluation Plan

Section	Description
Who are the stakeholders?	Identify and describe primary and secondary stakeholders.
What is being evaluated?	Articulate the items to be evaluated. Items may include design documentation, storyboards, flowcharts, instructional strategies, etc.
Who are the evaluators and reviewers?	
What are the evaluation methods?	Incorporate the evaluation matrix within this section.
When and how should this evaluation take place?	Describe the timing of the evaluation.
What types of decisions need to be made as the WBI design plan and prototype are developed and revised?	

These questions can be used to head the sections of the Formative Evaluation Plan (Fitzpatrick et al., 2004; Guba & Lincoln, 1989; Hale, 2002). Such documentation facilitates a clear understanding of the process and procedures to be undertaken by all involved in the WBI project. Ultimately, the Formative Evaluation Plan becomes part of the Design Document. In addition, this plan serves as the basis for reporting on the evaluation; results could provide a framework for a contractual agreement with the client (or stakeholder).

Who Are the Stakeholders?

The formative evaluation plan details not only the "what, when, and how" of the evaluation process but to whom the information is reported. These individuals typically form part of the stakeholder group and may include clients, employees (e.g., potential learners), managers, technology support staff, administrative support staff, and end users (Dean, 1999; Greer, 1999). The individuals or groups directly involved in the WBI production and delivery or who have a decision-making authority are considered **primary stakeholders.** Individuals or groups indirectly affected or only tangentially responsible or interested in the instructional situation are called **secondary stakeholders.** (Refer to Chapter 1 for more details.)

During a WBI formative evaluation, the primary stakeholders would be the instructor, designer, and other team members. The learners may be either secondary or primary stakeholders depending on their involvement in the WBI design. Administrators or managers may be either primary or secondary stakeholders depending on the organization and situation and, again, their level of involvement in the design. Because organizations and situations vary, others also may be identified as stakeholders.

In some situations, such as when a lone designer/instructor is creating the WBI, the primary stakeholders are the designer and possibly the students. Secondary stakeholders would be the principal and parents (when children or adolescents are the students). In a large school district, the curriculum or technology coordinators/directors would be included as stakeholders. In other cases involving a lone designer, the process of formative evaluation planning may be quite informal. For instance, college professors and instructors are left on their own to develop their courses. Some coordination among faculty may occur when multiple sections of the same course are involved; however, even then, it is usually left to each instructor to create and evaluate their own course materials.

GardenScapes

Elliott, with assistance from Kally, continues with formative evaluation planning for *GardenScapes.* They have identified the primary stakeholders as Kally, the course instructor, and Elliott, the designer; both make major decisions about the WBI and are directly affected by the project. The adult participants, especially those in the tryout group, are included as primary stakeholders because of their direct involvement in reviewing the WBI as it is designed and delivered.

The TLDC support personnel help support the development and implementation of *GardenScapes,* but have limited involvement and decision-making roles; they are considered as secondary stakeholders.

Two additional secondary stakeholders are included, TLDC Director Carlos Duartes, and an IDT professor, Judith Chauncy, Elliott's academic advisor. Because Elliott is a TLDC intern, he needs to provide internship reports to Mr. Duartes. Elliott will provide the same reports to his advisor, Dr. Chauncy, who also is his IDT program internship supervisor and will assign the internship grade.

Elliott follows the outline discussed in one of his evaluation courses, coincidentally taught by Dr. Chauncy.

GardenScapes General Stakeholders

Primary Stakeholders
- *Instructor: Kally Le Rue. She is responsible for the successful implementation of the course and for its content. She assists Elliott in WBI design and development.*
- *Designer: Elliott Kangas, TLDC intern. He is in charge of designing the course, developing the evaluation plans, and conducting the formative evaluation plan.*
- *Students: The adult participants of* GardenScapes *have direct impact on the success of the WBI implementation. Some will have direct impact on the WBI design as part of the tryout review. (Specific tryout participants will be named at a later date.)*

Secondary Stakeholders
- *Carlos Duartes, supervisor of the internship program. He will observe and review Elliott's design work, and will communicate with Dr. Chauncy on his progress.*
- *Dr. Judith Chauncy, IDT professor at Myers University: Dr. Chauncy is both Elliott's advisor and intern supervisor. She will observe and review his progress from the program's standpoint and communicate with Mr. Duartes. Dr. Chauncy will assign the internship grade.*

See this textbook's Companion Website (http://www.prenhall.com/davidson-shivers) for *GardenScapes* Design Document—Evaluation Planning.

ON YOUR OWN

Begin the formative evaluation planning for your WBI project. Address the section, "Who are your stakeholders?" Provide sufficient detail to clearly identify stakeholders as either primary or secondary based on their direct or indirect links to the WBI project. Add this description to your Formative Evaluation Plan.

(For illustrations of how other designers tackled these same issues, review the case studies appearing in the Extending Your Skills section at the end of this chapter.)

See this textbook's Companion Website (http://www.prenhall.com/davidson-shivers) for a printable template of the Formative Evaluation Plan.

What Is Being Evaluated?

The second section, "What is being evaluated?", focuses on the specific instructional materials, processes, or products that will be examined during formative evaluation. These materials may include design plans, storyboards, instructional content, instructional strategies, interface, navigational features, message and visual design features, WBI prototypes, assessment tools and scores, practice exercises, and more. The relevant questions for the WBI materials have already been identified and can be found in the formative evaluation matrix (refer to Table 5.4 and your own WBI evaluation matrix). Identifying and describing the specific instructional products and processes facilitates how the WBI design and formative evaluation are linked together.

GardenScapes

Elliott addresses the section, "What is being evaluated?", and incorporates his answer into the Formative Evaluation Plan.

During the *GardenScapes* design, Elliott and Kally review the objectives, assessment items, clustering of objectives, instructional strategies, and motivational strategies in relation to the specific questions that have been previously identified. If other questions arise and they need additional advice or expertise, they have identified two subject matter experts: Ms. Laila Gunnarson is head of the TLDC's technical support; Dr. Nikko Tamura is director of the Golden Valley Botanical Gardens.

As the WBI prototype and its website further develops the content information, practice exercises, assignments, and assessments are reviewed by the instructor (Kally), the designer (Elliott), and his internship supervisors. In the tryout, the participants will be asked to review and comment on the materials. In the evaluation, Elliott will determine the amount of time required for the instructor and learners to implement the WBI.

As a job aid, Elliott develops a chart that allows him to quickly identify the items to examine during formative evaluation:

	Materials to Be Examined
Design plans	• Objectives
	• Assessment items
	• Clustering of objectives
	• Instructional strategies
	• Motivational strategies
Prototype and website	• Storyboards
	• Interface
	• Navigation features
	• WBI prototype(s)

See this textbook's Companion Website (http://www.prenhall.com/davidson-shivers) for *GardenScapes* Design Document—Evaluation Planning.

ON YOUR OWN

Continue developing your Formative Evaluation Plan. Address the second section, "What is being evaluated?" Provide details.

(For illustrations of how other designers tackled these same issues, review the case studies appearing in the Extending Your Skills section at the end of this chapter.)

Who Are the Evaluators and Reviewers?

The Joint Committee on Standards for Educational Evaluation [Joint Committee] (1994) has developed responsibilities and requirements of evaluations for educational evaluation. According to the committee, an evaluator should be someone who is competent and trustworthy, who possesses substantive knowledge, technical competence, integrity, experience, public relations skills, and any other characteristics considered necessary by the stakeholders. Because only a few individuals possess all of these necessary characteristics, evaluation is often accomplished by teams, which meet those qualifications collectively.

The evaluators' role(s) are usually based on purpose(s) of the evaluation and the tasks that have to be accomplished to serve that purpose. In formative evaluation, the designers or design team members are typically the evaluators, which makes them both data gatherers and decision makers. Their responsibilities in formative evaluation are to identify strengths and weaknesses of the WBI and determine what, if any, revisions are necessary. This decision making is often shared with other stakeholders, such as the instructor, to ensure that the best WBI is produced.

With formative evaluation, the reviewers and their qualifications need to be identified. For instance, expert reviewers should be identified by their role (content, technical, etc.) and their qualifications. If learners will be participating in the formative evaluation, then their background information should be included in the Formative Evaluation Plan as well; information of a confidential nature should not be included unless identifying elements are removed or the information is reported in aggregate form.

GardenScapes

Although Elliott is "in charge" of developing the plans for formative and summative evaluations, he will be involved only in planning and conducting the formative evaluation and reporting its results. Elliott and Kally outline each member's duties and document their expertise. He and Kally will work together during formative evaluation, make necessary changes, and report evaluation progress to Carlos, with a final report sent to Dr. Chauncy.

Elliott includes the following information as part of the Design Document.

GardenScapes **Evaluators and Reviewers**

- *Evaluator/Designer: Elliott Kangas is the main evaluator. His expertise is both in WBI design and development and in formative evaluation. He has taken three graduate courses on evaluation methods and theory in his master's program at Myers University. Although he is not a member of the TLDC and therefore lacks general knowledge about the operations and culture of the Center and of CJC, he will work closely with experts from TLDC.*
- *Evaluator/Instructor: Kally Le Rue has been an instructor at CJC for several years. She holds several levels of expertise; she has the content knowledge because of her master gardening certification, has teaching experience with the target audience, and is participating in the WBI design and development. She is familiar with the Continuing and Distance Education Department and the CJC campus-at-large. As CJC lacks the financial resources to hire outside consultants, Kally as second evaluator is able to make effective use of available resources.*
- *Expert reviewer (technical support): Ms. Laila Gunnarson, coordinator of the TLDC technical staff, will review the technical aspects of the WBI prototype and website as needed. Laila has an associate degree in multimedia from CJC, bachelor's degree from Myers University, and has been on staff for 12 years. She is skilled in multimedia development and graphic design, and is the webmaster for CJC.*
- *Expert reviewer (subject matter): Dr. Nikko Tamura, director of the Golden Valley Botanical Gardens, will be the subject matter expert (SME) and expert reviewer as the WBI is designed and developed. Dr. Tamura has been employed with the Botanical Gardens for 10 years, has a terminal degree in Horticulture and Landscape Architecture, and is an active member of the ASLA (American Society of Landscape Architects). Dr. Tamura has extensive experience with the content area and has worked with Kally on other continuing education projects.*
- *Expert reviewer (instructional design): An ID expert will not review the materials per se. As part of Elliott's internship program, Dr. Chauncy and Mr. Duartes will review GardenScapes materials. Both have educational backgrounds and professional expertise in instructional design; adding additional ID experts is not necessary.*
- *End-User reviewer: Learners from the Garden Basics course will be asked to participate in end-user reviews during the formative evaluation. One or two learners will be asked to review the design plans as they develop; others will be asked to participate in tryout groups.*

    Learners will be chosen based on experience levels with gardening, technology skills, motivation levels, and dependability to complete the involved tasks. The exact number of learners who will be needed will be de-

termined by factors such as the methods and tools used and the time frame needed for data collection.

Elliott is drafting an invitation to participate letter, incorporating the standard consent form for participation required by CJC's Human Subject Committee.

See this textbook's Companion Website (http://www.prenhall.com/davidson-shivers) for *GardenScapes* Design Document—Evaluation Planning.

On Your Own

Continue planning formative evaluation. Provide the necessary details and documentation to include in your Design Document. Address the section "Who are the evaluators and reviewers?" Identify and explain the qualifications of those involved.

(For illustrations of how other designers tackled these same issues, review the case studies appearing in the Extending Your Skills section at the end of this chapter.)

What Are the Evaluation Methods?

Planning for formative evaluation continues by identifying methods and tools for gathering data. The purposes of the evaluation and the complexity of the WBI project often determine what methods are employed. These have been outlined previously (see Table 5.4). Practical matters such as time, budget, and logistics influence the selection of methods and tools.

A number of methods of data collection can be used in any evaluation; however, not all of them are viable for evaluating WBI. The methods appropriate for formative evaluations include testing, surveys, expert and end-user reviews, observations (during a trial implementation), and extant data (organizational reports, emails, discussions, etc.). Table 5.6 ties various methods and tools, or data sources, to the list of questions presented in Table 5.4.

See Appendix A for a description of data gathering methods and tools.

It is most often best to select the simplest methods for formative evaluation, especially when practical constraints exist. Simple evaluative methods maintain the integrity of the evaluation while staying pragmatic about the WBI project. For example, if time constraints exist, the evaluator can use questionnaires with end users rather than employing extensive interviews or observations. If the evaluation has a limited budget, then the number of end-user participants and types of formative evaluation methods can be restricted.

When identifying the methods and tools in the Formative Evaluation Plan, designers should explain or justify their use as well as provide samples of the actual instruments (in an appendix). They also must identify sources and obtain permissions as necessary for instruments that are copyright protected.

Table 5.6 Types of Methods and Tools for Formative Evaluation

Evaluation Criteria	SAMPLE QUESTIONS	METHODS AND TOOLS
Effectiveness		
Goals	Is the goal accurate? Are the goals and objectives clear? Are goals and objectives achievable? Are the goals and content appropriate for the method of delivery?	Expert review (SME, ID) Extant data (assessment scores, practice exercises, etc.) Interview Surveys
Content	Is the information complete, covering the content properly? Is there a match among content, objectives, activities, and assessment tools? Are reference citations provided? Do the instructional activities promote thoughtful and reflective responses or discussions? Do the activities promote learning?	Expert reviews (SME, ID) End-user review Surveys Extant data (practice exercises, discussions) Interviews
Technology	Do the technology applications function properly? Were materials easy to access by students? To modify by the instructor? Are copyright and intellectual property *not* violated?	Expert review (technical, ID, instructor) End-user review Observation
Message Design	Are messages an integrated whole? Do supporting graphics and features enhance the learning and are they without distractions? Is the appropriate voice used in expressing the content to the learners? Was humor used appropriately? Are directions clear? Was the time frame of the course appropriate? Does the text stand alone if graphics are unavailable?	Expert review (SME, technical, ID) End-user review Survey Interview
Efficiency		
Goals	Are the goals stated clearly and concisely? Is the purpose stated clearly and concisely? Is there congruence between the instructional goals and content?	Expert (ID, SME, instructor) and End-user reviews Interview Survey
Content	Is the content information clearly and concisely presented? Is it appropriate to the discipline? Is it timely, up to date?	Expert (ID instructor, SME) and End-user review Interview Survey

Table 5.6   Types of Methods and Tools for Formative Evaluation *(Concluded)*

Evaluation Criteria	SAMPLE QUESTIONS	METHODS AND TOOLS
Efficiency (cont.)		
Technology	Is access to the instructor or other learners provided? Is the website structured appropriately? Do the technology applications function easily and efficiently?	End-user survey Extant data (emails, discussions) Expert review (technical)
Message Design	Is the organization and structure of the message coherent? Are there titles and subtitles to organize the content? Are there asynchronous and synchronous types of activities for students and instructor?	Expert review (ID, instructor) End-user review Survey Interview
Appeal		
Goals	Are goals relevant to learners?	End-user survey
Content	Is the content interesting?	End-user review Survey
Technology	Any typographical, spelling, grammar, punctuation errors? Are there limited coding errors? Is the code written in a user-friendly protocol? Is navigation easy?	Expert review (ID, SME, technical) Observation
Message Design	Are the message and the media pleasing? Is the vocabulary level and tone appropriate for the content and audience? Are the screens uncluttered and with plenty of white space? Is the color, typeface, emphasis used appropriately and to enhance learning? Do supporting graphics and features enhance learning without distractions? Do the graphic devices function properly? Are the graphics, animations, or sound clear? Does it have good navigational design? Are the icons easy to use and clear as to their meaning? Are the screen layouts appropriate to the content and goals?	Expert review (SME, ID, instructor, technical) End-user review Survey Observation Interview

GardenScapes

Elliott adds a third column to his evaluation matrix, describing the data sources that he and Kally will use during their formative evaluation. They decide to use expert and participant reviews, surveys, and extant data collection as the main methods (and tools) for gathering data. They may, at certain points in time, use observation (mainly to focus on the technological aspects of the *GardenScapes* course).

GardenScapes Evaluation Methods

Elliott will survey the learners using a questionnaire that will relate to the instructional goal, instructional content, technology, and message design.

The content and technical expert reviewers will use a checklist as they review the WBI design plans and prototypes. Elliott will set up meetings with identified experts at designated times to clarify their checklist data and address questions about the data. Most of the expert reviewers are available for a reasonable fee and others are available at no charge.

At designated points in the formative evaluation, a representative sample of learners will be interviewed as they critique the WBI for its effectiveness, efficiency, and appeal. Later, the learners may be observed to identify where they experience difficulties, both instructionally and with the technology.

Evaluation Criteria and Categories	Specific Questions	Methods and Tools
Effectiveness		
Goals	Is the information accurate? Are the goals and objectives clear and achievable? Are the goals and content appropriate for Web delivery?	Expert (SME, ID, instructor with checklists) End-user survey Extant data (practice exercises, final garden plan)
Content	Is the information complete and accurate, covering the content properly? Are objectives, activities, and final project congruent? Do the activities promote learning? Does the information reflect the current views in landscape and garden planning?	Expert (SME, ID, instructor with checklists) End-user review & survey Extant data (discussions, emails, practice exercises, etc.)
Technology	Is there access to the instructor or other learners? Is the overall website appropriate for the content and learners? Are copyright and intellectual property *not* violated?	Expert (technical, SME and ID with checklists) End-user review Survey Observation

Evaluation Criteria and Categories	Specific Questions	Methods and Tools
Effectiveness *(continued)* Message Design	Is the appropriate voice used in expressing the content? Is humor used appropriately? Are the icons appropriate for adult learners? Are directions clearly stated? Does the text stand alone if graphics are unavailable?	Expert (SME and ID with checklists) End-user review Survey
Appeal Goals	Are goals relevant to participants?	Expert (SME and ID with checklists) End-user questionnaire
Content	Is the content interesting? Enjoyable?	Expert (SME, ID, instructor with checklists) End-user survey
Technology	Are there errors in typography, spelling, grammar, punctuation, etc.? Is navigation easy? Intuitive? Are materials easy to access by students? To modify by the instructor?	Expert (technical, SME, ID, instructor with checklists) End-user survey Observation
Message Design	Are the message and media pleasing? Is the language level and tone suitable for adults? Are the screens uncluttered and with good use of white space? Are color, typeface, emphasis, etc. aptly used? Do supporting graphics and features enhance the WBI? Are screen layouts appropriate to the garden content?	Expert (SME, ID, instructor, technical with checklists) End-user survey
Efficiency Goals	Is the purpose concisely stated? Are goals and lesson objectives congruent with each other and the content?	Expert (SME, ID with checklists,) End-user survey
Content	Is the information clearly, concisely presented?	Expert (SME, ID instructor with checklists) End-user survey

(continued)

Evaluation Criteria and Categories	Specific Questions	Methods and Tools
Efficiency (concluded)		
Technology	Is Web-based delivery efficient? Do the technology applications function properly? Do the graphic devices function properly?	Expert (technical, SME, ID, instructor with checklists) End-user survey Observation Extant data (amount of user activity, login time)
Message Design	Is the organization and structure of the message coherent? Do titles and subtitles help organize the content? Are there asynchronous and synchronous activities for students and instructor? Is the time frame for the WBI appropriate?	Expert (SME, ID, instructor with checklists) End-user survey Observation

Note: Elliott reordered the criteria according to the evaluation purposes.

Elliott must develop his own data-gathering tools, or instruments. He devises an opinion questionnaire and interview questions before beginning the design stage, and is developing the checklists for the expert reviewers and for the observations. These instruments will have items aligned to the list of questions.

Because Elliott plans to adapt instruments from other sources, he references the sources of each instrument in the Design Document. The instruments appear in an appendix called Formative Evaluation Instruments.

The questionnaires will be used to obtain learner opinions about the instructional, motivational, and technical aspects of the WBI. For reviews of initial design concepts, instructional strategy worksheets, storyboards, and screen designs will be used as a basis for discussion.

End users (acting as learners) or reviewers will mark on paper-based prototypes and use checklists for prototypes viewed through a browser. The checklists will identify areas that need improvement.

The final WBI and assessments completed in the field trial will be used to determine how well learners meet course goals and objectives. Learners and Kally will be asked to document time spent on activities and preparation of assignments. To evaluate the value-added aspects of the instruction, Elliott will interview Kally and other primary and secondary stakeholders.

ON YOUR OWN

Review the descriptions of methods and tools found in Appendix A. Determine the types that you will use with your own formative evaluation. Add a third column to your evaluation matrix to identify these methods and tools.

See Appendix A for additional information on data gathering methods and tools.

If you do not create your own questionnaires, checklists, and so on then you will need to obtain permission to use and/or purchase specific evaluation tools. If you adapt tools from other sources for your own use, be sure to identify the sources and, depending on how close they are to the original source, obtain written permission to use them. Add the materials to your Formative Evaluation Plan and place any materials and identified sources in an appendix. Use the overview given in Table 5.7 as a guide. (If you are using the printable template found on the text's Companion Website, note that the third column has been added, for your convenience.)

See this textbook's Companion Website (http://www.prenhall.com/davidson-shivers) for a printable template of the Formative Evaluation Plan.

(For illustrations of how other designers tackled these same issues, review the case studies appearing in the Extending Your Skills section at the end of this chapter.)

When and How Should Evaluation Take Place?

How the formative evaluation takes place to some degree depends on the type of evaluation methods being planned and when the data will be collected. The designer or, for some situations, a project manager, establishes early in the WBI project the beginning and ending dates of the formative evaluation. Formative evaluation data are collected throughout the WBID concurrent design stage and usually into initial implementation (see Table 6.1 in Chapter 6 for an example.) The results of the formative evaluation determine whether revision of the WBI design plan or prototypes (e.g., storyboards, WBI product, etc.) is necessary. Whenever possible, it is best to conduct a complete formative evaluation for WBI projects.

Formative Evaluation During WBI Design. The WBID Model recognizes that waiting until the development of the WBI prototype is rather late for revision to begin. Instead, this model allows for both experts and end users (instructor, learners, and others involved in the learning community) to review the WBI from the beginning of the design stage.

To begin, the designer and other members of the design team review the WBI design plans. This aspect of the formative evaluation may be conducted by the designer, another member of the design team, or the project manager. The evaluator also may use expert reviewers. When developing WBI as a course project, peer reviewers (paired classmates) may be used to evaluate and make recommendations to each other (Smith, 1990).

The design team, experts, and/or end users evaluate the WBI design plan for the clarity of its goals, meaningful examples, and relevant instructional activities (Kirkpatrick, 1998). These individuals may review the instructional and motivational strategies for their effectiveness, appropriateness, and potential learner motivation. The purpose of using these types of reviews is to improve the WBI design plans as they evolve.

Formative Evaluation During WBI Prototype Development.   Content and ID experts, as well as technical experts, can review the storyboards once they are developed; this review continues as screens and navigational structures emerge. As versions of the WBI prototypes are further developed, expert reviewers revisit the major instructional goals and objectives. SMEs and ID experts review the WBI for structure, content, graphics, and message design features even in noninteractive and nonfunctioning sites. Again, potential end users also may review these early renditions of the WBI.

Formative Evaluation in the Final WBI Prototype Development.   As the WBI shifts into final prototype development, tryouts with participants may begin. In traditional models, three types of tryouts—one-to-one, small-group, and field trial—are used to review instructional prototypes with the learners during the development stage (Dick et al., 2005; Gagné et al., 2005; Smith & Ragan, 2005).

One-to-One Tryout.   Typically, **one-to-one tryouts** are evaluations in which the evaluator and a learner review the materials together. Dick et al. (2005) suggest that three one-to-ones be conducted to gain different student perspectives about the instruction. One-to-one tryouts assist evaluators in making sure that the information is complete and that the message is appropriate for the learners (Smith & Ragan, 2005). Tryout participants review instructional strategies to determine whether they are satisfactory. Preliminary graphics can be viewed for relevance and appropriateness to the website. These reviewers can note errors in grammar, spelling, punctuation, and so on.

The WBID Model takes into consideration that until the website is constructed, design prototypes will be viewed using paper versions and then viewed on nonnetworked devices (Frick, Corry, & Bray, 1997). However, if the evaluator/designer has access to development servers, then these individuals can access both form and function of the WBI. The designer/evaluator is still present as the individual reviews the WBI on nonnetworked devices.

Small-Group Tryout.   With traditional ID models, the **small-group tryout** uses a small sample of the targeted audience (4–10 students) to work through the instruction more or less as intended, but most likely they are not in the actual setting (Dick et al., 2005; Gagné et al., 2005; Smith & Ragan, 2005). The materials have been revised based on the one-to-one results, but are still in prototype form. The evaluator observes the small group as they interact with the materials and may distribute evaluation instruments to the group members. In small-group evaluations, the WBI should be near completion so that reviewers gain an accurate view of how participants will interact with the lesson. With a small group, the evaluator gains a sense of the length of time learners require to complete the instruction and how well learners perform on the assignments and assessments.

Field Trial.   **Field trial** occurs after the major revisions to the prototype are made, based on small-group and one-to-one tryout results (Dick et al., 2005; Gagné et al., 2005; Smith & Ragan, 2005). Depending on the level of difficulty of the content, the extensiveness of the target audience, and the complexity of the Web-based learning environment, there may be several field trials to gain sufficient data prior to the "final" draft of the instruction being completed. The evaluator monitors the field trial, distributes evaluation instruments (or may have the instructor distribute them), and identifies what should be at this point only minor and minimal revisions to the WBI. Once these revisions are completed, the instruction goes into final production and full implementation.

In the field trial, the WBI materials are completely online and functional. Trials are conducted with participants who match or are a sample from the targeted audience and context. Results of the field trial identify any remaining errors and adjustments to take the WBI prototype to its "final" form.

The WBI or any other type of instruction is considered to be in final form when it is being fully implemented and disseminated to large numbers of learners (Gagné et al., 1992). Although designer and instructor may continue to make minor revisions (finding and reestablishing links to external websites, updating software, etc.), WBI is considered to be in its final form when no further substantive revisions are necessary at the end of the field trial.

Modifications to the "When and How" of Formative Evaluation.   Although the WBID Model allows for all three types of end-user tryouts for a complete formative evaluation to be conducted, it also allows for exceptions, such as those due to an organization not being able to support extensive WBI design and evaluation prior to implementation. Tryouts may not occur due to difficulty in locating a sufficient sampling of the targeted audience members, or because logistical problems with the Web-based learning environment do not allow for early access to the WBI.

While the WBID Model allows exceptions, it still requires that some form of tryout with end users be performed as a part of the formative evaluation. For example, one adaptation is that the evaluator/designer asks individuals who have similar characteristics to the targeted audience, instead of an actual sampling of the audience, to review the WBI design plans and prototypes. Only one or two of the three tryouts may be used instead of all three.

Finally, use of the WBID Model allows the initial implementation to serve as the formal tryout (to be discussed further in Chapter 8). For instance, it is commonplace for college and university professors to use first course offerings as a field trial. Often, higher education faculty members do not have the opportunity to fully design and develop a course prior to its initial offering. Once the initial implementation as the field trial is completed, then the WBI (or any instruction) can be put into final form based on the field trial results.

GardenScapes

Elliot and Kally add their plans for data collection to their Design Document.

GardenScapes Evaluation Methods and Schedule

Formative data will be collected throughout design, development, and initial implementation of GardenScapes. Based on the data collected, changes will be made to the WBI. Due to the unavailability of participants as well as time constraints, a small-group tryout will not take place; the initial implementation will serve as the field trial. Three learners will review the WBI design plan and at least 20 learners will participate in the field trial. Learners who participate in the design plan review will examine preliminary design drafts from goals to storyboards.

The evaluation audience will be recruited by distributing a letter to former participants of the Garden Basics *course, inviting them to participate in the evaluation. Individuals who volunteer and are selected will sign a standard consent form, provided by the Human Subjects Committee at CJC.*

See this textbook's Companion Website (http://www.prenhall.com/davidson-shivers) for *GardenScapes* Design Document—Evaluation Planning.

ON YOUR OWN

"When and how should the formative evaluation take place?" Address this question to determine the points at which you will collect formative data. Will you need to find expert reviewers and end users for the very beginnings of the concurrent design and development stage? Will you use all of the traditional tryout groups? Will your formative evaluation extend into the initial implementation? Whom will you need to select to participate in these processes? How will you gain their consent to participate? Are "invitation to participate" letters and consent forms needed?

Provide detailed, written documentation and justification for your decisions and include them in your Design Document.

(For illustrations of how other designers tackled these same issues, review the case studies appearing in the Extending Your Skills section at the end of this chapter.)

What Decisions Need to Be Made as the WBI Design Plan and Prototype Are Developed and Revised?

With each step in formative evaluation, the data are collected and must then be analyzed. In most cases, formative data will be rather easy to analyze: data such as performance assessments or quality-control measures can be quantified in frequency tables or as descriptive statistics (mean, mode, median, standard deviation) (Boulmetis & Dutwin, 2000). Questionnaires that use Likert-type scales can be presented with descriptive statistics or percentages (Hale, 2002; Kirkpatrick, 1998; Sherry, 2003).

Some data may be appropriate for use in inferential statistical tests such as the t-test, ANOVA, ANCOVA, linear regression, or multiple regression. Nonparametric tests such as Chi-square can be used for data that do not meet the assumptions for statistical analysis (Boulmetis & Dutwin, 2000; Gall, Gall, & Borg, 2003; Hale, 2002). An in-depth discussion of quantitative methods is beyond the scope of this book. It is best to consult research methods and statistical resources for additional information and direction.

From a qualitative perspective, interviews may have to be transcribed and coded so that common themes and patterns can be identified (Boulmetis & Dutwin, 2000; Hittleman & Simon, 2002; Stringer, 2004). The themes can then be interpreted, conclusions drawn, and recommendations made. Data from remarks made by the expert and end-user reviewers and observations may be evaluated in a similar fashion. Qualitative analysis processes can be quite complex (Denzin & Lincoln, 1994) and is beyond the scope of this discussion. It is best to consult other resources for specific information on qualitative research methods and analysis techniques.

Modifying the WBI Based on Results of the Data Analysis.   Based on results generated by data analysis, decisions are made as to instructional modifications. Some modifications are easy to integrate into the WBI project. In some cases where the modifications are a matter of editing the materials for errors, they are simply changed and documented. Other modifications may require interpretation by the designer and/or agreement with other stakeholders, such as data containing conflicting information. For instance, some end users may have responded that the information was too lengthy, others that it was too brief. The designer and other stakeholders must agree how to interpret mixed findings and, in those cases, determine what modifications, if any, should occur.

One way to determine which modifications should be made is to examine other data, such as the expert reviews, practice exercises, test scores, and the quality of completed assignments. The views of the instructor should be considered. Additional input from decision makers may be necessary when revisions require additional time and resources. Further discussion of formative evaluation (the reviews and revisions to the WBI design plan and prototypes) appears in Chapters 6, 7, and 8.

GardenScapes

Elliott and Kally add further details and explanations to their Formative Evaluation Plan. Once this last section is completed, they include it in their Design Document.

Ongoing Decisions Made while Developing and Revising the WBI Design and Prototype

For the formative evaluation, data analysis will occur as data are gathered. Elliott and Kally, as the expert reviewers, will analyze comments and written notes created by content and technical experts and the three end-user participants, and will modify the WBI based on their consensus of the meaning of the results. As data are gathered on the WBI prototypes, the results from the reviews will be analyzed to, determine what, if any, revisions are necessary.

Participants' final garden plans will be thoroughly reviewed during the field trial. To facilitate the review, Kally will ask participants to scan or attach illustrations of their design or provide digitized photos or videos of the actual sites (if created). Data that relate to perceptions and attitudes will be examined using a statistical software package to investigate descriptive results.

See this textbook's Companion Website (http://www.prenhall.com/davidson-shivers) for *GardenScapes* Design Document—Evaluation Planning.

ON YOUR OWN

Consider how you will address the question, "What decisions need to be made as the WBI design plan and prototype are developed and revised?" How will you analyze the data gathered during your formative evaluation? How will you document the decisions that you will make based on the findings? How will you resolve conflicts that occur when data show mixed results?

Make one final review of your entire Formative Evaluation Plan before you include it in your Design Document.

With your instructional goal and analyses in hand, check your completed On Your Own activities for this chapter, and verify that you have addressed the following questions:

- Who are the stakeholders?
- What is being evaluated?
- Who are the evaluators and reviewers?
- What are the evaluation methods?
- When and how should this evaluation take place?
- What decisions need to be made as the WBI design plans and prototypes are developed and revised?

Have you provided enough detail and explanation so others may follow your Formative Evaluation Plan, if necessary?

(For illustrations of how other designers tackled these same issues, review the case studies appearing in the Extending Your Skills section at the end of this chapter.)

Communicating Formative Evaluation Results

Communicating and reporting results of an evaluation are critical when designers work for a client (or stakeholder) who is paying the bills or when they are working in a design team on complex projects (Boulmetis & Dutwin, 2000; Kirkpatrick, 1998). Obviously, there may not be a need for detailed documentation when the WBI is being developed by lone designer/instructors and for their own use. However, documenting decisions, evaluation results, and revisions made is encouraged so that a historical record of the project is kept. Too often, memories fail and only vague recollections remain of WBI design processes and reasons for decisions.

Forms of Communication

The two basic forms for communicating evaluation processes and results are verbal and written reports. **Verbal reports** permit information to be shared quickly and informally with easily accessible stakeholders. **Written reports** take on a formal, permanent form. Written documents are static objects that record and communicate decisions. A combination of the two forms is often the best way to disseminate information about plans, procedures, and results of the project. When communication structures are complex, with multiple communications and channels, consistency should be maintained to make sure that the same message is shared. If, for some reason, changes occurred between a verbal report and its written documentation, then the written report should state what changes were made and why (Boulmetis & Dutwin, 2000; Joint Committee, 1994).

Other critical features of reporting practices include timeliness, brevity, clarity, and responsiveness to the audience. Stakeholders should be kept in mind when reporting results, especially when considering the amount of information that they receive (Joint Committee, 1994). Avoiding communication overload helps the evaluator's message to be heard (Kirkpatrick, 1998). A report may be given as the evaluation is in progress, at the end of the evaluation, or both.

Verbal Reports.   Verbal reports are often used to inform stakeholders and design team members about the progress being made, problems that have been encountered, and other issues requiring solutions. Verbal communications may be in the form of telephone conversations, presentations, or person-to-person conversations. These reports, however, are impermanent, and memory of what was actually said and heard is, of course, less reliable than written communication.

Written Reports.   Written documents, such as memos and letters, update stakeholders on the process of the evaluation and can be used as interim and final reports (Boulwetis & Dutwin, 2000; Joint Committee, 1994; Kirkpatrick, 1998). *Interim* reports keep clients and design teams informed of project progress. Interim reports provide incomplete or partial information based on their timing. These reports are static when they are sent and received; this delay does not allow for changes that continue to occur. Providing updated interim reports is valuable even though there is the risk that incomplete statements can be misinterpreted. Misconceptions can be clarified in subsequent reports.

Some designers use a report template (Table 5.7) to track decisions made during design and development. The template allows them to identify details pertaining to decisions or changes, including the person responsible for those decisions, the date, and the basis (rationale). If the WBI design project is contractual, then there may be an additional line for signatures or initials.

Table 5.7   Reporting Decisions Made Template

Stage or Phase of WBID	Decision Made	Responsible Person(s)	Date	Rationale for Decision or Modification

The *final* report typically includes an executive summary and full documentation of the evaluation. The executive summary highlights the evaluation activities, findings, and recommendations in a brief, concise manner. The executive summary appears at the beginning and provides a structure for the full body of the report. The full report describes the evaluation process in detail, beginning by describing the purpose(s), goals, and criteria used. The target audience, instructional resources, and instructional setting, evaluation methods, tools, and procedures are described as are the major questions identified in evaluation planning. The report presents a complete discussion of the results, including an explanation of data analysis procedures. In some cases, findings are not only interpreted, but recommendations based on those findings are offered.

Another way to disseminate information about formative evaluation is through professional presentations and publications (Joint Committee, 1994); these formats are often used in higher education settings. Papers may be presented at professional or scholarly conferences; evaluation description and results can be published in professional magazines or scholarly journals. Dissemination may occur through an organization's newsletter or through online publications. Some publishing houses report the results of evaluation activities as a marketing tool to provide information about instructional products to potential customers.

GardenScapes

Elliott and Kally plan to communicate and report results in *GardenScapes* using both verbal and written communications; they include these communication plans in the Design Document. Regular meetings will be held. For Elliott's internship, he will prepare two interim progress reports for Dr. Chauncy and Mr. Duartes, in which he will document major design decisions and subsequent modifications. He will use a report template (see Table 5.7) that allows space for decisions that have been made, the person responsible for those decisions, the date, and the basis (rationale) for those decisions or modifications. He will document any changes to the initial Formative Evaluation Plan.

Elliott's final formative report will include a brief overview of the evaluation in an executive summary. Since the structure of the final report will contain interim reports, he plans to save all documents to simplify writing the final report.

See this textbook's Companion Website (http://www.prenhall.com/davidson-shivers) for *GardenScapes* Design Document—Evaluation Planning.

ON YOUR OWN

Plan for the types of communication and reporting procedures used in your formative evaluation and explain them in your Design Document. Use the template in Table 5.7 as your guide. Identify the major elements of relevant reporting processes. Plan how you will organize the structure of your report of decisions made for easy dissemination to your stakeholders.

(For illustrations of how other designers tackled these same issues, review the case studies appearing in the Extending Your Skills section at the end of this chapter.)

See this textbook's Companion Website (http://www.prenhall.com/davidson-shivers) for a printable reporting decisions made template.

Preliminary Planning of Summative Evaluation

At this stage of the WBID Model, only preliminary plans for a summative evaluation are developed. (Chapter 10 is devoted to finalizing and conducting summative evaluation.) Recall that the main purpose of summative evaluation is to determine the overall value, or value added, of the WBI once it has been implemented for a specified period of time.

Summative evaluation generally occurs at some point during the life cycle of WBI. A formal summative evaluation may occur after the first full implementation or on a three- to five-year schedule, depending on the stability of the content, the learners, context, and/or technology (Dick et al., 2005, Gagné et al., 2005, Smith & Ragan, 2005). The timing of the summative evaluation is ultimately at the discretion of the client or primary stakeholder, based on their specific needs and requirements.

Although summative evaluation is conducted at a much later point, this preliminary planning plays an important role in subsequent events. First, it helps to ensure that this type of evaluation actually occurs. In many cases, summative evaluation is discussed but does not take place. By having plans—even very general ones—in place, clients may be encouraged to conduct an evaluation on the education or training that occurs within their organizations.

Second, planning facilitates necessary data collection related to the instructional situation currently in place. Often, data about instructional products or practices currently in use are *not* collected prior to a new innovation being introduced (Solomon & Gardner, 1986), which causes valuable information to be lost. Losing such data makes comparison of new and old interventions or innovations difficult, if not impossible, and the discussion of effectiveness of any new innovation becomes somewhat limited. Early preplanning allows for **baseline data** to be collected on existing instruction or program effectiveness for later comparison once the WBI has been fully implemented.

Baseline data collection and the later data collection during the summative evaluation are based on the criteria of effectiveness, efficiency, and appeal, just as in formative evaluation. Concurrently, a preliminary set of questions and potential methods and tools for the summative evaluation are identified. The evaluation plan can entail features similar to those found in the formative evaluation plan (Table 5.8).

Table 5.8 Preliminary Planning for Summative Evaluation

Evaluation Criteria	Main Questions	Data Sources (or Methods and Tools)
Effectiveness		
Efficiency		
Appeal		

Other Considerations for Evaluation Planning

In addition to the criteria previously discussed in formative evaluation, there are other considerations for collecting data for a summative evaluation. Presented in outline form here, we discuss these issues fully in Chapter 10 (Fitzpatrick et al., 2004; Fullan & Pomfret, 1977; Joint Committee, 1994):

- Establish a time frame for developing or purchasing instrumentation and tools, such as surveys, questionnaires, interview questions, observation checklists, review sheets, and assessments. This is especially important when gathering benchmark data.
- Determine if evaluators will be internal or external to the organization.
- Determine if evaluators require training in the selected evaluative methods or tools so that any training can occur before the start of the summative evaluation.
- Establish a procedure for collecting data.
- Identify additional experts external to the organization and document their competence areas.
- Obtain human subjects' approval, if necessary.
- Identify end users, explaining the evaluation process to them, sharing expectations, and obtaining any needed consent before the evaluation.
- Identify specific dates for data collection, as well as the quantity and types of materials and tools needed for each of those dates.
- Determine when experts are to complete and return their reviews.
- Allow time to collect, code, and analyze data as the evaluation occurs.
- Document data analysis procedures.
- Establish procedures, including dates and times, for communicating with clients and other stakeholders.

The evaluator/designer sufficiently describes and documents these considerations to allow for any baseline data collection on the current situation. If such data are collected and analyzed, then a description of the results are included in the preliminary summative evaluation planning. Adequate description allows future evaluators to follow and further detail them for later summative evaluation data collection.

As with any evaluation, summative evaluations should include a final report of the process, findings, and recommendations. The final report would be formatted with an executive summary followed by a full report. (We discuss the reporting of summative evaluation in Chapter 10.)

GardenScapes

To prepare for the summative evaluation that will occur after full implementation of the *GardenScapes* course, Elliott identifies several main questions and the data sources that will be needed to address those questions. These questions are based on the discussions he and Kally had with Carlos and Dr. Chauncy. They include the preliminary summative evaluation plan in the Design Document.

Preliminary Planning for Summative Evaluation

Evaluation Criteria	Main Questions	Data Sources
Effectiveness	How did final project meet course objectives?	Performance activities
	Do learners believe the WBI was worth attending?	Survey stakeholder perceptions
Efficiency	How long did learners participate in the WBI per session or activity?	Learner login and logout times
Appeal	Will learners take other distance courses at CJC?	Survey stakeholder perceptions

Because his internship at the TLDC will end long before the summative evaluation is scheduled to occur, Elliott devises only preliminary plans. He provides enough detail in an outline so that whoever conducts this evaluation will have a basis from which to work. *GardenScapes* is a new course offering at CJC; there are no data to obtain on a preexisting course.

Because of the lack of any comparison data, Elliott determines that using a pre- and posttest design for the summative evaluation will show whether the WBI was successful (which relates to effectiveness). Because of the extensive nature of a summative evaluation, Elliott adds the following methods for data collection to the outline:

- Opinion surveys (using questionnaires) will generate information about ease of use and interest (which relates to appeal). This information should be obtained from the instructor, participants, and the TLDC technical support staff.
- Periodic observation of discussions and emails will provide information on the efficiency aspects.

The results of this evaluation will be written in a formal report submitted to the stakeholders, who include the instructor, the TLDC director, and the Dean. This report will provide the evaluation methodology, results, and recommendations based on the findings.

Elliott, with assistance from Kally, plans for both formative and summative evaluations. The completed formative evaluation plan is made ready for implementation and the general purposes for the summative evaluation are identified. He presents the plans to Mr. Carlos for approval.

ON YOUR OWN

Make your preliminary plans for your own summative evaluation. Decide on its timing, general purposes, and data sources. Outline methods and tools you might use. Determine how you will communicate your results and recommendations. Describe these elements and supply a rationale for your decisions.

(For illustrations of how other designers tackled these same issues, review the case studies appearing in the Extending Your Skills section at the end of this chapter.)

Wrapping Up

Evaluating WBI is critical to its success. In many respects, the WBID Model is comparable to traditional ID models in that data sources and evaluation procedures are similar. However, the timing of planning the evaluation differs. Integrating evaluation planning into the early stages of the WBID Model facilitates successful design and delivery. Two types of evaluation planning occur at this stage: a detailed plan for formative evaluation and a preliminary plan for summative evaluation. Incorporating end users and expert reviews early into the design and development stages, rather at the end of the development stage, is another difference between the WBID Model and other ID models. The final difference is the recognition that it may not be feasible to conduct all three types of tryouts (one-to-one, small-group, and field trial) when developing WBI. Using all three types of tryouts in formative evaluation in WBI design greatly depends on availability of and access to potential members of the target audience and the functionality of the Web-based learning environment. Formative evaluation findings are documented and used to make modifications to the design plan and prototypes.

Preliminary planning for summative evaluation occurs at the onset of the WBID Model. The two main reasons for tentatively planning for this type of evaluation are (1) to be able to collect benchmark data and (2) help ensure that summative evaluation will occur. Summative evaluation findings will be used to make recommendations about the value of the WBI and whether it should continue to be used.

Expanding Your Expertise

1. How can evaluation criteria be used to organize evaluations? What are the most important evaluation criteria when designing and developing WBI? Justify your responses.
2. Why is planning for evaluation an important part of the WBID Model?
3. What methods of evaluation help evaluators obtain vital information to make decisions about revising WBI?
4. What is the purpose of documenting decisions and results in evaluation?
5. Why should there be a plan for communicating and reporting an evaluation?
6. How is evaluation of WBI different from evaluation for traditional instruction? How are they similar?
7. What features of the learning environment or WBI make conducting an evaluation difficult? How could these difficulties be overcome?

Extending Your Skills

Case Study 1   ## PK–12 Schools

Megan Bifford has completed her analysis for the Web-supported instruction targeted for elementary schools. After analyzing the fifth-grade science curriculum, her task is to develop a formative evaluation plan and begin the preliminary plan for a summative evaluation. After reviewing information on types of evaluation methods, she decides to focus on an objective-oriented evaluation because of the accountability requirements set by the state and district.

The Westport School has limited resources and Megan has a very small budget with which to work. Consequently, there is no funding for an external evaluator. Megan will act as the internal evaluator, with assistance from Cassie Angus, the district science coordinator. To begin the evaluation, Megan creates an initial set of formative evaluation questions:

- Are the technology supports effective?
- How does the lesson align to the curriculum frameworks and district standards?
- What are the students' perceptions of the instructional environment?
- Does student performance improve?

As Megan works through the formative evaluation, she outlines her communication plan. Her primary stakeholders are the superintendent and the school board, with Cassie serving as the liaison between Megan and those stakeholders. Secondary stakeholders include teachers, students, parents, and the business community. To communicate with the primary stakeholders, Megan will submit a series of written reports, culminating with a summative evaluation that follows a research methodology. For secondary stakeholders, Megan will give presentations to teachers and the PTA; in addition, she will create an informational flyer to send home with students. Megan begins to work on her summative evaluation plan before she starts to design her learning environment.

In Westport Schools, Megan is working with a motivated group of interested teachers at the fifth-grade level and a large pool of students. She has already identified two teachers to work with during formative evaluation as the Web-supported instruction is developed. Cassie will continue working with Megan during WSI design and development. Cassie will serve as the SME, as will the two designated fifth-grade teachers, Rhoda Cameron and Buzz Garrison. The remaining schools will be provided the WSI once revisions have been made to the prototype. All of the schools will be included in the summative evaluation of the WSI.

Case Study 2   ## Business and Industry

Homer Spotswood's safety training program for the M2 Company will combine online experiences with hands-on, face-to-face training. The employees are dispersed at several locations around the world and safety issues have recently mandated the new program. A fire safety program will be the focus of the first set of lessons. Because of the need to make sure that the goals of the organization are fully considered in the program, Homer uses the management orientation as a basis for his formative evaluation plan.

CEO Bud Cattrell is particularly interested in a return on investment (ROI) for this new training initiative. Subsequent training using a distributed format will be dependent upon the success of this program, both from cost and instructional perspectives. Homer plans to use Krathwohl's levels of evaluation to determine the project's effectiveness. Because keeping costs down is a major consideration, Homer needs to carefully monitor resources. The formative and summative evaluation plans that Homer creates must capture appropriate data to evaluate the project using an ROI model.

Homer determines that it is best to follow a straightforward evaluation plan. He designs major evaluation questions, defining *intervention* as Web-enhanced instruction:

- Does employee performance improve after the intervention?
- Is training time affected by the intervention?
- What costs are expended in the intervention?
- What costs are saved in the intervention?
- How does the face-to-face environment interact with the Web-enhanced materials?

Bud determines that the best way to justify the training initiatives is to hire an external evaluator who is a safety expert. He directs Homer to begin searching for such an individual. Homer continues to develop his Formative Evaluation Plan and begins to think about his summative evaluation preliminary plan.

Case Study 3   Military

Commander Rebekkah Feinstein has a progress briefing due to Captain Cameron Prentiss in one week, covering two aspects of the conversion program critical to the success of this conversion effort, the formative and summative evaluation plans.

The Formative Evaluation Plan includes an in-process evaluation of the developing product. The WBID Model, which the teams is using to develop the training product, calls for concurrent evaluation and design. Three development teams have been formed, each addressing one of the major topics. Part of the Formative Evaluation Plan, which Lieutenant Sandra Cole and her Curriculum and Instructional Standards counterpart, Lieutenant Rex Danielson, have developed, calls for a periodic review of the in-process product by another development team. Each team has the technical familiarity and educational background to provide substantive feedback as to accuracy and clarity of the material presented as well as the appropriateness of the sequencing, delivery, and assessment strategies. At predetermined points identified in the project management plan, the teams will exchange their products and record their comments on the learning content management system (LCMS). This system provides documentation of critiques of completed work and allows corrective actions to be logged and tracked. A bonus to this part of the Formative Evaluation Plan—to which they frequently refer to as "peer reviews"—is that it will allow the teams to develop a homogeneous presentation style.

The Formative Evaluation Plan will be conducted in conjunction with the rollout of the product on the Web. The LMS will be able to provide pre- and posttest scores, time-to-train (e.g., hours engaged in the lessons), and locations of the learners (ship, shore, or home). An LMS will require the completion of an end-of-lesson survey prior to recording that the individual lesson has been completed. This survey includes items asking what factors or characteristics of the online learning experience were most and least appealing. Lieutenants Cole and Danielson plan to conduct this part of the formative evaluation during the first two months that the products are available on Navy e-Learning. Results of the data will be provided to the original teams for analysis and revision.

A preliminary plan for summative evaluation is devised at the same time. The final summative evaluation will provide Commander Feinstein and her staff with key data to present a decision matrix to Captain Prentiss. This matrix will include much of the same data that is collected during the two-month field trial (test scores, time-to-train, training environment, and satisfaction survey), but over a one-year period after implementation. Additional data will come from surveys and interviews of Fleet commanders and senior enlisted personnel to determine how beneficial the instruction is to their organization's missions. The intent is that better-trained sailors perform better on the job and their supervisors recognize this. Captain Prentiss will take this information and provide refined guidance on the direction of the expansion of the classroom-to-WBI conversion project.

Case Study 4 # Higher Education

Dr. Joe Shawn and his teaching assistant, Brian, continue revamping his undergraduate course, *Introduction to Management,* for Web-enhanced delivery.

The University requires student evaluations for every course taught. However, this type of evaluation won't provide him with adequate information about the effectiveness, efficiency, and appeal of the Web-enhanced course. Dr. Shawn plans to survey the students at the beginning, during, and at the end of the WEI course when it is offered. He will develop a questionnaire based on others that he has used previously; it will focus on student opinions about the course content, the added Web activities, and other relevant aspects. He is particularly interested in their views about the integration of classroom and online activities. Other questions will solicit views on time and effort required for the Web activities, such as the chats and threaded discussions that he'll be using. He decides that he'll need to track the amount of time he spends in facilitating the online activities.

Because he is a researcher as well as an instructor, Joe is intrigued as to whether there are other value-added components of the Web-enhanced elements of the course. He plans to gather similar data with his current on-campus course offering, using similar self-report questionnaires. He may videotape selected class discussions for later comparison with chats and threaded discussions. Joe plans to compare performance scores on accomplishment of management objectives in the WEI course to scores from previous semesters and traditional courses that are concurrently taught.

These are just preliminary ideas and Joe will have to review the literature on teaching online in a business college to further detail this line of research. He plans to write and publish in this area so that he can advance his progress for promotion. Prior to collecting data, he will submit a Human Participants Form to the University's Institutional Research Board for their approval of the study.

The following applies to all case studies. Consider who you, as the designer, might act or respond in each case study.

- How does evaluation fit into the WBID Model and the presented cases?
- How do the evaluation procedures presented in this chapter affect the design and development of WBI? How do these procedures differ for each case?
- What you would do differently from each of the principals in the case studies?

6

Concurrent Design: WBI Preplanning and Design Tasks

Once the analyses have been conducted and evaluation plans formulated, attention turns to WBI design and development. Design and development tasks can be completed in tandem, a process known as concurrent design. At this stage of the WBID Model, the designer identifies the design, writes the objectives, and determines the instructional and motivational strategies. The development process then moves from design planning into WBI prototyping. Formative evaluation processes are also incorporated into the concurrent design stage in order to refine WBI plans and prototypes as they are created. We divide our discussion of the concurrent design stage into three chapters. Chapter 6 focuses on design-related tasks—from preplanning through clustering objectives. Chapter 7 explores instructional and motivational strategies and introduces a new tool, the WBI Strategy Worksheet. In this chapter we also discuss factors that affect WBI design. Chapter 8 culminates the discussion by focusing attention on development tasks such as storyboarding, flowcharting, and developing and evaluating prototypes.

Chapter 6 begins with a description of preplanning activities, which include identifying design tasks, identifying personnel, and establishing a timeline for design and development procedures. We then discuss writing objectives, after which we explore various types of assessment strategies and how to complete the TOAB with objectives and assessment items. We close with a discussion of how to cluster objectives.

Objectives

At the end of this chapter, you should be able to do the following:

- Explain the processes entailed in the concurrent design stage.
- Name the three main tasks involved in preplanning.
- Consider the specific design approach needed for a WBI project.
- Identify the concurrent design tasks and activities when using the WBID Model.
- Establish a timeline for WBI design.
- Identify the components in a three-component objective.
- Write the appropriate objectives for WBI.
- Determine what assessment strategies are appropriate for WBI.
- Develop assessments that correspond to identified objectives and outcome levels.
- Cluster the objectives into appropriate groupings and sequences.

Introduction

Up to this point, the instructional designer has established parameters for the Web-based learning environment and collected and analyzed data related to the four instructional components of goals, learners, context, and content. Formative and preliminary summative evaluation plans have been developed, as well. The concurrent design stage permits the designer to integrate design and development activities with formative evaluation tasks. The focus is first on preplanning design tasks and then on design activities, such as writing objectives, determining the appropriate type of assessment, and detailing instructional and motivational strategies, all of which affect WBI prototype development. The third focus of this stage is on development tasks, which become increasingly important as design decisions are finalized.

The design plan remains flexible in order to meet any unforeseen challenges that occur or that are found based on formative evaluation results (Figure 6.1). Recall that in Chapter 2 we described instructional design as an iterative process in that it allows the WBI to evolve and change as the stages of the WBID Model progress. This iterative process, similar to rapid prototyping techniques, can best be viewed as a linkage of design, development, and formative evaluation, with activities being conducted simultaneously (Davidson-Shivers & Rasmussen, 1999; Nixon & Lee, 2001). Wakefield, Frasciello, Tatnall, and Conover (2001) would concur, suggesting that such events occur at the "same time or acting in conjunction" (p. 2).

Rapid prototyping techniques balance a requirement for quality with the need to design and develop instruction swiftly (Danielson, Lockee, & Burton, 2000; Fisher & Peratino, 2001). However, key to success is a sufficient analysis or needs assessment of the instructional situation (Kraushaar & Shirland, 1985; Nixon & Lee, 2001). Rapid prototyping in-

Figure 6.1 Design processes of the concurrent design stage of the WBID Model.

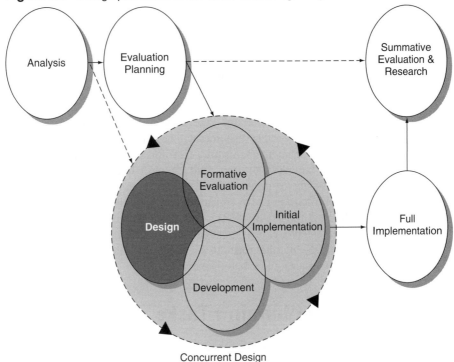

Concurrent Design

volves quickly developing a shell or portion of a final instructional product for review without waiting for final design specifications (Tripp & Bicklemeyer, 1990).

There are several ways to incorporate rapid prototyping (RP) into the WBID Model. First is the classic RP method of foregoing in-depth design specifications and moving into developing iterations of the WBI. Second is to design and develop units or lessons within a WBI project iteratively. For example, when WBI includes several instructional segments (units, lessons, modules, etc.), the objectives, assessments, and instructional and motivational strategies for one segment can be designed, developed into prototypic instruction (e.g., the lecture, threaded discussion questions, readings, etc.), and evaluated *en toto* rather than first designing all segments, then developing them, and finally evaluating the whole as in traditional ID models (Davidson-Shivers & Rasmussen, 1999; Nixon & Lee, 2001). As one instructional segment (unit or lesson) moves to prototype development, another is phased in for design. This "phasing in" of segments occurs until all have been designed and prototypes developed. Each segment prototype is evaluated and modified until the final WBI product is created. Early feedback, another aspect of rapid prototyping (Jones & Richey, 2000; Nixon & Lee), occurs throughout this process.

When applying the WBID Model, action on a design procedure, or task, is *not* conducted in isolation from the other tasks. Rather, the creation of an instructional strategy, for example, often leads to evaluating how that strategy might be implemented on the Web page. The design of an assessment tool may lead to reviewing the objectives and LTM items for congruency. Thus, a concurrent set of actions could lead to continuous formative evaluation and redesign of the WBI if boundaries are not established.

Consequently, it is important to set limits on the number of revisions to the WBI or to establish a contingency plan with the client. A contingency plan would state that the client will incur additional costs and experience additional time delays after a specified number of revisions, or that other resources will be required for the project to be completed on time. Establishing such agreements prior to WBI design minimizes continual changes and lack of progress. Likewise, it is important to require interim client approval at designated points throughout complex projects, as well as at the end of the project.

A second caution is that concurrent design could lead to too little formative evaluation and, ultimately, to a faulty WBI product being developed. There is a fine line between careful planning and overanalysis of each component in a WBI project. Designers should take care to not spend either too *little* or too *much* time on design and evaluation. Experience and skill helps designers negotiate this fine line.

WBI Preplanning Tasks

The concurrent design stage begins with three preplanning activities (Figure 6.2). The first is to finalize the design approach for the WBI project, the second is to identify the specific tasks associated with each concurrent design process. Identifying such tasks provides a framework for a project manager (or instructional designer) to be able to assign personnel to complete those tasks. The third activity is establishing the WBI project's timeline.

Finalizing the WBI Design Approach

The design approach guides the development of the WBI. Each decision can be integrated into the WBI prototype as it is made (Davidson-Shivers & Rasmussen, 1999). The WBID Model subscribes to this practical, yet grounded, ID approach. With many WBI projects, especially complex ones, it is not possible to complete all of the design activities for the entire project before starting development. Constraints of resources, time, and money, and the

Figure 6.2   Preplanning activities for the concurrent design stage.

Finalize the design approach	→	Identify specific tasks with concurrent design & development processes	→	Establish WBI project timeline

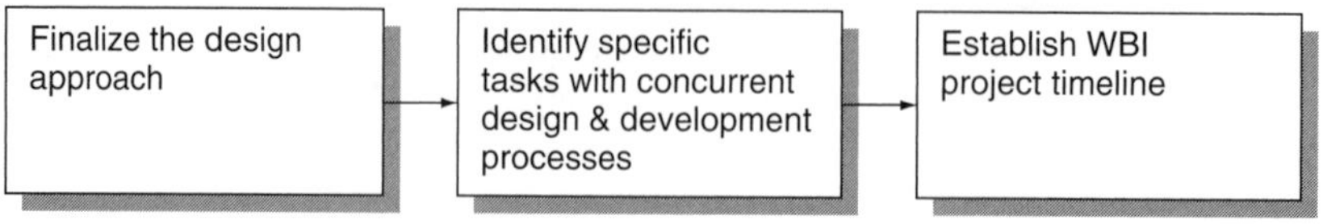

desire to be responsive to the customer suggest that concurrent design may be a good approach. Concurrent design also permits unforeseen technical difficulties to be resolved well before the final WBI is completed.

Identifying Tasks and Team Members

The project manager or instructional designer in complex WBI projects usually outlines the specific design and development tasks. Tasks related to design include writing objectives, creating assessments, determining appropriate instructional strategies, and selecting media. Tasks related to development include converting the plans into deliverable products: flowcharts, storyboards, prototypes, instruction, and the website. Table 6.1 provides an outline of specific tasks and the team members normally assigned to complete them. Team members are assigned to tasks based on their skills and the time frame of the project. This assignment chart may then serve as a stakeholder (or client) approval form.

Designers consider the following questions when preplanning personnel requirements:

- Will the designer be able to use the design approach as guide throughout the entire project?
- What skills will the tasks require?
- Who (which role or profession) should become a member of the design team?
- How will tasks and personnel be matched?

The designer will then use these or other questions as guidelines for completing the Design Document; providing adequate descriptions of the design team members, their expertise or competencies, and the duties (or tasks) that they will assume in the WBI project.

Table 6.1   Tasks and Team Members for Concurrent Design Stage

Tasks	Team Member	Required Duties
Summary of tasks of the initial WBID Stages		
Analysis	Project manager or Instructional designer (ID)	Performs analysis on instructional situation. Determines if WBI is appropriate solution. Analyzes the four instructional components.
Evaluation planning		Plans formative evaluation. Preliminary planning of summative.
	Client or Instructor	Provides access to data and personnel for both stages. Approves plans.

(continued)

Table 6.1   Tasks and Team Members for Concurrent Design Stage *(Continued)*

Tasks	Team Member	Required Duties
Concurrent Design Stage: Preplanning Tasks		
Recruit team Establish necessary budget, time frame, resources, etc. Approve project	Project Manager or ID	Finalizes the WBI design approach. Assembles team, budget, and resources. Establishes the project time frame. Manages the team. Reviews completed tasks. Approves any agreements and completed tasks.
	Client or Instructor	Explains design needs and wishes. Explains requirements (time, budget, resources, etc.). Reviews deliverables based on requirements. Approves any agreements and completed tasks. Approves payment for deliverables.
Concurrent Design Stage: Design Tasks		
Write objectives	ID	Develops objectives from the LTM. Modifies objectives as necessary with SME input.
	Expert reviewer or Instructor	Consults on appropriateness of learning content and objectives. Reviews and approves objectives.
Write assessment items and tools	ID	Determines if assessment tools are needed. Develops assessment items.
	Expert reviewer or Instructor	Consults by evaluating assessment items for congruence. Approves assessment plans.
Cluster objectives into instructional chunks	ID	Organizes objectives into small chunks for WBI development.
	Expert reviewer or Instructor	Consults on clustering of objectives. Approves instructional chunks.
Create WBI Strategy Worksheet (Planning instructional and motivational strategies)	ID	Determines appropriate instructional and motivational strategies for WBI. Selects appropriate media for WBI. Evaluates instructional strategies for congruence.
	Expert reviewer (Technical)	Identifies capabilities of WBI through the Web. Reviews Web learning environment.
	Expert reviewer	Evaluates instructional and motivational strategies for congruence.
	End-user reviewer	Reviews instructional strategies.
	Instructor	Reviews and approves worksheet.

Table 6.1 Tasks and Team Members for Concurrent Design Stage *(Concluded)*

Tasks	Team Member	Required Duties
Concurrent Design Stage: Development Tasks		
Create flowcharts	ID	Reviews design plan for structure and sequence.
Structure flowchart for use in LMS (if used)		
Create storyboards	ID	Converts instructional and motivational strategies (on the WBI Strategy Worksheet) to storyboards.
		Converts storyboards to WBI prototype(s).
	Instructor	Reviews and approves storyboards.
Design website	ID	Assists in designing interface and prototype development.
	Technical expert	Provides technical support as needed.
Convert instruction to Web-based documents	ID	Completes storyboard conversion to Web instruction.
	Technical expert	Provides technical support and programming.
	Instructor	Reviews and approves.
Incorporate appropriate media	ID	Integrates media into instruction.
	Technical expert	Provides technical support and programming.
Test website (Formative evaluation)	Project manager or ID	Performs quality control on website; tests links, evaluate navigation, load speed; tests sites various browsers, versions, and computer systems.
	SME/Instructor End-user reviewers	Conducts and participates in test. Identifies errors for revision.
Troubleshoot technology (Formative evaluation)	ID Technical expert	Fixes errors discovered through website testing.
Test instructional quality (Formative evaluation)	ID	Conducts trial runs of instruction and provides feedback, including completing assessments.
	Instructor End-user reviewer	Participates and reviews WBI and provides information on strengths and weaknesses.
Prior to Implementation Stage		
Major plan approval and sign-off	Project manager or ID	Consults with team and client. Approves WBI.
	Instructor or Client	Approves WBI.

GardenScapes

As they begin their design and development for *GardenScapes,* Elliott and Kally decide that the concurrent design approach facilitates their short design time frame. With this approach, they begin the design-develop-evaluate cycle immediately on completing their preplanning tasks.

The design team is made up of the instructional designer (Elliott), the instructor (Kally), and content and technical expert reviewers. Each member has the appropriate skills needed to successfully participate on the team. Carlos Duartes, director of the TLDC, gives his approval for the project, as does Dr. Judith Chauncy, Elliott's IDT advisor. Kally is both the content reviewer and instructor. Dr. Nikko Tamura will serve as an additional content reviewer. Elliott will conduct the instructional design reviews and Kally will assist. The TLDC staff provides the technical support, primarily through Ms. Laila Gunnarson. In addition, target audience members will be recruited for end-user reviews; they will most likely be identified from those individuals who have previously taken Kally's *Garden Basics* course.

Elliott and Kally create a matrix of the tasks, team members, and their duties. The first two sections appear here.

See this textbook's Companion Website (http://www.prenhall.com/davidson-shivers) for the complete table.

Concurrent Design Stage Tasks and Team Members for *GardenScapes* Project

Tasks	Team Member	Required Duties
Concurrent Design: Preplanning Tasks		
Preplanning activities	Carlos Durates—approves all TLDC projects (no designated project manager)	Approves teams and tasks for WBI projects for the TLDC. Approves design plan and oversees Elliott's internship.
	Dr. Judith Chauncy, Myers University	Approves WBI plan as an internship project for Elliott.
	Elliott Kangas, ID	Develops timeline and overall planning of WBI.
	Kally Le Rue, SME and instructor (could be considered client)	Assists overall planning the scope of the project from an ID perspective.

Concurrent Design Stage Tasks and Team Members for *GardenScapes* Project

Tasks	Team Member	Required Duties
Concurrent Design: Design Tasks		
Write objectives	Elliott	Develops objectives from the LTM. Modifies objectives as necessary with instructor and SME input.
	Kally Dr. Nikko Tamura, SME	Consults with ID on appropriateness of learning content and objectives.
Write assessment items and tools	Elliott	Determines assessment tools needed. Develops assessment items.
	Kally	Consults with ID and evaluates assessment items for congruence.
Cluster objectives	Elliott	Organizes objectives into small chunks for WBI development.
	Kally	Consults with ID regarding chunking of objectives.
Create WBI Strategy Worksheet	Elliott	Determines appropriate instructional and motivational strategies for WBI. Selects appropriate media for WBI. Evaluates instructional strategies for congruence with TOAB.
	Laila Gunnarson, Technology expert	Identifies capabilities of WBI through the Web. Reviews Web learning environment.
	Kally	Evaluates instructional strategies for congruence.
	Expert and End-user reviewers	Reviews instructional strategies and provides feedback.
Identify potential media	Elliott	Determines appropriate media by working with graphic artist or video expert.
	Laila and support staff at TLDC	Consults with ID about feasibility of media in the WBI.

ON YOUR OWN

Identify the design approach that you will use for your project and articulate it in your Design Document.

Reexamine the implications of your analysis findings and your evaluation plans and develop a list of WBI project tasks. Next, identify the skills needed to complete those tasks. Assign team members who have the skills and competencies to assume the specified duties. Be sure to provide adequate explanation or description of your team members in your Design Document. Identify individuals who could serve as expert and end-user reviewers as the WBI design and prototypes develop. Use Table 6.1 to guide you.

(For illustrations of how other designers tackled these same issues, review the case studies appearing in the Extending Your Skills section at the end of this chapter.)

 See this textbook's Companion Website (http://www.prenhall.com/davidson-shivers) for a printable template of the task/team member matrix.

WBI Project Timelines

The final preplanning activity is completing the WBI project timeline. A timeline helps project managers to sequence tasks, guide team members in completing tasks, and assess whether the WBI project is on time and on budget.

A timeline is based on the identified tasks and assigned team members. Additionally, the project manager must consider team members' other duties beyond this project (some individuals may be assigned to more than one project simultaneously) and other project constraints to establish a realistic timeline. Timelines should be flexible to allow for contingencies.

Key deadlines, called project **milestones,** are included in complex WBI projects; they indicate the deadlines when significant tasks must be completed to keep the project on schedule and to determine if the time frame needs to be adjusted. Milestones are used to gauge the success of the project in terms of being on time and within budget. In some projects, attainment of a milestone may elicit a client sign-off and payment.

Gantt charts visually illustrate the sequence of project tasks, the estimated (or projected) time, and the tracking of actual times to complete them. Depending on the life of the project, time periods in a Gantt chart may be displayed in hours, days, months, or years. The charts help a project manager identify where resources and efforts are being used and determine whether they are being used wisely. Such charts may be as simple or complex as the WBI project demands. Gantt charts can be easily created in word processors, spreadsheets, or programs such as *Inspiration*®, Microsoft *Visio*® or Microsoft *Project*®. Table 6.2 is a sample Gantt chart for a small WBI project with a quick turnaround time frame. This example indicates the concurrent design tasks (which include formative evaluation activities); highlighted times indicate the projected estimations for each task.

PERT charts are another way to illustrate the sequence of project tasks and the estimated (or projected) and actual times to complete them. PERT charts are often used with complex WBI projects. Developing PERT charts require the use of advanced extensive software programs such as Microsoft *Project*®. Our discussion in this text will employ only Gantt charts.

Table 6.2   Sample Gantt Chart for a Small WBI Project

Tasks		Week 1	Week 2	Week 3	Week 4	Week N*
Conduct Preplanning activities	Projected	▨				
	Actual					
Write objectives	Projected	▨▨				
	Actual					
Write assessment items and tools	Projected	▨▨				
	Actual					
Evaluate objectives and assessment items	Projected	▨▨				
	Actual					
Cluster and sequence objectives	Projected		▨			
	Actual					
Create WBI Strategy Worksheet	Projected		▨▨			
	Actual					
Identify media	Projected		▨▨			
	Actual					
Evaluate instructional strategies and media selections	Projected		▨▨			
	Actual					
Flowchart and storyboard lesson	Projected		▨			
	Actual					
Evaluate flowchart and storyboards	Projected			▨		
	Actual					
Design website	Projected			▨		
	Actual					
Convert storyboards to Web pages	Projected			▨▨		
	Actual					
Conduct evaluation (test website and instructional quality of WBI, troubleshoot technology, test)	Projected		▨▨▨			
	Actual					

N* = weekly columns added until project time frame is complete.

GardenScapes

In consultation with Carlos, Kally and Elliott create a timeline for design and development tasks, along with evaluation activities. They then estimate the time for completing each task, realizing that they may modify the timing as the project progresses. They leave spaces to identify the actual time expended on each task. The entire WBI project has a short time frame so that it can be implemented in the next term. Their approved Gantt chart appears here.

GardenScapes Timeline

Task	Person(s) Responsible	Week 1	Week 2	Week 3	Week 4	Week 5	Week 6	Week 7	Week 8
Review analysis to ensure correct framework for WBI	Kally, Elliott, Carlos	▮							
Write objectives	Kally, Elliott		▮						
Write assessment items and tools	Elliott		▮	▮					
Review objectives and assessment for formative evaluation	Kally, Carlos								
Cluster objectives, Create WBI Strategy Worksheet	Elliott, Kally		▮	▮	▮	▮			
Evaluate the WBI strategies	Nikko, End users								
Identify potential media	Elliott, Kally			▮	▮				
Evaluate media choices	Laila								
Flowchart and storyboard	Elliott					▮			
Review flowchart and storyboard	Kally, Carlos								
Convert prototypes to WBI	Kally, Elliott, Nikko, Carlos, End users				▮	▮	▮	▮	
Review website and WBI									
Test and troubleshoot WBI and site	Elliott, Laila					▮	▮	▮	
Final project due	Kally, Elliott, Carlos, Judith								▮

Italics indicates review process
Gray indicates projected time for each task

See this textbook's Companion Website (http://www.prenhall.com/davidson-shivers) for the *GardenScapes* Design Document.

ON YOUR OWN

Develop your WBI project timeline using a Gantt chart, using Table 6.2 as your template. Estimate time needed to complete each major task and provide a space for the actual time expended (label as appropriate by hour, day, week, etc.). Where possible, identify who (by name or title) will be responsible for completing the different tasks. If your project includes major deliverables, identify project milestones. Include your timeline in your Design Document with descriptions or explanations of the task, team members, and time periods.

(For illustrations of how other designers tackled these same issues, review the case studies appearing in the Extending Your Skills section at the end of this chapter.)

See this textbook's Companion Website (http://www.prenhall.com/davidson-shivers) for a printable Gantt chart template.

Essential Design Tasks

The foundational parts of the WBI design plan follow the preplanning activities. Six main tasks are considered essential to WBI design:

- Write objectives.
- Write assessments.
- Cluster objectives.
- Create the instructional strategies using the WBI Strategy Worksheet.
- Create motivational strategies using the WBI Strategy Worksheet.
- Identify media.

The first three tasks are discussed in this chapter; we explore the others in Chapter 7.

Writing Objectives

In the analysis stage, the relationships between and among the instructional content major steps and subskills were identified and illustrated on a learning task map (LTM). Each task was tagged with an identifying number. These items on the LTM serve as the basis for the instructional objectives.

Mager (1997) states that "an objective is a collection of words and/or pictures and diagrams intended to let others know what you intend for your students to achieve. It is related to the intended outcomes, rather than processes for achieving those outcomes; it is specific and measurable rather than broad and intangible; and it is concerned with students, not teachers" (p. 3). Gronlund (2004) states, "A more useful way to state instructional objectives is in terms of the intended outcomes of the instruction. This makes clear the types of student performance we are willing to accept as evidence that the students have learned what was expected of them" (p. 4).

Generally speaking, objectives are based on behavioral or cognitive learning principles or written from an objectivist rather than a constructivist perspective. At first glance, goals and objectives appear to be antithetical for a constructivist. However, because Jonassen (1992, 1999) mentions alternative assessment as a means to evaluate constructivist learning, it may be inferred that goals exist related to learning activities of exploration, articulation, and reflection, and are appropriate in constructivist learning environments. Jonassen (1999) suggests that goals must be "owned by the learner" (p. 216). Likewise, Riesbeck (1996) suggests that courses may be goals based or may employ goal-based scenarios, in which skills rather than facts are learned. He suggests two types of skills: process skills, which focuses on "multi-step, interrelated procedures" (p. 53), and outcome achievement skills, which "focus on results and the techniques to achieve those results" (p. 54). Yet, in most constructivist learning environments, goals are rather loosely defined and specific learning objectives may not be developed at all.

However, with learning environments that have a behavioral, cognitive or multi-theoretical learning approach, specific objectives can be useful. Most PK–12 school systems require that specific objectives or essential elements of the curriculum are stated and taught. The purpose of writing objectives is to describe expectations for student learning; stating objectives allows students, parents, and others in the community to understand what is taught over the course of a day, a term, or an entire year (Gronlund, 2004; Stiggins, 2005).

When developing objectives using one of these theoretical approaches, the designer focuses on the learner; the objective is not about what the *instructor* will "do," but what the *learner* will be able to "do" after the WBI or its units (or lessons) have been completed. In other words, an **objective** identifies particular skills in addition to facts, concepts, principles that are to be learned. Furthermore, they can be written in such a way as to allow for learner input.

Objectives, Learning Outcomes, and the Web

Recall that when writing the instructional goal statement, the designer also identifies its learning outcome. Likewise, when breaking down the goal, the designer aligns the LTM steps and subskills with coordinating outcome levels. For example, the LTM task item, "name the 50 U.S. state capitals," has an outcome level of verbal information (based on Gagné's [1985] Categories of Learning) or knowledge (based on Bloom et al., 1956). Naming state capitals is a lower-order cognitive task, but such knowledge can serve as building blocks for later higher-order thinking skills. By comparison, for the LTM task, "to produce a brochure," the appropriate outcome level is the intellectual skill of problem solving (Gagné et al., 2005) or synthesis (Bloom et al., 1956). With this latter example, learner input is involved in choosing the type and style of the brochure as well as its content; process skills are involved in finding a creative solution for producing an appropriate brochure.

The designer writes objectives based on the LTM steps and subskills to be congruent with outcome levels. This is not necessarily an easy design task even with the action verb (that is, performance) already identified in the LTM task items. It takes time and effort to develop well-constructed objectives that communicate the purposes of the WBI and emphasize expectations of student performance (Gagné et al., 2005; Popham, 2002). The designer may need to review and modify the LTM steps and skills that objectives and task items correspond with each other.

The two main formats for writing objectives are the five-component objective and the three-component objective. The five-component objective is not as well known and is used by designers, who follow Gagné's work. The three-component objective is generally attributed to Mager's (1997) work and is more commonly known and used by curriculum developers. Neely (2000) suggests that the Mager objective type is often the format of choice for PK–12 school environments, among others.

Five-Component Objectives

Gagné et al. (2005) advocate the use of a five-component objective in which a learned capability verb (LCV) is associated with each category of learning, or outcome level. LCVs are unique in that they are used to indicate the category of learning, *not* to indicate performance (or learner action). (Recall that Gagné's Categories of Learning and LCVs were discussed in Chapter 3.) A second action verb indicates learner performance. The other three components are the situation, which describes the condition in which the performance will occur, the object of the action, which describes content or object of the performance, and the tools, constraints, or special conditions that are applied to the performance. A five-component objective does not necessarily contain criteria for determining whether the learner has achieved the objective, although the tool, constraint, or special condition may indicate acceptable performance. Table 6.3 presents examples of five-component objectives from various WBI projects.

The advantage of writing five-component objectives is that they clearly identify the corresponding outcome levels with the LCV. However, the wording or phrasing can be cumbersome or awkward.

Three-Component Objectives

The three-component objective consists of a condition, a performance, and one or more criteria (Mager, 1997). Other terms may be used for these components, such as *situation* for condition, *behavior* for performance, and *standards* for criteria (Dick et al., 2005; Smith & Ragan, 2005).

Condition Component.   The **condition** sets the framework for the objective and is the situation in which the learning will occur or be assessed. It may suggest the type of tools required to perform the objective. The condition should identify a situation that is realistic and appropriate for a Web-based environment.

Performance Component.   The **performance** component stems from a learning task item and outcome level in the LTM. It is written as an action verb and identifies what the learner is to do or achieve. The performance is measurable and observable (or tangible). If

Table 6.3   Examples of Five-Component Objectives from WBI Projects with Various Topics

Objective	Learning Outcome
Topic: History	
Given an essay question on events leading to the Battle of Waterloo, the student will **classify** by **explaining** the important <u>events</u> that lead up to the battle *in a closed book exam.*	Intellectual Skill: Defined Concept (Gagné) Comprehension (Bloom)
Topic: Geography	
Given a map of the United States and a list of capitals, the student will be able to **state** by **matching** <u>capitals</u> to the states with at least *42 of 50 correct.*	Verbal Information (Gagné) Knowledge (Bloom)
Topic: Leaves	
Given 10 drawings of different tree leaves, the learner will be able to **identify** by **naming** <u>the tree type</u> from which it came, *in the blank space beside the leaf drawing.*	Intellectual Skill: Concrete Concept (Gagné) Comprehension (Bloom)
Topic: Résumé	
Given a sample of appropriate and inappropriate information for a résumé, the participant will **demonstrate** by **writing** a <u>résumé</u> for *a business environment and using only the appropriate information.*	Intellectual Skill: Rule using (Gagné) Application (Bloom)
Topic: Desktop Publishing	
Given websites and other supporting information, the employee will be able to **generate** by **producing** a uniquely designed <u>tourism brochure</u> *using a publishing software application.*	Intellectual Skill: Problem Solving (Gagné) Synthesis (Bloom)

Note: **<u>bold/underline</u> = LC verb;** **bold = action verb;** *Italics/**bold** = **situation**;* <u>underline = object</u>; *Italics = tools, special conditions, or constraints*

mental processes such as calculate, generate, and so on are the intended performance, then a learner's response must imply that such performances have occurred. Literally hundreds of appropriate verbs might be used, including *apply, calculate, develop, explain, jump, list, name, select,* and *type.* Per Smith and Ragan's (2005) notion, "fuzzy verbs" should not be used; verbs such as *appreciate, know, understand,* and *learn* are considered fuzzy and should not be used (refer to Chapter 4 for how to "de-fuzz" such verbs).

Criteria Component.   The final component of an objective is the **criteria,** or standard(s), by which the performance is judged. Without this part of the objective, the student's level of mastery, or performance, cannot be clearly determined. Neely (2000) suggests that teachers often use percents as *the* way to set standards for learning. Types of criteria include the quality of work, time in which the task is completed, number of correct responses, final product, or other criteria (Dick et al., 2005; Smith & Ragan, 2005). Table 6.4 shows examples of three-component objectives and outcome levels from various WBI situations.

The three-component objective identifies the standards for judging a learner's performance, but may use action verbs that do not always indicate the outcome level. For instance,

Table 6.4 Examples of Three-Component Objectives from WBI Projects, with Various Topics

Objective	Learning Outcome
Topic: History *Given an essay question about the events leading to the Battle of Waterloo,* the student will be able to **explain** the important events leading up to the battle according to their textbook.	Intellectual Skill: Defined Concept (Gagné) Comprehension (Bloom)
Topic: Geography *Given a map of the United States and a list of capitals,* the student will be able to **match** states with capitals with at least *42 of 50 correct.*	Verbal Information (Gagné) Knowledge (Bloom)
Topic: Leaves *Given 10 drawings of different leaves,* the learner will be able to **name** the type of tree from which it came with 80 percent accuracy.	Intellectual Skill: Concrete Concept (Gagné) Comprehension (Bloom)
Topic: Résumé *Given a sample of appropriate and inappropriate information for a résumé,* the participant will be able to **format** a résumé for a business environment using only appropriate information *with only one error.*	Intellectual Skill: Rule using (Gagné) Application (Bloom)
Topic: Desktop Publishing *Given websites, other supporting information, and a publishing software application,* the employee will be able to **produce** a tourism brochure *that has unique design and will increase marketing shares for beach businesses by 10 percent.*	Intellectual Skill: Problem Solving (Gagné) Synthesis (Bloom)

*Note: **Italics/bold** = **condition;** **bold** = **performance;** italics = criteria*

in the example on identifying tree leaves, the outcome level is the intellectual skill: concrete concepts or comprehension. However, the performance (or action verb), *name,* could be used in objectives related to verbal information or knowledge-level outcomes. It is important that three-component objectives correspond to an identified outcome level to clarify expectations for learning.

Writing Objectives Using the TOAB

No matter which type of objective (five- or three-component), each written objective must be congruent with the existing learning task items and outcome levels. In addition, the objectives must match the activity performed, its content, and its outcome-based intent. Again, the designer may spend a great deal of time and effort to make these elements correspond with each other. The TOAB tool, introduced in Chapter 4, can simplify this work. Table 6.5 shows examples of three-component objectives that correspond to the learning task items and outcome levels from the TOAB of various WBI situations.

Table 6.5 Examples of Three-Component Objectives from the TOAB of Various WBI Projects, with Various Topics

Learning Task Item and Number	Objective	Learning Outcome	Assessment Item
Topic: History 5.0 Explain Waterloo events.	Given the question about the events leading to the Battle of Waterloo, the student will be able to explain the important events leading up to the battle according to their textbook.	Intellectual Skill: Defined Concept (SWBAT)	
Topic: Geography 1.1 List state capitals.	Given a map of the United States and a list of capitals, the SWBAT to match states with capitals with at least 42 of 50 correct.	Verbal Information	
Topic: Leaves 2.6 Identify maple leaves.	Given 10 drawings of different leaves, the learner will be able to name the type of tree from which it came with 80 percent accuracy.	Intellectual Skill: Concrete Concept	
Topic: Résumé 4.2 Format résumé.	Given a sample of appropriate and inappropriate information for a résumé, the participant will be able to format a résumé for a business environment using only appropriate information with only one error.	Intellectual Skill: Rule—using	
Topic: Tourism Marketing 9.1 Create tourism brochure.	Given websites, other supporting information, and a publishing software application, the employee will be able to produce a tourism brochure that has unique design and will increase marketing shares for beach businesses by 10 percent.	Intellectual Skill: Problem Solving	

Once the objective column of the TOAB is completed, it is reviewed for clarity and accuracy and congruence. If significant modifications to any parts of the TOAB occur, the designer notes these changes in the Design Document and explains why they were made. Again, it is important to remember that in the WBID Model, design is not linear but iterative, and changes will occur from time to time during concurrent design. These changes often affect not only future procedures and decisions, but the results and decisions of previous steps as well. Communicating the changes and explaining why they occurred provides clarification to everyone on a WBI design team and even to a lone designer/instructor.

GardenScapes

Elliott and Kally write objectives for *GardenScapes* using Gagné's Categories of Learning. The following is a selection from their TOAB with the three-component objectives added. Because they have changed their final instructional goal statement (refer to the discussion in Chapter 4), their TOAB reflects this change in the learning task items and their corresponding outcomes. Due to time constraints, Elliott and Kally cross out and correct items on the original draft rather than complete a new one.

TOAB for the *GardenScapes* Course (selection)

Learning Task Item and Number	Objective	Outcome Level	Assessment Item
~~Design a garden.~~ Develop a garden design plan. *(Derived from final **goal** statement)*	Given a site for a garden, the *learner will be able to (LWBAT)* develop a garden plan that is appropriate to location and conditions.	Intellectual Skill: Problem solving	
1.0 Select garden theme. *(a main **step** from the LTM)*	Given a set of five potential themes, the LWBAT select one garden theme that is appropriate to the location and conditions.	Intellectual skill: defined concepts	
1.1 State color theme. *(a **subskill** from the LTM)*	When asked the question, What are the various types of garden themes?, the LWBAT state color theme as one of them.	Verbal information	
1.2 State cottage theme.	When asked the question, What are the various types of garden themes?, the LWBAT state cottage garden as one of them.	Verbal information	

This process continues until all skills and subskills have been listed.

Note: Strikethroughs and changes in wording by Elliott and Kally, are based on the final goal statement.

See this textbook's Companion Website (http://www.prenhall.com/davidson-shivers) for a complete list of *GardenScapes* objectives and the full TOAB document.

On Your Own

Using your LTM, write objectives for your WBI. Each LTM item should have an objective. Be sure that each objective is aligned with a learning outcome as well as with the learning task item. Refer to Tables 6.3 to 6.5 for proper formatting. Remember that each objective should contain a *condition, performance* (action verb), and *criteria*. Organize your objectives into the identified TOAB columns. Leave the assessment item column blank.

Note any changes to your TOAB as you review and revise your WBI design. If the changes are significant, you may need to create a new TOAB and explain the reasons for the modifications.

(For illustrations of how other designers tackled these same issues, review the case studies appearing in the Extending Your Skills section at the end of this chapter.)

See this textbook's Companion Website (http://www.prenhall.com/davidson-shivers) for a printable version of the TOAB template.

Writing Assessment Items

Assessment is the process of gathering information (Shrock & Coscarelli, 2000), which permits designers and instructors to determine the success of the learner, and, ultimately, the success of the WBI (Berge et al., 2000). In addition to the overall learner success, assessment can diagnose and monitor learner progress (Popham, 2002; Stiggins, 2005). Assessments can be used to help determine the reliability and validity of the WBI.

Purposes of Assessment

The three general reasons for assessing students include diagnostic, formative, and summative purposes (Johnson & Johnson, 2002; Linn & Gronlund, 1995). **Diagnostic assessment** determines learner readiness to participate in the new instructional activity; it is not used to assign value to student work (assigning grades *per se*). Typically these types of assessments are taken prior to or, at the beginning of, the instruction.

Formative assessment gauges learner progress towards meeting the instructional goal and is used to provide feedback (Figure 6.3). The feedback allows learners and instructors to make changes as needed to increase students' likelihood of mastering the stated goal. This type of assessment usually occurs throughout the WBI until the final assessment.

Final or **summative assessment** permits an instructor to judge the quality of learner's work and determine whether learners have achieved the instructional goal (Figure 6.4). This type of assessment allows assigning value to levels of performance, which can be used for grading.

Figure 6.3 Example of formative assessment tool.

Practice
_____

1. Evaluation is one of the ways that decision makers can improve their organization.

❑ True
❑ False
_____

2. Two types of evaluation are: _____ and _____.

_____

3. Decision makers need data to (Check all that apply)

❑ make decisions about continuing programs
❑ determine what's working in their organization
❑ determine what's not working in their organization
❑ determine worth of a program
_____

4. Views of the purposes of evaluation have been incorporated into program Evaluation Standards developed by The Joint Committee on Standards for Education Administration.

❑ True
❑ False
_____

Check

Practice
_____

Question#	Question	Correct Answer	Student Answer	Feedback
1	Evaluation is one of the ways that decision makers can improve their organization.	1	1	
2	Two types of evaluation are: _____ and _____.	formative OR summative OR formal OR informal	formal and informative	Types of evaluation include formative, summative or formal and informal.
3	Decision makers need data to	1, 2, 3, 4	2, 3, 4	
4	Views of the purposes of evaluation have been incorporated into Program Evaluation Standards developed by The Joint Committee on Standards for Education Administration.	2	2	

Score: 50

Figure 6.4   Summative assessment development options in an LMS.

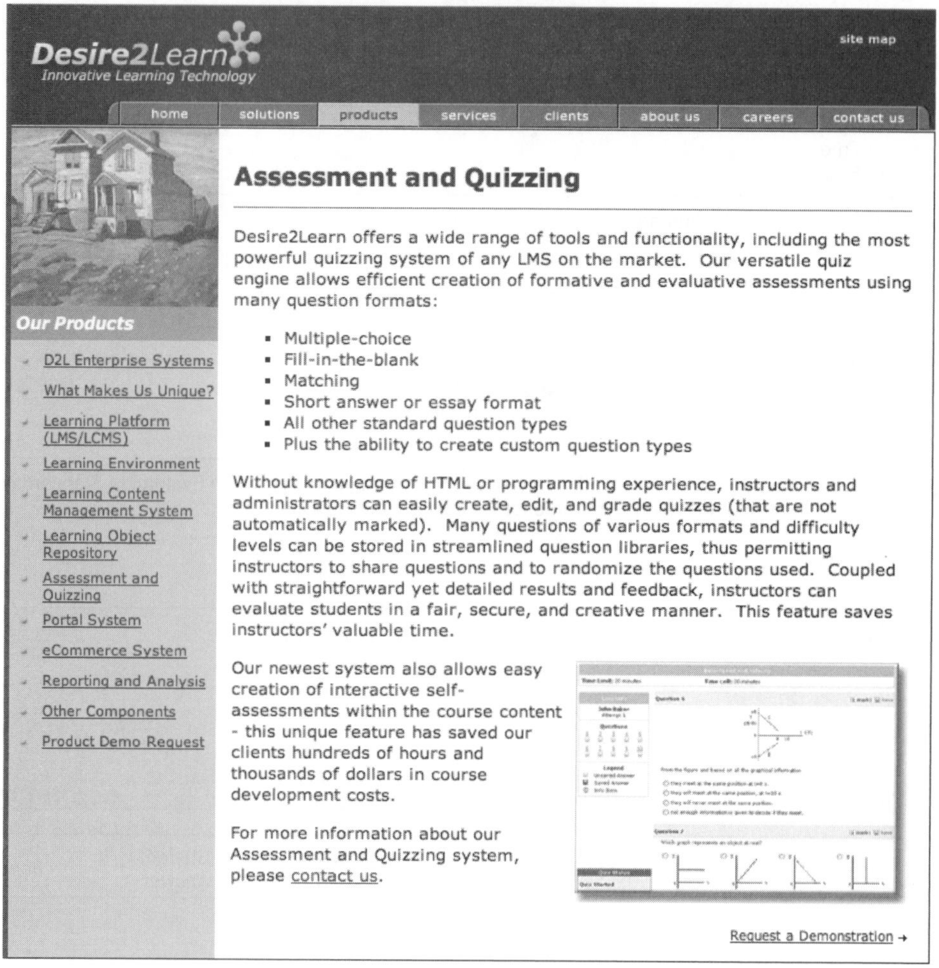

Source: Reprinted from http://www.Desire2Learn.com. Reprinted by permission of Desire2Learn, Inc.

Traditional Assessments

Traditional assessment items are familiar to most learners, instructors, and designers; they include multiple-choice, short answer, completion and true/false questions, and extended- or restricted-range essays. They are considered as either objective or subjective items (Kubiszyn & Borich, 1987; Shrock & Coscarelli, 2000; Smith & Ragan, 2005). With traditional assessments, answers are usually scored with an answer key (for fixed answer tests) or a scoring guide (for extended- or restricted-range essays).

These assessments can be formatted into WBI, especially when an LMS allows for uploading both the assessment tool and the scoring key. Learner feedback for fixed-answer assessments can be automated, saving the instructor time (Berge et al., 2000; Popham, 2002). Some LMSs permit advanced, automatic evaluation of word-based responses such as might be found in a fill-in-the-blank or short answer (restricted-range) essay. However, any computer-interpreted results should be reviewed to make sure that the scoring algorithm correctly evaluates learners' responses.

Alternative Assessments

Alternative assessments may be used in a Web-based environment (Brualdi, 2001; Davidson-Shivers & Rasmussen, 1999; Rasmussen & Northrup, 2000). Other terms, such as *performance* and *authentic,* are often interchanged with the term *alternative.* Popham (2002) opposes the use of *authentic* because it suggests that other types of tests are not genuine or valid. According to Popham, **alternative assessment** is defined as "meaningfully different tests intended for use with disabled or otherwise limited students so that more valid inference can be made about the students than if the original test were used" (p. 363). Yet, others (e.g., Fisher, 2000; Gronlund, 2003; Johnson & Johnson, 2002; Kubisyn & Borich, 1987; Rasmussen & Northrup, 1999) do not limit the term *alternative* to students with special needs and change the focus of the definition to any assessments that are not categorized as traditional.

Alternative assessments expand the possibilities for determining how learners meet objectives and include performance demonstrations, portfolios, and projects and products, such as papers, journals, and so on (Stiggins, 2005). Fisher (2000) suggests that this type of assessment assumes that there may be more than one product or type of product produced by the learners and rubrics or checklists may be a way to evaluate these types of assessments. Alternative assessments fit well with cognitive and constructivist approaches to learning (Jonassen, 1999; Ormrod, 2004), but are not limited to these two theory bases.

An LMS can facilitate the use of alternative assessments. Learners can submit work (including documents and multimedia products) and other assignments to the instructor via email, the Web, or through other LMS features such as drop boxes or document sharing (eCollege.com, 1999). If necessary, learners can submit work by postal services or faxes when electronic submission is not possible. The instructor can use the same means to provide feedback on the assignments and assessments.

Assessment Quantity and Quality

When considering quality and quantity of assessment, the needs of the learners must be met. Johnson and Johnson (2002) suggest that assessments must be meaningful. Assessments should align to the learning task and objective; they must be relevant to the learner, instructional content, and outcome (or expectations for student learning).

It can be difficult to evaluate learner performance due to the nature of WBI. Without the benefit of "seeing" the learner, there may be a tendency to include more assessment measures than necessary to verify that the objectives are mastered. For example, WBI instructors may attempt to assess every learner response because they are available for review; learners may expect that everything submitted must be evaluated as well. In face-to-face classrooms, where events such as discussions, small-group activities, and lectures predominate, learners are not assessed for every response or activity. Each individual objective does not have to be formally assessed to determine overall learner success. Instead, assessments can cover a set of objectives and course topics. Online assessments can mirror face-to-face learning environments.

It is not necessary to formally score all assessments, activities, and assignments within WBI. It is best to reserve scoring and feedback for those summative assessments that examine the student demonstration or final performance of a specified objective or instructional goal. Instructors and learners can be easily overwhelmed with excessive assessments. It is important that the designer remembers that every time an assessment is required of a student, the instructor must provide feedback and reinforcement to each WBI participant individually.

Two other factors to consider when determining the quantity and quality of assessments are the number of learners enrolled and the type(s) of assessment selected. With large course enrollments, evaluating essays or complex development projects may be too time consuming for a lone instructor. Instead, an objective type of assessment, such as a multiple-choice test, may be chosen as a feasible *and reasonable* alternative. In large classes where alternative assessments are used, teaching or graduate assistants may be employed to help in grading. However, the type of assessment chosen must remain congruent with the WBI goal and objectives.

The designer also must carefully consider the best placement of the assessments within the WBI. Formal courses tend to use midterms and final exams or final products to assess the value of student work. Measuring student performance within WBI can occur at major steps within the instructional task to ensure that learners are making progress toward the final instructional goal.

Assessment Security

One of the overriding issues of assessment relates to the security of the process itself (Alagumalai et al., 2000; Zhang, Khan, Gibbons, & Ni, 2001). When alternative assessment (essays, review of literature, papers, reports, projects, etc.) are used, **plagiarism** (stealing others' work) and other forms of cheating may all too easily occur. The advent of the Web has made access to and improper use of work written or produced by others a relatively recent and widespread phenomenon (*20/20*, 2004; CNN News, 2004; Fox News, 2004). Plagiarism, copying others' work, and not using proper documentation appear to be common problems on both college and PK–12 school campuses. Universities and PK–12 schools are taking necessary precautions to combat these forms of academic dishonesty by upgrading their student conduct policies, providing instruction on what is proper and improper use of others' work, and obtaining software that can be used to review student work for plagiarism. Software tools, such as those available from iThenticate.com and Turnitin.com (iParadigms LLC, 2005a, 2005b) are available to individuals and institutions for free or for purchase.

For the most part, an instructor cannot be absolutely sure that a learner "on the other end" is actually the registered learner or person performing the tasks. However, instructors in face-to-face classrooms may share similar difficulties (take-home tests, project-based assessments, etc.).

To reduce security breaches in assessment, the designer or instructor should address the following questions:

- How critical is personal performance?
- Will online learners be able to complete assessments at the host site or other resident sites?
- What types of assessment (traditional or alternative, formal or informal) will be used?

The answers to these questions depend to some degree on the type of WBI offered. Each situation requires that the designer determine the most appropriate assessment type. For example, when assessment is critical, learners may be required to attend proctored sessions where identification is mandatory. A less critical assessment might use open-book or timed tests.

A new technology that may heighten Web-based assessment security is the Webcam. This emerging technology has been proposed to meet the needs of instructional delivery for students who are at a distance either by choice or by mandate (Schouten, 2004). The logical extension of the use of Webcams is integrating them into a testing situation, which can provide an additional level of security to situations that require it.

See this textbook's Companion Website (http://www.prenhall.com/davidson-shivers) for links to websites related to assessment security.

Completing the TOAB with Assessment Items

The last column on the TOAB allows the designer to insert a sample assessment item or an explanation of how the objective and students' work (or performance) will be assessed. Again, the sample or the full assessment tool must be congruent with the other parts of the TOAB. The designer may include technological directions to assist the person who will create the final assessment tool(s). Assessment tool(s) can be completed at this time, which may be important when alternative assessments are being used or when rubrics, scoring guides, or checklists are needed to evaluate learner responses. Table 6.6 shows sample assessment items that correspond to the sample learning tasks and objectives previously shown.

Table 6.6 Examples of a Completed Row of a TOAB from Various WBI Projects, with Various Topics

Task Item	Objective	Learning Outcome	Assessment Item
Topic: History 5.0 Explain Waterloo events.	Given the question about the events leading to the Battle of Waterloo, the SWBAT explain the important events leading up to the battle according to their textbook.	Intellectual Skill: Defined Concept	In the following threaded discussion, select one event that led to the Battle of Waterloo. Explain how that event helped to lead up to the battle. INSERT THREADED DISCUSSION LINK

(continued)

Table 6.6   Examples of a Completed Row of a TOAB from Various WBI Projects, with Various Topics (*Continued*)

Task Item	Objective	Learning Outcome	Assessment Item
Topic: Geography			
1.1 List state capitals.	Given a map of the United States and a list of capitals, the SWBAT match states with capitals with at least 42 of 50 correct.	Verbal Information	In the following graphic, match the name of the state with its capital. INSERT GRAPHIC OF UNITED STATES
Topic: Leaves			
2.6 Identify maple leaves.	Given 10 drawings of different leaves, the LWBATname the type of tree from which it came with 80 percent accuracy.	Intellectual Skill: Concrete Concept	From the following drawings, select the leaf that is from a maple tree. INSERT EXAMPLES OF LEAVES, PROGRAM CORRECT AND INCORRECT RESPONSES
Topic: Résumé			
4.2 Format résumé.	Given a sample of appropriate and inappropriate information for a résumé, the participant will be able to format a résumé for a business environment using only appropriate information, with only one error.	Intellectual Skill: Rule-using	You are applying for a new position as an account executive for a marketing firm. Format a résumé that showcases your skills. Once completed, email the draft to your peer reviewer for feedback. After making changes, send your final résumé to the drop box.
Topic: Tourism Marketing			
9.1 Create tourism brochure.	Given websites, other supporting information, and publishing software application, the employee will be able to produce a tourism brochure that has unique design and will increase marketing shares for beach businesses by 10 percent.	Intellectual Skill: Problem Solving	You have been hired to create a brochure to encourage tourism in your town. Use the Web and your town's marketing materials to create your brochure. Share your creation with at least two other classmates for feedback. Incorporate their suggestions where possible. When you've completed your brochure, email it to the instructor.

GardenScapes

Kally and Elliott decide to use a performance-based, alternative assessment for *GardenScapes*. Because the participants are developing their own garden design plans, evidence of performance is required to evaluate their mastery of the goal. They will conduct a series of formative assessments using chats, threaded discussions, and email.

Learners will be encouraged to participate in a series of formative assessments to gauge their progress toward reaching the goal. Summative assessments will occur at the end of the course, when learners submit their garden plan. (Depending on the location of the participants, some may actually create their garden; although it will not be a course requirement.) Individual assessment security is not an issue because GardenScapes is a continuing education course and not a requirement of a degree program.

Elliott and Kally finish the TOAB; the following is a sample of their assessment items.

 See this textbook's Companion Website (http://www.prenhall.com/davidson-shivers) for the complete TOAB and assessment checklist.

Selected Items from the Completed TOAB for *GardenScapes*

Task Item and Number	Objective	Outcome Level	Assessment Item
Develop a garden design plan. End-of-course objective	Given a site for a garden, LWBAT develop a garden design plan that is appropriate to location and conditions.	Intellectual Skill: Problem solving	Garden Plan Checklist includes Plants appropriate to selected theme and site? Is there a focal point? Do proposed plants meet the requirements of the design plan? Do the color, size, and shape of proposed bloom or foliage complement each other? Is design in scale and appropriate to site, location, conditions, etc.? Does the plan provide appropriate legend?
1.0 Select garden theme.	Given an array of potential themes, LWBAT select a garden theme that is appropriate to location and conditions.	Intellectual Skill: Defined concepts	Which of the garden themes will you choose for your garden design plan? Why? (Insert list of garden themes) INSERT THREADED DISCUSSION LINK
1.1 State color theme.	When asked the question, What are the various types of garden themes?, LWBAT state color themed garden as one of them.	Verbal information	What are the various types of garden themes?
This process continues until all skills and subskills have been listed.			(Answer Key lists themes. Students will put in their journal.)

To help learners attain the desired performance and to assess their mastery, Elliott and Kally create a checklist and rubric with scoring descriptors for each final assessment scoring category.

Checklist Item for End of Course Objective	Score
Plants appropriate to selected theme and site?	5 4 3 2 1 COMMENTS:

Score descriptors:
5 = Theme and site well defined and all plants appropriate to theme/site
4 = Theme and site well defined and most plants appropriate to theme/site
3 = Theme and site satisfactorily defined and most plants appropriate to theme/site
2 = Theme and site less adequately defined and some plants appropriate to theme/site
1 = Theme and site minimally to poorly defined and few plants appropriate to theme/site

Is there a focal point?	5 4 3 2 1 COMMENTS:

Score descriptors:
5 = Focal point well defined and well placed on plan
4 = Focal point well defined and good placement on plan
3 = Focal point satisfactorily defined and placed on plan
2 = Focal point adequately defined and placed on plan
1 = Focal point minimally to poorly defined and placed on plan

This process continues until the complete objective checklist has been created.

On Your Own

Decide on the type(s) of assessment and schedule for assessing student performance for your WBI. Consider creating a checklist or rubric for authentic assessment tools. When creating a rubric be sure to define your scoring descriptors. If using subjective tests (e.g., essays, short answer items), consider developing the questions and the scoring key.

Complete the last column of the TOAB. For *each* objective create a sample test item or indicate how an alternative assessment will be used for the objective. Be sure that you use the TOAB to review the sample items for congruence with stated objectives, learning outcomes, and the learning task item. Make whatever adjustments needed so that all TOAB elements correspond with each other.

(For illustrations of how other designers tackled these same issues, review the case studies appearing in the Extending Your Skills section at the end of this chapter.)

See this textbook's Companion Website (http://www.prenhall.com/davidson-shivers) for a printable version of the TOAB template.

Clustering the Objectives

The third design task in this part of the concurrent design stage is clustering the objectives. The designer *clusters,* or groups together, the objectives to prepare for designing the instructional strategies (*how* the instructional content will be presented and taught) (Smith & Ragan, 2005). This clustering process is a means to *chunk* the objectives and the culminating instructional content activities into pieces of information (Ormrod, 2004). When organizing the objectives into chunks, note that Miller (1956) found that individuals hold only seven pieces of information, plus or minus two, in working memory at any given time. Similarly, Mayer (2003) states, "you can actively think about only five or so different things at one time" (p. 16). However, the size of the chunk depends greatly on the complexity and difficulty of the task or content, the expertise and prior knowledge of the learner, and context factors, such as time allotted for the WBI or types of media used (e.g., text, graphics, or video).

Once grouped, the designer organizes the clustered objectives into a logical presentation sequence. One tactic for organizing these clustered objectives is to analyze them from a variety of perspectives. Clusters can be organized based on the following criteria:

- Common themes
- Process-related or procedural relationships (e.g., one objective must occur before another)
- Strategies appropriate for the content and learners (e.g., addressing new terminology as a beginning chunk of information rather than having new terms dispersed throughout the WBI, or vice versa)

Each cluster can be classified by the learning task numbers, by a descriptive name that may later become a unit heading, or by both. Within the cluster, the designer sequences the objectives to promote the greatest learning. The actual sequence depends on the complexity of the content, relationship among the objectives, and learners' needs and abilities.

The designer retains and includes the associated task item numbers for the objectives from the TOAB, which will clearly specify the objectives that are grouped together. Retaining the task numbers is useful during small-group or field trial evaluations. The designer can compare the tagged objectives/test items with the LTM to pinpoint any problems with the organization or sequence of the WBI (Dick et al., 2005; Smith, 1990; Smith & Ragan, 2005). For example, perhaps the content and activities for a given objective or clustered set come too late in the instructional sequence or the instructional line is set too high or too low (recall the meaning of the *instructional line* from Chapter 4).

For the Design Document, the designer identifies how the objectives have been clustered together by a name and/or the learning task item numbers to begin developing the instructional strategies. In some cases, the designer may need to include in the Design Document an explanation of the changes from the LTM sequencing to the current clustering of objectives. For instance, a designer should explain a change based on a decision to cluster all new terminology and their definitions at the beginning of the WBI rather than providing these definitions throughout the WBI.

GardenScapes

In the instructional content task analysis for *GardenScapes,* Elliott determines four general topics based on the four main steps identified in the LTM and listed in the TOAB. Elliott then clusters the objectives into four sets, which will evolve into four main lessons. He adds two additional lessons to the WBI, one for providing an overview/getting started information and another for course wrap-up and conclusion. Kally reviews the clustering of objectives and approves.

Elliott prefers to name the lessons based on the phrases used in the main steps; Kally wants to add themed, fun names for each lesson. Her reasoning is that she used fun names in her *Garden Basics* course and they were well received by the adult learners. Furthermore, as she explains to Elliott, she watches (and names several) broadcast and cable TV home improvement programs that use "catchy" titles or ones that are plays on words. Even though Elliott thinks that the names will be "too cute," he, once again, defers to Kally's wishes, but makes a note to ask end users about the lesson titles as part of the formative evaluation.

For his lesson names, Elliott uses the six main instructional sections with the identifying objective task numbers, as follows:

1. *Taking Stock: Getting Started (an overview of the course)*
2. *How Does Your Garden Grow? Choosing a Garden Theme (Objectives 1.0–1.5)*
3. *Getting to the Root of the Problem: Determining the Types of Plants for the Garden (Objectives 2.0, 2.1.1–2.3)*
4. *An Eye-Catching Site: Create a Garden Sketch (Objectives 3.0–3.9)*
5. *Weed All About it: Maintenance Plan for Your Garden (Objectives 4.0–4.5)*
6. *Way to Grow as a Gardener! (course wrapup, including suggestions for completing the garden project)*

Within each unit, Elliott organizes the individual objectives hierarchically, with the lower-level subskills leading to the higher-level ones. Because the course objectives are somewhat procedural, the cluster of objectives is similar to the sequence found in the LTM.

 See this textbook's Companion Website (http://www.prenhall.com/davidson-shivers) for the clustered objectives for *GardenScapes.*

 ## ON YOUR OWN

Complete the organization of your proposed WBI by clustering objectives into major topics, regardless of their order in the LTM. Chunk and sequence objectives logically within each cluster. Define each cluster with a name that you may use later as a unit title. Preserve and include the task item/objective numbers from the TOAB in your Design Document for added clarity as to how you grouped the objectives together.

(For illustrations of how other designers tackled these same issues, review the case studies appearing in the Extending Your Skills section at the end of this chapter.)

Wrapping Up

In this chapter, we defined the tasks associated with the concurrent design stage, and noted the preplanning tasks—identifying the design approach, identifying the concurrent design tasks and team members, and developing a timeline. We discussed the essential design tasks of writing objectives, writing assessment items and tools, and clustering objectives. Objectives may be written using a five- or a three-component format. With WBI, traditional assessment tools (e.g., objective-type tests and essays) and alternative assessments (projects, papers, journals, etc.) may be used. However, the learning task items, objectives, outcomes, and assessment items must be congruent and the TOAB helps to align them. Chapter 7 continues with the design tasks in the concurrent design stage, as we explore designing the instructional and motivational strategies. In Chapter 8, we focus on the development tasks of the concurrent design stage.

Expanding Your Expertise

1. How do the data from analysis and evaluation influence the design of WBI?
2. Consider this statement: "I can create any kind of instruction in a Web-based environment." Would you agree or disagree? Why?
3. What are the main WBI design tasks? In a project team, who should be responsible for these tasks? What kinds of skills do you think project members should possess?
4. Assessment is a critical part of learning environments. How does assessment in Web-based learning environments compare to traditional assessment?
5. Is it important to cluster objectives, even though they have been delineated in the LTM and on the TOAB? Explain why or why not.
6. Can you identify ways to streamline these first few tasks of the concurrent design stage in addition to those discussed in this chapter? Review the literature on instructional design procedures to identify ways to make this part of the process more efficient.

Extending Your Skills

PK–12 Schools

Megan Bifford has begun the concurrent design stage for the elementary science curriculum. Her design team is made up of herself and two fifth-grade teachers, Rhoda Cameron and Buzz Garrison, and the district science coordinator, Cassie Angus. The teachers who are serving as the SMEs will field test the WSI in their classrooms. Because the Internet and Web will be used, access to those parts of the lesson will be available only to students who have an Acceptable Use Policy (AUP) form on file that indicates that the student can use the Internet.

The AUP outlines the responsibilities of the school, teacher, and student when using technology and includes a section on acceptable use of the Internet. Both parent and child sign the AUP. Forms are kept in the Media Center. Rhoda and Buzz will inform parents about the new unit through their weekly class newsletters. They will ask parents to review their child's AUP to make sure that it accurately reflects their wishes about their child's access to the Internet.

Megan will serve as both designer and evaluator of the project, working closely with her fifth-grade SMEs. She has outlined the major tasks that she thinks should be accomplished. Because she's part of a very small team, she will use her SMEs as a resource for ensuring that she aligns the WSI to classroom activities. The anticipated start date of the instruction is the middle of the following grading period. The first time the instruction will be delivered will be considered the field trial.

With input from the teachers, Megan completes the objectives and the assessments in her TOAB for the units that will be considered WSI. Cassie reviews the objectives and assessments to make sure that they correspond to the essential elements for science education curriculum for fifth grade. Rhoda and Buzz review them to see how they will fit into their curriculum plans. Together Megan, Rhoda, and Buzz cluster the objectives and check for congruence with to the district's curriculum framework. In the TOAB, they identify objectives that they think can be met by the WSI. They share the TOAB with Cassie for feedback and advice.

Business and Industry

Homer Spotswood feels overwhelmed with all of the information that has been gathered in the analysis stage. His CEO, Bud Cattrell, would like to see design plans soon. Homer devises a Gantt chart that outlines the time frame for the concurrent design stage, and evaluation phases. He uses the tasks that he has earlier identified to create the timeline. At the same time, he identifies the tasks that he will be responsible for and those that the in-house staff in the training department will complete. Homer will have support from an IDT intern, Stacey McGee, who will work with him throughout the project. Greta Dottman will serve as the SME for the content and work with the in-house trainers as they complete the face-to-face component.

Homer completes the project's timeline. For the TOAB he asks Stacey to detail the objectives, outcomes, and potential assessments, being sure to include all of the objectives for this course, including those to be delivered in the face-to-face experience. To aid development of the WEI portion of the program, he highlights the objectives that will be delivered via the Web. It is very important that the two parts of the training support each other. When the draft is finished, he and Stacey meet with Greta, who confirms the validity of the objectives. After clustering the objectives, Homer forwards them to the in-house trainers for their review and action.

Case Study 3   Military

The E^2C^2 development team is comprised of three groups, each with the responsibility to design the content of one of the three major topics. Each group's core includes a senior enlisted instructor/SME (a chief petty officer) and a civilian instructional designer. Graphic artists and animators support them.

Lts. Rex Danielson, Sandra Cole, and Bob Carroll work together to outline a timeline that includes tasks and task assignments to help their teams get started on the Web-based instruction project. Several tasks begin immediately. The SME from each team begins collecting instructional resources from current resident and text-based nonresident training courses that cover the selected, relevant topics. The instructional designers create draft objectives, based on the approved LTM. They develop a TOAB based on the LTM and insert the draft objectives. Working with the SMEs, they brainstorm ways to assess the objectives and create individual assessment items for each objective.

Case Study 4   Higher Education

Dr. Joe Shawn and his teaching assistant, Brian, use the *Introduction to Management* course syllabus as a base to finish revising the Web-enhanced course objectives and assessments. The syllabus is not as extensive as they need for this project. They expand objectives and develop specific assessments to meet these increasingly detailed objectives. Once they have finalized the objectives, Brian creates the TOAB to help organize the information. The university is scheduled to go through accreditation soon and course objectives must be in congruence with department, college, and university goals. The TOAB will be included in the course documentation. Based on the objectives and the textbook used for the class, he clusters the objectives into 10 groups. He uses the textbook chapter titles as his cluster names.

With the objectives completed and the clusters named, Dr. Shawn develops a course schedule, following the 16-week semester time frame in which he will deliver the class. He modifies his course assignment sheet to include a column where he will identify how the topic will be delivered. He reviews each cluster to see if it is appropriate to deliver via the Web. In some cases, he plans on lecturing on a topic and then using the University's LMS for discussion and assessment. For other sessions, the lecture and assignments will be entirely on the Web. Dr. Shawn feels that it is important for the students to know exactly what the class schedule and organization will be so that any confusion about class attendance is minimized. He uses the following form to help him get started.

Delivery (Web or Class)	Course Topic	Chapter	Class Assignments	Due Dates for Assignments
	Introduction			
	Overview of Management in a Dynamic World			
	Management as It Has Evolved			
	Global Environment of Management			
	Management and the Corporate Culture			
	Organizational Planning: Goal Setting, Strategy Implementation, and Decision Making			
	Organizing with Structural Design			
	Managing Human Resources and Diversity			
	Leadership in Action: Motivation, Communication, Conflict Resolution			
	Developing Teamwork with Empowerment Strategies			
	Controlling Information Technology, E-business, Operations, and Service Management			

The following applies to all case studies. Consider how you, as designer, might act or respond in each case study.

- What information is *not* presented that you would like to have had? How would you go about gathering that data?
- How do the earlier stages of the WBID Model influence the creation of the TOAB? How do these procedures differ for each case?
- What you would do differently from each of the principals in the case studies?

Chapter 7

Concurrent Design: Instructional and Motivational Strategy Planning

Once the objectives are clustered, the next set of essential design tasks in the concurrent design stage determine the instructional and motivational strategies for the WBI. Formative evaluation continues as the instructional strategies are described. To promote a sense of continuity, the designer uses a conceptual framework for describing these instructional and motivational strategies. The WBID Model provides the WBI Strategy Worksheet as the means to frame and document such strategies. While creating these strategies, the designer must bear in mind other factors that may impact the WBI and its delivery: class size, navigation, learner control, and feedback. The designer also must determine the types of media to incorporate into the WBI, if it hasn't already been pre-determined.

Chapter 7 begins with an overview of the main features in an LMS that influence the types of instructional and motivational strategies selected. A discussion of the conceptual framework guiding the design plan follows. We next describe the WBI Strategy Worksheet, which outlines the framework, and provide examples of how to use it. We then present two different motivational models and a description of basic WBI motivational strategies. The last section of this chapter presents several factors, including media selection, that affect the WBI design. Development tasks, the last part of the concurrent design stage, are the subject of Chapter 8.

Objectives

At the end of this chapter, you should be able to do the following:

- Identify the main features contained in an LMS.
- Identify the conceptual framework for the instructional and motivational strategies.
- Explain the purpose of the WBI Strategy Worksheet.
- State the purpose of providing an overview of the strategies for the entire WBI project.
- Identify the four main components of instructional strategies.
- Plan appropriate instructional strategies for each set of clustered objectives using the WBI Strategy Worksheet as a framework.
- Plan appropriate motivational strategies for each set of clustered objectives using the WBI Strategy Worksheet.
- Describe how factors such as class size, navigation, learner control, and feedback influence instructional and motivational strategies.
- Determine the appropriate media for a WBI project.

Introduction

This chapter focuses on selecting instructional and motivational strategies as part of the evolving WBI design plan (Figure 7.1). A major factor in designers' choice of strategies is whether they are using an LMS for the WBI. Each LMS has different features and capabilities, which mandate different strategic approaches. Certain features, however, are common to many LMSs.

- *Discussion forums* are features for asynchronous discussions. LMSs or free online discussion services may be able to track levels of discussion among individuals, display threads in a separate location and over the length of the course, permit connections to learner activities and other instructional features.
- *Chat rooms* are features for synchronous discussions. They may contain virtual whiteboards to show examples, means to monitor and discuss with individuals, archival capabilities, and so on.
- *Grouping capabilities* allow the instructor to divide the class into small groups. A small group may be able to discuss, chat, and share attachments among the group members, but not with the entire class. The instructor normally is able to monitor group activities.
- *Email capabilities* within the LMS permit broadcast and targeted communication among participants—learner to learner, learner to small group of learners, learner to instructor. Most systems allow senders to include attachments.

Figure 7.1 Design processes of the concurrent design stage of the WBID Model.

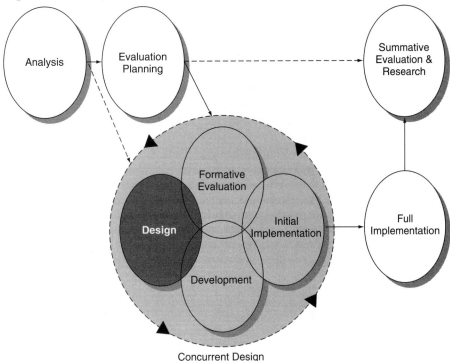

Concurrent Design

- *Lecture capabilities* allow instructional information to be presented via text, audio, and/or video. The LMS may allow inclusion of support materials such as *PowerPoint* or database documents. Lecture materials can typically be developed using a word processor or an HTML publisher, or may be added as an attachment.
- *Document sharing* permits readings, papers, videos, and so on to be shared by the instructor and the class participants. Generally, both learner and instructor are able to upload and download documents to and from the website.
- *Journals* allow learners to write their own reflections on content, activities, and so on as assigned. They may be reviewed by the instructor and the individual author, but not by other class members. Typically, instructors are able to append comments to the individual's entries.
- *Website linking* enables connections to external websites. Both instructor and student may identify and describe external sites.
- *Submission of assignments* allows assignments and assessments to be sent to the instructor. It may include the ability to attach files in a drop box. Individual students or the instructor may include a short message about the

assignment, and the instructor may provide feedback and send scores or grades to a gradebook and back to the individual.

- *Assessment capabilities* permit quizzes and exams to be designed and developed along with a scoring system. The LMS may allow instructors to designate a time frame for the exam to be accessed.
- *The gradebook* allows the instructor to assign, record, and distribute grades to each learner, documents user activity to various course activities, and records time spent in each activity. As the instructor posts scores for individual assignments, the gradebook calculates the percentage or points toward the final total. Generally, the instructor can access the gradebook as a whole or by individual class participant while maintaining privacy of individual student records.

Other LMS features may include management of participant registration, technical support, and so on, as briefly mentioned in Chapter 1. Because features and how they are set up differ, designers must evaluate the LMS for its capabilities and explore how they may facilitate designing the instructional strategies. Furthermore, LMSs continue to advance with each new upgrade or version. Not having an LMS available does not preclude a designer/instructor from incorporating such features into a WBI, although it may be more cumbersome to integrate disparate technologies together. Many of these features could be implemented without an LMS by using free tools available online such as *QuizStar* (4Teachers.org, 2004).

Conceptual Framework of the WBID Model

Up to this point, the emphasis has been on the "what" of the instruction (i.e., instructional content, learning task items, objectives, assessments). Now the designer must attend to the instructional strategies, the "how" of the WBI. Designers use instructional and motivational strategies to explain how the WBI will be developed and delivered. Appropriate instructional (and motivational) strategies promote a sense of continuity as learners progress from one section of the WBI to another and ensure that the information presented is clear and easy to read, see, or hear (Khan, 2001).

The kinds of strategies to incorporate into the WBI depends on the goals, objectives, and intent of the instruction. Goals that are aligned to upper levels of learning taxonomies, such as Bloom's Evaluation level, may require problem-solving techniques that are inherent in a constructivist learning environment. For example, learners might be presented with case studies or ill-structured problems to resolve. An added strategy might be to incorporate the use of experts and peers who work with learners to enhance social learning aspects of the WBI, following Vygotsky's theories (for an overview of these theories, see Kozulin, 2003).

The conceptual framework used in the WBID Model is based on several theories and models. The instructional strategies are based on Gagné's (1985) Nine Events of Instruction and the strategies of Dick et al. (2005), Gagné et al. (1992), and Smith and Ragan (2005). **Instructional strategies** are guidelines for presenting the instructional information and framing the WBI into a cohesive structure. Instructional strategies can be characterized as the structure of the learning community (Fisher, 2000). Many of the strategies used in traditional educational or training situations, such as lecture, discussion, question and answer, and reading assignments, can be used in WBI. Hall and Gottfredson (2001) suggest that other strategies, such as advance organizers or concept/site maps, be included. Innovative manipulation of these strategies to meet the technical requirements of the Web is dependent on the designer's and instructor's approach toward learning (i.e., behavioral, cognitive, constructivist, or multi-theoretical) and the purpose of the WBI (i.e., the instructional goal), and to some degree, on their abilities and imagination.

According to Pintrich and Schunk (2002), "motivation is a process whereby goal-directed activity is instigated and sustained" (p. 3). Alderman (1999) suggests that cognitive and emotional variables affect student achievement and would add that motivation has three functions, those of energizing or activating, directing, and regulating behavior. **Motivational strategies** are the methods related to those functions and are for encouraging learner participation, perseverance, and satisfaction in their learning. Both Keller's (1987, 1999) ARCS model and Wlodkowski and Ginsberg's (Wlodkowski, 1997; Wlodkowski & Ginsberg, 1995) theory on motivation could serve as the basis for the WBID conceptual framework.

There are four main components for the instructional strategies and four for the motivational strategies for the WBID Model. Generally speaking, the designer considers the instructional strategies first, although motivational strategies may come to mind while identifying instructional strategies. For clarity, our discussion of these two types of strategies will follow the same order; we begin with a description of the WBI Strategy Worksheet.

WBI Strategy Worksheet

The WBID Model provides another template, the WBI Strategy Worksheet, for describing the instructional and motivational strategies; this worksheet also becomes part of the Design Document. The worksheet is used to provide an overview of the instructional and motivational strategies of the entire WBI project and then may be used to further detail the design plans for each set of clustered objectives or unit of instruction (lesson, unit, module, etc.).

First, the WBI Strategy Worksheet allows the designer to provide the client/instructor and the other design team members with an overview, or outline, of how the four instructional strategy components are created and organized, what LMS or Web features will be employed, and when they will be used. Likewise, it provides an overview of the motivational strategies and explains how the WBI will direct learner motivation. Providing this overview early allows for the client/instructor and design team to develop a conceptual understanding of the WBI project. Additionally, this approach helps to elicit any necessary changes in the WBI design and ultimately, project design approval, when needed.

Second, the WBI Strategy Worksheet is used to describe the detailed design plans for each set of clustered objectives (i.e., unit of instruction). Once the overview is provided and approved, the design team uses the conceptual framework as stated in the worksheet to select and explain the strategies involved for each set.

The WBI Strategy Worksheet, however, is not a rigid, inflexible document, nor is the conceptual framework on which it is based. It may be adapted to include or exclude components (and subcomponents) according to the designer's or instructor's theoretical approach to learning. Table 7.1 presents the template for the WBI Strategy Worksheet.

The two components, Orientation to Learning and Instruction on the Content, will be described for each clustered objective (or unit of instruction) in the WBI. The component, Measurement of Learning, is detailed only when assessment is occurring in or at the end of that unit; otherwise, it is described in the WBI overview. Likewise, not every unit of instruction requires the final component, Summary and Close, because a subcomponent in Instruction on the Content provides for a review and closing of the module. However, short

Table 7.1 Instructional Strategy Components and Subcomponents of the Conceptual Framework as Identified on the WBI Strategy Worksheet

Orientation to Learning	**Instructional Strategies**
1. Provide an overview	
2. State the objectives	
3. Explain relevance of instruction	
4. Assist learner recall of prior knowledge, skills, and experiences	
5. Provide directions on how to start, navigate, and proceed through the unit of instruction	
Instruction on the Content	**Instructional Strategies**
1. Present instructional content	
2. Provide learning cues	
3. Present opportunities for practice	
4. Provide feedback on practice performance	
5. Provide review of and close the unit of instruction	
Measurement of Learning	**Instructional Strategies**
1. Assess performance	
2. Advise learner of performance scores	
Summary and Close	**Instructional Strategies**
1. Enhance and enrich learning	
2. Provide remediation for unmet objectives	
3. Provide opportunities for retention	

summaries may be appropriate to help learners make sense of the lesson and bridge their thoughts to the next section of instruction.

When working on a WBI that has multiple sets of clustered objectives, it is less confusing to detail the strategies for one unit of instruction before describing the strategies for the next unit. Nonetheless, if several designers are working on the project, then, of course, multiple units can be designed simultaneously. It is important to note that strategy development for each cluster of objectives is an iterative process and that these development tasks may begin once the design plan for that cluster is tentatively created.

Instructional Strategies for WBI

Within the WBID Model, the conceptual framework for the instructional strategies is comprised of four main components: Orientation to Learning, Instruction on the Content, Measurement of Learning, and Summary and Close. Each of these components contains several subcomponents, as shown in Table 7.1. The designer identifies and explains each included component so that the design team understands clearly the development of the WBI prototype(s) and the WBI delivery.

Yet, the amount of detail contained in the WBI Strategy Worksheet depends on the design team and how the design process functions. For example, when design is a collaborative and integrated effort, communication between and among team members can be open, with all members aware of each others' activities, design decisions, and so on. However, when the design team has individual members working on segregated parts of the project, careful documentation is required for the WBI to remain true to its design concept. In other words, the WBI Strategy Worksheet should provide enough explanation and description so that anyone on the design team could develop the WBI from it and any client/instructor would be able to conceptualize the WBI based on the descriptions. Again, the WBI Strategy Worksheet may be an outline of key concepts or information about the content and activities when used by a lone designer/instructor.

Although the four main components have a somewhat obvious specified order (i.e., Orientation implies a beginning and Summary and Close implies an ending), the subcomponents within each may be presented in any order, may be combined, or in some instances, omitted.

In the following discussion, we describe the instructional strategy components and subcomponents as being for a set of clustered objectives, or unit of instruction, rather than for an overview of the WBI.

Orientation to Learning

Orientation to Learning is an introduction to each unit of instruction within the WBI. This orientation sets the stage for the unit of instruction, outlines the instructional expectations, and facilitates the learner in completing the activities and assignments and learning the content. Additionally, this first component provides the general directions for proceeding through the unit by suggesting or mandating the order for completing activities and assignments.

Orientation to Learning, as the unit overview, is relatively short in terms of the amount of time learners spend in it as compared to the other three components. It has five subcomponents:

1. Provide an *overview* or advance organizer
2. State the unit *objectives* and desired performance outcomes
3. Explain the *relevance* of the unit for the learner
4. Assist in the learner's *recall* of prior knowledge, skills, or experiences
5. Provide the *directions* on how to get started and navigate through the unit activities

For the first unit of instruction, especially if it introduces the WBI course, these subcomponents need to direct learners toward important aspects of the entire WBI. Instructions for how to start the WBI may be needed for novice online learners; however, directions should be stated concisely and be optional for those with online experience. For the remaining units, the purposes of this component are to direct learners to the instructional content and purposes and to connect prior knowledge with new learning (Gagné & Medsker, 1996; Jonassen & Grabowksi, 1993; Mayer, 2003).

When drafting orientation strategies, placement of the units must be considered based on the sequencing of the clustered objectives (i.e., whether procedural, hierarchical, or a combination of both). For example, in a procedural sequence, units that appear early in the WBI may require extensive directions for how to use the website correctly. Later units that build on previous information do not have to repeat established directions and procedures. A random ordering of the units of instruction allows for the units to be opened and used in any sequence; in such instances, the directions and orientations may need to be explained on the home page of the WBI and minimally in each unit to not confuse the learner about how to proceed through the WBI.

The instructional strategies selected for the Orientation to Learning component must be meaningful and interesting to direct learners to the unit's content and purpose. Designing a flashy site that simply draws learners' attention, but is not related to content or purpose, is a waste of time (Bonk, 2004; Davidson-Shivers, 1998, 2001). The following instructional strategies are suitable for Orientation to Learning components:

- A relevant video or audio clip, or graphic describing the topic
- An opening question or problem related to the instructional objectives and content that is then addressed or resolved in the unit
- A relevant scenario or situation that is discussed throughout the unit
- Telling a pertinent story that illustrates the purpose of the unit
- A preview of the lesson (in text or graphics)
- An advance organizer

Table 7.2 Instructional Strategies for the Orientation to Learning Component as Indicated on the WBI Strategy Worksheet

Orientation to Learning Subcomponents	Instructional Strategies
1. **Provide an overview**	Text describing the lesson or course; Concept map; Graphical or text organizer; Course description; Story; Scenarios; etc. Demonstrate outcomes; Welcome and introductory statement; etc.
2. **State the objectives and desired performance outcomes**	Course syllabus or information; Icebreakers; List of goals and purposes; List of expected performance; Ask opening questions; Demonstrate outcomes; etc.
3. **Explain relevance of the instruction**	Scenarios; Examples; Games; Icebreaker; Stories; etc.
4. **Assist learner recall of prior knowledge, skills, and experiences**	Advance organizer; Pretest; Checklists; Share or recall relevant experiences; etc.
5. **Provide directions for how the learner is to start, navigate, and proceed through lesson**	Tutorial; Welcome letter; Site map; Site search; Specific directions for completing assignments; etc.

Source: Table data are from Bonk (2004), Davidson-Shivers (1998), Davidson-Shivers, Salazar, & Hamilton (2002; in press), Fisher (2000), Gagné (1985), Hall & Gottfredson (2001), Keller (1987), Khan (2001), Palloff & Pratt (1999), Rasmussen (2002), Smith & Ragan (2005).

Such instructional strategies draw awareness to the lesson by directing learners' attention to the lesson at hand and raising their expectations for learning. They provide relevance by evoking a sense of familiarity, confidence, or linkage to learners' own personal goals (Jonassen & Grabowski, 1993; Mayer, 2003; Ormrod, 2004). Table 7.2 provides examples of the instructional strategies for each of the five subcomponents; any duplication of strategies is intentional in that an instructional strategy may be relevant to one or more of the subcomponents.

GardenScapes

Elliott provides an overview for the entire WBI course using the WBI Strategy Worksheet. Kally reviews the strategies and offers suggestions that reflect her teaching style. Elliott and Kally discuss her suggested changes. Their results are as follows.

GardenScapes WBI Strategy Worksheet

Orientation to Learning	Overview of the Instructional Strategies for *GardenScapes*
1. Provide an overview for entire course	Learners will be introduced to the WBI by the following: • A welcome statement describes the benefits of having a beautiful outdoor garden where spring, summer, and perhaps, fall evenings are spent viewing their garden and nature (birds, butterflies, etc.). (Possibly a short audio clip as visuals are shown.) • Learners are invited into the outdoors through a beautiful doorway or arch. An animated garden with graphics will show different gardens with various themes. • After welcoming statement, 2 graphics will be displayed: Garden needing extensive help and a picturesque scene. (Pictures may be photos, line art, or clip art.) • A short overview of the content for the units is provided ***after*** their main objectives are presented. • Photos of instructor and other staff for the course are included.
2. State goal and main objectives 3. Explain relevance of WBI	• A short video addresses why create a themed garden. • The goal and main objectives of WBI are listed. • The pictures in the overview provide the idea that anyone can create a garden. • Learners will be invited to participate in an opening icebreaker.
4. Assist learner recall of prior knowledge, skills, and experience	• The opening icebreaker asks learners to share their prior gardening experiences. • The discussion helps them get to know each other. • Participants are to share their photos, a short biography, and gardening experiences.
5. Provide directions on how to proceed through WBI	• Directions on how to use the website are included. • A link to a site map is displayed. • A link is supplied to a tutorial on online learning and how to use the LMS.
Orientation to Learning for Lessons Strategies repeated at beginning of each lesson	**Overview of Instructional Strategies for Lessons 1–6** • A welcome statement is presented (audio clip by the instructor accompanying visuals). • A question is posed for recalling the last lesson and connecting to this one. • A scenario highlights topics in the content (includes pictures or short video clip). • The lesson objectives are presented. • Directions on getting the lesson started are provided.

Note: Rather than showing all of the overview at this point, the remaining sections will appear as we discuss each of the remaining three instructional strategy components.

Once the strategies for the entire WBI are reviewed and approved, Elliott and Kally begin work on the detailed descriptions for each of the *GardenScapes* units. They decide to incorporate most of the instructional strategies outlined in the course overview into the first lesson because it is the introduction to the WBI. Elliott varies the instructional strategies for the remaining units based on the course content and purposes. The instructional strategies detailed for the second lesson of *GardenScapes* follow.

GardenScapes WBI Strategy Worksheet

Orientation to Learning	Detailed Instructional Strategies for Lesson 2: How Does Your Garden Grow? Choosing a Garden Theme
1. **Provide an overview**	• A welcoming statement and introduction to Lesson 2 is presented. • (1- or 2-minute audio clip by the instructor over photos of themed gardens).
2. **State the objectives and desired performance outcomes**	• The main objective for Lesson 2: To select a garden theme from 5 types of gardens. • Other objectives relate to the naming the types of gardens. • Audio by instructor states the main objective. • All are listed at beginning of the text-based lecture notes in conversational tone of voice.
3. **Explain relevance of the instruction**	• Participants identify a garden shown in the welcome that they liked best. • Responses are posted to journal, document sharing, or email to instructor.
4. **Assist learner recall of prior knowledge, skills, and experiences**	• Ask participants to recall their favorite gardens from their past. • Either share later in discussion or post to journal.
5. **Provide directions on how to start, navigate, and proceed through the lesson**	• Directions for the Lesson 2 assignments are provided at the end of brief, text-based lecture. • Students are to refer back to Lesson 1 for general directions and to the tutorial. • *For technical problems or questions, a discussion site is provided for peers and mentor to use. If serious problems arise, students are directed to send email to the mentor.

*Although not an actual part of the content of this *GardenScapes* lesson, addressing technical problems facilitates learning.

Kally takes time to evaluate and comment on Lesson 1 as Elliott works on Lesson 2. As he works, Elliott thinks about strategies that might work in other *GardenScapes* lessons. However, he does *not* start working on them until he has moved into the development tasks for Lessons 1 and 2. Because he is the only designer on this project, it would be too confusing to work on all of the lessons simultaneously. He knows how good ideas "evaporate into thin air" if they aren't written down somewhere; he begins a tickler file for these ideas and stores them on a disk; he asks Kally to do the same thing.

See this textbook's Companion Website (http://www.prenhall.com/davidson-shivers) for the *GardenScapes* Design Document.

ON YOUR OWN

For your project, use the WBI Strategy Worksheet (see Table 7.1) to provide an overview of the entire WBI design for your project. Once that is completed (and possibly reviewed and approved), provide a detailed plan for each of your clustered objectives. The worksheet is a part of your Design Document and should provide enough explanation and description that *anyone* on the design team could develop the WBI from it. Be sure to have your design plans evaluated and approved as necessary.

Begin developing the instructional strategies for the Orientation to Learning for your first unit of instruction. Use the WBI Strategy Worksheet to detail and document the strategies, following the template given in Table 7.2. Create strategies that are appropriate to the instructional goal, learners, content, and learning tasks. Make sure that your orientation strategies reflect your theoretical approach to learning, as well. Describe the strategies in such a way that resulting Web pages can be developed. Remember, this part of concurrent design is a description of *how* to present the instruction, *not* the actual development of the plans.

For each unit of instruction, plan the instructional strategies for Orientation to Learning. If you are the lone designer/instructor, you may find it easiest to complete one unit's detailed description before starting another. If more than one designer is involved in the project, then multiple units may be started at the same time. Again, the detailed unit design plans are evaluated as designated in your formative evaluation plan and according to your project's timeline.

(For illustrations of how other designers tackled these same issues, review the case studies appearing in the Extending Your Skills section at the end of this chapter.)

See this textbook's Companion Website (http://www.prenhall.com/davidson-shivers) for a printable version of the WBI Strategy Worksheet template.

Instruction on the Content

The second instructional strategy component, Instruction on the Content, contains the subcomponents of presenting the content or information and providing learning cues, learner practice, and feedback. Instruction on the Content is the component where the major portion of teaching and learning takes place and is the most important component of any WBI. Because learners typically spend most of their time in this component per unit of instruction, a significant and proportional amount of design time should be spent in planning and developing these strategies.

Instruction on the Content is not presented in one large section; rather, it is broken into appropriately sized chunks (Mager, 1997; Mayer, 2003; Ormrod, 2004), based on the clustering of the objectives. The five subcomponents of Instruction on the Content appear within each unit or lesson. These subcomponents are repeated until all clustered objective sets and their associated objectives have been presented and practiced:

1. Present *content information*
2. Provide *learning cues*
3. Present opportunities for *practice*
4. Provide *feedback* on practice performance
5. Provide *review* of and close the unit of instruction

Similar to Orientation to Learning, these five subcomponents may be placed in any order, combined, or omitted. Table 7.3 presents examples of the instructional strategies for each subcomponent. Again, any duplication of the strategies is intentional in that an instructional strategy may be relevant to one or more subcomponent.

Table 7.3 Instructional Strategies for Instruction on the Content as Indicated on the WBI Strategy Worksheet

Instruction on the Content Subcomponents	Instructional Strategies

1. **Present content information**	• Direct instruction through presentations using text, audio, multimedia, streaming audio/video lectures, etc.
	 • Elaborate on the content by using
	  • explanation and
	  • examples and nonexamples with
	  • graphics and
	  • text-based descriptions
	 • Case studies or problems
	 • Project-based learning, inquiry-based learning, tutorials, etc.
	 • Simulations and games
	 • Interaction with experts, discovery learning
	 • Collaborative, cooperative, competitive, or independent learning situations
	 • Demonstrations
	 • Modeling
	 • Reading assignments or reviewing websites
	 • Library and Web searches for information
	 • Student-led presentations or discussions

2. **Provide learning cues**	• Socratic dialogue or method • Ask key questions via email, threaded discussion, chats, or within lecture • Use graphics or audio to guide the learner through the unit or WBI • Suggest appropriate learning strategies • Highlight key information visually or audibly (use *PowerPoint* slides, for instance) • Emphasize text (boldface, italics [but not underline unless hyperlinked to other information] etc.) • Use apprenticeship or mentoring to guide learning

(continued)

Table 7.3 Instructional Strategies for Instruction on the Content as Indicated on the WBI Strategy Worksheet *(Continued)*

Instruction on the Content Subcomponents	Instructional Strategies
3. **Present opportunities for practice**	• Games, simulations, laboratories • Role playing • WebQuests (Dodge, 1997) or Web research • Virtual field trips • Reciprocal teaching • Discussion groups, seminars • Group or individual investigations • Debates • Question and answer sessions • Drill and practice • Exercises (problems to work through, questions to respond to, reflective thinking exercises, etc.) • Reflection papers or journals • Projects, portfolios, papers • Case studies
4. **Provide feedback on the practice performance**	• Peer review • Discussions • Conferences • Instructor or mentor responses to learner practice • Feedback from LMS
5. **Provide review of and close the unit of instruction**	• Review previous learning throughout the unit or lesson • Summarize topic or lesson by instructor or students • End lesson with preview of next topic(s) or next task(s) • Use text, video, or audio Wrap-ups

Source: Table data are from Bonk, Daytner, Daytner, Dennen, & Malikowski (2001), Cheney, Warner, & Laing (2001), Chi-Yung & Shing-Chi (2000), Davidson-Shivers (1998; 2001), Davidson-Shivers, Salazar, & Hamilton (2002; in press), Dodge (1997), Gagné (1985), Gibbons, Lawless, Anderson & Duffin (2001), Hughes & Hewson (2001), Kemery (2001), Khan (2001), Northrup & Rasmussen (2001), Smith & Ragan (2005), Trentin (2001).

GardenScapes

Elliott and Kally's overview of the entire WBI project contains an outline for the Instruction on the Content strategies; it appears on their WBI Strategy Worksheet.

Instruction on the Content	Overview of the Instructional Strategies for *GardenScapes*
1. **Present content information**	For each lesson, the content will be structured so participants can move through the content in a specified order (based on LTM). The lessons will include: • Use of short, text-based lectures. • Use conversational tone with explanations, descriptions, etc. • Use of garden examples and nonexamples related to concepts and principles presented (e.g., garden themes, specific planning worksheets for a garden, etc.). • Graphics such as pictures, charts, etc. in examples and nonexamples. • Garden expert to present information. • Links to other websites for additional information. • Recommended readings or books on garden and landscape planning will be assigned for further study.
2. **Provide learning cues**	• Visuals to support main points of lectures. • Relevant examples of a variety of temporal zones will be presented. • Tap into prior knowledge of basic gardening as related to new content. • Provide a checklist (job aids) to keep participants on a track with weekly tasks or assignments. • Provide worksheets for assignments (planning sheet, etc.).
3. **Present opportunities for practice**	• Practice activities for learners in collaboration with partners. • Share ideas with each other (e.g., chosen themes, colors, plant choices, design planning sheets, etc.). • Question and answer (Q&A) sessions in occasional chats or threaded discussion (i.e., not every unit).
4. **Provide feedback on practice**	• Peers, instructor, or mentor provide feedback in Q&A sessions via chats or threaded discussions. • Specific questions will be addressed via email by instructor or mentor. • Instructor reviews assignments submitted in document sharing or drop box and returns feedback.
5. **Provide review of and close the lesson**	• Instructor creates summaries that highlight main points of content and activities at end of each lesson (by email or threaded discussion).

After the overview is approved by Carlos and Dr. Chauncy, Elliott and Kally design the instructional strategies for the Instruction on the Content for Lessons 1 and 2. The strategies for Lesson 2 follow. (The first theme only appears here.).

See this textbook's Companion Website (http://www.prenhall.com/davidson-shivers) for the complete WBI Strategy Worksheet in the *GardenScapes* Design Document.

WBI Strategy Worksheet

Instruction on the Content	Detailed Instructional Strategies for Lesson 2: *How Does Your Garden Grow? Choosing a Garden Theme*
1. **Present content information**	After the main objective is stated (audio), the text-based lecture notes for garden themes will • Define the term *garden theme*. • Identify and explain five themes: color, cottage, xeriscape, wildlife, and cutting garden. • Allow students to maneuver through the garden themes in any order of their choice (LTM indicated that this information was hierarchical). Explain features for each of the 5 garden themes in conversational tone. **Color Garden** (include following concepts through text and graphics): • A monochromatic or unified color theme. • Color choice based on personal preferences or to evoke a particular mood (pinks or blues have a calming effect, reds, yellows or oranges are stimulating). • White gardens allow plants to be viewed at night, also called a midnight garden. • Variation comes from differing hues of the color, shape, and size of blooms or foliage. • Differing plant heights and fragrance add interest. The list continues until all garden themes have been presented.
2. **Provide learning cues**	• Remind learners of how temporal zones, condition of designated site, etc. affect choice of theme. • Use garden examples and nonexamples to highlight differences among the five types of gardens. • Recommend that learners check their local garden centers, botanical gardens, and extension agencies for additional information, if necessary.

WBI Strategy Worksheet

Instruction on the Content	Detailed Instructional Strategies for Lesson 2: *How Does Your Garden Grow? Choosing a Garden Theme*
3. **Present opportunities for practice**	• Direct participants to websites to select gardens, themes, and plans that they like and will fit best for their location and climate. (Use journals.) • Participants select theme and explain why chosen based on preferences, site location and conditions, etc. They share their theme choice and which website most represents what they like and explain why it does. Share in a threaded discussion. • Set early deadline for website and journal assignment. • Set deadline for threaded discussion assignment. • *Remind students of discussion site for technical problems. If serious problems are experienced, remind them to send email to the mentor.
4. **Provide feedback on practice performance**	• Students provide feedback to each other on their choices. • Instructor provides feedback on choice based on information participants provided in first week about garden site, temporal zones, etc. • *Mentor (or technical support staff) answers any questions about technical problems.
5. **Provide review of and close the lesson**	For review of key concepts, the instructor will provide a summary: • Highlight main features of 5 types of garden themes and desirable conditions for each garden. • Comment on the activities and general progress of the group, in general. • Indicate next lesson topic and next steps in planning a garden.

*Although not an actual part of the *GardenScapes* content, addressing technical problems facilitates learning.

Kally and Elliott begin developing the storyboards for Lessons 1 and 2 with the strategies that have been formulated. Once they have prototypes of the first two lessons, they call in the expert reviewers and former students or end users to review them. As part of his tickler file, Elliott includes a reminder to ask former students or end users about their thoughts on the lesson titles.

Kally and Elliott then continue with the design and development of the remaining four lessons.

On Your Own

Determine the instructional strategies for Instruction on the Content subcomponents for each unit of your WBI, using Table 7.3 as your template. You can select different strategies for each lesson or establish a standard set of strategies based on your theoretical approach to learning, your instructional goal, and your design experience. The more specificity that you provide in this part of the Design Document, the easier your WBI development will be.

(For illustrations of how other designers tackled these same issues, review the case studies appearing in the Extending Your Skills section at the end of this chapter.)

See this textbook's Companion Website (http://www.prenhall.com/davidson-shivers) for a printable version of the WBI Strategy Worksheet template.

Measurement of Learning

The designer has already created sample assessment items or tools (refer to the TOAB discussion in Chapter 6). However, he or she now reviews the assessment tools to make sure that they and the timing of the assessments are still appropriate for the WBI. As part of the documentation in the WBI Strategy Worksheet, the Measurement of Learning component outlines the manner in which assessment will be integrated into the WBI by stating how and when learners will be assessed. Innovative approaches and tools for assessing learning performance may be required because traditional testing tools are not always feasible in WBI (refer to Chapter 6). The two subcomponents of Measurement of Learning are as follows:

1. *Assess learner performance* or progress toward mastering the instructional goal and objectives.
2. *Advise learners* of their progress or of performance scores.

Table 7.4 provides a partial list of strategies for assessing students and advising them on their progress. Refer to Chapter 6 for more detail.

A combination of diagnostic, formative, and summative assessments may be appropriate for the learning situation (Johnson & Johnson, 2002; Linn & Gronlund, 1995). Diagnostic and formative assessments may be structurally contained in other components of the WBI, such as the Orientation to Learning component (for diagnostic assessment), or as an embedded test at the end of a unit of instruction in the Instruction on the Content component (for formative assessment). Summative assessments usually occur at the end of the WBI once all of the units of instruction have been completed or at major time intervals within the term (i.e., midterms or finals); consequently, the component Measurement of Learning is included in the overview of the entire WBI project.

Table 7.4 Instructional Strategies for the Measurement of Learning Component as Indicated on the WBI Strategy Worksheet

Measurement of Learning Subcomponents	Instructional Strategies
1. **Assess performance or progress toward the goal**	• Use quizzes or tests using multiple-choice, completion, true/false, or matching items. • Use essays (several restricted-range questions to sample objectives or a single extended-range question). • Require completion of a project or term paper related to the goal. • Use LMS and other commercial programming tools (e.g., Java, CGI, C, Pascal) to create testing routines. • Use model answers to develop tests and scoring keys for learners to review.
2. **Advise learner of scores or progress**	• Provide checklists and rubrics to score essay tests, projects, or to score papers. • Use commercial tools for reporting grades, such as an LMS gradebook. • Use email, shared files, chat, mailing of reports and projects for feedback. • Encourage remediation, if necessary. • Provide project guidelines and rubrics for learners to self-check their work.

Source: Table data are from Alagumalai, Toh, & Wong (2000), Cucchiarelli, Panti, & Vanenti (2000), Davidson-Shivers (1998), Fisher (2000), Gagné (1985), Smith & Ragan (2005), Stiggins (2005).

The choice of assessment type (diagnostic, formative, or summative) depends on the nature of the instructional goal, its defined outcome level, instructional context, and the stated objectives (refer to the TOAB). For example, depending on the complexity and difficulty of the content and how the objectives have been stated and clustered, students may need to be assessed periodically throughout the WBI rather than at the end of the entire instructional content. In such cases, the designer will determine where to place the embedded assessment based on the clustered objective sets. For very complex and difficult content, such assessments may need to occur at the end of every unit of instruction. For others, traditional midterm and final examinations may suffice in terms of performance assessment. With relatively straightforward content, it may be satisfactory to provide an assessment of content and the goal and all of the objectives at the end of the WBI. Finally, formal assessments may require that assessments (entry and pretests) are given for diagnostic or evaluation purposes as well. Table 7.5 presents a rubric for the timing of formal assessments.

Complex WBI projects may require that the Measurement of Learning component be incorporated into the detailed description of instructional strategies for every unit of instruction within the WBI Strategy Worksheet. For less complex WBI courses, the description of

Table 7.5 Determining the Timing of Assessment

Timing of Formal Assessment	Complexity of Goals and Content
At the beginning of course	For diagnostic or formative evaluation purposes
After every unit of instruction	Very complex goals or objectives Very difficult content
At midpoint and end of course	Less complex and difficult goals, objectives, or content
At end of course	Straightforward, relatively simple goals, objectives, or content

this component's strategies may be placed after half of the units have been described and again at the end of the WBI. For straightforward (i.e., simple) goals, objectives, or content, the description may be included in the WBI Strategy Worksheet once the Orientation of Learning combined with the Instruction on the Content components have been detailed for all of the units of instruction.

Because formal assessment activities require a judgment of scores, learners may be required to access a designated Web-based host site or travel to an institution-defined remote site to take an exam. Other ways to control the assessment process are to provide a proctor who visits learners at their local site or have learners locate their own proctor who serves as the instructor's proxy. The use of a Webcam may also enhance assessment security. Directions for formal assessments must be clearly stated along with a time frame for when learners will be advised of their scores and/or grades.

An informal means of assessing student progress, rather than performance is through the use of practice exercises. These exercises (e.g., worksheets, peer review activities, responses in threaded discussions) could be considered as formative assessments (Johnson & Johnson, 2002; Linn & Gronlund, 1995). As indicated in the discussion on Instruction on the Content, feedback on such exercises is necessary, but they may not require a grade or score Administering such practice activities at a Web host site or a designated remote site does not require a proctor to be present.

GardenScapes

Most continuing education courses do not have the formal, summative assessments or "grading" typically required in an academic setting. Continuing education courses at CJC, especially those taken for pleasure, use formative assessment. However, Elliott and Kally include formal, summative assessments as a part of the evaluation plans (refer to Chapter 5).

Because the purpose of their formative evaluation plan is to improve the effectiveness of the *GardenScapes* course, Elliott devises short multiple-choice type of pretests and posttests that cover the goal and main objectives; these assessments will be given to the participants at the beginning of Lesson 1 and end of the WBI. At the end of Lesson 6 the course wrap up, Elliott will inform the learners that the tests' purposes are for evaluating the effectiveness of the course and not for evaluating the students' garden knowledge and skills; however, he will provide them with their own test scores on request.

WBI Strategy Worksheet

Measurement of Learning	Overview of the Instructional Strategies for *GardenScapes*
1. Assess performance or progress	A pretest in the form of a multiple-choice quiz on the concepts and procedures for planning a garden will be part of the orientation (for diagnostic purposes of assessing participant's current gardening skills and for formative evaluation purposes). It will be administered in Lesson 1.
	Informal, assessment tools in the remaining lessons will be used for formative purposes. • Questions that require the learner to make decisions about the development of their garden designs will be asked. These questions will be combined into a self-report journal on their progress. • A series of checklists that learners complete as they undertake the planning of their gardens will be used.
	At the end of the course, learners will submit their garden design plans.
2. Advise learners of scores	A posttest on *GardenScapes* concepts will be given at the end of the course (at the conclusion of Lesson 6). • The checklists and the self-report documents, other students, mentor, and instructor will provide feedback on student progress, but these are not graded. • The garden plans will be scored using the checklist and rubric developed in the TOAB. Scores for the garden plans will be returned to the learners via email within 1 week of the final day of class. • The formative evaluation quiz will be used to determine the effectiveness of the WBI. Elliott will analyze the pre- and posttest scores for gains. Students will be advised of their own scores if they so desire.

Elliott includes the strategies for Measurement of Learning subcomponents in the Overview of the entire WBI project. He includes the following Measurement of Learning strategies in the overview of the entire WBI project.

See this textbook's Companion Website (http://www.prenhall.com/davidson-shivers) for the WBI Strategy Workshop in *GardenScapes* Design Document.

ON YOUR OWN

Determine the instructional strategies for the Measurement of Learning component for your WBI project, using Table 7.4 as your template. Identify when and how often assessments will be conducted. Remember that the outlined strategies provide directions as to how the development team will construct the strategy. Add the information to your WBI Strategy Worksheet and include it in your Design Document.

(For illustrations of how other designers tackled these same issues, review the case studies appearing in the Extending Your Skills section at the end of this chapter.)

See this textbook's Companion Website (http://www.prenhall.com/davidson-shivers) for a printable version of the WBI Strategy Worksheet template.

Summary and Close

The Summary and Close component is the last part of the conceptual framework and instructional strategies included in the WBI Strategy Worksheet. Summary and Close strategies are designed to satisfy learners' expectancy for closure and redirect their attention back to the main points of the instruction. They enable learners to review their work, help them to uncover any errors to allow for relearning, and facilitate retention and transfer of learning (Dick et al., 2005; Gagné, 1985). Summary and Close has three subcomponents:

1. Provide opportunities for *retention.*
2. Provide *remediation* of unmet objectives.
3. Provide opportunities to *enhance* and *enrich performance.*

Because the detailed design for each unit or lesson already contains a review and close subcomponent, the Summary and Close strategies are included in the overview of the entire WBI project. Summarizing the main points at the end of the WBI facilitates retention and transfer of the new learning to other situations (Gagné, 1985; Gagné et al., 2005). This component provides an opportunity to review any objectives that were not mastered (Dick et al., 2005; Smith & Ragan, 2005).

With some LMSs, learners' access to the WBI and website may be denied after the course is completed and grades are posted. If that is a possibility, then the designer needs

Table 7.6 Strategies for the Summary and Close Component as indicated on the WBI Strategy Worksheet

Summary and Close Subcomponents	Instructional Strategies
1. Provide opportunities for retention	• Summarize and review the lesson through graphics and text. • Wrap-up remarks about the main points of lesson or WBI course. • Additional cases or examples to reinforce learning.
2. Provide remediation for unmet objectives	• Summarize and review the lesson through graphics and text. • Allow students to review assessment and their corresponding responses to understand their errors. • Directions to review instructional material based on unmet objectives. • Wrap-up remarks to close lesson or summary at the end of the entire WBI course.
3. Enhance and enrich learning	• Suggest additional exercises, case studies, and scenarios that extend the scope of the lesson. • Identify next steps, activities, etc. that go beyond the present lesson or WBI course. • Discuss how this WBI course or the lessons within relate to each other and future courses. • Wrap-up remarks to close lesson or WBI course.

Source: Table data are from Dick et al. (2005), Gagné (1985), Gagné et al. (2005), Khan (2001), Milheim & Bannan-Ritland (2001), Smith & Ragan (2005), Villalba & Romiszowski (2001).

to include provisions for alerting learners to check the website for their scores and to review any course information prior to the stated end date for access to the course website.

Again, the Summary and Close subcomponents may be combined with each other and presented in any order. For some instructional situations, it may not be necessary to use all of the assessment strategies. The instructional strategies for Summary and Close are presented in Table 7.6. Any duplication of the strategies is intentional in that an instructional strategy may be relevant to one or more of the subcomponents.

GardenScapes

Elliott and Kally design the instructional strategies for their Summary and Close component and include them in their WBI Strategy Worksheet.

WBI Strategy Worksheet

Summary and Close	Overview of the Instructional Strategies for *GardenScapes*
1. **Provide opportunities for retention**	• At the end of the course, a summary will highlight the goal and main objectives. • Learners will share their garden plans with each other in the LMS document sharing.
2. **Provide remediation for unmet objectives**	• Encourage learners to review the lecture notes and additional websites for unmet lesson objectives. • Scores for garden plans will be sent to each participant. • For areas where improvement is needed, participants will be encouraged to review the course summary prior to losing access to WBI.
3. **Enhance and enrich learning**	• Encourage continued learning at end of WBI by suggesting things such as becoming master gardeners; list other garden and landscape courses available through CJC, etc. • Encourage learners to mail photos of their gardens once planted to each other and the instructor. As an incentive, the photos will be archived for future offerings of *GardenScapes* and included in the website.

See this textbook's Companion Website (http://www.prenhall.com/davidson-shivers) for the WBI Strategy Workshop in *GardenScapes* Design Document.

ON YOUR OWN

Determine the instructional strategies for your Summary and Close component on the WBI Strategy Worksheet for your project, using Table 7.6 as your template. Include the details in your Design Document. Articulate the instructional strategies in a way that any members of the design team could develop them into the WBI.

(For illustrations of how other designers tackled these same issues, review the case studies appearing in the Extending Your Skills section at the end of this chapter.)

See this textbook's Companion Website (http://www.prenhall.com/davidson-shivers) for a printable version of the WBI Strategy Worksheet template.

Motivational Strategies for WBI

Theoretical Approaches to Motivation

There are many motivational theories that relate to student achievement and successful learning (e.g., Alderman, 1999; Eggen & Kauchak, 2003; Keller, 1987, 1999; Maslow, 1987; Slavin, 1991; Weiner, 1992; Wlodkowski, 1997, 1999) and are often discussed in the learning and instructional psychology literature. Each theorist has their own definition of **motivation** based on philosophical or psychological orientations. For instance, Pintrich and Schunk (2002) define it as "the process whereby goal-directed behavior is instigated and sustained" (p. 5). Weiner (1992) suggests that it can be defined as "the study of the determinants of thought and action—it addresses *why* behavior is initiated, persist, and stops, as well as what choices are made" (p. 17). From a cognitive psychology perspective, Ormrod (2004) describes *motivation* as "an internal state that arouses us to action, pushes us in particular directions, and keeps us engaged in certain activities" (p. 425).

Most theorists agree that there are two basic types of motivation: intrinsic and extrinsic. Ormrod (2004) suggests that *intrinsic motivation* is the source within an individual or task that promotes that individual to become engaged in the effort. An intrinsically motivated person is likely to pursue a task or goal without being prodded and values his or her achievement; the achievement is then reinforced by a personal sense of satisfaction. Several factors influence intrinsic motivation, such as personality characteristics; past experience; needs, desires, and preferences; anxiety levels; expectations; and attributions (Slavin, 1991; Weiner, 1992).

Extrinsic motivation is the source outside the individual and task that promotes the individual to perform (Ormrod, 2004). Alderman (1999) suggests that an extrinsically motivated person pursues or engages in the task to receive rewards or incentives (grades, praise, special privileges, material goods, etc.).

Both intrinsic and extrinsic motivation promote successful learning. However, Ormrod (2004) argues that most motivation theorists suggest that intrinsically motivated individuals have advantages such as being engaged in the task longer, willing to apply more effort, and persisting in the task longer than extrinsically motivated individuals. Alderman (1999) counters this argument by stating that "although intrinsic and extrinsic motivation have been viewed as polar opposites, current views acknowledge that these two sources represent a continuum from most to least extrinsic, not opposing forms" (p. 218). She suggests that individuals may shift from extrinsic to intrinsic or be motivated by both sources simultaneously.

Driscoll (2005) suggests that motivational theories can help designers consider the types of appropriate motivation conditions (extrinsic, intrinsic, or both) to incorporate into instruction. This is especially true with the reality of having distance between learners and instructors. Learners who do not see others regularly may feel isolated from the rest of the learning community and, thus, may not participate effectively or continue in the WBI (Sriwongkol, 2002). Various strategies that motivate and encourage may improve learners' participation (Hazari, 2000; Khan, 2001) and retention (Miller & Miller, 2000; Powers & Guan, 2000).

Among the various motivational theories that abound in the literature, there are two that correspond well with all types of instruction and to WBI design. They are Keller's (1987, 1999) Motivational Design Strategy (also known as the ARCS model) and Wlodkowski and Ginsberg's Motivational Framework for Culturally Responsive Teaching (Wlodkowski, 1997, 1999; Wlodkowski & Ginsberg, 1995).

Keller's ARCS Model.   Keller's (1987, 1999) *ARCS model* proposes four types of strategies that enhance learner motivation—those that focus learner *attention,* establish *relevance* for the learner, instill learner *confidence,* and facilitate learner *satisfaction.* In each of these four categories, Keller identifies several subcategories.

Focusing attention strategies are to gain and sustain learner attention on the instructional goal and the instructional materials (Keller, 1987). For WBI design, this strategy may occur in terms of providing something novel or unusual or interesting such as humorous stories that relate to the topic, or visually stimulating photos or videos that stimulate a learner's interest in the content. Driscoll (2005) suggests that for more lasting curiosity, Keller's attitude of inquiry needs to be invoked. This strategy can be accomplished by creating a sense of mystery or student involvement.

Keller suggests that *establishing relevance* allows individuals to view the WBI as being useful in meeting their needs and allows them to attain personal goals. Techniques for facilitating relevance in WBI include involving learners in their own goal setting or allowing them to choose how their progress is assessed. Driscoll (2005) suggests that "finding ways to engage students in learning can be effective means for motivating them, irrespective of whether they yet see the relevance of the learning activities" (p. 336). For WBI, these may include finding ways to challenge students either through competitive or cooperative group activities or through self-study activities.

Instilling confidence allows students to build their confidence in their own abilities as they successfully complete challenging tasks. These tasks need to be within Vygotsky's zone of proximal development (ZPD) for an individual (Driscoll, 2005). Ormrod (2004) suggests that a ZPD ranges somewhere between tasks that the individuals cannot do by themselves and can do with assistance from others. They accomplish such tasks by collaborating with others (usually by individuals who are more advanced and competent than themselves). Both Driscoll and Ormrod suggest that as students gain confidence and are able to do the work independently, assistance can be reduced. For example, learners may need more instructor or mentor assistance in getting started and working through assignments at the beginning of the WBI than toward the end.

The last category, *facilitating satisfaction,* allows learners to use acquired skills or knowledge meaningfully, or through a state of natural consequences (Keller, 1987, 1999). For WBI, learners may achieve satisfaction by using newly acquired skills in project-oriented or problem-solving tasks. Driscoll (2005) suggests that when instruction does not accommodate employing natural consequences, positive consequences (such as praise or other rewards or incentives) may be used instead. The WBI design strategy would allow for encouraging and motivating feedback.

Wlodkowski and Ginsberg's Motivational Framework.   The second motivational theory, which is less known by instructional designers, is Wlodkowski and Ginsberg's Motivational Framework for Culturally Responsive Teaching (Wlodkowski, 1997, 1999; Wlodkowski & Ginsberg, 1995). It focuses on motivations for learning for all learners and disciplines, and contains four major elements, which have some similarities to Keller's four categories. Table 7.7 highlights the elements in Wlodkowski and Ginsberg's motivational framework.

Their first element is *establishing inclusion* by creating a learning community and atmosphere that includes respect for learners and teachers and the interconnectedness they exhibit (Wlodkowski, 1997; Wlodkowski & Ginsberg, 1995). Applying this first element would circumvent one of the downsides of distance education—that of feelings of isolation (Sriwongkol, 2002). According to Vygotsky's theory, known as sociocultural perspective,

Table 7.7 Elements of Wlodkowski and Ginsberg's Motivational Framework

Element	Suggested Strategies
Establishing inclusion by creating a learning community and atmosphere that includes respect for learners and teachers and an interconnectedness they exhibit	• Use icebreaker activities to help learners get to know each other • Instructor hosts open chat or discussions to talk about the course, prior experiences, etc.
Developing of learner attitudes that facilitate the learning experience by emphasizing relevance and choice	• Have learners participate in determining paths of the class, including goals, content, assessments, as possible • Permit learners to select project topics that relate to their personal or professional interests
Creating challenging and reflective learning environments to enhance learner understanding	• Use case studies that present complex problems that require advanced critical thinking and problem-solving techniques • Encourage student reflection and application of real-world problems to academic frameworks
Promoting competence through continued learner success in the content, skills, and abilities that are valued by the learner	• Provide avenues for learner practice at various levels of learning taxonomies • Align practice activities with learner personal and professional interests

Source: Table data are from Wlodkowski (1997; 1999), Wlodkowski & Ginsberg (1995).

cognitive growth is influenced by society and culture and not performed in isolation (M. P. Driscoll, 2005; Ormrod, 2004). Ormrod maintains that knowledge construction (which some theorists view as constructivism and others view as information processing theory) may occur as an independent activity of the individual or when individuals work together (known as *social construction*). Furthermore, she posits that because people are social creatures by nature, part of their learning occurs by interacting with others (i.e., adults or peers). She states that "both Piaget and Vygotsky argued for the importance of peer interactions in learning and cognitive development" (p. 403). For WBI, motivational strategies that apply the element of *establishing inclusion* to help individuals become a community of learners include providing opening icebreakers, having students develop shared, common goals, and using collaborative activities that facilitate and promote student interaction. Requiring student biographies or personal Web pages let students connect names with faces. Another strategy would be to allow students to establish their own discussion forums to help each other with technical issues or ask questions about the content amongst themselves. These WBI discussion groups are sometimes called student lounges, lobbies, open discussions, cafés, and so on.

Wlodkowski and Ginsberg's second element is *developing [learner] attitudes* that facilitate the learning experience by emphasizing relevance and choice (Wlodkowski, 1997; Wlodkowski & Ginsberg, 1995). This element is similar to Keller's relevance category in its emphasis on promoting learning that is personally meaningful and allowing for individual choices. Motivational strategies for WBI would be to provide learners with examples, practice exercises, and so on that they see as relevant to their needs, abilities, and goals. Providing them opportunities to choose throughout their learning experience is another strategy.

Creating challenging and reflective learning environments *for enhancing [learner] meaning* is their third element (Wlodkowski, 1997; Wlodkowski & Ginsberg, 1995). This element seems comparable to Keller's categories of instilling confidence because both relate to challenging learners and building or enhancing their understanding of the content. Shared experiences through group interactions (discussions, group projects, etc.) and independent activities (reflective journaling, Web searches, etc.) can help learners make sense of the WBI based on their own and shared perspectives. Providing feedback that promotes understanding and encourages them would also facilitate their understanding.

Their fourth element is *engendering competence* through continued learner success in the content, skills, and abilities that are valued by the learner (Wlodkowski, 1997; Wlodkowski & Ginsberg, 1995). This last element appears to bring Keller's categories of confidence and satisfaction together. Motivational strategies include providing opportunities for practice and for demonstrating skills throughout instructional activities. Another strategy is to provide relatively simple or easy practice at the beginning of a lesson and increase the level of difficulty as the learners demonstrate success, so their confidence increases as the WBI progresses.

Driscoll (2005) maintains that "[student] motivation is enhanced when [their] expectancies are satisfied and when they attribute their successes to their own efforts and effective learning strategies" (p. 331). Additionally, she suggests that designers understand motivational theories and approaches to include in instruction. Both Keller's and Wlodkowski and Ginsberg's motivational theories provide the WBI designer with strategies that facilitate learner engagement, participation, and retention.

GardenScapes

Elliott and Kally identify the motivational strategies for *GardenScapes,* adding them to their WBI project overview right after the instructional strategies section. They include explanations of how their strategies will motivate the participants.

WBI Strategy Worksheet

Overview of the Motivational Strategies for *GardenScapes*

For Orientation to Learning
- Use an icebreaker as one of the first activities in *GardenScapes.*
- Include short biography and photos of the participants.
  (*help establish inclusion within a learning community*)

WBI Strategy Worksheet

Overview of the Motivational Strategies for *GardenScapes*

Instruction on the Content
- Permit learners to choose their own garden theme.
- The content of each lesson is highly relevant since it is of personal interest to them.
  (*develop learner attitudes because of relevance and choice*)
- Learners will be encouraged to share experiences, to reflect on the plant choices for their garden plan.
- Learners can share ideas in chats, threaded discussions, and email.
  (*help establish inclusion within a learning community*)
- Lesson content will be conversational in tone.
  (*promote confidence*)
- Examples and scenarios will provide ideas and suggestions for their own garden design.
  (*create challenges to promote learner understanding*)
- Learners will be encouraged to practice the skills outlined in the lesson through instructor emails.
  (*promote competence*)
- Instructor will model active participation and positive attitudes.
  (*help establish inclusion within a learning community and develop learner attitudes*)

Measurement of Learning
- Instructor will provide constructive feedback and upbeat email messages.
  (*continue to establish inclusion within a learning community*)
- Feedback will be used throughout the lessons and scoring of the garden design plans will occur at the end of the course.
  (*promote competence and develop learner attitudes*)

Summary and Close
- Learners will be encouraged to keep in touch with their learning community to share future garden successes.
- An archive website will be created that will showcase garden designs and pictures of resulting gardens.
  (*both promote competence and develop learner attitudes*)

Elliott and Kally are aware that they must incorporate all strategies stated in the overview into each lesson as well.

See this textbook's Companion Website (http://www.prenhall.com/davidson-shivers) for the WBI Strategy Workshop in *GardenScapes* Design Document.

On Your Own

State which motivational framework you are using for your WBI project. Identify the motivational strategies for each of the four instructional strategy components and explain how they facilitate learner motivation. As a part of your design documentation, incorporate them into the WBI Strategy Worksheet already written or add them as a separate worksheet.

(For illustrations of how other designers tackled these same issues, review the case studies appearing in the Extending Your Skills section at the end of this chapter.)

See this textbook's Companion Website (http://www.prenhall.com/davidson-shivers) for a printable version of the WBI Strategy Worksheet template.

Other Factors to Consider for WBI Design

Good instruction, regardless of the delivery system, rests on the use of innovative and appropriate instructional and motivational strategies for the learning situation. The challenge in a Web-based environment is to select appropriate strategies that facilitate learners' abilities to meet the stated instructional or learner-determined goals. However, designing good instructional and motivational strategies is not an isolated activity and requires that other factors surrounding the WBI be considered simultaneously. Identifying the factors that influence the WBI's design and conversely, the design's impact on the factors, are parts of this process. The main factors to consider in WBI design include class size, navigation and learner control, feedback, and interactivity. Determining media is another factor that must be considered; we address it in the last section of this chapter.

Class Size

A pragmatic matter in WBI design is how many learners will be enrolled in the WBI per offering. To determine appropriate class size, the designer reviews organizational policies on class size, course demand and sequencing, and the support and technology infrastructures for the Web environment. Within the WBI and learning community, the designer takes into account the complexity of the content and the availability and experience level of the learning community team members (instructor, mentor, learner). For instance, the instructor's overall workload (not just teaching load) and experience with online instruction as well as learner motivation and experience with online learning should be taken into consideration when planning WBI delivery (Collison, Elbaum, Haavind, & Tinker, 2000). The type of online instruction (i.e., WBI, WEI, or WSI), level of interactivity, and difficulty of course assignments also impact the number of learners that should be enrolled.

Any combination of these factors affects and determines appropriate class size. For example, if a course were to have a strong support and low level of interactivity, but very inexperienced learners and instructor, then a lower learner–teacher ratio may be warranted than if the instructor were dealing with experienced learners. If a course were to cover basic introductory content, require simple assignments, objective-type of assessments, and low-level interaction, then a larger enrollment may be appropriate than if the reverse were true. Highly interactive courses that cover complex content and complicated assignments justify small class sizes.

WBI class size can, in many cases, mirror sizes of traditional education and training courses. In the preceding examples, the first scenario presented is similar to seminar-type courses. The second scenario is similar to large lecture courses and the third corresponds to project-based or problem-based courses or labs.

An experienced online instructor can without extreme difficulty effectively work in a moderately interactive WBI course with class size ranging from 10 to 25 students. With the addition of a mentor, increasing the class size may be possible, as long as the complexity of course content and assignments remain at a lower level, the interactive level is moderate, and the learners have had previous online learning experience. Part of the task of determining class size or establishing organizational policy is taking into account the challenges faced by the online instructor (refer to Chapter 1).

Navigation and Learner Control

A second factor surrounding WBI design and delivery is navigation and learner control, which govern how learners maneuver through the WBI. **Navigation** is, fundamentally, the path that end users take to move around the instructional website. Navigational paths should be easy for learners to understand and locate so that they do not have an additional task of determining how to get to various activities (Hannum, 2001; Khan, 2001). Navigation elements (e.g., site maps, indexes, buttons or icons to different parts of the instruction [assignments, lessons, quizzes]) should be prominently displayed on the website and be intuitive or logical to minimize cognitive overload (Berry, 2000; Nielsen, 2000). When navigation is challenging, learners divert their attention from learning to solving the encountered navigation problems.

Learner control refers to the amount of personal regulation an individual exerts over the learning environment. Learner control may permit selection and control of what is learned, how it is learned, and when it is learned (Lin & Davidson, 1996; Rasmussen & Davidson, 1996). Learner control can be defined by variables such as sequence, pace, display mode, content, instructional strategy, completion time, amount of practice, and level of difficulty (Hannafin & Peck, 1988; Yoon, 1993–1994).

See Appendix B for additional information on navigation and learner control.

Feedback

Even though feedback has been mentioned in the instructional and motivational strategies, it bears additional emphasis by repeating it; feedback greatly influences the WBI design and delivery. **Feedback** is the process by which learners receive responses to their questions or comments about assigned WBI activities (Figure 7.2). Identifying feedback needs is one way to prepare instructors for the demands of the learning community (Persichitte,

Figure 7.2   Examples of email feedback.

Example 1: Global Feedback to the Class

To: class
Cc:
Bcc:
Subject: Your Instrument Discussion

I wanted everyone to know how much I appreciate all of your hard work and feedback on each other's instruments. I am extremely happy and pleased—and can see how the feedback has been increasingly detailed and effective as we've gone through this exercise.

Thank you for all of your efforts.

Example 2: Automatic Feedback to an Individual Student

To: student
Cc: instructor
Bcc:
Subject: Your Assignment

You have successfully uploaded your file to the drop box. You are ready to move to the next lesson.

2000). Balance must be maintained between the feedback desired by learners and the ability of the instructor to respond in a timely fashion. Providing personal and responsive types of feedback to large numbers of learners adds to instructor workload; active learning communities need to use other types of feedback to reduce the load.

Participants and their peers as well as mentors can provide feedback through email, chats, or threaded discussion. A WBI also can employ automatic feedback such as automated email, Web pages that include answers to frequently asked questions (FAQs), listservs for global responses, and links displaying a Web page with correct answers or additional information about the activities. Feedback can be programmed through an LMS (Darbyshire, 2000) and this type of technical support may alleviate learner concerns and instructor work overloads.

Interactivity

Similarly, interactivity needs additional emphasis here even though we have previously discussed it in the WBI strategies sections. Interaction, as the transaction(s) between and among participants in the learning communities and with the WBI, is defined in a variety of fashions, depending on the structure and focus of the interaction (Wagner, 2001) (refer to Chapter 1). The levels of interaction and the type of learning community help determine which instructional and motivational strategies will be used in the WBI.

Figure 7.3   Proactive interaction discussion.

Example of Proactive Interaction: Learners are presented with a problem and directed to make sense of the situation as they discuss with others.

Review the information in the case study and the supporting documents. Take the perspective of one of the stakeholders in your view of the data. Interpret the data, based on your perspective and develop recommendations that go along with those interpretations. Share your interpretations and recommendations with your group. Collectively, develop a group set of interpretations and recommendations to share with the class. Individually critique at least one other group's summary. In your comments, identify strengths and weaknesses and explain why.

```
<threaded discussion>
        <reply>
        <reply>
                <reply>
        <reply>
                <reply>
<threaded discussion>
        <reply>
                <reply>
                <reply>
                        <reply>
        <reply>
                <reply>
        <reply>
<etc.>
```

Schwier and Misanchuk (1993) use a taxonomy that includes reactive, proactive, and mutual types of interactivity. *Reactive interactivity* occurs when learners respond to stimuli or answer questions. In *proactive interaction,* learners generate their own knowledge constructions beyond the expectations of the designer or the instructor (Figure 7.3). *Mutual interaction* revolves around the use of artificial intelligence or virtual reality, where learners become part of the learning environment itself. The most applicable type of interaction in a learning community model is proactive interaction, as it focuses on active rather than passive learning.

Furthermore, the discussions on interactivity offer three modes of interactions: student to student, student to instructor, student to instruction (Beer, 2000; Davidson-Shivers et al., 2001; Davidson-Shivers, Morris, & Sriwongkol, 2003; M. Driscoll, 1998; Fisher, 2000; Horton, 2000; Moore, 1989; Rasmussen & Northrup, 2000). Rasmussen and Northrup (2000) provide a fourth type of interaction, that of student-to-management system. Interactivity strategies for these four modes can be incorporated into the WBI Strategy Worksheet. Table 7.8 presents a sampling of strategies that may promote interaction in each of the four interaction modes. Using a combination of strategies for these four modes enhances and strengthens WBI experience of learners. Planning for levels of interaction promotes both independent work within the WBI and development of extensive, broad-based learning communities.

Table 7.8 Potential Strategies for Interaction Modes

Learner–Content	Learner–Learner	Learner–Authority	Learner–Management
• Include text and/or audio based presentations • Clearly organize content • Use advance organizers • Use embedded learning strategies such as highlighting, outlining, questioning • Use hyperlinked table of contents • Provide rich relevant examples	• Assign group projects • Require peer feedback • Establish study buddies • Require sharing and/or reflecting on content in threaded discussions • Use icebreakers early in the class • Encourage social interaction in and out of class	• Email notes to individual to entire class • Use chat rooms as online office hours • Use chat rooms for focused class discussions • Distribute agenda or questions prior to chat • Have mentors available for assistance • Summarize threaded discussions • Use journals to monitor student progress	• Use gradebooks • Notify learners when assignments are due • Notify learners when scoring is completed • Post files for grading and distribute to individual • Have central point of access for course announcements, information and due dates

Source: Table data are from Brooks (1997), Cecez-Kecmanovic & Webb (2000), Hedberg et al. (2001), MacKnight (2001), Malaga (2000), Moore (1989), Norman (2000), Northrup & Rasmussen (2000); Palloff & Pratt (1999), Spector & Davidsen (2000).

Table 7.9 Factors to Consider During WBI Design and Delivery

Factors Affecting WBI Design
Class Size Identify plans or realities relating to class size. **Navigation and Learner Control** Identify plans or realities for handling navigation and learner control. **Feedback** Identify plans or realities relating to feedback strategies. **Interactivity** Identify plans or realities relating to interactivity. **Other Factors** Identify plans or realities relating to any other factors that need consideration.

The designer takes into consideration these four interaction factors and others while planning strategies for WBI design and delivery. When an ideal design situation is in place, the WBI design strategies are the driving force that affects the factors (Smith & Ragan, 2005). Often these factors are considered in tandem as the strategies are identified by the situation. However, in other situations, some factors may already be predetermined and then they drive the instructional and motivational strategies to be employed. As with all parts of design documentation, there is a place to identify interaction factors within the WBI Strategy Worksheet (Table 7.9).

GardenScapes

Elliott and Kally consider the factors of navigation, learner control, feedback, and interactivity in relation to the *GardenScapes* course. The following outlines their plans to deal with these factors.

Plans for Handling Other Factors Related to WBI Project

Class Size
- The class size is limited to 25 learners because of the interactivity level designed into the course and the experience level of both Kally and the targeted learners.
- Although there are no intensive written assignments to be graded, Kally and the class mentor will be providing feedback for the participants' assignments leading to the final plans as well as the actual garden design.
- A final consideration for class size is that the class is in its first offering online and the instructional strategies are being tested as part of the formative evaluation. Subsequent class sizes may be increased as Kally gains experience in online teaching and learners become acquainted with the Web and online learning.
- The CDE, in its *Policy Handbook,* sets the class size of lifelong learning course offerings to a maximum of 35. This limit was established for WBI courses with low interactivity, learners and instructors who have average online learning skills, and a mentor being part of the learning community.

Navigation and Learner Control
- A great amount of learner control will be used. An open navigation system with random access to different areas of LMS will be used.
- Buttons and links will be located at the same place on each page for ease in navigation.
- The same icons and graphics will identify these links and buttons.

Feedback
- Web pages that contain answers to common questions.
- Embedded questions and answers.
- Access links to instructor and expert databases.
- Instructor or automatic email (weekend strategy) returns message within 24 hours of delivery.
- Instructor holds weekly chats to provide feedback.
- Mentor responds to questions within 24 hours.
- Mentor will hold weekly chat to provide feedback.

Interactivity
- Participation is over an extended period. Lessons have potential for high degrees of interactivity.
- Learners share prior experiences, instructional or technical problems (if any) and questions with each other. Email, chats, and threaded discussion will be used.
- Interaction with content will occur through advance organizers, content organizational strategies, including listing and questioning.
- Grades will be posted in the LMS and feedback distributed via the LMS.

Elliott and Kally submit their Design Document to Mr. Carlos for his approval. They continue their design plans and move to their final consideration, media selection.

See this textbook's Companion Website (http://www.prenhall.com/davidson-shivers) for the WBI Strategy Workshop in *GardenScapes* Design Document.

On Your Own

Develop a plan for handling factors such as navigation and learner control, feedback, and interactivity that may impact your WBI Design. Describe the elements of this plan in your Design Document.

(For illustrations of how other designers tackled these same issues, review the case studies appearing in the Extending Your Skills section at the end of this chapter.)

See this textbook's Companion Website (http://www.prenhall.com/davidson-shivers) for a printable version of the WBI Strategy Worksheet template.

Media Selection for WBI

The promise of the Web includes the expansion of available technologies to WBI learning environments (refer to Chapters 1 and 2). At the beginning of the online environment, the Internet was primarily text based: with hyperlinks, certainly, but no graphics, audio, or video until the advent of the Web (Crumlish, 1998; Smaldino et al., 2005). With improved computer systems and servers, improved access, and increased bandwidth, the possibilities of incorporating a variety of media into WBI exist and will continue to be enhanced. The main options for media relate to text, graphics, audio, and video (including products such as Microsoft *PowerPoint* and Macromedia *Flash* and *Director*).

The following factors determine the types of media to use in the WBI:

- Instructional and motivational strategies delineated in the WBI Strategy Worksheet
- Technological aspects of the Web environment (specifically bandwidth and computer system capabilities) for both learners and instructors and the organization hosting the WBI
- Designer expertise in media development or the inclusion of or access to media specialists (graphic designers, videographers, etc.) in the design team

Often, these considerations and selecting the appropriate media have a highly reciprocal relationship. Sometimes the designer (or design team) is able to design the strategies and then choose the media; other times, the media selection has been determined prior to the instructional and motivational strategy planning. Because the primary purpose of this Web-based learning environment is to support learners in achieving the instructional goals, any type of media selected must add value to the WBI. Table 7.10 identifies instructional and technical questions that designers may consider when selecting media for WBI.

Table 7.10 Questions to Consider for Identifying Types of Media for WBI

Instructional Questions	Technical Questions
• Do the media help learners understand the content? • Do the media help motivate learners? • Do the media support (or detract) from the WBI environment? • Will training be needed for learners or instructor to use the media? • Are the media congruent with the objectives, content, and instructional strategies?	• Are the media easy to access? • Are additional supports needed to access and use the media (e.g., plug-ins, special programs)? • What bandwidths are available to learners? • Who will create the media?

GardenScapes

Previously Elliott came up with several questions related to media selection; Kally and he use them to determine the types of media to incorporate into *GardenScapes:*

- Are the media relevant to the content?
- Do the media support the content?
- What kind of training will learners need to use the media?
- Who will create the media?

They base their decisions on the information contained in their WBI Strategy Worksheet, the technology available in the website, and the TLDC staff members' expertise in media development.

Identifying Types of Media for *GardenScapes*
- Short video clips and photos will be used for garden examples.
- Audio and stills will be used in the welcome statements and introductions of each lesson.
- Content will be delivered with text and graphics.
- TDLC staff will create the media that will be housed on the TDLC Web media server.
- Media created will be activated through the LMS so learners will not need to download plug-ins. Linking objects in the LMS reduces the need for additional learner training.

 See this textbook's Companion Website (http://www.prenhall.com/davidson-shivers) for the WBI Strategy Workshop in *GardenScapes* Design Document.

ON YOUR OWN

Identify questions to address for media selection and then use those questions to identify the types of media that are appropriate for your WBI. On what basis did you make your selection? Incorporate these ideas and explain them on your WBI Strategy Worksheet.

(For illustrations of how other designers tackled these same issues, review the case studies appearing in the Extending Your Skills section at the end of this chapter.)

See this textbook's Companion Website (http://www.prenhall.com/davidson-shivers) for a printable version of the WBI Strategy Worksheet template.

Wrapping Up

This chapter discussed the remaining essential design tasks in the concurrent design stage. Features of an LMS were briefly outlined; although LMSs are valuable tools, many of these features are available even when the designer does not use an LMS. We introduced the WBI Strategy Worksheet as a way to identify and document appropriate instructional and motivational strategies to be used in WBI. We discussed the conceptual framework for designing the instructional strategies—Orientation to Learning, Instruction on the Content, Measurement of Learning, and Summary and Close. We explored employing motivational strategies in WBI. Such strategies could be based on Keller's (1987, 1999) ARCS model, Wlodkowski and Ginsberg's Motivational Framework (Wlodkowski, 1997, 1999; Wlodkowski & Ginsberg, 1995), or some other motivational theory. The additional factors of class size, navigation and learner control, feedback, and interactivity were discussed as being considerations that may affect the WBI design and delivery, or vice versa. Similarly, media selection and identification of instructional and motivational strategies have a reciprocal relationship.

Expanding Your Expertise

1. Is it important to have a comprehensive strategy plan for design? Justify your answer.
2. Consider the flexibility built into the conceptual framework for instructional strategies (as outlined in the WBI Strategy Worksheet). How could a constructivist (or behaviorist or cognitivist) use this framework for creating a Web-based learning environment?
3. Two motivational theories were discussed in this chapter. What other motivational theories or frameworks could be used in WBI design (or any instructional innovation, for that matter)? Conduct a review of literature to find other motivational theories.
4. Because motivational strategies are closely aligned with instructional strategies, is it necessary to delineate them separately in a design plan? Explain why or why not.
5. How much learner feedback is enough? What factors will make the amount and timing of feedback vary? Explain why.
6. Interactivity in Web-based learning helps to keep learners engaged in the community. What interactive strategies are most important to consider in the design of WBI? Describe strategies for the various types of interactivity.

7. In less interactive environments, what instructional strategies are important to create a WBI in which the independent learner succeeds and thrives?

8. Should the factors of class size, navigation and learner control, feedback, and interaction determine the design of instructional and motivational strategies or should it be the reverse? Explain and support your answer.

Extending Your Skills

Case Study 1 ## PK–12 Schools

Megan Bifford has begun detailing the instructional strategies she will need to present her WSI (Web-supported instruction). Based on the design decisions made so far, the overall instructional strategy design that she plans on implementing is based on a WebQuest, as proposed by Dodge (1997).

WebQuest Structure	Strategy
Introduction	Establish framework for the lesson; highlight objectives that will be met. Tie WebQuest activities to those that will be completed in class.
Tasks	Present the task to be completed, including a description of the final project.
Process	Provide directions, Web links, content, worksheets, and a general structure of the activity.
Evaluation	Provide a rubric that specifically outlines expectations of the product to be developed.
Conclusion	Summarize lesson. Make additional linkages to classroom activities.

The WebQuest aligns to the components on the WBI Strategy Worksheet. Since inquiry skills are at the center of the learning experience, a WebQuest where students will explore a topic with the intent of developing the identified skills is an appropriate framework.

Megan explores the WebQuest strategy and finds that they are generally designed to provide students with a great deal of learner control, within broad parameters. Students will access the Internet and Web to locate information to resolve the presented problem. Students are provided with a task and general guidelines, but they may fashion their own path. In this WebQuest, where developing inquiry-based skills is a major focus, students will be provided with worksheets that will help them solve the task. In this Web-supported activity, the classroom teacher will provide feedback.

Megan, Rhoda, and Buzz expand the WBI Strategy Worksheet to specifically detail all of the strategies that will be used in the WSI. Once they have a solid idea of what they want to do, they will share their ideas with Cassie for her feedback.

Megan meets with the district's staff person in charge of the Computer Center, Victor Gracie. They discuss how to make sure that the technical ramifications of her media selection are considered, especially when students access websites outside the district's network.

Rhoda and Buzz believe that their students will be highly motivated in the Web-supported instruction. The fifth graders like to use technology in class and because they will be working in cooperative groups, they will encourage each other throughout the project. To promote motivation, they are planning on incorporating strategies from Keller's ARCS model into online and in-class experiences.

Case Study 2   Business and Industry

Homer Spotswood's intern, Stacey McGee, reviews the TOAB to begin to brainstorm appropriate instructional strategies for their WBI. Homer and Stacey meet to talk about the strategies.

As part of the Orientation to Learning strategies, Homer emphasizes to Stacey that it is very important that employees realize the importance of fire safety and are motivated to change poor performance behaviors. Because of the nature of the course, employees will have very little learner control; navigation will be highly structured to make sure that employees go through the lesson in a similar fashion. Automatic feedback will be provided throughout the online portion of the class; specific performance feedback will be obtained during the face-to-face experience.

In the content area, employees must be able to quickly implement safety procedures. The Web-based portion of the class must be closely aligned to and support the hands-on activities of the face-to-face sessions. Assessment is a twofold process: employees must pass a cognitive test online and a practical performance assessment.

Plant administrators, specifically Bud Cattrell, must be able to document that employees have successfully completed the program. Consequently, performance is going to be closely monitored and tracked.

Case Study 3   Military

The design strategy directed by the Commander, Naval Education and Training Command, employs reusable learning object (RLO) technology. Each component of this design—text, graphic, animation, video, and audio—is stored in a central database allowing sharing of the resources and continuity of presentation. The different elements will be grouped together to form the instructional materials. The individual elements of the RLOs, the reusable information objects (RIOs) will be coded using metadata, identifying their associated instructional or motivational strategy. When the RLOs are formed, they will conform to the identified strategies. This information is input to the database via a commercially procured LCMS.

After each team proposes instructional and motivational strategies, Commander Rebekkah Feinstein and Lieutenants Sandra Cole, Rex Danielson, and Bob Carroll meet to review team progress. While not all of the strategies have to be the same, they must be complementary. Once the strategies have been reviewed and approved by the parties, Commander Feinstein will provide an update brief to Captain Prentiss.

Commander Feinstein gives the teams the direction to review policy for class size and to develop implications for different class sizes in light of the instructional strategies. In addition, they will propose strategies for navigation, learner control, and feedback while keeping in mind the objectives and the learning context.

Lt. Carroll begins to work with the graphic artists in the media pool to identify media that will be used in the E^2C^2 course. He provides the graphic artists with the materials that have been developed so far and schedules a meeting for all of the teams to get together to discuss expectations of media.

Case Study 4   ## Higher Education

Joe Shawn thinks that whatever he selects as instructional strategies will be very important to the future success of the course and, ultimately, the undergraduate management program. Brian, his teaching assistant, and he spend a great deal of time brainstorming types of instructional strategies for the WEI design, as well as motivational strategies for this targeted group. In general, they determine that they will need to clearly identify how the materials can be used in students' future business endeavors, and to make sure that the students realize how the content relates to them and their future careers. In addition, they plan on making sure that students have the opportunity through practice and assessments to demonstrate their level of achievement.

They use the modified class assignment page to help them brainstorm and organize the strategies. Dr. Shawn already has presentations created for the majority of the identified clusters. He plans to audio-narrate these presentations to provide content, so that he does not have to create a significant amount of text. He has many different class activities that he is going to try to repurpose for the online portion of the Web-enhanced class.

Because the course is Web enhanced, the class size will be the same as when it is taught in a face-to-face setting. With that in mind, he knows that he will have to consider limiting the level of student–instructor interaction unless he can convince his chair that a teaching assistant would help him monitor and facilitate discussions.

The following applies to all case studies. Consider how you, as a designer, might act or respond in each case study.

- What information is not presented that you would like to have had? How would you go about gathering that data?
- How do the earlier stages of the WBID Model influence the creation of the instructional strategies? What kinds of implications do issues of class size, navigation, learner control, and feedback have on the Web-based learning environment?
- What are the implications of media on each case?
- What would you do differently from each of the principals in the case studies? What advice would you offer the participants in each case?

Chapter **8**

Concurrent Design: Putting Design Plans into Development Action

In the WBID Model, design and development activities are completed concurrently. The design planning, which results in the WBI Strategy Worksheet, is the basis for developing the WBI and its prototypes. Additionally, message and visual design principles help guide the development, assembly, and organization of the Web page and website. In the concurrent design stage, initial development tasks include developing an interface prototype, creating flowcharts, and developing the storyboards. Later development tasks include developing the website, converting the instructional prototypes into Web pages, and incorporating media into the pages. Formative evaluation procedures are included to ensure that resulting WBI meets design specifications.

Chapter 8 begins with a discussion on basic principles related to message and visual design in WBI. We then present a brief description of an interface, including the use of visual metaphor and analogy, which culminates in sketching an interface and revising the initial prototype based on message design. We then introduce and discuss types of flowcharts and two types of storyboards that can be used in WBI development. A discussion on the technical issues associated with website development follows. The chapter closes with an overview of final developmental tasks related to formative evaluation.

Objectives

At the end of this chapter, you should be able to do the following:

- Identify appropriate principles of message and visual design for use in WBI development.
- Define interface.
- Explain when a visual analogy or metaphor should be used in WBI.
- Sketch an interface prototype.
- Develop flowcharts for the WBI.
- Explain two types of storyboards and their purposes.
- Develop a storyboard as an initial WBI prototype.
- Develop the WBI prototype.
- Identify any technical problems with WBI.
- Establish parameters for developing WBI.
- Continue formative evaluation while developing WBI prototypes.

Introduction

The last part of the concurrent design stage is development (Figure 8.1). Recall that in Chapter 6 we identified specific development tasks in the preplanning activities. They include creating, assembling and organizing the Web pages and website based on the WBI design. McClelland, Eisman, and Stone (2000) characterize a website as a "random assemblage of unrelated documents" (p. 23) and suggest that a designer must take advantage of technological capabilities to develop a successful website. In other words, part of the development process is to coordinate the WBI and its website into a cohesive environment.

Although the actual development of the Web pages and website is important and certainly impacts the WBI, this is not the main focus of this discussion, for several reasons. First, a considerable number of institutions are moving toward the use of LMSs, which lessens the demand or need for designers/instructors to create their own Web pages or websites. In addition, a number of Web tools are available for page and site development. For instance, a designer can use Web editors (*Composer, DreamWeaver, FrontPage, Fusion, GoLive, PageMill,* among others) and other tools, such as courseware tools, text editors, and conversion utilities to develop the WBI (Horton, 2000). Some of these popular tools can be purchased, and others are available for free. Finally, there are a number of resources available for designers to increase their technical skills and creative talents. Technical skills can be learned through technology-based courses, books, and self-paced tutorials. Creative skills are more difficult to learn. We suggest that designers read about message and visual design, examine other websites for their visual composition, and continue to practice, practice, practice. For some of us who are creatively challenged, Web artists/developers sell templates and sample websites.

The main focus of this discussion is to provide a general overview of the development tasks. The purpose of these tasks is to produce an innovative, educationally sound WBI that allows participants to navigate intuitively.

Figure 8.1   Development and formative evaluation processes of the concurrent design stage of the WBID Model.

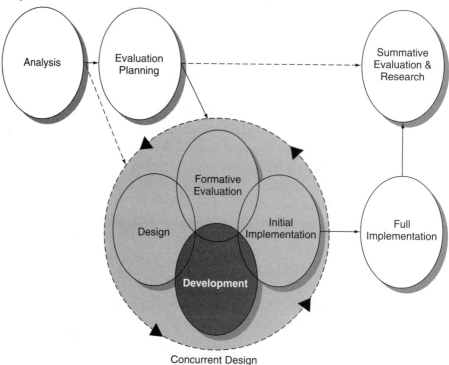

Concurrent Design

A general progression of WBI development is to sketch the interface, develop the flow-chart and storyboards, and produce the prototype Web pages and website or incorporate the prototypes into a LMS. Concurrently, formative evaluation procedures continue to identify technical problems within the WBI prototypes. However, this ordering of tasks may vary at the designer's discretion and in response to the WBI project's evolution.

To understand these tasks and their purposes, the designer must take into consideration how message design influences WBI development. We begin with a brief discussion on message and visual design.

Applying Message and Visual Design to WBI

The presentation of WBI content and activities is based not only on sound instructional design (ID) principles, but also on communication principles. According to Grabowski (1995), these principles facilitate carrying out the ID blueprint (i.e., plans documented in the WBI Strategy Worksheet).

Message design encompasses the visual features of text and graphics as well as their placement on the page. In a Web-based environment, proper use of message design allows designers to create appealing and suitable layouts for Web pages and websites, and to ensure smooth navigation within these virtual environments by the use of buttons, icons, and hypermedia links and through text and media (e.g., audio, video, and multimedia). Ideas based on message design help designers ensure effective dialogue and interchange of information between instructor and learners (Grabowski, 1995; Lohr, 2003; Ormrod, 2004; Richey, 1986; Seels & Richey, 1994).

Message Design

WBI is comprised of instructional content, directions, activities, and other types of information provided for learners. Learners and instructor communicate with each other using emails, chats, threaded discussions, and other Web technologies. The instruction is developed through a combination of text and graphical elements (buttons, icons, charts, tables, etc.), and media (graphics, illustrations, photos, video, audio, etc.).

Message design in WBI requires special considerations due in part to the separation of learner and instructor. Directions must be clear, the information must be organized so that it is easy to understand, feedback should be readily available, and navigation should be easy and straightforward (Nielson, 2000).

The designer concentrates on the text, graphical elements, and media to make sure that any noise is reduced and that the instructional message is clear and understood (Grabowski, 1995; Lohr, 2003; Ormrod, 2004; Richey, 1986). **Noise,** or interference, includes unclear directions, inappropriate or irrelevant visuals or text, poor navigational metaphors, and inadequate visual elements such as poor backgrounds, unreadable font styles and sizes, and uncomplementary color combinations. Table 8.1 outlines basic principles to guide designers when making these initial WBI development decisions.

Part of developing an effective instructional message is to make it appealing. To develop an attractive WBI, the designer needs a conceptual understanding of the principles related to visual design.

Visual Design

Visual design is often associated with both the aesthetics of the Web page features and the website's functionality (Alexander & Tate, 1999; Clark & Mayer, 2003). Aesthetics and functionality must balance to create a WBI that is visually pleasing, technically precise, and educationally sound. Clean, crisp, and clear designs help learners accurately receive and interpret the instructional message. However, determining what "looks good" is not only in the eye of the beholder, it also is based on principles related to visual design (Alexander & Tate, 1999; Grabowski, 1995; Simonson et al., 2000; Smaldino et al., 2005).

Fonts and Styles. An example of identifying visually pleasing and instructionally sound elements is the selection of fonts (often called *typefaces*) and type style. A huge number of fonts are available, and designers must select one or two that are best for their WBI. They must choose based on the readability and legibility of the font, which can vary due to size, the type style (boldface, italics, etc.), and use of upper and lower case (Lynch & Horton, 1999; Smaldino et al., 2005). Readability and legibility of fonts will vary by

Table 8.1   Guiding Principles of Message Design

Feature	Guidelines
Text elements	1. Write clearly and concisely. 2. Provide directions for how to proceed through WBI, practice exercises, and assessments. 3. Web pages should not be long listings of text. Besides being boring, this is difficult to read. 4. Scrolling should be minimized. 5. The font and its size should be selected based on learners' reading abilities and the font's legibility. 6. Tables should be used to highlight important information. 7. Use white space so that the page does not seem crowded, too complex, or too difficult to read.
Graphical elements: Charts, tables, image maps, icons and buttons	1. Locate buttons in a consistent place on the Web page. 2. Relate icons to the instructional content or function. 3. Clearly identify all links. 4. Include a return link to the WBI. 5. Use default color settings or clearly identify differences. 6. Use tables and charts to organize information.
Media: Graphics, illustrations, photos, video, audio, and animated features	1. Use media that are relevant and meaningful. 2. Be consistent with the size of the graphics in relation to the Web pages. 3. Use adequate white space in graphics. 4. Limit the use of animated GIFs, repeating Flash files, and blinking text. 5. Permit users to bypass repeating files.

Source: Table data are from Boling & Frick (1997), Grabowski (1995), Hannum (2001), Jones & Farquhar (1997), Lynch & Horton (1999), Nielson (2000).

learner opinion and delivery system (Lohr, 2003); in other words, what is pleasing and appropriate for one individual may not be for another. What is suitable for one delivery system (books, computers, etc.) may not be suitable for another. For WBI, both Lynch and Horton and Lohr suggest that the designer select commonly used typefaces (either serif or sans serif) so that the WBI will load properly. Figure 8.2 shows selected font examples and nonexamples for WBI.

The examples on the left in Figure 8.2 are commonly used fonts that work well because of their legibility on a monitor and because of clarity of the typeface. The nonexamples (on the right) are in the same point size as the examples; however, most are too small or complex to be read clearly and easily. While attention getting, they will be difficult to read on a computer screen.

Charts, Tables, and Other Illustrations.   Charts, tables, and other types of illustrations in WBI also may facilitate comprehension and learning. Lohr (2003) maintains that

Figure 8.2   Font style examples and nonexamples for WBI (shown in 12 point size).

Suitable Fonts for WBI	Fonts Not Suitable for WBI
Arial	Decorative styles:
Bookman	Caslon Open Face
Times New Roman	HERCULANUM
Courier New	Bernard Fashion
New Bakersville	Script:
Frutiger	Charme
Helvetica	**Brush Script**
	Isadora
	Free Style Script

when designing or adding graphics to instruction, they should be not only interesting, but functional. She further suggests that graphics that are driven by the technology rather than by the instruction are generally not well designed or meaningful. Figure 8.3 provides several graphics that are *not* appropriate for WBI because they lack contrast and have visual clutter.

Ultimately, well-designed graphics provide a visual perspective of the information presented, are practical, and support the message and add meaning to the content. Examples of clear, uncluttered graphics are shown in Figure 8.4.

The graphics in both Figure 8.3 and 8.4 are presented here in grayscale to illustrate the need for clarity, simplicity, and contrast within the confines of this text. They may be seen in their original colors on this text's Companion Website.

Color.   Although appropriate color adds to aesthetic appeal, graphics may not add to or enhance the instructional message. The use of color may create visual clutter for some learners; other participants may not be able to see details within the image due to color blindness. Finally, even when graphics are visually appealing, clear, and meaningful, the designer must consider whether visual complexity (e.g., visual effects of blurring, washing out, or transparency) has been added. Adding visual complexity also can increase file size; large files can be slow to up- and download (Nielson, 2000).

Figure 8.3   Graphical nonexamples containing low contrast, shadowing, or other visual clutter that do not clearly convey the message of connecting to the Web.

Figure 8.4   Graphics that convey the message of connecting to the Web with clarity and without visual clutter.

Overall, a general guideline for designers is to select (or create) graphics that reduce the noise inherent in visually cluttered or complex graphic files. Simple, clear graphics of a small file size will load quickly; they reduce noise and minimize participant frustration.

See this textbook's Companion Website (http://www.prenhall.com/davidson-shivers) for color version's of figures 8.3 and 8.4.

Other Communication Principles.   Other communication principles associated with good visual design are those of simplicity, balance, emphasis, and harmony (or unity) (Nielsen, 2000; Savenye, Smith, & Davidson, 1989; Simonson et al., 2000). Used in combination, these principles allow designers to create a visually attractive Web page and website. A detailed description of the many visual design principles is beyond the scope of this discussion. Table 8.2 presents a basic overview of important design considerations.

See Appendix B for additional information on message and visual design principles.

Consistency.   The use of consistent text, graphics, and media is fundamental to developing a well-designed WBI. Consistency among graphics and text reduces cognitive overload by removing unnecessary complexity and making the WBI easier for learners to use (Berry, 2000; M. Hughes & Burke, 2000; Nielson, 2000; Zwaga, Boersema, & Hoonhout, 1999). By contrast, an inconsistently developed WBI creates confusion and is harder to navigate. Inconsistency occurs when different fonts (styles and sizes) graphic types, and random links have neither rhyme nor reason for their placement and use, creating a dis-

Table 8.2 Basic Principles of Visual Design: Explanations and Guidelines

Principle	Explanation	Guidelines
Simplicity	Elements essential to the instruction; avoid extraneous features	1. Keep page easy to read. 2. Follow general reading patterns (left to right, top to bottom). 3. Use the idea of less is more. 4. Avoid overcrowding. 5. Follow flow patterns for text and graphics, such as in the shape of the letters C, S, or Z. These patterns allow the learner to see/read information from right to left and top to bottom and have visual appeal. 6. Apply two rules of thumb. *Rule of thirds:* mentally divide screen or page into thirds; placing elements on imaginary lines may be more balanced and pleasing to the eye. *7 × 7 rule:* include 7 lines of text down by 7 words across (a slide or screen) to reduce overcrowding. 7. Limit the color variation of text and borders.
Balance	Sense of equilibrium in a graphic or visual Symmetrical: left and right of the visual's center contain equally weighted and spaced objects Asymmetrical: larger objects are placed closer to center than smaller ones	1. Avoid off-balance designs; they are disturbing to the eye. 2. Asymmetrical visuals are more interesting, but could be more difficult to create. 3. Use color, contrast, size, and position when creating visual balance.
Emphasis	Essential, or key, elements to the idea presented are displayed as important and are the main visual focus	1. Use color, contrast, size, shapes, etc. to add emphasis to important features. 2. Use cues such as arrows, boldface, italics, etc. to add emphasis. 3. Highlight important elements.
Harmony (or unity)	Important elements coordinated for a specific purpose	1. Overlap items. 2. Use a single color to suggest connections. 3. Repeated shapes, objects, sizes, and colors suggest unity. 4. Objects that are close together are viewed as connected.

Source: Table data are from Boling & Frick (1997), Hall & Gottfredson (2001), Hannum (2001), Jones & Farquhar (1997), Khan (2001), Lohr (2003), Nielsen (2000), Rice et al (2001), Savenye, Smith, & Davidson (1989), Simonson et al. (2000).

jointed appearance throughout the WBI environment. Likewise, inappropriate visuals, flashing GIF animations, scrolling text, and odd color combinations decrease the full potential of WBI. Instead of enhancing learning, extended use of such elements only distracts learners. However, some embellishments can be added to a consistent layout to create visual interest and style. Lohr (2003) suggests that a consistent layout without some embellishments is too predictable and boring. The skill is in knowing the right amount of embellishments to add to Web page layouts.

GardenScapes

Elliott and Kally agree to general message and visual design guidelines for developing their WBI prototypes (from storyboard to final product). As they choose specific fonts, color choices, and so on and when and where they will place them on the Web page layouts, they create a job aid to help ensure consistency.

Message and Visual Design Guidelines for *GardenScapes*

Feature/Principle	Application Ideas for Lessons
Text elements	• Text will be clearly written. • Text on Web pages will be concise and focused. • If scrolling is necessary, it will be minimized as much as possible. • Directions on how to use the WBI, LMS, and assignments will be included.
Graphical elements: Charts, tables, image maps, icons and buttons	• Buttons and links will appear in the same places on each Web page. • Graphics will relate to garden themes and the chosen metaphor. • Default settings for links will be used. • Where needed, tables will be used to organize text for easy examination.
Media: Graphics, illustrations, photos, video, audio, and animated features	• Graphics will be relatively small. • Graphics will be sized similarly throughout the website. • No blinking text will be used. • If animation is incorporated, learners will be able to access it.
Simplicity	• Text colors will be limited to black, green, and blue. • Text, graphical elements, and media will be formatted to read like a book, from left to right. • Long pages will be subdivided, with buttons and links to move to next sections.
Balance	• The pages will vary in symmetry to add interest, but still remain consistent. • Text and figures will be used to organize the information.
Emphasis	• New terms, assignment due dates, and important information will be highlighted using bold and italics. • New items will be highlighted in red. • Some embellishments will be added to Web pages to add variety and interest.
Harmony (or unity)	• Consistent coloring schemes will be used. • The same set of icons will be used throughout the website to unify the site. • Circles and ovals in the background may be used to signify unity among objects.

See this textbook's Companion Website (http://www.prenhall.com/davidson-shivers) for the *GardenScapes* Design Document.

On Your Own

Consider how you will apply message and visual design principles in your WBI project. What specific principles will you use? Use tables 8.1 and 8.2 and the GardenScapes example as your guides. Add this information to your Design Document.

(For illustrations of how other designers tackled these same issues, review the case studies appearing in the Extending Your Skills section at the end of this chapter.)

See this textbook's Companion Website (http://www.prenhall.com/davidson-shivers) for a printable version of the design principles template.

The Interface

The "look" of the WBI and the navigational and structural features of a Web page influence its usability (Nielsen, 2000).

An **interface** is composed of the pieces of information displayed and the arrangement of presented information. Designers must decide how that arrangement is perceived and experienced by the user in an instructional product (Jones & Farquhar, 1997; McClelland et al., 2000). In other words, the interface is what the learner sees when viewing a Web page and is made up of text, graphical elements, and other media. The interface should be designed in such a fashion that the learner doesn't even notice it; interface elements that facilitate intuitive navigation include consistent placement and behavior (Khan, 1997; McClelland et al.).

An interface that is structurally sound allows learners to use it intuitively. This intuitiveness helps learners succeed, not only in navigating through the website, but in learning the instructional content.

Use of Metaphors and Analogies

One of the first considerations in developing the interface is to decide whether to use a visual analogy or metaphor. **Visual analogies** are ways to describe or illustrate the unfamiliar by comparing it with something familiar (Simonson et al., 2000). An instructional **metaphor** is a representation of a mental model that helps guide learners through a learning experience (Driscoll, 2005; Lohr, 2003). A visual analogy or a metaphorical representation should be something familiar to the learner and should complement the content or the idea being presented in the WBI. Analogies and metaphors are often used in computer-based training and WBI to help learners recognize some particular aspect of the instruction. For instance, throughout this text, we use icons to indicate when additional information appears either in an appendix or on this text's Companion Website.

According to Nielson (2000), metaphors are useful for providing a unifying framework for a Web page and its associated website; they promote learning by permitting individuals

Figure 8.5 Icons used in metaphors and analogies.

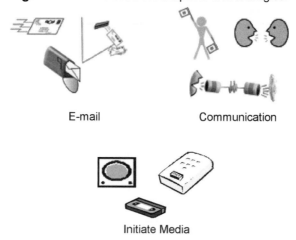

E-mail   Communication

Initiate Media

to use prior knowledge to complete instructional materials. An example of a metaphor is the use of VCR or DVD controls to move through the WBI. Figure 8.5 shows several icons that can be used for certain aspects or features of the WBI.

Yet, the use of metaphors or analogies is not without controversy. Not everyone agrees that metaphors or analogies are necessary in WBI; there are many examples of the misuse or inappropriate use of metaphors (Nielson, 2000). Lohr (2003) suggests that designers will often spend too much time and effort trying to be clever with metaphors and analogies when a simple, straightforward interface would be most appropriate. When developing or using a metaphor, designers must carefully determine whether and how well it represents the related content, context, or idea.

Sketching the Interface

The basic elements of an interface include the analogy (or metaphor) components, text, graphics, media, and navigational placeholders; designers must define each of these elements. When sketching the interface, the designer gathers the graphics, icons, text, and other elements together; once gathered, the process of fitting them together can begin.

To create prototypes quickly, Rudd, Stern, and Isensee (1996) suggest that prototype development may start out with low-fidelity images such as, an interface produced as a paper and pencil sketch has low fidelity. Low fidelity allows the designer and others to generate visual ideas quickly and thus agree without delay on the direction of the prototype. As the development progresses toward final draft, high-fidelity prototypes are created. An interface developed as a computer-generated document has higher fidelity. Using presentation or graphics software, designers can manipulate the location or arrangement of the interface elements as a part of a rapid prototyping technique. When using an LMS, the interface may be already defined, permitting little designer modification. In this event, designers should concentrate on the arrangement of information that they have control over.

GardenScapes

Elliott and Kally discuss the interface for their WBI project. Because Kally wants to emphasize creating a garden, they decide to develop a metaphor of a growing garden as the general interface. Their initial idea is to use different aspects of gardening to identify the various class activities within the WBI's six lessons and supplemental resources. They plan to design icons to use as buttons that will link the learner to the various lessons and the subcomponents.

Elliott and Kally begin gathering graphics, including garden tools, seed packets, plants, butterflies, and birdbaths, and examples of fonts and type styles. Elliot starts sketching the initial interface.

Initial Interface Sketches for Main Page of *GardenScapes* (*without their placement*)

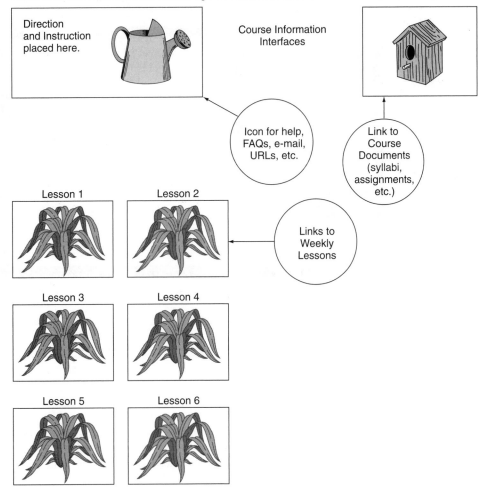

Elliott refers to his message and visual design notes while he develops the interface. As Kally and he review the various prototypes, they revise or select other options for icons. In their latest version, the chosen graphics relate to the garden themes, common buttons and links will be found on all Web pages. They plan to use text, graphical elements, and media to present information. Blinking text will *not* be used. Scrolling will be limited as much as possible. Adequate white space on Web pages will reduce density and complexity.

Elliot designs the Web pages with complementary colors to add unity to the message. He chooses to use only four colors for text, borders, and so on; they will be applied consistently throughout the WBI. He chooses to employ garden-based icons; for example, a hand cultivator and hoe might signify an activity. Buttons will be located at the left side of the screen in a menu format. To the right of the menu will be space for the content presentation, activities, and directions. Elliott's revised interface follows:

Interface Prototype for *GardenScapes* (Revisions based on message and visual design descriptions and formative reviews)

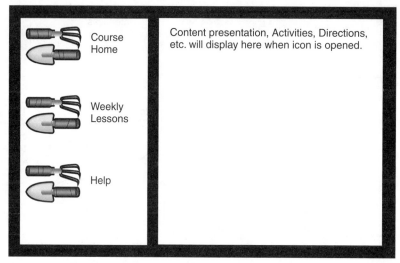

See this textbook's Companion Website (http://www.prenhall.com/davidson-shivers) for the *GardenScapes* Design Document.

ON YOUR OWN

Consider whether it is appropriate to use a metaphor or an analogy for your WBI. If so, briefly describe the metaphor or analogy. Make an initial sketch of your interface. What colors will you use? Where will you locate the buttons on the Web page? Are you being consistent with colors, fonts, styles, placement of links, icons, and so on? Is your design aesthetically appealing?

(For illustrations of how other designers tackled these same issues, review the case studies appearing in the Extending Your Skills section at the end of this chapter.)

Flowcharting

Flowcharting illustrates the structure of the WBI as a single lesson or as a collection of lessons (or units) within a course and identifies the instructional flow. This flowchart does *not* contain instructional text or content, which were identified in the LTM or on the WBI Strategy Worksheet. Rather, it establishes navigational specifications for the website and provides an outline of the instructional sequence. Maddux and Cummings (2000) suggest that designers develop flowcharts before committing resources to full WBI development.

A flowchart for a simple WBI lesson is shown in Figure 8.6. In this sequence, learners are guided step by step through a lesson, beginning with a set of directions. As outlined in

Figure 8.6   Flowchart that outlines the navigation in a simple WBI lesson.

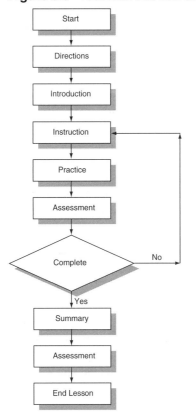

the WBI Strategy Worksheet, learners are presented with an introduction, a series of concepts, and opportunities for practice. The learners complete a summary and final assessment as they end the lesson.

Flowcharting is directly related to website navigation. The flowchart indicates the types of decisions that end users will be able to make based on how the units of instruction (or lessons) are sequenced and linked together. The example in Figure 8.6 is linear navigational flow. Appendix B contains nonlinear examples.

See Appendix B for additional flowcharting examples.

Flowcharts can be created using a variety of applications, including *PowerPoint, Inspiration, Visio, Image Composer,* and most word processing applications. Websites may be designed in one of four ways: linear, hierarchical, hierarchical with association, and random (Lin & Davidson, 1996; Rasmussen & Davidson, 1996).

Designers must answer the following questions when developing the flowchart:

- How will the learning sequence be organized?
- How will learners navigate the website?
- Will learners access the instruction in random or predetermined order?
- Will access to various sections of the instruction be restricted?
- Will there be a conclusion and assessment for each section of the instruction or will there be one conclusion and assessment for the entire course or lesson?

Flowcharts and Learning Management Systems

Most LMSs provide a structure that assists designers in organizing instructional websites. Although LMSs usually provide consistent structure, they can restrict creativity by not allowing designers or instructors input on page or website organization. While developing the flowchart, the designer examines the structure of the LMS, including how content is displayed and how features such as chat and discussions are accessed, to minimize conflict between the proposed structure of the WBI and the requirements of the LMS.

GardenScapes

Elliott evaluates the different types of instructional sequences. The design most closely related to the conceptualization of the course is hierarchical with association (found in Appendix B). The course will be embedded into an LMS. Using the structural framework of the LMS, Elliott creates the following flowchart to represent how learners will progress through the lesson.

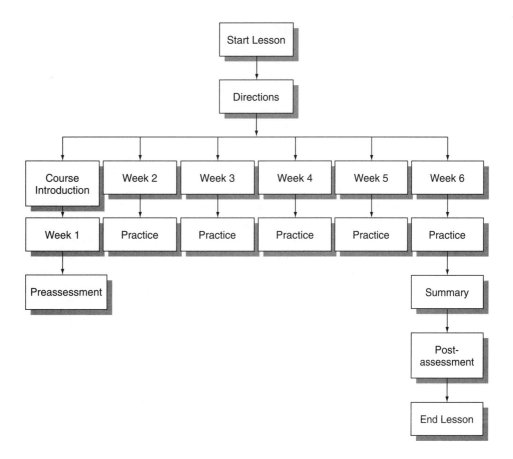

See this textbook's Companion Website (http://www.prenhall.com/davidson-shivers) for the *GardenScapes* Design Document.

ON YOUR OWN

Create a flowchart for your WBI project. (If you are using an LMS, make the flowchart fit its structure.) Present how the learner will move through the units of instruction (or lessons) and show the types of decisions that they are allowed to make. What types of Web pages will you need to create? Review Appendix B and identify the design type your flowchart depicts. Add the flowchart and accompanying description to your Design Document.

(For illustrations of how other designers tackled these same issues, review the case studies appearing in the Extending Your Skills section at the end of this chapter.)

Storyboarding

Storyboards organize the directions, instructional content, and supporting information of the WBI into a meaningful structure (Maddux & Cummings, 2000). Designers use storyboards to define what each created Web page will look like and, consequently, they serve as another type of prototype. In essence, storyboards formalize the interface and show how all of the Web page elements will function together.

Storyboarding is the development step that illustrates how the instructional text, media, and graphical elements will be found on each Web page. The text contains the directions, instructional content, practice, and feedback that have been proposed in the WBI Strategy Worksheet (refer to Chapter 7). The proposed media, also identified in the worksheet, include the graphics, video, and audio for these pages. The graphical elements include items such as charts, tables, image maps, icons, and buttons.

Storyboarding permits quick product development, and provides a means for making decisions about the entire website based on the planned strategies (i.e., the WBI Strategy Worksheet) before the WBI is taken to the next level of development. Documenting these decisions (and their approval) on storyboards ensures consistency of content and uniformity of style, color, and element location (Instructional Technology Research Center, 2004).

A style guide can be used with storyboarding. **Style guides** outline policy decisions of font, style, size, color, and placement; size of graphics; and conversational style (formal or informal). Style guides help organizations create uniformity among WBI products. A style guide is especially useful when a design team is involved and when the WBI project is complex or is part of a series. The resulting consistency enables end users to navigate from one WBI to another without having to relearn icon, button, and so on meaning and placement.

Types of Storyboards

There are several formats for storyboards. Two types useful in WBI development are the detailed storyboard and the streamlined storyboard.

Detailed Storyboard.   A **detailed storyboard** contains all the details about the Web page, including all graphics, fonts, styles, color, size, background color or image name, and navigational buttons. This storyboard should look very similar to the resulting Web page, although design changes may occur after storyboards are created. Figure 8.7 shows a sample of a detailed storyboard. The storyboard displays the font choices (Comic Sans) and the relative sizes (e.g., headings, 14 point; text, 12 point), and visually depicts the relationship of the interface elements for each page. Any graphics can be sketched or any clip art can be placed on the storyboard as well.

The resulting Web page from this detailed storyboard is illustrated in Figure 8.8. Note the ways in which the storyboard and the Web page are alike, and how they differ.

Streamlined Storyboard.   The **streamlined storyboard,** which can be formatted as a table or a matrix, helps to organize all the Web pages in the WBI. In a streamlined storyboard, the instructional pages for each lesson, based on the content and strategies provided in the WBI Strategy Worksheet, are identified for every Web page being developed. These pages state the alignment of the objectives, the instructional text, and media (graphics, animations,

Figure 8.7 Detailed storyboard (not full scale).

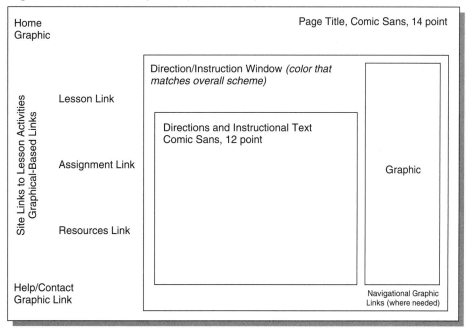

Figure 8.8 Example of a Web page from storyboards.

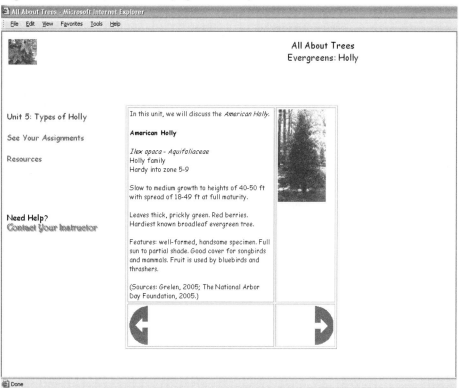

Table 8.3 Sample Streamlined Storyboard

Objective/Title of Page	Text Summary	Navigation/Sites	Other/Comments
5.3.1 Identify a Holly Tree Unit 5: Types of Holly	Give Latin name, *Ilex opaca-Aquifoliaceae* State interesting facts about the holly. Discuss types of holly trees, identifying specimen shown. Describe growth habit, identifying characteristics, environmental requirements. Discuss characteristics of holly that distinguish them from other evergreens. Include other pertinent facts. Cite sources of all information.	Links to: • See Your Assignments • Resources Graphic Link to Home Forward Arrow goes to next Evergreen Tree Lesson screen Back Arrow goes to Unit Introduction	Include graphics for heading and links and holder graphic next to text.

videos, etc.), and include any URLs. If the information on content and strategies appears in the WBI Strategy Worksheet in sufficient detail, then the designer may simply copy and paste that information into the appropriate cells of a streamlined storyboard and add other information to the other cells such as type of page (objective/concept), navigation/sites, and so on. In addition to the instructional Web pages, other pages, such as a course title page, directions pages, and assignment pages facilitate the WBI and they, too, must be created. Table 8.3 presents a sample streamlined storyboard for an individual web page within a unit of a WBI. Figure 8.8 (previously shown) also is the resulting Web page for the Lesson 5.1.3 page as described in the streamlined storyboard. (See Table 8.3).

It is good practice to create both detailed and streamlined storyboards because their combined use ensures that the client identifies and reviews all information needed for the Web pages, simplifying subsequent approval. Using both types of storyboards ensures that the design team has access to all of the necessary information to go forward.

GardenScapes

Elliott decides to use both detailed and streamlined storyboards to guide the development of *GardenScapes*. The detailed storyboard is based on the previously defined interface.

Storyboard for *GardenScapes* **Lesson 2:** How Does Your Garden Grow? Choosing a Garden Theme

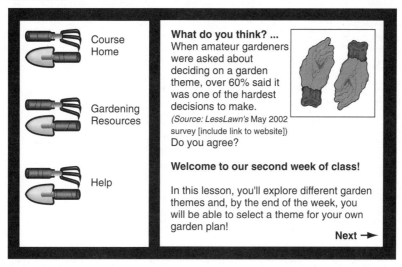

Screen Instructions:
Text: Web Default (Georgia)
Text Color: Black
Message Block: Black with 40% white fill
Horizontal Rule: Green
Back/Next Icons: Dk. Green
New Information Icon: Dk. Blue

Elliott develops streamlined storyboards using the LTM, clustered objectives, and the WBI Strategy Worksheet. He works with Kally on how the instructional strategies and course content can be converted into Web pages and a website. The following is part of his streamlined storyboard.

Objective/Concept	Text Summary	Navigation/Sites	Other
Title Page	Welcome to our course, *GardenScapes*. To begin the lesson, first visit the introduction link. Then review the syllabus. Once you've finished those sections, you're ready to begin your garden planning! Go to Week 1 to get started.	Other main sites (syllabus, introduction, week's lesson, etc.)	Garden Visual— main site email to support for technical assistance email to instructor

(continued)

Objective/Concept	Text Summary	Navigation/Sites	Other
About This Course	This course is designed to provide both new and experienced gardeners with skills to create exciting cutting gardens. You're ready to be a part of our garden club if you have both the desire to begin your own garden and design a location that you want to transform.	Return to main page	Garden Visual—transparent version
			email to support for technical assistance
			email to instructor
	If you're ready to get started, check out the syllabus and then begin with Week 1's lesson. If you have any technical problems, email our technical support team. If you have any questions about the class, send them to your instructor.		
	Welcome to Class!		
Syllabus	In process of being approved by CJC Administration. (to be added on approval)	Return to main page	Garden Visual—transparent version
			email to support for technical assistance
			email to instructor
Four Major Topics from WBI Strategy Worksheet	Check the textbook website for the completed streamlined storyboard.	Return to main page	Garden Visual—transparent version
			email to support for technical assistance
			email to instructor

See this textbook's Companion Website (http://www.prenhall.com/davidson-shivers) for additional storyboards for *GardenScapes.* in the Design Document.

ON YOUR OWN

Create storyboards for your WBI project, selecting the type (s) that will be most useful to you. In most cases, you will need to use a combination of detailed and streamlined storyboards. Create text, identify graphics, and specify navigational points. Align instructional material to the clusters of objectives that you have already defined. For informational messages (e.g., title pages, directions, etc.), use a streamlined storyboard and list the title of the page and create the text that the learners will see. Add the storyboards to your Design Document.

(For illustrations of how other designers tackled these same issues, review the case studies appearing in the Extending Your Skills section at the end of this chapter.)

Creating Web Pages and the Website

The commercial adage, "Just Do It" (Nike, Inc., 2004), is an important consideration when it comes to Web development. The process cannot move forward until the designer begins to actually produce the instructional text and other elements that will appear on the Web page.

In some instances, some designers may be more comfortable with and enjoy the early design and development tasks of concurrent design, and then pay less attention to the actual Web page production. They are concerned with making sure those important elements are included on the storyboards and that most decisions are made prior to Web page prototyping. However, the emphasis on these aspects of the development tasks may extend the length of the concurrent design process.

In some instances, designers may be too eager for Web page prototyping and rush into actual page development with little time spent on these early tasks. Emphasis on Web page production may cause the WBI project to have faulty starts that require numerous revisions and costly overruns, which could have been avoided by spending more time on the early tasks of concurrent design.

When the design team (whether one person or many) has thought through the design and development tasks and made appropriate decisions throughout the concurrent design stage, the WBI project should be on track in terms of resources, budget, and time with the quality of the WBI maintained.

The next step is to develop the WBI prototype. Because formative evaluation procedures are built into concurrent design, development decisions, prototypes, and final WBI are reviewed similar to the way the WBI design plans were evaluated. The designer must take care of the technical issues that could affect prototype development.

Technical Issues Associated with Website Development

The technical issues associated with website development are load speeds, server capabilities, and cross-browser functionality. Other issues related to user access, copyright, maintenance, and use of Web page editors, should be considered in website development. Jones and Farquhar (1997) describe the Web as an open system, which adds an element of complexity to WBI development. At the point of development, the environmental information from the analysis stage should be reviewed to determine if any changes with the facilities or equipment have occurred since the actual analysis. Different organizations will have specific technical issues that should be investigated in this part of development. The issues outlined in this chapter should be used as a starting point for identifying organization-specific issues.

Download Speeds

Download speeds are affected by how the site is accessed (e.g., modem, broadband, or direct connection) and the complexity of the Web page. Pages should download as quickly as possible to decrease participants' frustration levels (Nielsen, 2000). Some editors, such as

Microsoft *FrontPage,* display download times on pages as they are developed. Nielsen suggests that the simple rule is the faster the page is displayed, the better.

The elements contained on a Web page influence how fast it appears on a user's computer system. For instance, text documents, unless unusually lengthy, download quickly. However, animated GIFs, music, graphics, and graphical devices such as tables, *Flash* animations, or downloaded or streaming video increase the amount of display time needed. Large file sizes and graphics (e.g., tables, photos, clip art) and media (e.g., streaming video) increase a page's complexity, and it will take longer to appear (or load).

It is easy for the novice or "technology happy" designers and stakeholders (sometimes called *techno-romantics*) to include far more media and graphics on a Web page than are really necessary. Designers must consider carefully each item to make certain that it is relevant and necessary to the learning environment (Berry, 2000; Clark & Mayer, 2003; Lynch & Horton, 1999).

Servers

As a website is developed, the capabilities of the server are identified to ensure that the site will function as planned. Not all servers have the capabilities required by the design plan. Special server software, called *extensions,* must be installed to implement various Web-based functions (Dashti, Kim, Shahabi, & Zimmerman, 2003). For example, videos have special server requirements and extensions such as Real Media *Server* or Microsoft *Media Player* must be installed (Real Media, 2004).

Another concern to be addressed is determining from which server(s) the WBI will be stored and accessed. In many organizations, one server is used for development and another for delivery and implementation. Working closely with the technical staff of the host (or LMS) organization is critical to ensure that the website is fully functional and located on the proper servers.

Technical staff members provide server access, security protocols, and other information valuable to maintaining the website. All of these elements require specialized technical knowledge and skills that most designers do not (nor need to) possess. Designers, however, need to know what to ask about these technical issues. Table 8.4 provides an outline to guide the designer on technical issues. The list is *not* comprehensive; other questions, pertinent to the organization and situation, certainly can and should be added.

Cross-Browser Functionality

Different browsers and different versions of a browser will inevitably be used by learners and instructors to access the website. In other words, all participants may not upgrade browsers at the same rate, and types and versions of browser being used may not be fully compatible. The most up-to-date version of the browser will not always be needed; many individuals prefer to keep a stable browser, rather than often updating it. In a class, learners may have many different browser versions. The website should meet a common denominator of technology as determined in the environmental analysis.

Also, although HTML (hypertext markup language), XML (extensible markup language), and other Web editing languages create *platform-independent* (i.e., not tied to a specific operating system) Web pages, designers should be aware that different operating systems display content using different rules, and should design their websites accordingly.

Table 8.4 Suggested Questions to Ask About the Technical Issues

Questions About the Server	Questions Related to Website Support
1. How do I get access to the development server?	1. How is the site backed up?
2. What server should I develop on?	2. When is the site backed up?
3. Will that server be the production server?	3. What are the server access hours?
4. What security concerns should I be concerned with?	4. Is there a mirror server/site?
5. What security authority do I need to develop the site?	5. Who will provide help when problems arise?
6. What will my URL be?	
7. Will my learners need any special access or security authority?	
8. What access and use policies do I need to know?	
9. How can the LMS (if any) be used?	
10. Are there protocols for file organization?	
11. Are there download timeout parameters for large graphics?	

(For example, text formatted specifically for Windows-based browsers may appear several sizes smaller and be unreadable when displayed on Apple Mac OS–based browsers.)

ADA Requirements

The Americans with Disabilities Act (ADA) (U.S. Department of Justice, 1990) and the Web Accessibility Initiative (W3C, 2001) are very important to designers. The ADA's implications for information distribution on the Web were quickly noted, creating the need for several levels of accommodation. In the development stage, the website not only must meet ADA requirements, but also meet the Web Accessibility Initiative's Priority 1 checkpoints. The Web Accessibility Initiative outlines three priority levels; each level has specific checkpoints that guide the development process and ultimately, the website.

Copyright Issues

The Technology, Education, and Copyright Harmonization Act (2002) extends the fair use guidelines of the Copyright Act of 1976 to distance education settings and ensures that WBI instructors have the same rights and responsibilities of educators in traditional classrooms. The Copyright Act of 1976 refers to "the legal rights to an original work [and] set the conditions under which anyone may copy, in whole or part, original works transmittable in any medium" (Smaldino et al., 2005, p. 11). Regarding the "fair use" exception, Smaldino et al. state that "there are no absolute guidelines for determining what constitutes fair use in an educational setting. The law sets forth four basic criteria for determining fair use" (p. 87).

However, use of these "four basic criteria" does not mean that an instructor or instructional designer has *carte blanche* in the use of materials. Authorized use requires express, written permission that specifies the conditions for use of copyrighted materials. If questions arise about the use of copyright, designers should investigate ramifications of using the material (Zobel, 1997).

Some copyrighted materials, including the WBI being developed, can require password access to guarantee that only the appropriate users (e.g., instructor, author, learners) can access the information. Most LMSs limit access to the WBI and its website by requiring security passwords for login.

To avoid copyright entanglements, designers can use works in the public domain, create their own content, or obtain written permission to use copyrighted works (which may incur a fee to the copyright owner). In addition, many organizations have policies related to intellectual property that must be followed. Libraries in organizations offering distance programs are a prime source of information and support in the area of copyright.

Maintenance Issues

Another technical concern experienced when developing WBI is maintaining the website. External links that are active during development may not continue to work during implementation because the Internet and the Web are ever-changing entities. Review and testing of such links and sites is required for the instruction's continued success. Some editors, such as Microsoft *FrontPage®,* test links automatically and return reports to the designer so that updates can be made.

In many ways, WBI can be viewed as in a continual state of development. The notion that the instruction is never actually completed requires that the instructor or someone at the client's location be responsible for the website after its development. A maintenance plan should be instituted to ensure that the website remains current each time it is implemented. Maintenance concerns related to implementation will be explored in Chapter 9.

Use of Web Editors

A **Web page editor,** or simply *editor,* is a tool that assists designers in Web page and website development. There are many editors available either as freeware or shareware, or as commercial products. Netscape *Composer,* Microsoft *FrontPage,* and Macromedia *DreamWeaver* are examples of commercial products. Some LMSs include simple editors that ease Web page development or allow editors to connect to them, thus enhancing development. Regardless of the type of editor used, the complexities of developing websites and pages are lessened with their use. Editors greatly enhance the ability of novice and experienced designers to develop Web pages and websites because skills in programming in HTML or other markup languages are not required.

GardenScapes

Elliott is investigating the technical issues that the design team may face. He identifies questions to ask Laila Gunnarson, the technical support staff member, working on this project.

Server Questions	Site Support Questions
• Do I need a password to access the development server? • Will the development site need to be transferred to a production server? • What will my URL be? • Are there requirements for file organization? • Are there learner access concerns I should be aware of? • How will learners be entered into the LMS? • Are there other policies that I need to know?	• When is the site backed up? • What are the server access hours? • Is there a mirror site? • Who will provide help when problems arise?

His other concerns are related to ADA, copyright, and use of Web page editors. Working with Laila and her staff, Elliott identifies the most appropriate solutions for his technical and other concerns.

Solution Summary

General Technical Issues

Learners will be able to access the site via home computers; learner access ranges from 56KB dial-up to T-1 and DSL connections. Learners who do not have access from their home or office can participate in the course from the main computer lab at CJC.

Visuals and video will be kept to a minimum to ensure that download speed is maximized.

Access to systems will be maintained 24 hours, 7 days per week.

Server Capabilities

Learners will be entered into the LMS by the Dept. of CDE staff.

The TLDC will be responsible for initial technology support. The College's information technology and computer support personnel will address concerns that TLDC cannot resolve.

Cross-Browser Functionality

Learners will use two primary browsers to access the instruction. The instructional product will be able to be viewed in both Netscape *Navigator* and Internet *Explorer*. Based on the analysis, with assistance from the computer support staff, a minimum version will be established.

ADA Requirements

CJC mandates that all instruction meet ADA requirements. In addition, all of the site will meet Priority 2 of the Web Accessibility Initiative, with the desire to meet as many Priority 3 checkpoints as possible.

Copyright Issues

The TLDC or the SMEs will generate all visuals and pictures on the site. In the case of a copyrighted visual being acquired, written permission of the copyright holder will be obtained and filed with the lesson documentation.

Use of Web Editors

The development team will use an editor when developing the WBI.

See this textbook's Companion Website (http://www.prenhall.com/davidson-shivers) for additional storyboards for *GardenScapes*. in the Design Document.

ON YOUR OWN

Identify technical and other website concerns for your project. Specify questions that need to be answered by the technical support staff. Identify potential solutions to these issues. Use the following chart to help organize the relevant issues.

(For illustrations of how other designers tackled these same issues, review the case studies appearing in the Extending Your Skills section at the end of this chapter.)

See this textbook's Companion Website (http://www.prenhall.com/davidson-shivers) for the *GardenScapes* Design Document.

Formative Evaluation and WBI Development

In the evaluation planning stage, the plans for conducting the formative evaluation process were completed and placed in the Design Document (see Chapter 5). Formative evaluation began with the design tasks in the concurrent design stage and continues with the development tasks. As the WBI evolves from design plans to prototypes (interface, storyboards, etc.) to final WBI product, the last phase of formative evaluation, end-user tryouts, occurs.

This may include all or some of the target member tryouts (i.e., one-to-one, small-group, and field trials). As discussed in chapters 2 and 5, the field trial may be the initial WBI implementation. These tryouts allow the designer, instructor, expert reviewers, and learners to work through the WBI to identify instructional and technical problems.

Modifications are made to the directions, instructional content, and activities as needed to improve the WBI. Support resources, such as technical directions, are integrated into the learning environment as needed. The more attention that is paid to the WBI and its learning environment during this last phase, the better the implemented WBI and its website will be.

GardenScapes

Throughout the concurrent design stage, Elliott, with Kally's assistance, has conducted formative evaluation on their plans and deliverables to make sure that all of the instructional elements that they are working on align to their plan. For their formal formative evaluation efforts, they perform the tryout group activities (one-to-one and field trials):

The formative evaluation tryouts

Conduct one-to-one evaluations where the target audience will review design drafts and storyboards:

- A novice Internet learner who is a beginning gardener
- An expert Internet learner who is a novice gardener
- An expert Internet learner who is a knowledgeable gardener

The field trial will consist of working with 17 members of the target audience who will work through the completed lesson during the first offering of the *GardenScapes* course.

The progression of *GardenScapes* design plan to WBI prototype requires some changes based on the tryouts. Reviewers, for example, propose changes for the interface design. Elliott also asks about lesson titles; based on the results of the one-to-ones and other reviews, the titles are kept as is. Formative evaluation continues through the field trial, where the questions detailed in the evaluation plan are addressed by a larger sample of participants.

See this textbook's Companion Website (http://www.prenhall.com/davidson-shivers) for the *GardenScapes* Design Document.

ON YOUR OWN

Review your plans for formative evaluation. As you go through your WBI development activities, put the last phase(s) of your formative evaluation plan into action and make modifications to the WBI as needed.

(For illustrations of how other designers tackled these same issues, review the case studies appearing in the Extending Your Skills section at the end of this chapter.)

Wrapping Up

In this chapter, we described the concerns related to developing instruction and the Web pages that comprise the website. Using the specifications from the WBI Strategy Worksheet and principles related to message and visual design, the Web development tasks of the concurrent design stage begin. The interface, flowcharts, and storyboards are initial prototypes of the WBI and are used to develop effective and attractive Web pages and website, gain client approval, and provide the design team a conceptual understanding of the WBI project. The designer uses these prototypes to develop the WBI's website. Questions on technical issues ranging from load speed, server capabilities, cross-browser functionality and issues related to ADA requirements, copyright, and use of web editors were identified. Formative evaluation is integrated into the entire Web development process.

Expanding Your Expertise

1. What are the main development tasks that should be accomplished in a WBI project? In a project team, who should be responsible for those tasks?

2. What development tasks do you think are the most critical to the success of the WBI project?

3. What strategies do designers need to employ as they convert design plans into WBI prototypes and then to having the WBI ready for implementation?

4. Describe the process for developing an interface using a metaphor or analogy. How does this process transfer into action? How do you go about developing your Web-based interface?

5. Do you think that use of a visual metaphor or analogy is necessary? Explain your point of view and support it with evidence drawn from the literature.

6. What technical or other issues do you consider to be the most important when considering WBI? How do you accommodate them?

7. How do you integrate or coordinate formative evaluation with Web development tasks?

8. Is conducting formative evaluation important to Web development? Why or why not? Explain your response.

Extending Your Skills

Case Study 1

PK–12 Schools

Megan Bifford has begun the development of her WebQuest, using Dodge's (1997) structure. Cassie, Rhoda, and Buzz, as well as their students have provided input into her design and provided feedback during the formative evaluation of her Design Document.

She is working on her interface, which will be fairly simple, using the major sections of a WebQuest: Introduction, Tasks, Process, Evaluation, and Conclusion.

Because the focus of the WebQuest is inquiry and science, icons will include graphics of scientists, scientific tools, and question marks. Each icon that is selected will relate to the concepts in the WebQuest. A simple visual design that includes all WebQuest sections will make up the interface. Because the WebQuest will be used in the classroom, extensive directions are not required: teachers will use the WSI as a supplement to their class materials and partially direct the WebQuest.

Megan uses a commercial Web editor to create her website. She is planning on storing her Web pages on the district server. She has a meeting scheduled with the county's computer support/information technology staff to address server and technical concerns and is starting to identify the questions she wants have answered.

Throughout this development, Megan will test her links, graphics, and Web pages. Of particular interest to Megan are issues related to ADA. Many children in the schools have varying exceptionalities and will require accommodations for full use of the website. When she has a working prototype, she will share it with Cassie, Rhoda, and Buzz for feedback.

Case Study 2   ## Business and Industry

With Stacey McGee's assistance, Homer Spotswood's program on safety is ready for development. Stacey has completed the TOAB. Homer's next task is to sketch an interface and select appropriate graphics that will support learners while they participate in the online portion of the class. A range of computer skills are held by M2 employees and the interface must be intuitive to all employees. In addition, since some employees may access the instruction through dial-up connections, the website should load quickly to minimize learner frustration. Homer wants to integrate a metaphor into the visual design to help employees link plant safety operations and the WBI. Homer and Stacey talk about how to design the interface as a representation of the plant floor. They sketch their ideas to share with the graphic artist who has been hired to work with a contracted Web programmer. Based on the interface ideas and the instructional strategies, Stacey will create a flowchart and a set of storyboards.

Homer has several meetings scheduled with the technical support group, headed by Nancy Wells, to address the concerns that the development team and plant employees will face. The Web programmer will create the website on the plant's backup server and will need access to technology resources. For implementation, however, the website will be hosted on an outsourced server that contains an LMS; funding for this outsourcing will flow through the technology group and will be part of the ROI calculations that CEO Bud Cattrell is interested in. The Web programmer will create documentation to assist M2 programmers in updating the website after development is completed and Homer will ask for guidance on what information M2 programmers will need for that continuing support.

Case Study 3   ## Military

The commanding officer of the Training Support Center, Captain Prentiss, has been impressed by the thoroughness of planning by Commander Rebekkah Feinstein's team. Their analysis, evaluation plans, and design strategies are consistent with the vision and direction of the Naval Education and Training Command and the Naval Personnel Development Command.

The three E^2C^2 major-topic teams press on with their development of functional prototypes of their individual courses. A great advantage they enjoy is their use of the learning content management system (LCMS). This system allows them to author content, import media, link to external resources, create assessment items, and develop glossaries—all within a collaborative digital environment even while some may be traveling. An additional advantage is that the periodic peer reviews (from the formative evaluation plan) are conducted on the same LCMS. This integrated design and development architecture enhances their production efficiency.

As prototype development continues, the teams determine the requirements for multimedia. Storyboards and scripts are developed to explain their instructional strategy to the supporting teams of graphic artists and animators. They determine that the information provided in several of the animations can be enhanced by explanatory narrations and contract with a professional to provide those narrations. Format standards for visuals, animations, and videography are agreed to and applied across the board. Finally, the LCMS development templates include an interface design and navigation scheme that is the same Navywide. What results is a seamless transition from one lesson to the other with continuity of style.

Although peer reviews provide valuable information, each of the teams voices concern that a "prototypical" learner would not have had input before the products went online. Since the development teams are co-located with the TSC's "A" schools, Lieutenant Bob Carroll is able to enlist the help of 21 junior sailors in the "pool" waiting to commence their training. These sailors provide valuable insight as to what visual designs, amount of information per visual, and practice items appeal to and work for them. Suggestions are incorporated in the WBI where possible.

Case Study 4   Higher Education

Based on the syllabi, the objectives and assessment for *Introduction to Management* have been completed and a set of instructional and motivational strategies has been established. Dr. Joe Shawn and his TA, Brian Cody, are ready to flowchart and storyboard each of the WEI class sessions, using the course schedule that has been created. Each will have similar types of Web pages: introduction, objectives, lesson materials (including presentations and activities), a practice assignment, and a summary. In addition, supporting Web pages for the face-to-face classes will be included.

The development of the website will occur within the University's LMS, minimizing the need for interface design. However, message design, instructional content, directions, and assignments must be exceptionally clear and concise. Because the course is Web enhanced, students participation and assignments in the online sessions will not have the immediate feedback from Dr. Shawn, which is similar to their oncampus sessions. Clear messages will assist students in completing the online work.

As part of his development duties, Brian works with the University's Information Technology Center to make sure that Dr. Shawn has all of the tools and access that he needs to begin creating Web pages. Brian uploads all of Dr. Shawn's presentations to the LMS. For the online sessions, Dr. Shawn creates the audio narrations for the presentations; these narrations must be completed before uploading.

Before Dr. Shawn actually creates the Web pages, he investigates how he can incorporate publisher materials into his lessons. His textbook publisher has *cartridges* that can be imported into the university's LMS. Depending on the materials that he can import without breaking copyright laws, the actual materials that he develops may be different than originally planned.

The following applies to all case studies. Consider how you, as designer, might act or respond in each case study.

- What is the relationship between the development tasks and the other concurrent design activities as outlined in the WBID Model? Is there a connection to activities of other stages within the WBID Model?
- How do design decisions influence development tasks?
- For each case, what other tasks need to be completed in developing the WBI?
- What would you do differently from each of the principals in the case study?

PART 3

IMPLEMENTATION AND EVALUATION OF WEB-BASED INSTRUCTION

Chapter **9**

Implementation: Establishing A Sense of Community

The implementation stage of the WBID Model brings the results of previous stages to fruition. Implementation procedures begin after concurrent design activities are completed. The major focus of implementation is creating the learning community, however it is designed. For implementation to be a success, each member of the learning community must understand online teaching and learning and must employ appropriate facilitation and management strategies. Personnel, budget, and time allocations are also critical to successful implementation. Final preparation activities include initial learner contact, a final check on WBI technical requirements, and participant training on online learning/teaching skills.

Chapter 9 begins with a brief overview of online teaching and learning, followed by a discussion of the activities and preparations needed for successful implementation. We devote the rest of the chapter to describing strategies for facilitating and managing an online learning community.

Objectives

At the end of this chapter, you should be able to do the following:
- Explain the online teaching and learning process.
- State the preplanning activities for implementation.
- Identify personnel who make up the implementation team.
- Identify budget and time allocations for WBI implementation.
- Identify final preparation activities for WBI implementation.
- Classify the two main aspects of implementation.
- Explain the facilitation strategies that support a Web-based learning community.
- Explain the management strategies that support WBI implementation.

Introduction

After WBI has been developed and formatively evaluated, implementation of the instruction begins (Figure 9.1). The major focus of implementation is creating an online learning

Figure 9.1   Implementation state of WBID Model; processes for either initial or full implementation.

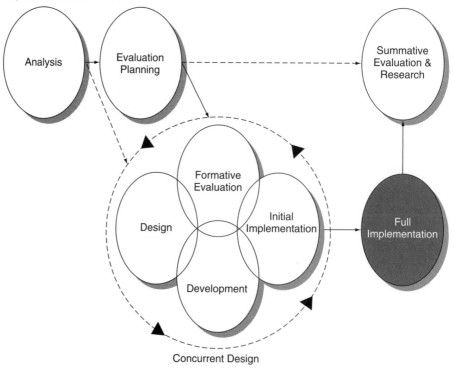

community based on the interactions among learners and instructor and the shared sense of purpose developed by the WBI participants. Successful implementation results in an active, flourishing online learning community.

Web-based learning communities take on different forms, from highly interactive environments to highly independent instruction with any number of variations in between (as discussed in Chapter 1). A learning community is formed when the instructor and learners have established their own group identity regardless of their level of interaction. To successfully establish such a community, instructors need a conceptual understanding of teaching and learning processes in an online environment.

A multitude of activities are involved in online teaching and learning. It is impossible to present in a single chapter everything that might occur during WBI implementation; rather, this chapter is simply a guide for implementing WBI.

Understanding Teaching and Learning in an Online Environment

Good teaching practices transcend delivery systems; a good instructor in an online learning environment will have traits to be a good instructor in a face-to-face classroom setting (e.g., dependability; clarity of policy; preparedness; subject matter knowledge; concern for learners' welfare; positive attitude toward teaching and learning; skill as an effective moderator; articulate, understandable delivery; etc.). Many instructors are well versed in strategies for the traditional classroom; however, the WBI environment requires additional or alternative instructional methods (Spector & de la Teja, 2001).

Online teaching and learning can be very personalized when instructor–learner activities are highly interactive and collaborative. Even when the WBI activities are independent and noncollaborative, individual online learners cannot become lost among the many. Although online learners may seem faceless, they are "known" by the instructor and the other learners. WBI participants are well aware of who is and is not participating in the learning community assignments and activities (Collison et al., 2000).

In online environments, contacts between learner and instructor tend to be quite individualized and independent of other whole-group assignments, activities, and interactions (Spitzer, 2001). In traditional classrooms much of the interaction occurs through questions or comments by an individual, which is heard by all participants in the room. By contrast, online learner–instructor interactions are usually written (e.g., email, discussions, feedback on assignments), and most do not involve other learners.

Additionally, WBI instructors can find the sheer volume of student communication overwhelming. Even with the majority of online instruction being independent learning (Clark & Mayer, 2003), these courses still require the instructor to interact in some manner with learners, typically on an individual basis.

Dempsey (2002) and Northrup (2002) maintain that online teaching is based on interaction, which can be characterized by the immediacy or perceived immediacy of a response. Learners, taking the course at their convenience, are able to contact instructors at all hours of the day or night. This may raise expectations in novice learners for immediate instructor response; similarly, a novice instructor may feel compelled to respond immediately to each and every learner message.

In contrast to traditional face-to-face environments, where college instructors teach one to three courses per week or teachers teach various courses on a daily basis, lessons in the online environment are accessed anytime, anywhere. This characteristic may create an expectation that the instructor is always "at the other end of the line" and available. Instructors must clear up any such misconceptions early in the course to manage their time and workload properly. Collison et al. (2000) suggest that instructors guard against responding immediately to learners so as to *not* raise unrealistic expectations.

As learners become experienced in online learning, their expectations may change and their need of instructor support may diminish. Prior experience with online instruction furnishes learners with a framework that helps them work through technical issues and problems. However, additional instructor guidance may be necessary, even for experienced online learners, when a new Web-based activity occurs or when there is a change in the LMS.

Another way for instructors to lessen unrealistic expectations is to establish designated times for responding to learners through online office hours or for checking email while still maintaining other types of instructional support (Davidson-Shivers, 1998, 2001). We advise instructors to encourage learners to develop their own support systems and troubleshooting strategies.

Understanding Online Mentoring

Mentors are individuals who work part time to assist instructors (they also may be referred to as teaching or graduate assistants, teacher aides, or tutors). If an instructor is fortunate enough to have the assistance of a mentor, then it is important that the mentor's role is clearly established and understood by all participants. A mentor is *not* a surrogate instructor; rather, a mentor supports and assists the instructor and learners. A mentor must be viewed as an essential part of the WBI community to be effective (Rasmussen, 2002). This integration occurs when the instructor explicitly defines to all participants the mentor's role and duties. Such definition has the added benefit of avoiding potential conflicts or duplication of effort.

Mentors may focus specifically on resolving technical issues, moderating online discussions, or tracking learner progress by scoring assignments and posting scores to the gradebook and to the learner (Gilbert, 2001; Zacbary, 2000). With requisite background knowledge or teaching experience, a mentor may be asked to help learners by providing content tutoring or by elaborating on ideas and concepts presented in the lectures or assigned readings (Marable, 1999; Rasmussen, 2002).

Implementation: Preplanning Activities

The WBI and its website have now been developed (or the WBI incorporated into an LMS). The WBI design team must now engage in preplanning activities and final preparations necessary to ensure that the online instruction is ready for implementation.

WBI implementation depends on the expertise of its personnel, and one of the preplanning activities is identifying the implementation team. Although this team may have some of the same members as the design team, it differs in terms of its purpose. The assigned personnel form a core group that addresses aspects of implementing the WBI and facilitating teaching and learning. In addition to the instructor, this team may include instructional support staff, such as the mentor. An instructional designer or evaluator may be involved if formative reviews, summative evaluations, or research activities are being conducted. Administrative and technical support staff also are usually a part of the implementation team; these staff members concentrate on managing the administrative infrastructure and operating the website.

Implementation Personnel

WBI Instructor.   The online instructor is the most "visible" individual to the learners and has the major responsibility for the WBI's success. The instructor provides the information on course goals and requirements and directs the learning events and activities. As a part of implementation tasks, the instructor needs to review and be well versed in the features of the developed WBI as well as with the instructional content, and is responsible for building rapport with learners through communication, established office hours (times for individual learners to share questions or concerns), synchronous discussions, group meetings, and other activities.

In addition, the instructor may need to develop personal information (e.g., a short biography with a photo, or a personalized video), the course schedule, and associated house-keeping documents (Collison et al., 2000; Davidson-Shivers, 1998, 2001; Davidson-Shivers & Rasmussen, 1999).

Depending on the organization's structure, the instructor may be responsible for delegating activities to and monitoring the mentor and support personnel (technical staff, administrative staff, etc.) and for making sure that links to the support team are activated.

WBI Mentors.   Although not all online instruction has mentors, when present, they play an important role in establishing a learning community. In fact, they may have a critical role when the student enrollment is large, learning tools are complex, and course assignments are complicated. Mentors work closely with instructors and, depending on the instructor's needs, may be involved with the WBI learning activities (moderating discussions, tutoring, etc.) rather than just the "behind the scenes" activities (addressing technical questions, scoring tests, etc.). Mentors should be helpful and accessible, and should be able to solve technical problems.

Their duties will vary by instructor and online course and will change over time (Salmon, 2000). Mentor duties may include tasks such as logging onto the system at least once a day to see if learners are having problems and keeping records of problems and technical issues for easy review and reference. They may contact learners as the course starts to begin developing rapport. By being especially responsive early in the course, mentors can reduce learner frustration.

Administrative and Technical Personnel.   WBI implementation is supported by the infrastructure of the organization. This infrastructure is not only the physical composition of an organization, but also the management and operation of that entity (Davidson-Shivers, 2002), and includes three types of personnel: midlevel to upper management, administrative support, and technical support personnel.

Manager or Administrator.   Support from mid- and upper-level management is critical for successful implementation and dissemination of any innovation (Barker, 1999; Davidson-Shivers, 2002; Lee & Johnson, 1998; Ritchie & Hoffman, 1997). Without such commitment, WBI cannot be implemented at a sophisticated, comprehensive, systemwide level. Managers do not need to take hands-on roles in the day-to-day activities of the actual WBI. Instead, they provide the infrastructure needed to institute and maintain a systemwide online educational or training programs.

As part of preparing for implementation, managers focus on allocating funding and other resources. For instance, they must find the funding to finance capital outlays for equipment (servers, computers, etc.) and appropriate software for the information technology or computer service centers, classrooms, office buildings, and libraries. Such facilities may even require retrofitting to extend the reach of technology access and support throughout the institution. Additionally, the technology will need to be upgraded periodically. Finally, managers are responsible for overseeing the necessary training of staff members (Candiotti & Clarke, 1998; Davidson-Shivers, 2002; Horgan, 1998; Microsoft Corporation, 1999; Morrison, 1996; Saunders, 1997; Zastrow, 1997).

Without this commitment by management, WBI initiatives may be consigned to delivery on a limited or *ad hoc* basis.

Administrative Staff Members.   The administrative staff personnel are the "behind-the-scenes" individuals who work with registration, enrollment, fees, and other operations. Their positions range from clerks and secretaries to coordinators and directors. As part of their implementation responsibilities, they contact learners, provide them access to the Web-based learning environment, coordinate registration, fees, and payments, and maintain student or employee records (Collis, 2001). Other responsibilities may be to distribute course materials, record and send grades or test scores to students or trainees, and distribute and analyze instructor/course evaluations (Burgess, 2002; Davidson-Shivers & Rasmussen, 1999; Rasmussen, Northrup, & Lee, 1997).

Technical Staff Members.   The final management and operations personnel group is the technical support staff, which includes programmers, technicians, and Web developers. Programmers work on the system software, ensure that the systems operate properly, and may supervise LMS operations. Technicians are primarily concerned with network infrastructure and computer access to that infrastructure. They are responsible for providing technical assistance to online participants, including identifying the adequacy of participant computer equipment and software, downloading and installing software, and troubleshooting problems as they arise (Collis, 2001; Hanuum, 2001; Khan, 2001). Web developers and webmasters work closely with instructors, especially in modifying the website, maintaining current outside Web resources, and updating software necessary for instruction (Collis; Robinson & Borkowski, 2000). Based on the organizational resources and complexity of the WBI and its implementation, one person can take on one or more of these technical duties.

In many cases, it is the instructor who will take on these additional duties. For instance, instructors act as technical or administrative support by solving technical problems or working through administrative tasks for individual learners. Yet, to fulfill these additional duties, the instructor must have the appropriate training to meet technical and administrative challenges (Fisher & Peratino, 2001; Robinson & Borkowski, 2000).

Identifying personnel required to fulfill implementation duties is only the beginning of meeting implementation challenges; other preplanning tasks involve budget and time allocations. Implementation costs are influenced by time constraints and demands and are comprised of personnel and the requirements for the technical infrastructure and WBI distribution.

Implementation Budget and Time Allocations

The organization's commitment to a WBI initiative can often be measured by the budget and time allocations awarded. Sufficient money and time must be committed for WBI to be implemented successfully, just as they are required for its design and development (Berge et al., 2001; Khan, 2001). Budget requirements for implementation fall into three general areas: technical infrastructure, materials distribution, and personnel.

Technical Infrastructure.   The infrastructure may be part of an organization's in-house service or it may be outsourced to another company. The technical infrastructure budget is associated with equipment such as servers, computers, network access, and other support systems for instructor and learner access. Licensing of software applications may include software needed for instructors' or learners' productivity, access, or communication needs. Other budget items are related to admissions, registration, fee collection, and maintenance of learner/employee records.

Time Allocations.   Most elements of a technical infrastructure require a long-term commitment. It may take years to develop the infrastructure required to support Web-based instructional efforts. Therefore, time requirements related to technical infrastructure must be built into an organization's overall strategic plans.

Materials Distribution.   Learner and instructor materials such as print and electronic media (texts, flash cards, DVDs, CDs, etc.), or other resources may need to be distributed to members of the learning community. Distribution costs depend on the design of both the online environment and any support materials, and their duplication for instructors and learners (Greer, 1992). For example, some WBI require learners to use workbooks or specialized software.

Organizations may send instructors, facilitators, and mentors textbooks, workbooks, or software. Online learners may return or submit materials in nonelectronic formats (e.g., hard copy through mail systems or courier delivery services); if so, such costs can be incorporated into the budget of the organization.

Time Allocations.   The distribution timeframe depends on the complexity of packaging the materials, the number of individuals who will receive the materials, and those who can help distribute them (Greer, 1992). The resources committed to distribution dictate the amount of time required; the greater the number of personnel who distribute materials, the less time will be needed.

Implementation Personnel.   A significant portion of the budget is with the core personnel for implementation. The corresponding amount that team members spend on WBI implementation depends on the length of the course, complexity of the instructional system, and the number of personnel available. The budget is directly related to the amount of time that individuals are required to work on implementation and the number of people involved.

Often, individuals are reassigned from other projects to start up a new implementation; in these cases, the organization would not provide additional funding for the reassignments. However, if such implementation tasks become a part of regular job duties, then reallocation of time and budget for other employees' duties may become necessary (Mourier & Smith, 2001). In other situations, where assignments are added to the workloads of individuals already involved in implementation projects, the budget should allow them additional compensation for the extra work. However, the reality is that additional assignments do not always lead to additional compensation, especially in periods of tight budgets and reduced resources (Davidson-Shivers 2002; Mourier & Smith).

An alternative to reassigning duties to current employees is to hire new staff, either permanent or temporary. Time and budget requirements for these new hires will depend on their scope of duties. Costs for new hires are functions of salary and fringe benefits, orientation, and training. These costs will vary with their specified duties and experience level. Salary and fringe benefits differ from one organization to another, as well as from one region to another. Costs for project personnel should align to both industry and local salary rates and employee qualifications.

Other Budget Items Associated with Personnel.   Employee reward systems and incentive structures for instructors, technical support, and administrative staff are another part of the budget. Appropriate incentive and reward systems enhance morale and commitment to the project. Conversely, not rewarding employees appropriately can lead to low morale and low motivation (Esque, 2001; McLagan, 2002; Mourier & Smith, 2001). If monies are tight, management may consider alternative incentives such as new equipment for employees, improved workplace setting, time off after project completion, special recognition, and so on (Esque; Mourier & Smith). Of course, costs are associated with these alternatives, but they may be less than direct funding of raises or bonuses.

Time Allocations.   Time requirements for personnel vary widely, depending on the needs of the organization, complexity of technology systems, number of other online courses or programs being offered, number of learners and instructors involved, and the amount of other personnel involved. Time estimates for WBI activities are projected based on task complexity, length of the project implementation, and the selected personnel roles involved in the implementation. Table 9.1 provides questions and suggestions for identifying personnel, time, and budget allocation needs.

For the lone instructor, allocating personnel, time, and budget may be immaterial because it comes back to that one person performing related tasks. However, completing this exercise may help the lone instructor identify specific activities, roles, and duties involved in implementing WBI. Further, for instructors who teach part time, identifying these tasks can help them determine the appropriate fee for their teaching services.

Table 9.1　Time and Budget Allocations for Personnel

Personnel and Duties	Estimating Time Strategies	Costs
Instructor What are expectations of the instructor? What activities will be completed?	Estimate time involved with completing activities: • How complex is the learning environment? • How many learners? • What personnel are available to assist the instructor? • What other duties must the instructor fulfill?	Review salary schedules. Compare instructor costs for different programs and courses.
Mentor If a mentor is available, what are the duties?	Estimate time involved with completing activities: • How many learners are involved? • How complex are the tasks?	Review salary schedules. Compare mentor costs for different programs and courses.
Operations Manager or Administrator What type of support do midlevel to upper-level management need to offer?	Estimate time required to complete required tasks: • What tasks can be delegated?	Review salary schedules, including fringe benefits. Identify surcharges for management services.
Administrative Support Staff What support does the administrative support staff need to offer?	Consider number of individuals involved, complexity of task, and time constraints of project.	Review salary schedules, including fringe benefits. Identify surcharges for administrative personnel services. Include other costs for resources needed during implementation.
Technical Support Staff How will technical support staff work with the learning community?	Estimate time involved with completing activities: • How many people are on the support team? • How many systems does the team support?	Review salary schedules, including fringe benefits. Identify any surcharges for technical personnel.

GardenScapes

The time has arrived for *GardenScapes* to be implemented. As part of preplanning activities, an implementation team is put into place and the budget and time allocations are made.

The implementation team addresses a series of questions prior to the start date of *Garden-Scapes* and other scheduled online instruction.

Personnel

The implementation team is similar to the design team. Deb Scarletti is hired for 10 hours per week to serve as mentor (teaching assistant) for *GardenScapes* participants. Lee Shallot, of the Continuing and Distance Education Department (CDE) administrative support staff, supervises online registration and related administrative functions. Implementation tasks related to administrative support are now a part of CDE staff duties while the online course is being offered.

Both Kally and Deb have computer access at home and at their CJC offices, which permits them to access the website at their convenience.

Budget and Time Allocations

The online program budget is funded from several sources within CJC. Allocations for CDE personnel such as Lee, Kally, and Deb are funded by CDE and Laila (technical support staff) by TLDC as part of the department's or center's operating expenses. The appropriate department or center of CJC funds other technical or administrative infrastructure expenses for online programs as needed.

The team estimates the time required for the general implementation tasks for *Garden-Scapes,* basing the estimates on past experience and best guesses. The actual time commitments will vary depending on the expertise of the staff (and learners) and the scope of other tasks assigned to the staff and instructors.

Time and Budget Allocations for *GardenScapes*

Personnel and Duties	Estimated Time Requirement	Costs
Instructor: Kally Le Rue		Salary determined by the CDE, under policy of CJC
• Teach course	3 hours	
• Answer email	2 hours	
• Hold online office hours	2 hours	
• Troubleshoot instructional problems	2 hours	
• Review, score, and provide feedback on assignments and final design project	3–6 hours	
• Miscellaneous activities	2–5 hours Total: 14–20 hours per week	

Time and Budget Allocations for *GardenScapes (Continued)*

Personnel and Duties	Estimated Time Requirement	Costs
Mentor: Deb Scarletti		
• Troubleshoot technical problems (more time in first 2 weeks)	2–4 hours	Salary determined by CJC; Graduate Assistant stipend
• Answer email	3 hours	
• Assist Kally and Laila as needed (includes making weekly links active)	3–5 hours	
	Total: 8–12 hours per week	
TLDC Manager: Carlos Duartes		
• System funding and resource allocation	Part of general management duties	Salary determined by CJC
• Planning for professional development		
Admin. Support: Lee Shallot		
• Duplicate materials	3 hours per mailing	Salary determined by CJC Mailing costs Duplicating costs
• Prepare mailings		
• Supervise registration	3 hours registration Total: 9 hours	
Technical Support: Laila Gunnarson		
• Develop online training materials (development of online tutorial)	(Total of 30–40 hours for online tutorial development)	Salary Schedule determined by CJC; Technical support charge assessed by TLDC.
• Troubleshoot technical problems	3–4 hours	
• Work with mentor and instructor as needed	1–2 hours	
	Total: 4–5 hours per week	

Carlos approves the online program personnel and budget and time allocations for the TLDC. The CDE director approves the budget portion for the online programs allocations, and the CJC central administration approves the overall budget.

See this textbook's Companion Website (http://www.prenhall.com/davidson-shivers) for *GardenScapes* Implementation Documents.

ON YOUR OWN

Identify the personnel and their assigned duties for your implementation team. If adding new members, be sure to identify their qualifications, their title/department, and so on. Estimate time and budget allocations required for completing the tasks involved. Forecast each team member's salaries and other associated costs.

If you are the lone instructor, most of the duties will be yours. However, by completing this exercise, you may be able to identify other people who can help you effectively implement your own WBI.

Using Table 9.1 as your template, list personnel and their duties for your project. Identify other expenses that may occur with an implementation (print or other materials, mailings, etc.). Estimate the time needed to complete the defined tasks. Add these estimates to the documentation for your WBI project.

(For illustrations of how other designers tackled these same issues, review the case studies appearing in the Extending Your Skills section at the end of this chapter.)

See this textbook's Companion Website (http://www.prenhall.com/davidson-shivers) for a printable template of the personnel time and budget table.

Final Preparations for Implementation

Once personnel and budget and time allocations are in place, it is time to make final preparations for the WBI and its website. There are four main questions to consider for a smooth WBI implementation:

1. What is the initial contact for learners?
2. Are the technical requirements for access, communication, and distribution in place?
3. Are the communication tools for participants in place?
4. Do participants need online skills training?

Identifying the Initial Learner Contact

Initial learner contacts are associated with how to market the WBI (or online programs) and how learners register for the course (or courses). Because learners may be anywhere, advertising and registration do not have to be bound to a particular location. Advertising the course can be completed through flyers, email, the Web, and publications such as newspapers, magazines, or journals.

Depending on the organization's policies and procedures, registration for online courses should be via the mail, telephone, or Web. After registration and before the WBI begins, learners should be contacted and provided with relevant information about the course and how to get started.

Sending enrolled learners a welcome message informs them how to access the WBI and ensures that they have the information they need to get ready for the online course (Burgess, 2002;

Table 9.2   Initial Learner Contact and Registration

Initial Learner Contact and Registration	Potential Responses
How will the WBI be advertised?	Use email, listservs, bulletin boards, postal mailings, newspapers, brochures, flyers, TV ads, radio ads, journals, magazines, conferences
When does the WBI start/stop?	Use organization's course schedule; set dates far enough in advance to accommodate completion of startup tasks
Who makes initial contact?	Delegate specific responsibilities to administrative staff, help staff, or instructor
How are learners initially contacted?	Distribute welcome letter, email; make telephone contact; WBI announcement or automated message
How do learners know where/when to register? To access WBI?	Obtain information in course schedule, brochure, website, welcome letter or email; provide URL and directions for accessing the WBI
How do learners identify the software or plug-ins that they need?	Identify plug-ins required, e.g., *Acrobat Reader, Real Player, QuickTime Player, Windows Media Player, Flash Player,* etc. and make available on site or include link to download site
How do learners know their roles and responsibilities?	Include information provided by instructor in the online tutorial at website, syllabus, in welcome letter
Who do learners contact for technical or administrative assistance?	Use LMS's technical services; identify organization administrative or technical support staff, instructor, mentor
How will learners obtain any support materials?	Identify online library services; establish links to bookstore, website, relevant external links; confirm email and postal mail addresses for sending attachments of support materials

Davidson-Shivers, 1998, 2001). These initial contacts may occur through automated messages or emails, in an announcement on the opening page of the WBI, or as part of course bulletins or schedules. Table 9.2 summarizes these initial contact considerations.

Because multiple members of the implementation team may contact the enrolled learners for various reasons (support staff for registration, instructor to welcome students, etc.), it is imperative that information is consistent. Conflicting or inaccurate information will only confuse and frustrate learners. Administrative staff, or whoever is in charge of this task, may use a *tickler* (reminder) file to ensure that these events are taken care of; these events are especially important when learners are new to WBI (Simonson et al., 2003).

Final Technical Requirement Preparations

All technical requirements for the WBI and its website must be in place prior to implementation. Table 9.3 outlines the technical requirements considered in WBI final preparation.

Table 9.3 Technical Requirements for Communication and Distribution

Technical Requirements	Potential Responses
How does the instructor access it?	Define the LMS procedures for instructor access, LMS instructor support and resources
What software or plug-ins are needed to use the WBI?	Identify plug-ins required, e.g., *Acrobat Reader, Real Player, QuickTime Player, Windows Media Player, Flash Player,* etc. and make available on site or include link to download site
How does the instructor send and share documents or feedback on assignments?	Specify digital drop boxes, email attachments, LMS, file sharing within website, FTP, chat rooms, threaded discussions, automated processes (e.g., LMS or automated mail responses), gradebook
How will instructor or learners access online skills training?	Links needed to online instructor/learner training; LMS instructor support and resources; establish instructor/learner FAQ and communication website
How will the WBI team distribute support materials?	Links needed to online library services, bookstore, website, external website; send attachments through email and postal service
How will instructor or learners report technical problems?	Include mechanism for reporting bad links, missing graphics, or other technical problems that creates automated message to point of contact person

In addition, some colleges and universities require the use of particular software products (Microsoft *Office*®, Corel *WordPerfect*®, etc.) to reduce incompatibility when sending and receiving documents. If such requirements exist, then the software must be made available both to instructors and others involved in WBI implementation and in learner-accessible computer labs. Learners may be required to purchase or have access to the software to participate in the online environment. These requirements need to be stated in online course schedules and catalogs (or training schedules), university or organizational websites, and all other relevant documentation.

Preparing for Communication Among WBI Participants

Preparing for communication among the instructor, mentor, support staff, and learners is another preimplementation task. The necessary communication tools must be in place, and all tools for distributing materials, assignments, and so on must be readied for implementation. Table 9.4 identifies communication and distribution tools needed for implementation.

Online Skills Training for Participants

A final pragmatic aspect of preparing for the WBI startup is online training for all participants (instructor, mentor, support staff, and learners). Periodically, instructors and technical and administrative support staff need to upgrade skills and knowledge. According to Spitzer (2001), online participants must learn how to interact with the system and be able to use the available

Table 9.4 Tools for Communication and Distribution

Participants	Communication Tools
How will learners, instructor, and mentor contact each other?	Identify locations of chat rooms, threaded discussions within website, listserv, email, telephone, face-to-face meetings
How are course expectations shared?	Clearly define class requirements in syllabus and through email, chat rooms, presentations (lectures), announcements
How do learners and instructor share files?	Specify digital drop box, email attachments, file sharing systems in LMS, FTP up- and download sites

technology tools to meet online environmental demands. Providing for professional development within the organization is an additional responsibility of managers or administrators.

Teaching online requires complex technical knowledge and skills that most instructors do not currently possess (Davidson-Shivers, 2002; Young, 1997). Furthermore, instructors need to have an understanding of andragogy or pedagogy (Davidson-Shivers,; Maxwell & Kazlauskas, 1992; Tsunoda, 1992). Likewise, staff members need to update their skills to meet the challenges of new technologies. Technical support staff also may need to become familiar with online instructional methods when working with instructors and students. On-line skills training for learners may be similar in content to that of instructor training, but with a slant toward learning rather than teaching.

Ideally, instructors, mentors, and support staff who are new to online instruction complete skills training prior to implementing the online course. The best option for online learners, especially new learners, would be to complete training before they start the WBI. However, it may not be possible to provide such training before enrollment. Some organizations may not be able to anticipate who will be enrolling in courses and/or what type of training those learners may need. In these situations, learners should complete the tutorials once they are enrolled and have access to the website or complete tutorials as part of initial course assignments.

Common Delivery Options for Training. The four most common options for delivering online skills training are (1) face-to-face workshops or orientation meetings, (2) peer tutoring, (3) books or workbooks, and (4) online tutorials. *Face-to-face workshops or orientation meetings* provide information on how to be an online participant with hands-on experience accessing a website and experimenting with new technologies used in the WBI. These types of workshops may be mandated for distance residency programs and may be convenient for learners to attend who are near the organization. Face-to-face workshops or meetings permit participant questions to be addressed immediately with other attendees benefiting from hearing the responses.

In the second option for training, *peer tutoring,* experts work with novices. For instructors, a novice instructor could monitor another more experienced, online instructor's learning environment to see the WBI in action. The activities, pace, and interactions of the course can be observed. By "sitting in" on an established online course, the new instructor can ask critical questions about what is transpiring and how the instructor manages learners and incoming assignments, develops personal notes or commentary, and establishes a communication style

Table 9.5   Training Options for Online Participants

Participant	Online Skills Training
Instructor	• Provide hands-on practice through F2F and online tutoring. • Include opportunities for instructors to integrate content into websites. • Use just-in-time online tutorials to explore online topics (how to teach online and technology topics [video, text, html, uploading, downloading, FTPing, etc.]). • Pair with expert instructor. • Increase knowledge of pedagogy and andragogy through workshops, books, etc.
Mentor	• Provide tutorials containing expectations and how to work with instructors and students. • Participate in peer tutoring.
Learners	• Complete distance learning tutorials (online or print-based materials). • Participate in orientation sessions (online). • Participate in face-to-face orientations. • Complete online tutorials or workbooks. • Be allowed to observe a sample class.
Support staff	• Increase knowledge of pedagogy and andragogy through workshops, books, etc. • Update skills through workshop training, technical books, and online tutorials.

Source: Table data are from Davidson-Shivers (1998, 2001), Ko & Rossen (2001), Simonson et al. (2003).

(Davidson-Shivers, 1998, 2001; Salmon, 2000). Novice instructors may be able to adopt (or adapt) the expert instructor's style to their own situation. Novice learners could follow a similar process, being paired with expert (or experienced) online learners.

The third option, *books or workbooks,* is the least interactive, but perhaps the most readily available. Although print-based materials explain the processes that occur in online teaching and learning and provide suggestions for using media, time management, and so on, they suffer from not being online. Of course, these limitations are lessened when support materials, such as WBI simulations, are included on a CD or website. Otherwise, novice instructors (and other participants) will need to visit an instructional website (or several) to see examples and gain an experiential sense of how these virtual environments operate.

The final training option, *online tutorials,* provide participants with just-in-time support and training (Blackboard, Inc., 2000; eCollege.com, 1999; Northrup, 2003). Training modules guide participants through processes, activities, and online concepts by modeling strategies for online learning and teaching. Most LMSs have online tutorials available to participants. Table 9.5 identifies the needs of the different online training participants.

Carefully preparing the WBI and its website for implementation minimizes potential problems and allows the focus to shift to the course content itself once implementation is underway. Rather than worrying about technical and functionality problems, the members of the learning community can concentrate on and become proficient in online teaching and learning.

GardenScapes

The team prepares for the WBI startup events. *GardenScapes* is specifically designed as a lifelong learning experience for adults interested in developing their gardening skills.

The CDE advertisements indicate that the course begins in the upcoming term. The course is listed in CDE's online course schedule, is featured on the home page of the CJC website as a news event, and is listed in the *Continuing and Distance Education Course Schedule Bulletin,* which is distributed through regional newspapers.

Learners register for the course in the same manner as they do for on-campus courses—in person, over the phone, or online. Learners receive directions on where, when, and how to go to the instructional website at the time of registration. There is a single entry URL for the course, accessible through the CJC main website.

The CDE administrative staff, with Lee supervising, mail informative welcome letters to learners. The welcome letters contain the start date and length of the course, the course URL, and a welcome statement from Kally. Toward the end of the course, the administrative staff will distribute via email a reminder for learners to complete the online course and instructor evaluation.

Course participants use the LMS tools and email system to communicate with each other. Kally emails the entire class to reiterate major course policies and to encourage learners to ask questions. Deb emails the class for the first couple of weeks to make sure learners are not having any technical problems. The following table summarizes the team's WBI startup preparations.

Preparation Tasks for Implementation	Responses
What is the initial contact for learners?	
How is the WBI advertised?	Advertising is through CJC website, course schedule, continuing education marketing in local newspapers.
When does the course begin/end?	The upcoming term and ends in 6 weeks.
Who makes initial contact? and How? What information will the contact contain?	Lee's staff will send registration materials and a welcome statement, respectively. Registration materials include how to sign onto LMS, including URL, class time frame, type of computer system and access requirements, and the course URL. The welcome includes an outline of major class goals, roles and responsibilities of participants, and identifies the contacts.
What are the roles of the instructor and mentors?	Kally focuses on content questions and answers. Deb's focus is on technical issues related to the WBI and online learning.

(continued)

Preparation Tasks for Implementation	Responses
Are the technical requirements for communication and distribution in place?	
How will participants access the LMS? What assistance is needed? What plug-ins are needed?	LMS is used for communication and file sharing. Some materials are in PDF format; access to *Acrobat Reader* is included on the website.
How does instructor send and share documents with learners?	Learners submit assignments in the online drop box. Kally will provide feedback similarly.
How will feedback on assignments and assessments be provided?	Kally and Deb will collaborate on addressing questions and resolving problems with assignments.
How will support materials be supplied to students?	All materials are available on the website. Support materials are in PDF and HTML formats.
What are the communication tools for participants?	
What will learners and instructor need to communicate?	All participants require access to the Internet and Web and an email address. Communication will be through email, threaded discussion, and a chat room.
How will course expectations be shared?	Kally will hold 3 open-class chats during week 1 to answer questions about the course. (Some information is in her letter.)
How do participants send and share documents?	Files will be shared through the LMS or distributed via email.
Do participants need online skills training?	
How will the instructor and mentor be trained?	Kally worked extensively with the TLDC and the CJC's LMS training, which relates to technical and online teaching skills. Deb participated in LMS training and has participated in a previous online class.
How will learners be trained?	CDE's online learner training is available through CJC's website as a PDF file for easy downloading and printing. Learners may download this guide prior to the course's start date.

See this textbook's Companion Website (http://www.prenhall.com/davidson-shivers) for *GardenScapes* Implementation Documents.

ON YOUR OWN

Identify the pertinent questions that relate to preparing your project for WBI implementation. Using Tables 9.2–9.4 as your template, organize your ideas. Include this information in your project documentation.

(For illustrations of how other designers tackled these same issues, review the case studies appearing in the Extending Your Skills section at the end of this chapter.)

See this textbook's Companion Website (http://www.prenhall.com/davidson-shivers) for a printable template of the preparation tasks table.

Early Events in WBI Implementation

Once initial contact is made and learners are enrolled and able to access the website, the early activities—the initial interactions between the instructor and learners—engender rapport and a sense of community among the participants. These activities are based on the Orientation to Learning strategies designed and developed during the concurrent design stage (refer to Chapter 7). These initial events orient learners to the WBI goal and content while not overwhelming them with too much information too soon. They also orient learners to the instructor's teaching style.

The course syllabus provides overview information about the course goals and purposes, requirements, schedule, deadlines for assignments, and scoring/grading systems. The instructor uses this initial time to explain additional course procedures, furnish learners with tips on how to improve their online learning skills, explain the various ways to communicate, and describe the first assignments. Participant roles and responsibilities also are described at this time (Burgess, 2002; Davidson-Shivers & Rasmussen, 1999; Simonson et al., 2003).

Implementation: Facilitation and Management

Once the WBI has been introduced to the learners and participants begin interacting with each other, the next part of implementation is to provide Instruction on the Content (as discussed in Chapter 7) and, simultaneously, continue building the learning community. Creating a sense of community within the online learning environment requires that two aspects of implementation run smoothly: facilitation and management.

As noted previously, **facilitation** is the execution of the WBI and the establishment of the learning community, and **management** refers to the learning environment administration and operation. For clarity, we discuss these aspects of implementation separately even though they are actually intertwined, due in part to the system requirements of the WBI environment.

Implementation: The Aspect of Facilitation

Facilitation may be the most important aspect of WBI implementation because, as Spitzer (2001) suggests, it serves as the main connection between learners and instructors, and is where participants consider, reflect, and learn content knowledge and skills (Ko & Rossen, 2001). Facilitation consists of events and activities that explore issues, discuss topics, and address questions. Building contacts between and among participants helps form their learning community.

Good facilitation processes expedite and advance the sense of community among participants, according to Collison et al. (2000), and promote student learning. The instructor's concerns should be to maintain the connection of the instructional activities to their related objectives and course goal and promote timely and relevant communication among all course participants (Davidson-Shivers & Rasmussen, 1999; Ko & Rossen, 2001; Northrup, 2003). Mentors, depending on their role, assist the instructor. Table 9.6 highlights facilitation strategies that keep online teaching and learning effective. The choice of strategies will vary for each online course.

Table 9.6 Strategies for Effective Facilitation

Facilitation Activities	Possible Strategies
Keep synchronous discussions on track and relevant	Schedule discussions and publish an agenda with beginning and ending times stated.
	Invite guest speakers and change format to general participation when speakers are finished. Use chats format and include a question and answer session at the end.
	Make chats private or password protected for course participants only.
	Allow learners and instructor to "settle" into the chat through greetings, welcomes, and personal interactions prior to the discussion.
	Establish netiquette rules and procedures to cue for specific chat functions, such as a question mark (?) to stop a discussion and allow someone to ask questions, etc.
	Provide guidance when discussion begins.
	Establish the tone of conversation.
	Provide shortcuts to terminology with emoticons (LOL, STS, BTW, ☺, ☹, . . . etc.).
	Summarize discussions periodically to ensure that learners follow the discussion.
	Privately warn individuals of inappropriate behavior. If it continues, ask them to leave.
	Escort discourteous or unwelcome visitors out of chat room.
	Make entrances and exits silent, especially when there are late arrivals.
	For late arrivals to the chat, summarize discussion privately and provide directions on how to join the chat, if necessary.
	Close session with short summary of the highlights. The facilitator may ask participants to summarize main points or highlights.
	Close the session by allowing learners to continue to chat with each other in order to finalize their thoughts, even though the formal session ends.
Keep asynchronous discussions on track and meaningful	Identify the discussion agenda with beginning and ending times stated.
	Inform learners of participation expectations early on. Identify minimum amount of interaction required for the discussion, if necessary.
	Pose questions and provide direction on the content to be discussed.
	Use debates, questions and responses, and other types of discourses to add interest and variety while maintaining relevance.
	Have learners be discussion moderators, or leaders as part of course requirements.
	Give learners another venue (such as another discussion area) for personal and unrelated course concerns.
	Review flow of the discussion, interject comments as needed, and encourage participation as required.
	Balance the amount of instructor intervention so that it is not too much (more than 25%) or too little (less than 3%).
	Encourage continued discussion through other communication tools such as listservs, chat rooms, emails, etc.

Table 9.6 Strategies for Effective Facilitation *(Continued)*

Facilitation Activities	Possible Strategies
Keep asynchronous discussions on track and meaningful *(continued)*	Follow netiquette guidelines in the discussion.
	At the end of the discussion, summarize major concepts and ideas; correct misconceptions that may have occurred, and expand on areas that may not have been covered well. Post summary to the discussion or document sharing area or use email.
	Assign learners to summarize discussions as part of the course requirements.
Creating group synergy	Provide opportunities for participants to get to know, help, and learn from each other. Setting up a separate chat room or threaded discussion for learners to use may help.
	Provide opportunities that allow learners to assist each other with technical support and share general technology tips, etc.
	Ask learners to post biographies with photos to build a sense of community.
	At the beginning of the course, and perhaps each unit, use "icebreakers" to help learners get to know each other.
	Make initial online activities easy but meaningful and then assign more difficult tasks as the course progresses.
	Allow for a mix of small-group and whole-group activities on collaborative efforts such as group writing, group presentations, group problem-solving tasks, etc.
	Include independent activities for the individual learner as well.
	Place learners or allow them to self-select into groups early in the course.
	Rotate group membership for different course assignments for interest and community building.
	Discuss the expectations for students working in groups.
	Train learners how to work in groups; provide nonthreatening practice to promote group interaction.
	For major group projects, allow same group membership to continue in order for them to develop their system for working together and completing the project.
	Share collaboration and cooperation strategies with groups.
	Build individual and collective accountability into group projects. Assign roles. Rotate assigned roles as the course progresses (moderator, data gatherers, reviewers, etc.). Have groups peer evaluate as well.
Provide timely feedback on activities, assignments, and assessments	State due dates and provide expectations of when feedback will be received for assignments.
	Provide directions for submitting assignments and assessments.
	Define timeframe for feedback. Meet organizational policies and procedures for responding to feedback; policies may range from 24 hour return to instructor-defined day/time.
	State whether feedback is provided in documents sent back to students.

(continued)

Table 9.6 Strategies for Effective Facilitation *(Continued)*

Facilitation Activities	Possible Strategies
Provide timely feedback on activities, assignments, and assessments *(continued)*	Personalize feedback to acknowledge individuals and their work.
	Send feedback on assignments to each individual. Keep the content of feedback between instructor and learner. (This is required if scores or grades are involved.)
	Use summaries of weekly activities, participation, performance, etc. as feedback on the group as a whole.
	Use automatic responses available via email systems or LMS to notify learners of receipt of work.
Provide feedback on quality	Focus on student activities (participation, performance, etc.) that specifically relate to objectives.
	Differentiate between "chatter" that should not be assessed and responses that contribute to knowledge gain.
Engage learners in instruction and learning	Have learners contact instructor and mentor as one of the initial assignments.
	Avoid meaningless activities or interactions that are busywork.
	Provide activities during the first week or session to allow learners to practice using required technology tools and explore the site.
	Email learners periodically through the course to maintain their interest.
	Summarize group discussions, answer general questions, and notify learners of class events (use emails or document sharing features).
	Notify learners of class events (use news functions, calendars, announcements, etc.).
	Interact with learners at least once a week (or session) to help them stay engaged.
	Novices may need additional encouragement, especially at the beginning of the course. Such encouragements can decrease as learners gain confidence.
	Encourage learner contact with mentor, technical support, or library services if help is needed.

Source: Table data are from Blackboard, Inc. (2000), Bonk (2004), Brooks (1997), Burgess (2002), Collison et al. (2000), Davidson-Shivers (1998, 2001), Davidson-Shivers & Rasmussen (1998, 1999), Ko & Rossen (2001), Northrup, Rasmussen, & Burgess (2001), Palloff & Pratt (1999), Salmon (2000), Simonson et al., (2003) Southard (2001).

GardenScapes

The instructional strategies for *GardenScapes* emphasize developing a learning community, with Kally in charge of facilitating that community. CJC and CDE have established a general policy of contacting learners within 24 hours of their inquiry, especially if it is a technical concern. Depending on the contact person, it may be an automated response ("out of the office" statements, acknowledgement of receipt of message, etc.). The actual solution, certainly, may take longer, but early contact will help to minimize learner frustration.

The first week brings a series of challenges because most of the learners are new to Web-based learning. Both Kally and Deb know that their flexibility and ability to problem solve will be key to easing learner apprehension and frustration. Kally and Deb work closely with the participants to instill a level of comfort with the technology and encourage willingness to share ideas and offer helpful suggestions to each other. Kally responds to questions about the content and Deb responds to technical problems. They distribute answers to general questions to the entire class in case others have the same question.

The facilitation activities for Kally include interaction with the participants, leading discussions, and guiding learning experiences. She realizes that these learners are not traditional students and may not have been in "the classroom" for a long time. She engages in the following major activities:

- Send (or include) the welcome note in the packet distributed by Lee and her staff.
- Send an introductory email for each lesson to indicate that the week has started, note any upcoming due dates, and state that learners should contact Kally or Deb if they have questions.
- Host one online chat session each week as part of her office hours.
- Send an email to update class and encourage work on assigned activities sometime during the week.
- Establish a regular schedule to check emails and respond to individual questions or concerns.
- Send an end-of-week email to summarize major weekly topics and encourage learners to submit work.
- Score or provide feedback to any assignments related to the weekly garden topics and respond within a week.

Other facilitating strategies appear in the following table.

Facilitation Activity	Strategies
Keeping discussions alive and on track	Some discussions take place asynchronously in the LMS. Kally poses a question and participants respond to it. To encourage discussion, participants may be asked to respond to others in addition to posting their own ideas.
	Use of threaded discussion permits participants to share garden experiences, gardening tips and suggestions to others, and ask questions among themselves.
	For each synchronous discussion (chat), Kally or Deb ask for general questions or comments and learners can informally interact. The formal chat begins a few minutes into the session to allow for all to log in.
	If participants enter late, they are welcomed privately and a short synopsis of the chat is provided to them. This mediation permits the flow of the chat without interruption.
	Periodically, a short summary recaps the discussion and Deb or Kally ask if there are questions.
	Toward the end of the chat, Kally or Deb summarize and conclude the session, or they may ask learners to close with a summary remark on what they learned or found interesting or provide a highlight of the discussion.

(continued)

Facilitation Activity	Strategies
Creating group synergy	Group discussions take place in chat rooms, threaded discussion, or via emails with learners participating in them.
	Kally provides the structure for the discussions early in the course with guiding questions and specific direction for responding to questions and/or reply to others' comments.
	In later sessions, small groups determine what method of discussion they prefer and structure their own discussions.
	Groups are created to share ideas and tips on gardening. The groups remain consistent throughout the entire course.
	Learners are encouraged to find a "garden pal" to work with on class projects. Garden pals also evaluate each other's garden plan.
Provide timely feedback	In the first session, Kally indicates that assignment feedback should be received in 5–7 days.
	Kally explains that she or Deb's responses to emails will be sent within 24 hours, following CDE policies. If they occur on the weekend, an automated response will be sent. Resolving any problems may take longer, but an initial response will be within the 24 hours.
	She establishes online office hours as two designated points in the week when she will address emails.
	For graded assignments, feedback is returned within a week unless the assignment is submitted at the end of the term. At that time, the project feedback is returned to the learner when grades are due to the Registrar's office.
Engage learners in the WBI	New learners may require additional assistance with technology and learning at a distance. Deb contacts those individuals directly to minimize such problems.
	Learners with access problems are given specific instructions on website access from Deb Scarletti or Laila Gunnarson.
	Kally encourages participation by setting dates and times for chats and encourages learners to form small support groups or select partners.
	Both Kally and Deb have weekly office hour sessions to answer questions. At the end of the course, a one-hour concluding session (again in the chat room) will be held for learners to debrief the things that they have learned in the course.
	For continued access problems, Deb contacts learners via phone to walk them through. Deb works with Laila to confirm URLs, user IDs, and passwords.
	If problems continue and participants are local, they may be sent to TDLC for one-on-one assistance. If learners are not local, *NetMeeting* is used to access their computer and guide them through procedures.
	Learners are encouraged to download and correctly install current versions of browser and needed plug-ins. Notifications of these requirements are included in welcome letter and on the LMS.
	If a learner is on a network ISP with a firewall, multimedia or chat technologies may not work. Network administrators at the ISP must be contacted to permit access.

See this textbook's Companion Website (http://www.prenhall.com/davidson-shivers) for *GardenScapes* Implementation Documents.

ON YOUR OWN

You are at the facilitation phase of your WBI. Using Table 9.6 as your template, list the facilitation activities you expect to implement for your own project. How will you respond to those activities? Describe facilitation roles of your instructor and mentor, if available. What strategies will you suggest for your instructors and learners?

(For illustrations of how other designers tackled these same issues, review the case studies appearing in the Extending Your Skills section at the end of this chapter.)

See this textbook's Companion Website (http://www.prenhall.com/davidson-shivers) for a printable template of the facilitation activity table.

Implementation: The Aspect of Management

Another aspect of implementation is management, the administration and operation of a Web-based course (Dabbagh, Bannan-Ritland, & Silc, 2001; Kahn, 2001). Management events include day-to-day operation of technology systems, updating course information, and tracking learner progress (Dabbagh et al.; Khan,). Khan characterizes maintenance as an element of management, and notes that specific tasks include website and server maintenance, software updates, and content changes. Management activities affect all participants of the learning environment (Brooks, 1997); making sure that the WBI and its website functions properly is vital for the success of online teaching and learning.

Whether the system is simple or complex, learners and instructor are considered a part of it. The same management tools used for planning WBI design and development can assist in managing the learning environment, coordinating tasks, and maintaining learner and instructor roles and responsibilities.

System Management.   The complexity of website management is dependent on both website and network infrastructure. At a minimum, a system will have a server and access to the Web. Even small WBI systems require coordinating technology and networking systems so that they function smoothly. System complexity naturally increases as the number of individuals and integrated networks increase.

For the most part, implementation team handle systems management activities so that instructors and teachers do not have to work on the system level. However, lone designer/instructor may need to contend with systems management, often without help of any kind.

Management by Instructors.   The day-to-day learning situations within the WBI require that the instructor and the support team are ready to react to technical problems. Because they are the "visible" entity to learners, instructors generally bear the brunt of identifying maintenance problems even though they may not actually perform the specific maintenance activities. Instead, they are the liaison to the technical support staff who resolves technical problems and maintains the system (Brooks, 1997; Darbyshire, 2000). These staff members are responsible for upgrading new versions of server software, browsers, LMS, and plug-ins. When these parts of the Web system are upgraded, they may create new problems for the participants because they may change how the WBI is viewed or displayed; support staff resolves any problems created by upgrading the system.

In some organizations, the instructor is responsible for maintaining the website in addition to facilitating the instruction. When wearing two hats, the instructor must resolve technical problems in a timely fashion to minimize learner frustration and maximize learner access.

In addition to the daily WBI situation, instructors manage their own time and set limits on when they will be actively working on WBI. To make their time more manageable, instructors may use computer resources to organize and monitor student information by creating folders for learners' assignments or emails (Northrup et al., 2001). The LMS may have a gradebook that can be used for this purpose as well. Instructors also may monitor mentor activities (Darbyshire, 2000; Ko & Rossen, 2001; Simonson et al., 2003). Table 9.7 outlines strategies instructors can use to manage WBI day-to-day activities.

With all of the issues and concerns raised thus far, it is obvious that facilitation and management tasks for the instructor are vast and varied. When compared to instruction in a face-to-face classroom setting, WBI may seem overwhelming. However, these issues and concerns are not insurmountable and the responsibility for successful implementation does not reside with the instructor alone. Learners also have a responsibility for their own learning and a shared responsibility with the group to create the community. They can do these if they manage their time and workload well.

Management by Learners.   Learners, outside of the shared online environment, must manage their own personal time and workload (Gilbert, 2001). Since WBI has flexible time requirements, learners generally establish their own schedules within the established course parameters. However, learners must accept the responsibility for meeting assignments and course deadlines (Gilbert). Although the instructor may encourage them to review course calendars, keep up to date with class activities, and monitor their own progress, they must manage and organize their time.

As learners move through WBI environments, they are often the ones who initially find technical problems related to WBI and website maintenance. A mechanism that allows learners to report bad links, missing graphics, or other technical problems should be included in the LMS. This link can send an automated message to the person who performs the maintenance. Table 9.8 shows management strategies for online learners.

Table 9.7 Strategies for the Instructor to Manage Day-to-Day Activities

Activity	Strategies
Activate links	• Notify learners when links are active.
Establish deadlines	• Share deadlines for assignments.
Find lost learners	• Contact learners via email, telephone, or traditional mail if they are not attending class on a regular basis.
Assess learners	• Have learners assessed in secure locations (host or remote sites). • Use LMS to have learners authenticate their access.
System failures or technology failures	• Be flexible, have backup plan. • For short-term server problems, use email to communicate and send assignments until technology resources are back in operation. • For long-term problems, use backup servers or access; advise learners.
Track learner participation, assignments, assessments, etc.	• Use LMS or Web-supported tools (gradebooks or spreadsheets) to organize learner data. • Track data related to course goals and requirements.
Monitor mentor activities	• Identify mentor's (teaching assistant) role and specify their tasks for the WBI community. • Require a time log of tasks completed. • Have learners evaluate quality of mentor activities.

Source: Table data are from Barron & Lyskawa (2001), Cucchiarelli et al. (2000), Hazari (2001), Wagner (2001).

Table 9.8 Strategies for the Learner to Manage Day-to-Day Activities

Activity	Strategies
Identify class activities	• Review class activities early in the class session. • Print schedules and keep in binder, highlighting due dates. • List session activities to be completed. • Ask questions of instructor, mentor, or technical support as appropriate when needed.
Participate in class activities Complete class assignments	• Schedule time to participate in chats or threaded discussions. • Find "study buddy" for support. • Create class calendar to keep track of assignments. • Practice with submission technology (email, drop boxes, etc.). • Keep in contact with instructor if technology problems occur.

Management by Mentors.   Although the instructor defines the mentor's duties, mentors must manage their own time and workload. One way is to set up a schedule that includes times to check email, confer with the instructor, and contact technical support personnel. Using computer resources (computer folders, etc.) assists mentors in organizing student work and makes it easier to find and score learner documents, post scores/grades, and provide feedback. Mentors can create databases of technical problems for easy recall of FAQs and solutions.

When the mentor's responsibility is only to collect, but not resolve, website link problems, then he or she acts as the liaison and reports them to the instructor or technical support team to fix or update. However, mentors may perform simple maintenance activities such as updating URLs to Web resources. Table 9.9 highlights management strategies for mentors.

Table 9.9   Strategies for the Mentor to Manage Day-to-Day Activities

Activity	Strategies
Monitor or maintain links	• Search for new links for inactive URLs. • Repair broken links. • Notify learners and instructor when links are reactivated. • Create a database for responses to common technical problems and FAQs.
Manage time and duties	• Establish a schedule to confer with instructor. • Set up times to monitor emails. • Set up times to contact technical support staff. • Set up office hours for learners.
Score assignments and assessments	• Use computer resources for student assignments, posting scores, and providing feedback to learners.
Assess learners	• Have learners assessed in secure locations (host or remote sites). • Use LMS to have learners authenticate their access.
System failures or technology failures	• Be flexible, have backup plan. • In short term, the WBI continues until the technology is back in operation. • For long-term problems, use backup servers or access; advise learners.
Track learner participation, assignments, assessments, etc.	• Use LMS or technology supported (gradebooks or spreadsheets) to organize learner data. • Track the data that is related to course goals and requirements.
Monitor mentor activities	• Have mentor responsible for specific tasks for the WBI community. • Require a time log of mentor duties and tasks completed. • Have students evaluate quality of mentor activities.

GardenScapes

At the beginning of the course, Kally and Deb monitor the WBI and its website daily. Based on their preplanning activities, the implementation team begins their duties. Laila, Deb, and Kally use the management strategies for their designated roles.

Laila manages the technical support staff as they perform tasks related to servers and software management. She schedules the system outages, which, unless there is an emergency, occur during breaks between terms. All network and technology enhancements (e.g., plug-in, server, and server software upgrades) are planned for those same breaks to maximize learner and instructor access during the WBI course offering. Servers are backed up every night to guard against information loss as part of standard operating procedures in the TLDC.

Most of the potential problems can be averted if the implementation team is prepared and ready. A link on the main course page permits learners to report to Kally questions regarding the content or assignments. Kally makes modifications or provides further explanations as necessary.

Deb corrects links and makes sure that the graphics are active. A link on the main course page permits learners to report URL problems to Deb. Deb makes modifications to the website as determined. Website resources included in the course are well known and established entities (e.g., governmental agencies and long-standing companies) and are expected to be fairly stable. If a link to an outside source is no longer active, then Deb searches for a new one to replace it.

Activities	Strategies
To be completed by Laila (system; technical support)	
Failing technology	The CDE has a backup server that mirrors the primary servers in the TLDC. In the event of a long-term systemic server outage, assignments will be distributed via email.
To be completed by Kally (instructor)	
Activating links	Send an email when the weekly lessons are available. Class will begin on Mondays. Learners have the week (7 days) to complete assignments.
Sharing time expectations	Reiterate expectations found in welcome letter and the introductory materials. Inform learners on approximate time commitment for weekly lesson activities.
Finding lost learners	Contact learners who do not participate for 2 consecutive weeks.
Assessing learners	Review written work or projects submitted to her via email or electronic drop boxes.

(continued)

Activities	Strategies
To be completed by Deb (mentor)	
Activating links	Make the links active.
Tracking learner participation	Review threaded discussions and chat logs to track learner participation. The electronic grade book in the LMS will be used.
To be completed by Lee (administration)	
Finding lost learners	Lee will supervise finding "lost" learners.
	Staff makes reasonable efforts to contact learners who have not participated during the first week of the WBI by email and then by telephone. Learners who do not pay course fees will be automatically dropped from the course roster by the system. Lee will send a letter to any learners still unavailable or unresponsive.
	Some attrition is expected. Those who do not continue in the course will receive an evaluation form so that they can share their reasons for leaving the course.
To be completed by learners	
Participation	Access WBI and complete activities in timely fashion.
	Responsible for participating in building a sense of community for the group.
	Responsible for their own learning and soliciting help if necessary.
	Obtain necessary skills and knowledge to be an effective online learner.
	Become a self-starter and use self-regulation skills.

As for the content, it is relatively stable. Kally does not expect it will need to be altered for the next two to three years. Other management activities for the implementation team appear in the table above.

As the *GardenScapes* course progresses through the remaining weeks, monitoring activities that occurred during the first week or two are reduced. Kally and Deb establish designated schedules for office hours, while maintaining their facilitation and management activities.

See this textbook's Companion Website (http://www.prenhall.com/davidson-shivers) for *GardenScapes* Implementation Documents.

ON YOUR OWN

Consider the tasks related to management that will be required for your own WBI project. Identify the personnel responsible for managing the WBI implementation. Document the strategies that each will use to maintain the WBI, its website, and the system. Use tables 9.7–9.9 as your template for documenting activities.

(For illustrations of how other designers tackled these same issues, review the case studies appearing in the Extending Your Skills section at the end of this chapter.)

 See this textbook's Companion Website (http://www.prenhall.com/davidson-shivers) for a printable template of the management activities table.

Wrapping Up

The implementation stage brings the WBI to life, so to speak. Without implementation, the rest of the activities in the WBID Model are simply an exercise in futility (and without utility). Understanding online teaching and learning assists in successful implementation. Several preplanning and final preparations are required before WBI implementation begins; they include identifying personnel for the implementation team, planning budget and time allocations, and preparing the WBI and its website to meet technical requirements for all participants. Once learners are enrolled and the WBI starts, the focus shifts to student learning and establishing a sense of community among participants. The two closely interwoven aspects of WBI implementation are facilitation and management. The implementation stage of the WBID Model is, in actuality, only the beginning of online learning and instruction. However the challenge is continue to offer the WBI as long as it remains relevant and timely for the participants. To determine relevance and timeliness of a WBI requires a summative evaluation. Chapter 10 focuses on conducting summative evaluation and research.

Expanding Your Expertise

1. Define implementation and differentiate the various tasks involved in this stage of the WBID Model.

2. How do events and processes in facilitation and management interact?

3. Take a systematic perspective and explore the roles of personnel involved in WBI implementation. How do these roles compare to those from other stages of the WBID Model?

4. How do decisions made and activities completed in previous stages of the WBID Model impact the implementation stage?

5. Is it important or necessary to train all participants *prior* to implementation? Justify your views.

6. Identify what you think are the most critical activities of the implementation stage. Explain why they are vital to implementing WBI successfully.

7. How would you determine whether an implementation is successful?

Extending Your Skills

PK–12 Schools

Megan Bifford has begun to implement her lesson. The fifth graders in Rhoda and Buzz's classrooms have begun to use the WebQuest. As the WebQuest becomes available by being placed on the district's server, Megan works closely with Cassie, Rhoda, and Buzz. Several other teachers have been recruited by Cassie to use the Web-supported instruction so that it can be implemented in several schools. This group of teachers, plus Megan and Cassie, make up the implementation team. The WSI is part of the district-sponsored curriculum, so budget is not an issue: additional materials are not required. All of the technology resources needed for the WebQuest are found in the schools.

To facilitate the WebQuest, each teacher has established centers in their classroom called Internet, Presentation, Research, and Drawing. Megan advises the teachers to tell the students about the WebQuest, provide directions, link the WebQuest to activities in class, and divide the class into teams. Teachers follow their normal classroom management strategies throughout the experience.

Megan sends out newsletters and email to participating teachers, providing them with links to the website and tips on using it in their classrooms. She encounters the following difficulties:

- Server access is not available on the second day of the implementation (a cable to the main school board building was cut). [Solution: repair cable]
- Some browsers in schools will not open the instruction. [Solution: Upgrade browsers to newer version]
- Some graphics do not show up on all computers. [Solution: Make sure that graphics are in right folder location on the server; review browser specifications to make sure that graphics are shown]

Megan works through these problems with the school system's support teams.

Megan observes students in Rhoda and Buzz's classrooms. She notes more ideas on how to integrate the WSI into the classroom, to include in her Formative Evaluation Report and as data for summative evaluation. Any tips that she generates she includes in her newsletters. Using all of this information, Megan and Cassie plan a future professional development workshop to offer to teachers so that they can effectively integrate the WSI into their science classrooms.

Business and Industry

Homer Spotswood is deeply focused on implementation activities of the safety training initiative. Homer is working with M2's trainers, who are serving as the face-to-face facilitators as well as online facilitators. Before the program began, he had two training sessions, one face-to-face and one online, with the facilitators so that they would be comfortable with the technology and their roles and responsibilities.

Employees at all plant locations have begun the mandatory training. The implementation has begun smoothly. Access has been no problem and the instruction seems to be working properly. In the first days of online training, facilitators respond quickly to questions, attempting to minimize as much frustration as possible. Questions are answered both online and in the face-to-face sessions. Online group discussions and questions are encouraged to address global issues across the different plant locations. Facilitators share tips for online learning (how to manage time and materials) in the online environment and in face-to-face sessions.

The course facilitators are using the LMS to help manage data that Homer will need for the summative evaluation. Using the LMS, they are tracking logins, performance, and participation. They create data files that include data from the face-to-face portion of the training. At the end of the training, these files will be sent to Homer, who will aggregate the data.

On the horizon, however, Bud Cattrell notifies Homer and other plant supervisors that a new issue has emerged: three of the plants will be receiving new equipment that will greatly impact the procedures for using the safety equipment and protocols. Homer's immediate task is to determine exactly how the new equipment will change the instructional content; immediate changes must occur during ongoing maintenance of the WBI.

Case Study 3   ## Military

Commander Rebekkah Feinstein and Lieutenants Danielson, Carroll, and Cole and their E^2C^2 teams have worked on the training for close to four months and their hard work is paying off. Captain Prentiss has received several progress reports throughout the development effort and these reports have been sent up the chain of command and warmly received. Relative to classroom-based, instructor-led training, development has progressed rapidly.

According to the Formative Evaluation Plan, the first two months of WBI implementation involved widespread formative evaluation, with usage and satisfaction survey data collected. Enrollment for the three courses was limited to three groups of sailors during the first two months of implementation:

- Sailors at shore establishments in the continental United States (CONUS) awaiting assignment to "A" school
- Sailors on two designated ships underway off the East Coast of the United States who are awaiting assignment to "A" school
- Sailors at TSC ready to enter the core courses of the four local "A" schools

In addition to the LMS data and survey results, Commander Feinstein's team deploy team members as facilitators and onsite data gatherers of implementation issues to two CONUS shore bases and the two designated deployed ships. Meanwhile, other team members monitor and facilitate the process at the TSC "A" schools. To assist the sailors in resolving technical problems, the command sets up a 24-hour help desk staffed by instructors (in three shifts), available as a link through Navy e-Learning. As the groups of facilitators compare notes during weekly threaded discussions, mediated by their Navy Knowledge Online (NKO) portal, they identify common implementation problems:

- The start-up/welcome email needs additional, specific instructions on accessing the LMS.
- Initially, facilitators are spending a combined total of 10–20 hours online each day with learners because of individual issues related to content and technology. This time is forecast to decrease as learners become acquainted with the online environment.
- As anticipated, shipboard learners have limited access to the Web-based products, but the extent to which this is a limitation was not foreseen.

At the conclusion of the two months, implementation data are gathered and incorporated in updated versions of the three lessons. These corrections are documented on the LCMS for future reference.

Case Study 4   Higher Education

Dr. Joe Shawn's *Introduction to Management* course is offered during the upcoming term. Dr. Shawn's implementation team is made up of himself, his TA Brian, and the university's online help desk that handles technical problems.

Students register for the class using the university's registration system, which is available via the Web or in person at the Registrar's office. Registered students receive an email telling them that their class will be Web-enhanced and that they will be expected to have regular access to the Internet. If they don't have access at home, the university's computer labs are open 24/7. This email outlines the specific technology resources needed to participate in the class. For students who have not participated in an online class, the email directs them to complete an online tutorial before class begins.

The class meets first in a face-to-face, traditional classroom. Prior to that meeting, Dr. Shawn distributes an email welcoming students to class and telling them how to access the class website. Additional information and directions for accessing the Web-enhanced materials will be given in class. Additional in-class or office meetings will be scheduled if students need additional help.

In the face-to-face class, Dr. Shawn discusses how online learning differs from in-class experiences. The class discusses learner management strategies and expectations of online learning. After Dr. Shawn's class meeting, Brian sends out an introductory email, in which he shares some management tips for learning in an online environment. Students are instructed to ask Brian for technical help; all content and course questions are sent to Dr. Shawn. Brian answers questions through a technical issues threaded discussion, so all students can benefit from his responses. For questions that Brian cannot answer, the help desk is brought in for additional assistance. Brian keeps a log of technical issues that will be used as a resource for subsequent classes. To manage his time, Dr. Shawn schedules online office hours that he posts on the course website. He identifies two times during the week that he will answer email and work on course issues. He talks with Brian, who also posts hours when he will be available to help students (times differ from Dr. Shawn's hours).

The following applies to all case studies. Consider how you, as designer, might act or respond in each case study.

- What information is *not* presented that you would like to have had? How would you go about gathering that data?
- For each case, what is the relationship of implementation to the rest of the WBID Model?
- What other implementation issues do you envision for each of the cases?
- What would you do differently from each of the principals in the case studies?

Chapter 10

Conducting Summative Evaluation and Research: The Final Stage

In the evaluation planning stage (refer to Chapter 5), the preliminary plans for the summative evaluation were developed. These plans provide a framework to prepare for and carry out summative evaluation. At the same time, research can be conducted on the project. Summative evaluation occurs at a predetermined point in the WBI life cycle, usually when major revisions are no longer taking place and the WBI has been used by a large number or percentage of the target population. Its purpose is to determine the value or worth of the WBI. Planning, conducting, and reporting summative evaluation and research comprise the last stage of the WBID Model.

Chapter 10 begins with a description of the purposes of summative evaluation and its main steps, followed by strategies for reporting results.

Objectives

At the end of this chapter, you should be able to do the following:
- Describe the purpose of summative evaluation in the WBID Model.
- Describe the final planning of summative evaluation.
- Determine basic methods and tools used for summative evaluation and research.
- Develop strategies for analyzing and reporting data.
- Prepare a report of findings.

Introduction

In Chapter 5, we suggested that it might not be necessary nor possible for the designer to conduct all of the traditional phases of formative evaluation (i.e., one-to-one, small-group, and field trials) for all WBI development situations. Similarly, it may not be necessary to conduct summative evaluation for every situation even though this process has utility. Savenye (2004) maintains that summative data is helpful in making decisions about online instruction. However, she acknowledges that WBI designers tend to be more interested in collecting formative data than conducting summative evaluations and that this may be partly due to ever-changing systems and designer concerns for improving WBI. However, there are situations in which summative evaluation should be planned and implemented (Figure 10.1). Summative evaluation is appropriate when stakeholders make decisions about the WBI's continuation or document its value or worth. In this chapter, we discuss final planning and reporting for summative evaluation, which is the final stage of the WBID Model. We have added the term *research* to the chapter title because of the strong emphasis on research methodology in summative evaluation.

At the designated point during its life cycle when summative evaluation occurs, an instructional designer may take on the task or a professional evaluator may complete the evaluation. Because either may plan and conduct a summative evaluation, in this discussion we will use the term *evaluator* throughout.

As noted in Chapter 5, although summative evaluation is conducted later in the WBI's life cycle, its planning, according to the WBID Model, began prior to WBI design and development. This preplanning allowed baseline data to be collected on the existing instruction or program for later comparison with the fully implemented WBI. In addition to collecting baseline data, this preliminary planning identified the main purposes, based on the criteria of effectiveness, efficiency, and appeal, and identified potential evaluation methods and tools. At this last stage of the WBID Model, summative evaluation plans are finalized and carried out. Summative evaluation is a major undertaking, and requires documentation of purposes, data collection, and analysis procedures. The results of the evaluation are recorded and reported to stakeholders so that they may make appropriate decisions about the WBI.

Figure 10.1   Summative evaluation and research stage of the WBID Model.

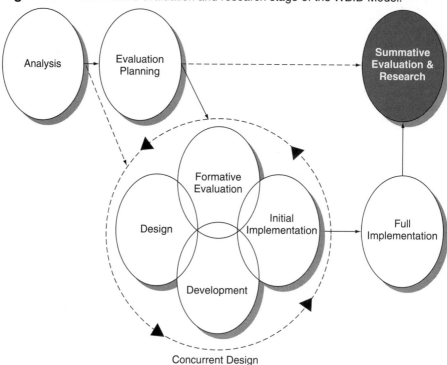

Concurrent Design

Summative Evaluation Planning: Detailing the Purposes

The main purposes for evaluating WBI at this stage are to determine (1) its value, (2) if it provided a "value added," and (3) whether it should be continued, either as is or modified in some manner. The **value,** or worth, of the WBI is considered in relation to its goals and content, instructors and learners, and context (refer to Chapter 5). To determine worth, evaluators judge critical aspects of the WBI in terms of its effectiveness, efficiency, and appeal (Palloff & Pratt, 1999; Patton, 2002; Rossi, Freeman, & Lipsey, 1999, Savenye, 2004). The following are general, overarching questions for summative evaluation:

- Have the instructional goals of the WBI been met?
- Were the stakeholders satisfied with its outcomes?
- Was the WBI cost effective?
- Were time efficiencies gained?

In addition to these questions, evaluators will consider whether the level of use of the WBI corresponds to its intended use and whether any adaptations were made to it during implementation (Fullan, 1990; Fullan & Pomfret, 1977), and if so, were they effective. Table 10.1 presents sample questions that relate to a few of evaluators' general concerns.

Table 10.1 Summative Evaluation Questions for Determining the Effectiveness, Efficiency, and Appeal of WBI

Areas of Consideration	Sample Questions
Instructional Goals and Content	**Effectiveness** Did learners master the objectives? Were the goals of the WBI met? Is there evidence that the project was developed using an instructional design process? **Efficiency** Were the goals achieved? How well were goals achieved? Did the WBI facilitate learning faster than other delivery methods? Were costs reduced? Were there costly technical support issues related to the WBI? **Appeal** What recommendations can be made for future improvements? Did the message design provide clarity?
Learners and Instructors	**Effectiveness** Was the instruction informative to learners? Were stakeholders satisfied with the outcomes? Was the instructor satisfied with the outcomes? Did learners drop out of the WBI due to incompatible technology? Lack of technological support? **Efficiency** Did the instructor find the website easy to use? Did learners find the website easy to access? Were there design features (i.e., scrolling text, constantly running animations, etc.) that reduced the efficiency of the WBI? **Appeal** Did learners find the WBI interesting? Did learners find the WBI helpful? Did learners find the WBI satisfactory?
Context	**Effectiveness** Did the WBI fit the website environment? Is the course on a stable system? Does the site work with the lowest specifications of computer or Web browser? Were the participants' computers and server compatible? **Efficiency** Was there easy, smooth access to the website? Were time efficiencies realized? **Appeal** Did technical support meet participant needs? Are disclaimers and cautions provided? Are the authors clearly identified? Did the photos, videos, etc. enhance the WBI?

Source: Table data are from Dick et al. (2005), Henke (2001), Palloff & Pratt (1999), Patton (2002), Rossi et al. (1999), Rumble (2003), Savenye (2004).

The thoroughness in detailing such questions depends on the specific WBI situation and stakeholder requirements. It also depends on whether the WBI was developed using an integrated design and evaluation approach (i.e., concurrent design). Consequently, message and interface design and technical considerations should not be overlooked during a summative evaluation (Henke, 2001). Even when WBI has been formatively evaluated, its present value is based on whether its currency and relevancy have been maintained using similar considerations.

A second purpose for conducting a summative evaluation is to determine whether there was value added as a result of implementing WBI (Weston & Barker, 2001); in other words, was value added because of the instruction? **Value added** occurs when something of significant worth or merit is gained due to the WBI. The overarching questions related to this type of purpose are, *What might have happened if WBI had not been implemented?* and, *Was the individual learner's performance enhanced in some manner because the instruction was delivered through the WBI?* For instance, value added would mean that some individuals were able to access and participate in the instruction only because of its online availability (Savenye, 2004).

A third purpose of summative evaluation is to decide whether the instruction should be continued as is, modified, or discontinued (McMillan & Schumacher, 1997). Typically, this third purpose is relevant within a cyclical maintenance schedule, as mentioned in Chapter 9. Not all instruction, including WBI, is meant to last forever; summative evaluation helps stakeholders decide whether it has served its purpose. If the decision is to continue, additional findings will help the stakeholders decide whether the WBI can be maintained in its present state or if changes are necessary.

GardenScapes

Percy Davis, a doctoral IDT student at Myers University, is hired as a TLDC intern this year; his assignment is to evaluate the CDE online program. Part of his task is to evaluate several WBI courses that have been offered by CJC over the last three or four years. The *GardenScapes* course is one of the courses slated for this evaluation.

Kally Le Rue is still the instructor for this course and provides Percy with the preliminary summative evaluation plans that Elliott Kangas drew up during his internship at the TLDC (refer to the summative evaluation preplanning in Chapter 5). Percy reviews the plan and develops a list of specific questions for his evaluation of *GardenScapes,* as well as for the other courses slated for evaluation. He organizes the questions by areas of consideration.

Questions for the Summative Evaluation Plans for the *GardenScapes* Course[*]

Areas of Consideration	Questions
Instructional Goals and Content	**Effectiveness** Did the participants create a garden plan? ***How did final project meet course objectives?***[†] How well did participants learn the garden concepts and procedures? **Efficiency** Was the WBI efficient? Did the WBI delivery provide easy access for participants from other parts of the country?[*] ***How long did learners participate in the WBI per session or activity?***[*] **Appeal** ***Will learners take other distance courses at CJC?***[†]
Learners and Instructors	**Effectiveness** Were the stakeholders satisfied with the course outcomes, activities, and products?[*] Did Kally find the course satisfactory and informative in terms of teaching? ***Do learners believe the WBI was worth attending?***[†] **Efficiency** Did Kally find the WBI easy to use? Did learners find the WBI easy to use?[*] **Appeal** Would Kally teach this course and others again using this delivery? Did the participants find the course interesting and motivational, appropriate to their backgrounds, and helpful?[*] ***Would learners take another course in this format?***[†]
Context	**Effectiveness** Did *GradenScapes* fit Web delivery? Were the computers of the learners, instructor, and server compatible? Was the course on a stable system? ***Were technical problems minimized?***[*] ***Were technical problems taken care of quickly?***[†] Was there appropriate technical support?[*] Did the website work with the lowest specifications of computer and Web browser? **Efficiency** Was access to the website smooth and easy for learners and the instructor?[*] Was access restricted to participants who had registered for the course?[*] **Appeal** Were disclaimers and cautions provided to participants, especially first-time users?[*] Were the authors clearly identified? Were references cited properly and permission for use clearly visible?[*]

[*] Evaluation of other WBI courses offered at CJC will use similar questions to make comparisons among them.
[†] Questions from preliminary plans proposed by Elliott Kangas.

See this textbook's Companion Website (http://www.prenhall.com/davidson-shivers) for *GardenScapes* Summative Evaluation Documents.

ON YOUR OWN

Review your preliminary plans for the summative evaluation of your project. Are they still appropriate? Modify your plans, if necessary, and finalize the list of questions to be addressed in your summative evaluation. Base your questions on the main criteria of effectiveness, efficiency, and appeal that are specific and relevant to your WBI situation. Begin documenting your final summative evaluation with this information.

(For illustrations of how other designers tackled these same issues, review the case studies appearing in the Extending Your Skills section at the end of this chapter.)

See this textbook's Companion Website (http://www.prenhall.com/davidson-shivers) for a printable template of the summative evaluation considerations table.

Summative Evaluation Planning: Detailing the Main Steps

The main aspects of the Summative Evaluation Plan are similar to those of the Formative Evaluation Plan. This plan identifies and describes the people, materials, and resources involved; the data gathering and analysis procedures; and the reporting process (Fitzpatrick et al., 2004; Guba & Lincoln, 1989; Hale, 2002; Patton, 2002; Rossi et al., 1999). This final similarity between formative and summative evaluation is indicated in the questions that guide the procedures:

- Who are the stakeholders?
- What is being evaluated?
- Who are the evaluators?
- What are the evaluation methods and tools?
- How are data collected and analyzed?
- How are evaluation results reported?

These six questions form the basis for final summative evaluation plans. As evaluators address each guiding question, they provide written documentation. One way to document this plan is to write it in narrative fashion; another is to use an Evaluation Planning Worksheet, such as the one shown in Figure 10.2. The choice depends on how formal the document must be, who the evaluator and client/stakeholders are, and whether the document will serve as the basis of a contractual agreement between client and evaluator.

Who Are the Stakeholders?

As discussed previously, individuals considered part of the stakeholder group include clients, managers, support staff (administrative, technical, and instructional), instructor/trainer, and learners, students or employees (Dean, 1999; Greer, 1999). Depending on

Figure 10.2   Evaluation Planning Worksheet for summative evaluation.

(Title Page)

Evaluation Planning Worksheet for:

_____

by
(Name, Location, Date)

(Worksheet Pages)

The Summative Evaluation Plan
Who are the stakeholders?
• Primary: • Secondary:
What is being evaluated?
Who are the evaluators?
• Internal or external evaluator(s) • Who will be asked to participate in the evaluation?
What are the evaluation methods and tools?
How are data collected and analyzed?
How are evaluation results reported?

when the summative evaluation takes place, an instructional designer may or may not be involved. Generally speaking, the role of an instructional designer may no longer be needed once the WBI is in full implementation and, consequently, this individual may or may not be a part of the stakeholder group.

Individuals with decision-making authority about the WBI are considered **primary stakeholders.** Individuals or groups indirectly affected by the WBI are **secondary stakeholders.** During summative evaluation, primary stakeholders are those individuals or groups who make decisions about the value, value added, and continuation of the WBI (Fitzpatrick et al., 2004). Specifically, they may include the administrator(s) and instructor within formal school settings or the managers and trainers within business settings. In some situations, the instructor and/or trainer has input but will not make the ultimate decision about WBI continuation. The learners or participants in the WBI are part of the secondary stakeholder group. Others tangentially associated with the WBI may include technical support staff, community and civic leaders, and, for public PK–12 school systems, parents, state departments of education, and state legislative bodies. In higher education, the legislative bodies and accrediting agencies may be involved indirectly by asking for reports about the curriculum or the programs; if so, they could be considered secondary stakeholders. Other organizations may have secondary stakeholders, such as stockholders for corporations and other business entities, and legislators and taxpayers for the military and governmental agencies.

GardenScapes

Continuing with his Summative Evaluation Plan, Percy identifies the stakeholders in *GardenScapes.*

Who Are the Stakeholders?

Primary stakeholders include Kally Le Rue, the instructor, and Carlos Duartes, the director of TLDC. Percy is obtaining short bios from each of them and stating in his report why they are the primary stakeholders.

Secondary stakeholders include Dr. Ford, director of CDE, and other college administrators, the president of CJC, its board of trustees, the technical support staff of the TLDC, and the participants of the GardenScapes course. In addition, some evaluation results may appear in the various reports to supervisory state and accrediting agencies of CJC.

See this textbook's Companion Website (http://www.prenhall.com/davidson-shivers) for *GardenScapes* Summative Evaluation Documents.

ON YOUR OWN

For your summative evaluation, address the question, Who are the stakeholders? Identify and describe your primary and secondary stakeholders based on those individuals or groups who are responsible for making decisions about continuation of the WBI. Add this information to your Summative Evaluation Plan, either in a narrative format or using the Evaluation Planning Worksheet, as shown in Figure 10.2.

(For illustrations of how other designers tackled these same issues, review the case studies appearing in the Extending Your Skills section at the end of this chapter.)

See this textbook's Companion Website (http://www.prenhall.com/davidson-shivers) for a printable version of the Evaluation Planning Worksheet.

What Is Being Evaluated?

The second question, *What is being evaluated?*, is asked to determine the focus of the evaluation. For summative evaluation, the focus may be on specific instructional materials and/or instructional processes. Instructional materials include the instructional content as provided in the lectures, reading assignments, the discussions, and other group and independent activities. Processes examined include the instructional activities (such as assignments and assessments), interaction of the participants, and the feedback provided by the instructor. The technology and the features of the website and Web page (e.g., text, graphics, etc.) should be evaluated as well (Palloff & Pratt, 1999; Savenye, 2004).

Although it is necessary to consider the technological aspects of the WBI, Weston and Barker (2001) suggest that the primary focus of this evaluation is to be on the content and the instructional quality. Identifying specific aspects of the WBI and its website as a secondary focus refocuses attention on main criteria of effectiveness, efficiency, and appeal; they should correspond to the identified, detailed questions (refer to Table 10.1). These questions further help evaluators identify the appropriate methods and tools for collecting appropriate data.

GardenScapes

Continuing with the Summative Evaluation Plan, Percy identifies the aspects of the *GardenScapes* course to be evaluated.

What Is Being Evaluated?

The course, GardenScapes, is the instructional situation to be examined; products to be evaluated are the lectures and the instructional support materials, directions for activities and assignments, and instructor feedback. Processes to be evaluated are the exercises, discussion activities, and assessments. The graphics, videos, and audio clips will be examined for their quality in promoting and supporting the instruction.

Some of the instruments, such as the opinion survey, developed for the formative evaluation will be used with slight modifications. Data on learner and instructor login time will be tracked and collected by the LMS. Observation of discussions (through transcripts) will be used to assess the quality of the responses, based on the evaluation questions identified.

See this textbook's Companion Website (http://www.prenhall.com/davidson-shivers) for *GardenScapes* Summative Evaluation Documents.

ON YOUR OWN

Continue preparing your Summative Evaluation Plan. Address the second question, *What is being evaluated?* Identify the specific instructional products and processes that will be the main focus of your evaluation. Describe the WBI products and processes in your plan. Identify any technical features as a secondary focus of the study.

(For illustrations of how other designers tackled these same issues, review the case studies appearing in the Extending Your Skills section at the end of this chapter.)

See this textbook's Companion Website (http://www.prenhall.com/davidson-shivers) for a printable template of the Evaluation Planning Worksheet.

Who Are the Evaluators?

In Chapter 5 we briefly discussed the qualifications and requirements for evaluators for formative evaluation; these same characteristics are required for the evaluators who conduct summative evaluation. For instance, competent and trustworthy evaluators are particularly important to summative evaluation simply because decisions are being made about the WBI viability. Evaluators should have strong public relations skills and possess technical competence, integrity, and prior relevant experience (Joint Committee, 1994). Again, few individuals possess all of the necessary characteristics needed in a comprehensive evaluation project, so it is more likely that a team will be formed.

Evaluator roles depend on the purpose(s) of the evaluation and the activities accomplished to serve that purpose. The role may be to gather information and report findings. In this situation, evaluators describe and explain the evaluation process and results and report them to the decision makers. Additionally, they may be asked to make recommendations. In other instances, the evaluators may be called on to provide data and decide whether the WBI should remain the same, be modified, or be discontinued.

In either of these two roles, those involved in the evaluation may view the evaluator as either an advocate or a critic (Joint Committee, 1994). This perception is based on how the evaluation has come about, what the outcomes of the evaluation will be, and the rapport that the evaluator establishes. Evaluators, however, should be neutral agents, focusing objectively on the merits of the project.

Internal or External Evaluators.   Evaluation teams may be made up of either internal or external evaluators, or a combination of the two. An **internal evaluator** is an individual who is involved in the WBI development or implementation. The internal evaluator could be the instructional designer, the facilitator of the course, or an in-house administrator. An **external evaluator** has not taken part in the WBI design or implementation and does not work at the organization. This individual is considered to be independent of the host organization (Fitzpatrick et al., 2004; Van Tiem et al., 2001), even though they may be paid by that organization.

Who Will Participate in the Evaluation?   A second part of identifying who is involved in the evaluation is to determine the evaluation participants or respondents (Fitzpatrick et al., 2004). In other words, who will be asked to provide information about the WBI? One group to consult with would be the experts (SMEs or instructional design experts) and ask them to review the WBI for its currency of content and instructional soundness. Another group would be comprised of those individuals who have been directly or indirectly involved in the implementation and use of the WBI. This group could include instructors, mentors, past and present learners, and administrative, technical, instructional support staff members, and administrators.

GardenScapes

Continuing with the Summative Evaluation Plan, Percy identifies the evaluators.

Who Are the Evaluators?

Percy Davis has been designated as the external evaluator to the WBI summative evaluation project. The chair of the CDE, Dr. Bill Ford, approves the final plans for summative evaluation before the evaluation begins. Percy's Summative Evaluation Plan will serve as a template for evaluating the other WBI that are undergoing review.

Originally, it had been suggested that Kally be an evaluator as well. However, because she has been so closely involved with the design and implementation of *GardenScapes,* Kally is considered as a resource during data collection, rather than as a formal evaluator.

Expert reviewers are not used in this particular evaluation. The content is assessed based on the instructor and participant responses to survey questions, analyses of the discussions, and learner scores on the assessments.

Percy asks past course participants and members of the current course to participate in this evaluation. Prior learners have been surveyed for their opinions about the WBI and its content, instructional activities, and delivery. Percy observes a sample of the current learners during a portion of their interaction with the WBI; they in turn complete the performance assessments and an opinion survey, which are similar to those used in the past.

The technical support staff at TLDC provides data on the technical applications and their tasks related to supporting the WBI for the summative evaluation. The technical staff provides access to the current course offering so that Percy can virtually observe the class sessions.

See this textbook's Companion Website (http://www.prenhall.com/davidson-shivers) for *GardenScapes* Summative Evaluation Documents.

ON YOUR OWN

Continue your final planning of summative evaluation and the written documentation for your Summative Evaluation Plan. Address the question, *Who are the evaluators?* Describe who will participate in the evaluation. Be sure to describe their qualifications and the purpose of their involvement in this evaluation.

(For illustrations of how other designers tackled these same issues, review the case studies appearing in the Extending Your Skills section at the end of this chapter.)

See this textbook's Companion Website (http://www.prenhall.com/davidson-shivers) for a printable template of the Evaluation Planning Worksheet.

What Are the Evaluation Methods and Tools?

Throughout this last stage of the WBID Model, data collection protocols are followed based on the requirements of the evaluation questions and the preliminary plan. The methodology used in a summative evaluation may be similar to that used in formative evaluation with the addition of conducting an evaluation study. The selected evaluation methods and tools for data gathering will address the questions posed in the study. (Refer to Chapter 5 and Appendix A. For further information, consult other resources on evaluation methodology.)

See Appendix A for brief descriptions of methods and tools appropriate for gathering data.

Data may be collected from the performance measures (assessments, practice activities, etc.), surveys, interviews, and observations (Mills, 2002; Smith & Ragan, 2005). This data will be in raw form—numbers and words that have not yet been interpreted. Data will take many forms: test scores, survey responses, interview question responses and answers, and interview notes.

In summative evaluation, data are typically focused on learner performance (Dabbagh, 2000; Ko & Rossen, 2001) and opinions about the WBI content, delivery, and usability (Savenye, 2004). Performance scores can be used to infer how well learners have met the instructional goal and objectives. Learner perceptions, measured by attitude scales, must be monitored; these scales or instruments may be focused on content, learning environment, or both. Other data that might be collected, depending on the evaluation plan, include navigational pathways, time on task, or other statistics available through an LMS (e.g., number of individual interactions, group interactions, assignment tracking).

Data from the perspective of other individuals involved in the WBI (i.e., instructor, administrator or manager, support staff) will help triangulate the data gathered from learners. **Triangulation** allows information to be verified by using multiple data sources or multiple methods (or tools) for data gathering. Triangulating data from various perspectives helps evaluators obtain accurate and appropriate data and assist decision makers in rendering a judgment of the WBI's worth. Triangulation strengthens both the design of the analysis or evaluation and the information it yields (Creswell, 1994; Johnson, 1997; Patton, 1990).

Data organization begins as soon as data collection begins, which may be well before any analysis (Mills, 2002). For example, categorization of technical problems, threaded discussion responses, or mentor emails can begin as soon as the data are collected. New data can be integrated into the categorization system. Quantitative data can be organized into spreadsheets or statistical programs in preparation for final data collection and analysis.

It is important to provide careful documentation of this part of the Summative Evaluation Plan. The documentation should explain what methods were selected and why they were chosen. Evaluators should state whether they developed or selected (and purchased) the instruments used. The instruments should be described and, when appropriate, the actual instruments placed in an appendix. If evaluators use instruments other than their own, then they should gain written permission for use. Evaluators need to reference the original source on the instrument in their documentation and, if necessary, that permission was granted. Even when adapting their own instruments from other sources, evaluators must acknowledge the source(s) in their documentation and identify the source(s) on their own version.

GardenScapes

Percy identifies the methods and tools for the summative evaluation.

What Are the Evaluation Methods and Tools?

Because of the lack of historical data, the preliminary plan indicated that a pre- and posttest design would be the main method for determining whether the WBI was successful. Because of the extensive nature of a summative evaluation, other data collection methods are added:

- Use of opinion surveys (using questionnaires) to obtain information about ease of use and interest (this information is obtained from the instructor, participants, and the TLDC technical support staff)
- Observation of discussions and emails for a current course offering
- Interviews with a random sample of participants from a current course offering

Percy's plan describes the methods and instruments; he places copies of the instruments in an appendix. These questionnaires and observation checklists were used in the formative evaluation and are adapted for use in the summative evaluation. Percy provides a rationale for why he selected the methods and tools as part of the Summative Evaluation Plan (this information also appears in the final report). Percy identifies and gives credit to Elliott as the author of the opinion questionnaire.

See this textbook's Companion Website (http://www.prenhall.com/davidson-shivers) for *GardenScapes* Summative Evaluation plan.

ON YOUR OWN

Review the evaluation methods and tools you selected in your preliminary Summative Evaluation Plan (refer to your work from Chapter 5). Further define and refine these methods and document them in your Summative Evaluation Plan.

Develop the tools/instruments you will use to collect data. Place a copy of them as an appendix to your plan (they will be included in the evaluation report as well). It may be necessary to select or adapt instruments produced by others for your WBI situation. If so, be sure to gain permission for their use, identify and acknowledge your sources appropriately, and cite all references in your Summative Evaluation Plan.

(For illustrations of how other designers tackled these same issues, review the case studies appearing in the Extending Your Skills section at the end of this chapter.)

See this textbook's Companion Website (http://www.prenhall.com/davidson-shivers) for a printable template of the Evaluation Planning Worksheet.

How Are Data Collected and Analyzed?

There are two factors to consider in data collection. The first is to determine at what point in the life cycle of the WBI summative evaluation occurs. As noted previously, it typically is after the WBI has been implemented for a period of time (Fitzpatrick et al., 2004; Hale, 2002). The timing of the summative evaluation depends on the WBI's preliminary plan, organizational requirements, the project requirements, and the needs of stakeholders. Summative evaluation might be conducted at the end of the initial WBI implementation or at the end of a semester, year, or some other cyclical time period. One way to determine when to conduct summative evaluation is to consider whether the final production is finished (e.g., the WBI is no longer going through major revision). Another criterion is when the WBI has been delivered to a significant number of the intended audience (Gagné et al., 2005; Smith & Ragan, 2005).

The second factor is to identify the time frame of the actual data collection procedures. This follows procedures similar to those for formative evaluation (see Chapter 5). The timeline includes identifying specific points to collect data, which may include when to administer questionnaires or assessments, observe course activities, or conduct interviews. For instance, the evaluator may decide to collect data only at the end of the course, at both the beginning and end of the course (i.e., pre- and postassessment data gathering), or at additional designated points between the start and end dates of a course (i.e., a repeated measures design). Time requirements must consider who will participate in this data collection, such as experts or course participants. Another consideration is gaining approval of the primary stakeholders for the evaluation. Furthermore, data cannot be gathered until the instruments have been developed, or purchased and permission for use received. Likewise, any required evaluator training in data collection methods or tools must occur.

When determining the data collection time frame, evaluators must allow enough time to code and analyze data. Depending on the methods and design of the evaluation, data analysis may begin at various points. Traditionally, analysis is conducted after the course has ended and grades or scores presented to learners. However, with action research or qualitative methods, data collection and analysis may occur more or less simultaneously (Gall et al., 2003; Guba & Lincoln, 1989; Mills, 2002). Another aspect of this timing is preparing communications and writing a final report, which also should allow time for evaluators and primary stakeholders to discuss the findings and general recommendations once they have received them.

A Gantt or PERT chart can be a useful tool to identify the estimated and actual timeline for summative evaluation. On the timeline, the evaluator documents the proposed time frame for each procedure. Each of the tasks is described in the Summative Evaluation Plan and the order of those tasks is outlined to improve how the evaluation is carried out. When conducting the summative evaluation, the evaluator notes the actual time used to complete each task and any deviations from planned procedures, and explains in the final report why those changes occurred.

Table 10.2 shows a sample Gantt chart that outlines a sequence of tasks often performed in summative evaluations. Specific tasks and their ordering will vary depending on the WBI situation.

Table 10.2 Gantt Chart of Summative Evaluation Timeline

Tasks	Time Frame	Week 1	Week 2	Week 3	Week 4	Week N
Distribute consent forms to evaluation participants	*Proposed*					
	Actual					
New learners complete preassessments or surveys	*Proposed*					
	Actual					
Gather old preassessment or survey data	*Proposed*					
	Actual					
Conduct interviews with learners	*Proposed*					
	Actual					
Conduct interviews with learners	*Proposed*					
	Actual					
Observe current learners in WBI	*Proposed*					
	Actual					
Collect data on Time on task	*Proposed*					
	Actual					
Gather midpoints data as identified	*Proposed*					
	Actual					
Interview instructor	*Proposed*					
	Actual					
Interview mentor, other staff, or administrators	*Proposed*					
	Actual					
Code data	*Proposed*					
	Actual					
Analyze data	*Proposed*					
	Actual					
If needed, identify recommendations and write Evaluation Report	*Proposed*					
	Actual					
Communicate and discuss results to stakeholders	*Proposed*					
	Actual					

GardenScapes

Continuing with his Summative Evaluation Plan, Percy determines when to conduct the evaluation and outlines the procedures he uses to collect and analyze the data.

When Are Data Collected and Analyzed?

Consent forms, containing an explanation of the evaluation study, will be sent to learners who have previously taken the course and learners who sign up for the fourth offering of GardenScapes. Learners in the current offering will receive the consent form in their welcome packet.

The timing of the summative evaluation is short and so the plan requires that data gathering materials are ready at the start of the current offering. The pretest will be administered at the beginning of the current offering of the WBI. Once the pretest is completed, current learners gain access to the WBI.

The summative evaluation time frame coincides with the *GardenScapes* course offering. However, data coding and analysis occur after the course has ended. Percy's plan allows additional time for data analysis, writing the final evaluation report, and communicating the evaluation results to the primary stakeholders. Using a Gantt chart, Percy reports proposed times for each task in terms of when the task takes place and the amount of time taken to complete it.

Data Collection and Analysis Timeline

Tasks	Time Frame	Week 1	Week 2	Week 3	Week 4	Week 5	Week 6	Week 7	Weeks 8–12
Obtain consent	Proposed	░							
	Actual								
Learners complete pretest	Proposed	░							
	Actual								
Gather old pretest data	Proposed	░							
	Actual								
Interview previous learners	Proposed		░	░	░				
	Actual								
Interview current learners	Proposed			░	░				
	Actual								
Observe current learners in WBI	Proposed		░	░	░	░			
	Actual								
Distribute opinion survey to learners	Proposed					░	░		
	Actual								

Data Collection and Analysis Timeline

Tasks	Time Frame	Week 1	Week 2	Week 3	Week 4	Week 5	Week 6	Week 7	Weeks 8–12
Gather prior opinion survey data	Proposed	▓							
	Actual								
Interview instructor	Proposed			▓					
	Actual								
Interview mentors and staff	Proposed				▓				
	Actual								
Interview decision makers	Proposed					▓			
	Actual								
Analyze data	Proposed							▓	
	Actual								
Develop report	Proposed								▓
	Actual								
Develop recommendations	Proposed								▓
	Actual								
Communicate results to stakeholder	Proposed								▓
	Actual								

See this textbook's Companion Website (http://www.prenhall.com/davidson-shivers) for *GardenScapes* Summative Evaluation Documents.

ON YOUR OWN

Address the question, *When are data collected and analyzed,* in your Summative Evaluation Plan. Identify when summative evaluation will occur during the WBI life span and once decided, develop a timeline for your evaluation procedures.

Describe the tasks that you will perform during the summative evaluation. Use a Gantt or PERT chart format such as the one shown in Table 10.2 to highlight the task sequence. Include your documentation in your Summative Evaluation Plan.

When actually conducting the summative evaluation, note when each task occurred and how much time was taken. Document whether any changes in the procedures occurred, what they were, and why they happened. Place this information into your Summative Evaluation Report.

(For illustrations of how other designers tackled these same issues, review the case studies appearing in the Extending Your Skills section at the end of this chapter.)

See this textbook's Companion Website (http://www.prenhall.com/davidson-shivers) for a printable Gantt chart template.

Table 10.3   Alignment of Evaluation Questions and Data Sources

Main Evaluation Question	Data Sources
Was the instruction effective?	• Performance measures (pretest and posttest scores, final products, practice tasks) • Surveys to evaluation participants
Was the instruction efficient?	• Instructor reports on preparation time, time spent on feedback, scoring student products, emails, etc. • Student reports time spent on lesson activities (interviews, email, chat logs) • LMS tabulations and records on instructor and student time within the system • Interviews (e.g., instructor, mentor, staff)
Was the instruction appealing?	• Student satisfaction measures (survey and questionnaire results, etc.) • Student retention rates, course evaluation measures • Instructor perceptions • Interviews with evaluation participants

How Are the Data Analyzed and Reported?

Data can be analyzed and reported in a variety of fashions. Data analysis strategies should be based on the evaluation questions and the types of methods and tools selected, as documented in the Summative Evaluation Plan. For specific methods of analyzing data, refer to references on research or evaluation design and methods, such as Cresswell (1994, 2005), Fitzpatrick et al. (2004), Leedy and Ormrod (2005), and Patton (1990, 2002). Table 10.3 shows examples of types of data to collect and their sources.

See Appendix A for additional information on data analysis methods.

Reporting Evaluation Results.   A full Summative Evalution Report presents the procedures of data collection and analysis from the evaluation as they occurred. The body of the report is written in a similar format and sequence to the Summative Evaluation Plan. However, even though it is similar, it should be a separate document. This allows changes to the plan or procedures to be noted along with explanations as to why those changes occurred. The Summative Evaluation Report provides results such as descriptive statistics and frequency distributions of performance scores and opinion data. Inferences using statistics can be incorporated as well. If recommendations are to be provided, they are included after the results of the evaluation are stated. Finally, a summary of the information is presented, highlighting the main points and findings of the evaluation.

This summary, known as an **executive summary,** is often placed at the beginning of the report with the detailed, full report following. An executive summary provides an overview of the evaluation, the results, and any recommendations to stakeholders to allow them to read the full report at their leisure or when they desire additional details on specific evaluation items. Table 10.4 provides tips for presenting data and reporting results.

The written report can be enhanced through the use of graphs and charts. Numbers can be visually depicted through charts, graphics, and tables. Calculations of performance gain

Table 10.4   Tips for Data Presentation and Summative Evaluation Reports

Data Presentation	Writing Results
Define and explain type and meaning of graphical data representations.	Follow desktop publishing guidelines for print document creation.
Use legends to describe complex data.	Include an executive summary that details important evaluation findings.
Place complex data tables, graphics, and information in appendices and refer reader to them.	Write to the appropriate audience.
Follow formatting guides contained in style guides (e.g., APA, MLA, etc.) to present data.	Proofread carefully.
Follow good presentation style by stating clearly the issues and findings as well as the methodology.	Write concisely, yet explain issues and findings completely.
Make sure that the presentations (visual and text) parallel and support evaluation questions, discussion of results.	Answer evaluation questions.

Figure 10.3   Learner performance scores.

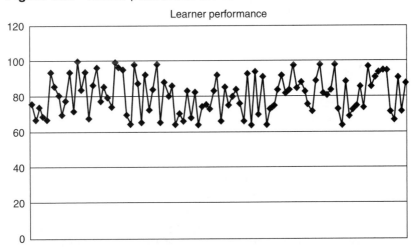

scores (i.e., pretest scores subtracted from posttest scores) or changes of opinion (subtracting pre- from postscores) can quantify these performance or opinion changes. Examples of data presentations follow.

Figure 10.3 is a sample line graph that displays learners' performance scores on a single test. Scores range from 100 to the low 60s. The purpose of this type of graph is to visually depict where the individuals scored in comparison to each other. In this example, learners generally performed well, with the majority of learners scoring above 80.

Figure 10.4   Learner performance and gain scores.

COURSE OFFERINGS	Average Pretest	Average Posttest	Gain Score
Course 1	50.6	89.3	38.7
Course 2	59.3	90.5	31.2
Course 3	35.3	75.2	39.9

$N = 20$ students per course offering

Figure 10.5   Data presentation of learner perceptions.
Learner Perceptions of Learning Online

QUESTIONNAIRE ITEM	Strongly Agree N (%)	Agree N (%)	Disagree N (%)	Strongly Disagree N (%)
The instruction met my needs.	17 (42.5%)	20 (50%)	2 (5%)	1 (2.5%)
I was able to apply the content at my work.	12 (30%)	27 (67.5%)	0 (0%)	1 (2.5%)
I liked learning in an online environment.	10 (25%)	27 (67.5%)	2 (5%)	1 (2.5%)

$N = 40$ learners

Descriptive data of gain scores show performance. Overall course scores and averages can be used to investigate how (and if) scores improve after the WBI has been completed. Course averages and gain scores are presented in Figure 10.4. These data show that individuals in Course 3 exhibited the largest gain score. They began the program with the lowest average pretest score. An analysis of variance (ANOVA) or analysis of covariance (ANCOVA) could be conducted on the raw data to evaluate statistical significance.

Survey data can be reported as frequency and percentages in a table format. Learner perceptions are shown in Figure 10.5. In this example, the great majority (over 90%) agreed or strongly agreed with the survey statements, which are presented in the left column.

Regardless of the reporting techniques used, explanations of findings should be written and presented in a clear, concise fashion that showcases their meaning. Charts and graphics should display data that facilitate understanding of the findings and that can be used for widespread organizational distribution. Reports should highlight significant findings (statistical and otherwise) and offer judgments about the relative value of the WBI, as determined by the summative evaluation purposes and requests of the stakeholders.

GardenScapes

Percy is conducting the summative evaluation of *GardenScapes,* which has been taught three times, once in each of the past three terms. The course is currently in its fourth offering.

How Are the Data Analyzed and Reported?

Prior to Percy coming on board, Kally collected data during each of the past three course offerings. Data were collected from online surveys at the end of each term; data relating to performance scores were gathered. Registration data were collected through the LMS. Percy begins analyzing these data and writing his report.

The TLDC staff members have downloaded survey and performance data into electronic spreadsheets for manipulation and analysis. To ensure that the evaluation is as free of bias as possible, Percy analyzes this data and collects additional data during the fourth course offering. Based on the questions and the data collected, he generates findings for these areas:

- Was the WBI effective?
- Was the WBI efficient?
- Was the WBI appealing?

Using the preliminary evaluation plan, Percy identifies the main questions on a chart. He aligns his data sources to these questions.

Main Evaluation Question	Data Sources
Was the instruction effective?	Participant pre- and posttest scores, final product grade, practice tasks
Was the instruction efficient?	Instructor prep time, scoring products, other feedback, etc.
	Participant time spent on lesson activities
	LMS records of instructor & student time in system
	Interviews (e.g., TLDC staff)
Was the instruction appealing?	Student opinion surveys (past students and pre- and postsurvey of current students
	Retention rates for the 4 offerings of *GardenScapes* Instructor perceptions

To address the evaluation questions, Percy analyzes data using traditional qualitative and quantitative processes. Pre- and posttest scores are one data measure. Performance scores for the final project are included. He presents these scores in a table that identifies course averages (means).

Retention is an important issue for CJC; Percy examines course retention rates. Because satisfaction is critical to a continuing education course such as this one, he pays special attention to learner perceptions and opinions.

After completing his summative evaluation, Percy generates an executive summary of his findings and recommendations. He provides the complete report to Kally Le Rue and Carlos Duartes and sets up a meeting to discuss the results. Once discussed and approved, he retains a copy for his own records. Kally and Carlos distribute copies to the designated stakeholders such as Dr. Ford, chair of CDE and other CJC administrators as deemed necessary.

An excerpt of the executive summary follows:

In the four terms that GardenScapes has been offered, 83 individuals successfully completed the course out of 101 who initially registered (see TCE Records 2003, on class size). In general, attrition can be attributed to personal- and/or work-related reasons, rather than dissatisfaction with the course. Learner performance was excellent. Due to the nature of the course, involving performance and explicit feedback, all learners who completed the course met the course requirements. Learners were highly satisfied with the course; 87 percent rated it above average or excellent. It is recommended that the course continue to be part of the offerings of CDE.

The following data table depicts student enrollment, completion rates, and average scores.

Learner Completion Rate and Average Final Performance Scores

Course Offering	Number of Learners	Number Who Completed Course	Completion Rate (%)	Average Final Score
Term 1	24	17	71%*	93
Term 2	25	18	72%	97
Term 3	27	25	91%	90
Term 4	25	23	92%	90

*Percentages rounded up

Percy includes important findings based on the opinion questionnaire sent to learners. An excerpt of key items appears here:

Learner Satisfaction

Questionnaire Item	Strongly Agree N (%)	Agree N (%)	Disagree N (%)	Strongly Disagree N (%)
I was able to complete the assignments based on the instruction.	48 (60%)*	28 (35%)	2 (3%)	2 (3%)
The mentor was able to solve my problems.	60 (75%)	18 (22%)	1 (1%)	1 (1%)
I liked learning in an online environment.	40 (50%)	32 (40%)	6 (7%)	2 (3%)
The instructor was accessible.	64 (80%)	14 (18%)	2 (3%)	0 (0%)
Feedback was provided in an acceptable amount of time.	44 (55%)	32 (40%)	4 (4%)	0 (0%)
The assignments were reasonable.	66 (83%)	14 (17%)	0 (0%)	0 (0%)

Total number of learners responding for all terms (N = 80) *
Any inconsistency between frequency and percentage is because of rounding

See this textbook's Companion Website (http://www.prenhall.com/davidson-shivers) for the Summative Evaluation Documents for *GardenScapes*.

On Your Own

Answer the question, *How are the data analyzed and reported,* by including in your Summative Evaluation Plan the data sources related to the main questions. Explain how you will gather, organize, and analyze data. Describe how you will write the full report and what type of graphics representations you will use. If you have time, conduct your summative evaluation and write the final report. In the report, include information about what took place in the summative evaluation, any changes to the original plan and why they occurred, the evaluation results and any recommendations. Develop an executive summary of the process and findings.

If you are unable to collect data, invent data and develop tables and graphics that illustrate your findings. Describe data tables that you generate. Develop an executive summary based on your findings. Tailor the executive summary to a stakeholder who would be receiving your report.

(For illustrations of how other designers tackled these same issues, review the case studies appearing in the Extending Your Skills section at the end of this chapter.)

Wrapping Up

The summative evaluation stage "closes the loop" to the WBID Model by determining the value of the WBI being implemented and used. Summative evaluation provides justification for whether the WBI continues, changes are mandated, or WBI discontinued. A

Summative Evaluation Plan follows a format similar to a Formative Evaluation Plan, except that the methods and tools may vary due to research design and methodology being used. Evaluators define the WBI's purpose(s), the stakeholders, materials to be used, the evaluators and participants in the evaluation, and evaluation methods and procedures. In addition, a timeline for data collection is developed. Finally, the procedures for data collection, analysis, and reporting are developed.

Summative evaluation is conducted to address questions regarding whether the goals were met, the stakeholders were satisfied, and the WBI was effective, efficient, and appealing. The report addresses these guiding questions to provide information to decision makers who will ultimately determine the fate of the WBI.

Expanding Your Expertise

1. At what point in the WBI life span should summative evaluation be conducted for WBI projects? Why?

2. Why is it necessary to continue to follow the preliminary plan for summative evaluation? Why would an evaluator abandon that plan and start a new one?

3. How would you justify summative evaluation to a group of stakeholders who do not see its value?

4. Why is important to document summative evaluation plans?

5. What would be reasons to develop a separate Summative Evaluation Report when the plan has already been documented?

6. Why should an executive summary to an evaluation report be developed?

7. How would including data charts and graphs improve a Summative Evaluation Report?

8. Under what conditions would you report and recommend the discontinuation of a WBI? Explain what justifications you would provide for this recommendation.

9. Should summative evaluations even be conducted for WBI projects? Explain and provide evidence that supports your response based on a review of the literature. Document your sources.

Extending Your Skills

Case Study 1   ## K–12 Schools

Half of the fifth graders in the Westport Schools have begun using the WSI, which has been designed to help them develop inquiry skills. Stakeholders have requested that a summative report be presented to the school board during the fall term, after full implementation. In this time frame, half of the students will have participated in the WSI for an entire school year and standardized test scores will have been delivered to the schools.

Since the stakeholders want to see if the WSI makes a difference in student performance, scores of students who have completed the WSI will be compared to those who have not completed the WSI.

Megan Bifford has gathered data outlined in her Summative Evaluation Plan. As she approaches the beginning of summative evaluation, she frames her investigation using this evaluation question (which is of prime concern to the stakeholders): *How did the WSI influence student performance?* She uses student performance scores on classroom assessments and high-stakes tests to answer this question, analyzing scores for gains. In addition, she codes students as having gone through the WSI or not and analyzes their scores statistically to see if there are significant differences between the two groups.

In addition, Megan is curious to see if student motivation is affected by integrating technology such as this Web-supported instruction into the curriculum. Consequently, she asks the question, *How is student motivation affected by the WSI?* She interviews a purposeful sample of students and teachers to investigate their motivations. Students and teachers complete a survey framed from a motivational perspective.

Following the protocol she established during formative evaluation, Megan submits written reports and summaries to stakeholder groups. She makes herself available for questions at the school board and PTA meetings. Summative Evaluation Reports are forwarded to the district school superintendent and then to the school board for their review. Data analysis and reporting focuses on gain scores and student performance on standardized tests. For the question on motivation, Megan analyzes interviews for themes and patterns and uses survey responses (frequencies and percentages) for data analysis. She generates a final report when the WSI is fully implemented in all schools.

Case Study 2   **Business and Industry**

Ira "Bud" Cattrell has hired an external evaluator, John Coxel, to conduct the summative evaluation of the new training intitiative, the Web-enhanced safety training program. Homer shares with John his preliminary Summative Evaluation Plan and all of the initial data gathered during the analysis, concurrent design and development, and implementation stages, including performance scores, training time, development costs, and plant safety information (before and after the training). M2 has defined the parameters of the summative evaluation:

1. How does the training initiative affect plan safety?
2. What is the return on investment (ROI) of the training initiative?

John reviews the evaluation questions and creates an Evaluation Planning Worksheet to align the questions and data sources. He uses this worksheet as the basis for his contract with M2. He identifies additional data that he will need and who he will gather that data from. John submits the worksheet to Bud and Homer for approval.

John makes preliminary presentation to Bud and Homer within one month of the completion of the training program and the subsequent distribution of data to John. A full report is made to the board of directors at the next regularly scheduled quarterly meeting after the preliminary presentation.

Case Study 3 **Military**

One year after full implementation, the initial WBI conversion project is scheduled for summative evaluation. Fortunately, the original core staff and principals remain at TSC. Although some of the development team members have received transfer orders, their replacements are oriented to the project's planning and development through a review of the planning documents, historical briefings, and the documentation existing on the LCMS. In fact, while awaiting summative evaluation, the teams select followon projects for conversion and start the analysis and development cycles for these new products.

Commander Rebekkah Feinstein contacts Central Enrollment of Navy e-Learning and receives a large quantity of usage, achievement, and satisfaction survey data from sailors who have completed the lessons. She requests data on the numbers of sailors who started the lessons but dropped before completion. Additionally, she sends out and receives command surveys from 50 major commands throughout the Navy. These commands are identified by the Unit Identification Code (UICs) of the individual sailors who took the online courses. The 50 UICs/commands with the highest number of completions are sent surveys.

Commander Feinstein appoints Lieutenant Bob Carroll as lead for the statistical analysis. His background in operational research and systems analysis from the Naval Postgraduate School makes him the obvious choice. Lieutenant Bob Carroll consolidates his findings in a formal written report that is forwarded up the chain of command after a formal presentation to Captain Prentiss.

As a result of the evaluation, the final recommendation is to continue the development of more lessons with the same format until all of the core courses are online. The evaluators make the following specific issues and comments:

- Delivery of online instruction while afloat was severely limited by both bandwidth and computer access. Until improvements can be made to the communication and instructional architecture, it is recommended that WBI material be reformatted to work on the ships' internal local area networks (LAN). Course progress and test scores can be recorded on the LAN server using a runtime LMS and downloaded when the ship arrives dockside and is connected to landlines.
- Sailors were pleased that they were able to access the instruction while on base and later finish up while at home; this capability received many positive comments.
- Though few videos were employed, those that were used incurred imagery degradation due to the streaming codec used. Alternative delivery means of videos requires additional research.
- Navigation was generally considered simple and intuitive and the interface design made presentation of the material appealing.
- The 24-hour help desk proved extremely valuable, first for online technical issues and, later, for content-related questions.
- The feature, "Ask the Chief," was particularly useful in answering content questions and its use served to develop a sense of a learning community and infuse a Navy culture into the ongoing lessons.

Case Study 4   # Higher Education

Dr. Joe Shawn uses an evaluative study that compares his Web-enhanced management course to on-campus versions of the course. He revises the opinion survey form from the initial implementation for this study to compare demographics, computer and Web skills, and student attitudes toward the course content, activities, and preferences. He uses extant data of course grades (and scores on various texts and exams) as part of the instruments for comparison.

Once the study is completed, Dr. Shawn analyzes the data and then presents his evaluation results to his department chair, Dr. Amber Wolfgang. Data and recommendations focus on learner performance, satisfaction and motivation, attainment of learning objectives, and cost effectiveness. Dr. Wolfgang is particularly interested to identify significant differences between the two delivery systems.

There were no significant differences in learner performance in the Web-enhanced and face-to-face versions of the *Introduction to Management* course and satisfaction scores were also equivalent. However, students wrote comments that they enjoyed the convenience and flexibility of the Web-enhanced class, especially not having to come to campus every week. Also, although not clearly indicated, WEI may add to the cost of course delivery.

Based on the findings and Dr. Shawn's recommendations, the department faculty and administration decides to pursue enhancing the entire management program with WEI and other forms of online instruction. These findings will become part of the accreditation documentation that technology is being integrated into teaching; the American Association of Collegiate Schools of Business (AACSG), the accrediting agency, will use this documentation for the college's review.

The following applies to all case studies. Consider how you, as a designer/evaluator, might act or respond in each case study.

- What information is *not* presented that you would like to have had? How would you go about gathering that data?
- What is the relationship of summative evaluation to the rest of the WBID Model, especially to formative evaluation?
- What other evaluation issues do you envision for each of the cases?
- What would you do differently from each of the principals in the case studies?

Appendix A

Methods and Tools for Gathering Data and Information

Introduction

The methods and tools (also called *instruments*) used for a WBI analysis are similar to the methods and tools used for an evaluation. The five main methods are surveys, reviews, observations, extant data collection, and empirical studies (quantitative and qualitative) (Boulmetis & Dutwin, 2000; Sherry, 2003), with the latter method being most appropriate for summative evaluation. Each method is described in Table A.1, which lists data-gathering methods and tools for the three stages (analysis, formative evaluation, and summative evaluation).

WBI Data Gathering with Surveys

Surveys are used to canvas a targeted population or representative sample pools for respondents' views or opinions about a given topic or issue. By surveying more than one source or a large pool of participants, designers acquire a more complete picture of the variety of perspectives on the instructional situation.

For example, a designer/evaluator may investigate the technological functions of a WBI design project by interviewing stakeholders, such as the students, instructor(s), technical support staff, and administrators. The designer may find that each group holds similar views about how the technology functioned or may find that opinions diverge among the sample groups. For instance, a technical support staff member might state that the technology was easy to install and had little operating difficulties, while learners may state that they encountered major technical difficulties during the WBI. Both opinions, in one sense, may be "right" in that each individual's perspective is based on their experience levels with the technology, responsibilities within the WBI, and their comfort level with the instructional material.

Table A.1 Analysis and Evaluation Methods and Tools

Stage	Method	Tool	Sample Question(s)	Sample Data
Analysis	Surveys	Questionnaire Interview	Are goal(s), content, etc. Accurate? Adequate?	Identify opinions, self-report of skills
	Observation	Site visits, audio taping, video, etc.	How are tasks performed?	Record skills procedures, time, etc.
	Reviews	Experts and learners or employees	Where are the problems occurring? Is content complete? Current?	Performance gaps, content needed, instructional situation
	Extant Data	Assessment tools: tests, reports related to work, student/personnel files, etc.	Does current process, instruction, technology, etc. work?	Test scores, absenteeism, customer complaints, public opinion, errors made, etc.
Formative Evaluation	Surveys	Questionnaire Interview	Is WBI accurate? Complete? Appealing? If not, what needs to be changed?	Identify opinions, report of skills, etc.
	Observation	WBI in action and website	Is technology functioning? Are student and instructor interactions effective?	Eliminate technical problems Effective instructional strategies employed
	Reviews	Experts and end users	Are WBI goal(s), content, etc. accurate? Complete? Current? If not, what needs to be changed?	Determine if goals, instructional strategies are congruent
	Extant Data	Performance measures Navigation devices and technology issues Time measures	Is the WBI usable, timely, successful? If not, what needs to be changed?	Identify learner's mastery of goal, ease of use, etc.
Summative Evaluation	Surveys	Questionnaire Interview	Is WBI still effective, appealing, efficient etc.?	Identify opinions, self-reports
	Observation	Website and WBI in action	How do students and instructor perform in WBI?	Congruency, of goals, instructional strategies, etc.
	Reviews	Experts and end Users	Are WBI goal(s), content, etc. still accurate? Complete? Current?	Identify learner's mastery of goal, ease of use, etc.
	Extant Data	Performance measures Technology tools	Is the WBI still usable, timely, successful?	Record skills procedures, time, etc.
	Evaluation Studies	Pretest–posttest comparisons, Comparative studies, Case studies, etc.		Compare pre- and posttest scores on performance, attitudes Compare current to previous instructional delivery

Gathering data through surveys provides a broad perspective of the Web-based instructional situation and is a way to triangulate data. (Recall that *triangulation* allows designers to verify information using multiple sources for data or multiple methods or tools for data gathering.) Triangulating data prevents reliance on a single data source or method and helps strengthen both the design of the analysis or evaluation and the information it yields (Creswell, 1994; Johnson, 1997; Patton, 1990). In the previous technological functions example, the triangulated data may reveal differing opinions among the technical support staff and the WBI participants. If this result occurs during a formative evaluation, the designer may deem it necessary to correct the apparent technical "glitches" and/or install tutorials on the technology. Such decisions are made once all pertinent data is gathered and analyzed during the formative evaluation.

Types of Questions

Surveys use the tools of questionnaires (e.g., Web-based surveys) or interviews (e.g., telephone or face-to-face) for gathering *cross-sectional data,* data that is collected at a single point in time (Johnson & Christenson, 2003). Designers may ask three main types of questions in a questionnaire or an interview—closed ended, open ended, and high gain.

Closed-Ended Questions.   *Anchored statements* provide defined words that explain, or anchor, a range of numerical choices. Respondents may find a range of choices more meaningful than a ranking or rating number alone. For example, an item stem may state that "online chats are . . . " and have response values ranging from 1 to 5, with the 1 anchored with "extremely informative to me" and the 5 anchored with "not informative at all."

These types of statements are termed **closed-ended questions** because respondents are restricted to the choices in the rating scale. In some cases, such as a fixed alternative question, the responses are limited to yes/no or agree/disagree (Boulmetis & Dutwin, 2000). Closed-ended questions allow designers to quantify received information in terms of percentages, averages, or frequencies of responses (Davidson-Shivers, 1998).

Open-Ended Questions.   **Open-ended questions** allow individuals to provide their thoughts and ideas about the given question. Individuals respond in their own words and data take on a qualitative tone (Davidson-Shivers, 1998). Open-ended questions are useful in gathering specific information about learners' and instructors' experiences with the WBI. However, note also that responses can be very different from each other and may require further analysis by the analyst or evaluator. It can be difficult to determine how different individuals' comments compare to each other because of the subjectivity of both vocabulary and interpretation. Evaluators must devise a scheme to categorize data into themes or factors. Several design team members should review the data to strengthen commonality of interpretation; in other words, to provide inter-rater reliability (Johnson & Christenson, 2003). Open-ended responses, on the other hand, can provide rich data for explaining how learners perceive the WBI.

High-Gain Questions.   The third type of question, **high-gain questions,** allow the designer/evaluator to move beyond the initial response to an open-ended question and to

Table A.2   Types of Questions

Questions	Definition	Examples	Survey Tool
Closed-ended questions	Questions or statements that yield restricted responses	Was the site easy for you to access? Do you have a computer at home?	Questionnaires Interviews
Open-ended questions	Specific questions or statements that allow individuals to answer in their own words	What were your favorite topics? What learning activities were the most beneficial for you?	Questionnaires Interviews
High-gain questions	Followup questions or statements that allow probing for additional information	What changes would you make to the site? What other topics need to be covered?	Interviews

Source: Table data are from Boulmetis & Dutwin (2000), Davidson-Shivers (1998).

probe for further details (Davidson-Shivers, 1998). For example, if the responses to the question, "What were your favorite aspects of the course?" were either "I like the convenience of responding to questions and doing activities within my own time frame," or "I enjoyed the topic on equity and access of computers," the designer or evaluator could ask each respondent targeted followup questions. With the first response, the followup question might be, "Does that mean you prefer the threaded discussions to the online chats? If so, why?" Followup for the second response could be, "Did you enjoy the topic because of a personal interest or because of the way we presented it? Please explain."

The targeted nature of high-gain questions means that the designer/evaluator must generate them on the fly as an interview takes place. The advantage is that well-constructed questions may yield additional insight into the perceptions, experiences, beliefs and attitudes of the learners, instructor, or other stakeholders.

Table A.2 presents examples of the three question types.

Questionnaires

One of the main survey instruments is the questionnaire. It is most often used to obtain opinions about the content, instructional strategies, and the technological elements of the WBI or demographic data on the instructor and/or participants (Boulmetis & Dutwin, 2000; Ciavarelli, 2003; Savenye, 2004). Questionnaire items generally are in the form of a statement with limited, or closed-ended, choices. Sometimes, questionnaires contain open-ended items that allow participants to make additional comments. Table A.3 presents examples of each item type.

Questionnaires are used to gather information quickly about participants' experience level with computers, the Web, and the instructional content, and pertinent demographic data prior to the start of the WBI project. Designers may then have participants fill out followup questionnaires during formative or summative evaluation to find out whether their skills (and other information) have changed in any way that may significantly affect the WBI design or delivery. Gathering such data ensures that the WBI meets the needs of the

Table A.3 Types of Questionnaire Items

Type	Example of Item Type
Limited-choice, or closed-ended statement	Do you access the Internet and Web on a daily basis? Yes _____ no _____
Open-ended statement	How you will use the information in your teaching?

learners, the instructor, and the organization. Designers also use questionnaires to determine whether participants found the WBI interesting, efficient, and effective. It is a tool to acquire benchmark and followup data for identifying trends in opinions, skill levels, and so on. A **benchmark** is a preestablished criterion for quality or success that guides the evaluation process (Boulmetis & Dutwin, 2000). Benchmarks provide baseline data for statistical analysis of questionnaire (or other instrument) responses. **Baseline data** is information gathered on the existing instructional situation that is then compared with data gathered about new interventions or innovations.

The main purpose of preliminary planning of summative evaluation (see Chapter 5) is to ensure that baseline data on the existing instructional situation can be obtained prior to the WBI being adopted and implemented (Boultmetis & Dutwin, 2000; Salomon & Gardner, 1986; Sherry, 2003). Again, the purpose is to determine whether (and how) learners' opinions about the WBI have changed over a specified time period regarding such topics as directions provided, topics covered, information presented, and the instructional strategies used.

Anonymity and Confidentiality.   To protect participants' anonymity and confidentiality, it is good practice to have an external individual collect and compile the data (Joint Committee, 1994). Information identifying participants should be removed and not used in subsequent communications and reports. When surveying respondents more than once, the evaluator may set up a coded identification system to identify respondents each time they are surveyed while maintaining confidentiality.

Distribution and Return Rate.   Questionnaires for a WBI design project can be sent via email, distributed through a Web survey, via postal services, or at an onsite meeting when situations permit.

Questionnaires are considered a relatively easy way of collecting data, but the rate of return is usually low; a return rate of approximately 25 percent or higher is considered good. The response rate for students in online graduate courses or programs may be somewhat higher, in some cases as much as 80–85 percent. This high rate may be due to having a "captive" audience; these results are not typical.

Developing Questionnaires.   Questionnaires can be developed to provide quantitative or qualitative data, or both. Items anchored with numerical rankings or ratings can be quantified by totaling points or computing percentages. Items anchored by words are more qualitative in nature, but may provide quantitative data if responses are aggregated and reported in percentages. See Table A.4 for sample questionnaire items.

Table A.4 Quantitative and Qualitative Questionnaire Items

Items	Examples	Reporting Results
Quantitative	Rate ease of use with WBI technology (1 being difficult and 5 being easy): 1 2 3 4 5	Find frequencies, mean, median, and mode for the ratings.
Qualitative	Describe how well the technology worked for you. Explain whether you had any difficulties.	Classify information into categories or conduct a factor analysis on the information.

Table A.5 Example of Checklist and Likert Scale Items

Type of Item	Example of Item
Checklist	Mark with an X the age group to which you belong: __ 25 & under __ 26–35 __ 36–45 __46–55 __ over 56
Likert Scale	I find the video lectures extremely valuable (1 = strongly disagree, 5 = strongly agree): 1 2 3 4 5

Questionnaries may be developed as checklists, wherein participants mark the most appropriate items that reflect their opinions, abilities, and so on. Checklists tend to be easier to answer than other types of questionnaires.

Another format is the Likert scale. For example, the item, "I find the video lectures extremely valuable" could have responses ranging from a 1 ("strongly disagree") to 5 ("strongly agree"). There is some debate over whether an odd or even number of responses is best. An even number of responses forces respondents to choose whether they agree or disagree with the statement; an odd number allows for a middle ground, either neutral or undecided. Table A.5 presents sample checklist and Likert scale items.

Supplying respondents with choices of "not applicable" or "do not know" may be beneficial when surveying for amount of skills and knowledge about the technology and/or content. A sample questionnaire for evaluating an online course is shown in Figure A.1.

Face Value of the Questionnaire.   Face value, or face *validity,* is another feature to consider when using questionnaires. Popham (2002) points out that this notion has been around for decades and that "all that is meant by face validity is that the appearance of a text [or other measures] seems to coincide with the use to which the test is being put" (p. 65). If items on a questionnaire do not appear to address its purpose, respondents might question its face validity. However, appearances can be deceiving; the validity of an instrument is in fact determined by the evidence that allows for confidence in the score-based inferences drawn from using it (Gronlund, 2003; Popham).

Another consideration with this type of data collection is the evaluator's confidence that participants have responded to each item appropriately and that the data are accurate. Questionnaires require an honest self-report of information; without this expectation, the results

Figure A.1 Questionnaire for WBI formative evaluation that includes items relating to demographics, prior knowledge and skills, and student opinions about course content, activities, and delivery.

Student Number _____

Name of Course _____

Student Survey

I will periodically ask you to respond to this questionnaire so that I can make comparisons for modifying the course as necessary. Your input will be helpful and is greatly appreciated! Thank you, (Instructor's name).

I. **Please fill out the following demographic data:**

Gender: _____ Male _____ Female

Age: _____ less than 25 _____ 25–34 _____ 35–44 _____ 45+

Degree plan: _____ Master's student _____ Ph.D. student

II. **Please type an "X" on the line next to the choice that best matches your response <u>at this point in the quarter.</u>**

I have a great deal of computer experience.

_____ Strongly Agree _____ Agree _____ Don't Know _____ Disagree _____ Strongly Disagree

The pace of this class is too rapid.

_____ Strongly Agree _____ Agree _____ Don't Know _____ Disagree _____ Strongly Disagree

I use the Internet and Web frequently.

_____ Strongly Agree _____ Agree _____ Don't Know _____ Disagree _____ Strongly Disagree

The feedback I received was constructive.

_____ Strongly Agree _____ Agree _____ Don't Know _____ Disagree _____ Strongly Disagree

I have taken a Web-based course before.

_____ Strongly Agree _____ Agree _____ Don't Know _____ Disagree _____ Strongly Disagree

I expected immediate help from my instructor when I had problems.

_____ Strongly Agree _____ Agree _____ Don't Know _____ Disagree _____ Strongly Disagree

I sought help from my instructor.

_____ Strongly Agree _____ Agree _____ Don't Know _____ Disagree _____ Strongly Disagree

The topics in this course interest me.

_____ Strongly Agree _____ Agree _____ Don't Know _____ Disagree _____ Strongly Disagree

I like being able to work at my own pace on course assignments.

_____ Strongly Agree _____ Agree _____ Don't Know _____ Disagree _____ Strongly Disagree

I liked the small- or whole-group chats.

_____ Strongly Agree _____ Agree _____ Don't Know _____ Disagree _____ Strongly Disagree

There were too few scheduled class meetings.

_____ Strongly Agree _____ Agree _____ Don't Know _____ Disagree _____ Strongly Disagree

Figure A.1 Questionnaire for WBI formative evaluation that includes items relating to demographics, prior knowledge and skills, and student opinions about course content, activities, and delivery. (*Continued*)

I could get help when I had technical problems.

____ Strongly Agree ____ Agree ____ Don't Know ____ Disagree ____ Strongly Disagree

The course is well organized.

____ Strongly Agree ____ Agree ____ Don't Know ____ Disagree ____ Strongly Disagree

I strongly recommend this course to other students in the field.

____ Strongly Agree ____ Agree ____ Don't Know ____ Disagree ____ Strongly Disagree

I had very few technical problems.

____ Strongly Agree ____ Agree ____ Don't Know ____ Disagree ____ Strongly Disagree

We didn't need to have a face-to-face orientation meeting.

____ Strongly Agree ____ Agree ____ Don't Know ____ Disagree ____ Strongly Disagree

The amount of feedback was appropriate.

____ Strongly Agree ____ Agree ____ Don't Know ____ Disagree ____ Strongly Disagree

I like working in groups or with partners.

____ Strongly Agree ____ Agree ____ Don't Know ____ Disagree ____ Strongly Disagree

The technical problems I experienced were detrimental to my understanding.

____ Strongly Agree ____ Agree ____ Don't Know ____ Disagree ____ Strongly Disagree

I am satisfied with this course.

____ Strongly Agree ____ Agree ____ Don't Know ____ Disagree ____ Strongly Disagree

III. Please enter any additional comments that might help me revise the course.

Source: Davidson-Shivers (1998, 2001).

are suspect (Kirkpatrick, 1998). When developing and administering a questionnaire, the designer/evaluator needs to stress the need for honest responses.

Determine How to Sample the Population. For the analysis or evaluation, the designer/evaluator must determine whether to survey the whole group (if small in number) or a sample. If the course has many students, it may not be necessary or even possible to survey all participants. When conducting a random or stratified random sampling of a population, it is important that respondents are representative of the entire population and any of its subgroups (Boulmetis & Dutwin, 2000). Using sample groups reduces the costs involved with surveying a whole population.

Benefits of Using Questionnaires.   The great advantage of using questionnaires is the amount of information that can be covered in a short period of time from a cross-section of the target population.

Furthermore, respondents can answer with relative ease (especially if items are specified and ranked statements rather than open ended), and answers are relatively easy to score.

Drawbacks of Using Questionnaires.   As with any tool, there are drawbacks to using a questionnaire. One is the lack of security regarding who is in fact responding when the instrument is sent through email, or an LMS or online survey system. Palloff and Pratt (1999) suggest that it is virtually impossible to make online environments completely secure. However, security can be increased by specifying a limited time frame for responding and by requiring respondents to reply using access codes.

Lack of confidentiality may also be a drawback for individuals returning the questionnaires. When learners share their opinions or beliefs about the course and/or instructor, they need to be assured that their comments and their personal identity and privacy are protected (Palloff & Pratt, 1999).

Using a variety of strategies can minimize confidentiality breaches. The designer/evaluator can provide participants with a code to be used in place of their names, especially useful when participants are surveyed more than once in a designated period. The LMS subsystem or Web applications such as *Free Online Surveys, Create Survey, WebMonkey* or *Cool Surveys* can be used to create the instruments. With these applications, individual responses and identity can be confidential. Finally, having another individual collect the data and remove identifying information before sharing the results with the instructor, designer, or other stakeholders enhances the degree of confidentiality. With questionnaires relating to opinions about the course, aggregate data should be reported rather than raw data from individual participants.

As with traditional delivery of questionnaires, the lack of responses and problems of returning forms are always a drawback. Knowing who has completed a questionnaire via return email and then sending a followup reminder to nonrespondents may reduce this lack of response (Boulmetis & Dutwin, 2000). Kirkpatrick (1998) stresses the importance of getting 100 percent response to increase the value of the questionnaires. Making responding easier by using Web-based applications and automated tracking of respondents may promote higher response levels.

Finally, questionnaires are *self-report instruments,* in which individuals record their own recollections, opinions, attitudes, and judgements (Wheeler, Haertel, & Scriven, 1992) about the WBI situation. They also may be subject to anecdotal bias (Sherry, 2003).

Interviews

Developing Interview Questions and Checklists.   As with questionnaires, interviews can use close-ended, open-ended, or high-gain questions to survey participants about the WBI (Davidson-Shivers, 1998). For example, a closed-ended question in an interview may be, "Do you have a computer at home?" This yields a specific answer, but is limited in quality of information. An example of an open-ended interview question is, "What types of technology do you use at home, work, or school?" This type of question allows respondents to provide details.

Interviews may be either standardized or semistructured. With a *standardized* interview, every repetition is administered and scored in the same manner. A *semistructured* interview uses a set of questions that allows respondents to respond in a number of directions. Each subsequent direction leads to a prescribed set of questions for the interviewer to ask (Boulmetis & Dutwin, 2000).

Surveying small groups or individuals through interviews allows high-gain questions to be asked, the responses recorded, and followup questions added when necessary. These followup questions may be already devised (as in a semistructured interview), which supplies consistent interview data. Interviewers also may generate questions at the time the interview takes place, which is a less consistent way to gather data. If the latter type of questioning occurs, it is then a form of unstructured interview. An *unstructured* interview allows the interviewer complete freedom to ask any questions as long as it relates to the interview's purpose (Boulmetis & Dutwin, 2000).

To help facilitate data collection during an interview session, the interviewer could have a checklist with each question and its corresponding answer set (including space for unanticipated responses), and would mark responses as they occurred. A sample interview checklist is shown in Figure A.2.

Conducting Interviews.   Interviews may be conducted via the telephone or at face-to-face meetings. Desktop conferencing software such as Microsoft *NetMeeting* can be used to electronically interview groups or individuals. Conferencing software alleviates the need for participants to be in a specific location for the interview; however, everyone must be online at the same time. Chats can be used as well for interviews. Chat applications and LMSs have different capabilities for sharing information; these characteristics need to be explored so that the most appropriate tool can be used to gather data.

During an interview, questions should not cue, or lead, respondents to answer in a particular way. Interviewers must take care to not make comments, provide nonverbal cues, or use tone of voice or text to trigger participants' responses.

Interviews can be used with both individuals and small focus groups (Fitzpatrick et al., 2004). Organizational stakeholders possess different perspectives on WBI and should participate in evaluations. Teachers, technical and administrative support staff, students, administrators, and parents may all have differing views about the use of WBI in a PK–12 school district. Individuals at differing status levels, such as top managers, division leaders, and staff, would likely have different opinions within an organization. To draw out perspectives from stakeholders at different status levels, the evaluator/designer may need to interview separately a representative group from each constituency (Joint Committee, 1994). Separate meetings with small, homogeneous focus groups may encourage respondents' comfort level in responding to sensitive questions (Fitzpatrick et al.).

The interviewer records all responses regardless of the interview format or method. Of course, interviewees must agree to being recorded and should be informed before the interview begins how the information will be used. Confidentiality should be discussed with interviewees at that same time.

Benefits of Interviewing.   Interviews allow the collection of in-depth, rich data. Such data can be informative by providing positive and negative examples, allowing additional probes into statements, and permitting participants to share additional information. The quality of the data gathered depends on the quality of the questions and the experience level of the interviewer.

Figure A.2 Sample interview checklist.

Interview Checklist

Date: **Time:**

Subject: **School:**

Title: **City/State:**

Interviewer: **Tape #**

Others Present:

Question	*Responses*					
How long have you been a principal/teacher/aide? *(circle one)*	1 year	2–5 years	6–10 years	11–15 years	16–20 years	21+ years
How long have you been at this school?	1 year	2–5 years	6–10 years	11–15 years	16–20 years	21+ years
What did you do before coming to this school?						
Which best describes your computer skills?	Novice	I get by	I'm pretty good	Expert		
What kinds of informal technology training have you had?						
What kinds of formal technology training have you had?						
How do you think technology should be used in classrooms?						
How was your official technology plan created?						
What was your role in developing the technology plan?						
When was your technology plan first created?	Within the last 6 months	6 mos.– 1 year	1–3 years	4–6 years	7–10 years	Over 10 years
When was your technology plan last updated?	Within the last 6 months	6 mos.– 1 year	1–3 years	4–6 years	7–10 years	Over 10 years
Who gets a copy of the technology plan?						

Figure A.2   Sample interview checklist. (*Continued*)

Question	Responses					
How do you use the technology plan?						
How closely is the technology plan followed?						
What kinds of activities occur in the school that involve technology?						
Where are training sessions held?	In classrooms	In labs	At other schools	At a central district office	At a company lab	Other
When are training lessons held?	Planning days	Early release days	After school	During school	At conferences	Other
Other comments:						

When small-group interviews are used, the comments of one respondent may trigger responses by others and thus allow a brainstorming effect to take place. Such brainstorming may help generate additional and valuable information that might never appear when interviewing one person at a time.

Drawbacks of Interviewing.   Time constraints are the major hindrance when using interviews for data collection. The breadth of information gathered, in turn, can be limited. Interviews cannot last for long periods of time: a maximum of an hour and a half is recommended to limit fatigue among adults (20 to 30 minutes would be the maximum when interviewing children).

The number of people who can be interviewed (whether individually or in small groups) is limited due to the nature of this tool and the difficulty in following a discussion when too many individuals are involved at one time. Because only a small number of respondents may be involved in an interview, evaluators need to ensure that they fairly represent the organization's population.

Another drawback to using interviews is the time it takes to transcribe and code data into meaningful information, which depends on the skill of the interviewer, accuracy of the transcripts, and the evaluator's ability to code, analyze, and interpret the data. In addition, bias may influence both the questioning and interpretation; potential sources of bias should be identified in the evaluation documentation.

As noted, group interviews may spark brainstorming; however, they also can trigger the phenomenon of groupthink. **Groupthink** occurs when individuals respond in complete agreement with one another and accept discussed information or decisions without asking questions or providing any contradictory opinions (Esser, 1998; Janis, 1973). If this phenomenon occurs, the interviewer must attempt to break the cycle, perhaps by posing a controversial question or playing devil's advocate.

WBI Data Gathering Through Observation

Methods of Observation

Observations can provide rich, detailed description of WBI experiences. In traditional classrooms, observation is a method for viewing teacher and learners in live (or videotaped) instruction. However, with online instruction, most actions and interactions (discussions, group work, etc.) are recorded (Boulmetis & Dutwin, 2000; Hallett & Essex, 2002; Savenye, 2004; Sherry, 2003) and available for observation. Thus, observation can occur by reviewing the archived material or by lurking. *Lurking* occurs when an individual subscribes to and watches the discussion or group activity, but does not interact with the group directly.

Other messages, such as emails from the instructor to the group or to individuals, provide information about the clarity of directions, the type and amount of technical problems, and the type and amount of instructor feedback. Access to email allows evaluators to track when and how often difficulties occur and if those difficulties change as the course progresses. Evaluators can become part of the class and receive course emails through the LMS or the course listserv. If using an LMS, programs can be installed that capture email that is distributed through the system.

It may be difficult to capture all of the interactions among participants using only email systems. Email logbooks or journals might be a solution. Logbooks provide a way for learners and instructors to track what activities are performed daily or weekly (Ravitz, 1997) and the amount of time required to prepare, score, and complete assignments from the learner's perspective. Logbooks can be submitted to the evaluator or analyst for examination. Logbooks may not be completely accurate in that items may be forgotten and the information is subjective.

Through observation, the evaluator can monitor the level of participation. Some LMSs track the number of times that an individual posts information, when they post, and the total number of postings over time. An LMS may record user activity such as identifying what pages are being accessed, how much time is spent in individual pages, and any incorporated activities.

In addition to monitoring the frequency of participation, the quality of the participation can be observed and analyzed through discourse analysis of transcriptions (Ravitz, 1997). In discourse analysis, classification systems are used to place the participant responses into categories. For instance, Davidson-Shivers et al. (2001, 2003) classify online discussions into substantive and nonsubstantive categories that facilitate data analysis (Table A.6).

Ethics of Observing.   When using observation, the designer/evaluator should bear in mind the ethical consideration of learner and instructor privacy. In some respects, observa-

Table A.6   Classification System for Online Discussions

Code# and Name	Definition	Example
Level 1: Substantive		
Structure types: Messages that relate to the discussion topic (questions posed) or course content		
1. Structuring	Statements that initiate a discussion and focus attention on the topic of the discussion, often made by the discussion leader or instructor	"Today we are going to discuss . . . " or "Well with only a few minutes left, I want us to conclude by . . . "
2. Soliciting	Any content-related question, command, or request that attempts to solicit a response or draw attention to something.	"How would you make IT attractive to . . . ?" or "How long does it take to implement a change in . . . ?"
3. Responding	A statement in direct response to a solicitation (i.e., answers to questions, commands, or requests); generally, these are the first response to the initial statements by the discussion leader or a direct response to a question by another student about the topic	"From the assigned readings, I believe that the ID is a solution . . . for educational system restructuring. However, the main burden for the restructuring is that . . . " or "I think ownership is an internal motivation, if they think they are part of the design and it is their product, they can make instruction have a significant positive impact on . . . "
4. Reacting	A reaction to either a structuring statement or to another person's comments, but not a direct response to the question	"Your earlier statement got me to thinking about . . . " or "You said . . . I think important ingredients to helping employees, teachers, etc. adjust to new technology would be . . . "
Level 2: Nonsubstantive		
Structure types: Messages that do not relate to the discussion topic (questions posed) or course content		
5. Procedural	Scheduling information, announcements, logistics, listserv membership procedures, etc.	"The final paper is due on . . . " or "The assignment can be sent via email."
6. Technical	Computer-related questions, content, suggestions of how to do something not related to the topic directly	"Some of you have experienced some difficulty recently in getting email back from the listserv . . . " or "How do I copy and paste the chat?"
7. Chatting	Personal statements, jokes, introductions, greetings, etc. to individuals or the group	"How was your weekend?" or "What is the matter with my typing tonight!"
8. Uncodable	Statements that consist of too little information or too unreadable to be coded meaningfully	Typographical errors were the majority of the uncodable responses
9. Supportive	Statements that although similar to chatting, contain an underlying positive reinforcement to the comment (*Note:* This category was added when researchers met about their coded transcripts)	"You always give such a well written answer! I enjoy reading your ideas and thoughts." or "lol . . . cool idea!"

Source: Table data are from Davidson-Shivers et al. (2001), Davidson-Shivers et al. (2003).

tion by lurking is far less intrusive than observing in a face-to-face classroom setting because of the level of invisibility to the WBI participants. With regard to privacy, it can be very intrusive. Ethically, online participants must be notified that they will be observed, of the purpose of the observation, and that confidentiality will be maintained (Joint Committee, 1994; Palloff & Pratt, 1999; Sherry, 2003). Participant permission should be gained before observations begins.

Benefits of Using Observations

One of the obvious benefits of observation is being able to see the context of the information and the richness of detail that might not be available through other methods of data collection. Conducting several observations enables an examination of changes that have occurred over time, such as development of a community through *esprit de corps,* improved computer skills, improved skills of argumentation, and so on.

Drawbacks of Using Observations

Observing and transcribing and coding data are time-consuming tasks. The amount of information, although rich in detail, may be not be easily analyzed and may not yield useful information.

The Joint Committee (1994) suggests that evaluation of instruction affects people in a variety of ways and that observations could be construed as quite invasive in the learning environment. Evaluators must take care to safeguard the rights of individuals (the right to know, the right to privacy, etc.) (Palloff & Pratt, 1999). Advising participants that they may be observed, maintaining confidentiality, and limiting access to such information protects these rights (Sherry, 2003).

WBI Data Gathering Through Extant Data Collection

Extant data are products that already exist within the organization, the WBI, or its website. Documentation of the WBI at the website can be reviewed for the instructional effectiveness and ease of use by instructors and learners. These materials can be evaluated in terms of relevancy, timeliness, and completeness. For instance, navigation devices may be installed into the website (or may already be included in the LMS) to determine the pathways that participants use. Evaluators may thus investigate how learners and instructors move through a lesson.

Some Web services and LMSs, including *WebCT, Blackboard,* and *eCollege,* record the time in and out of the system. This timing feature provides a gross estimate only of online time, since it is impossible to determine whether individuals are actually working on the lesson, attending to something else, or have stepped out for coffee.

Participant assignments, tests, independent work, and any resulting scores are considered extant data. For example, completed tests and assignments allow the evaluator to investigate how well learners performed based on the stated goals and objectives. These types of documents differ from observations, which may be archived records because of the intended focus: With extant data, the designer/evaluator is focused on the scores in order to make inferences on the success of the WBI; with observation data, the focus is on the interaction and activity of the participants.

Benefits of Using Extant Data

Extant data provides documentation on performance during the instructional period. When required throughout a course offering, assessments show performance over time. Combined with other assignments, these performance tests help determine whether the WBI facilitated the attainment of the instructional goals and objectives. Such data may help explain why instructional goals were or were not achieved.

Drawbacks of Using Extant Data

A concern with extant data collection is that the data are only a snapshot of the information. The samples that an evaluator selects may not be typical for that group or individual nor might they reflect changes within the group across time. A random or stratified random sampling of the data may help increase the likelihood the data sample will fairly represent the population.

A second drawback relates to concerns about privacy and electronic data-collecting devices. Sherry (2003) states that "the availability of data does not imply open access" (p. 443). As previously stated, participants have the right to know what is being reviewed and for what purposes (Joint Committee, 1994; Palloff & Pratt, 1999). Maintaining privacy for individuals who share information is essential, especially when it is pertinent to an individual's personal life or professional career. Electronic communications can carry names, URLs, and other personal information and should be *scrubbed* (stripped of identifying information) before sharing data with others.

WBI Data Gathering with Expert and End-User Reviews

Evaluation can be conducted through expert and end-user reviews. Experts review the design plan, product, and/or the implementation for the WBI's effectiveness, efficiency, and appeal. Subject matter, instructional design, and technical experts are just three types of reviewers typically used in WBI evaluation. End-user review is useful because these individuals provide information about the WBI or instructional situation from a learner's perspective.

Subject Matter Expert Reviews

A subject matter expert (SME) reviews materials for accuracy, completeness, and clarity of the content. SMEs either know the instructional content or have teaching/training expertise with the target audience. SMEs provide background information and review the instruction for accuracy. They identify additional information, both that is necessary or essential to make the content complete and that is helpful but not necessarily essential for learning. Experts also may identify additional resources for the instruction (Dick et al., 2005; Smith & Ragan, 2005).

Teaching or training experts could help determine logical sequencing of the content presentation, provide information about specific instructional strategies that facilitate learning, and identify any errors of clarity or accuracy (Smith & Ragan, 2005). They could help determine how easily the WBI can be modified. They also are a resource for identifying pertinent characteristics of prospective learners.

Instructional Design Expert Reviews

Instructional design (ID) experts review the instructional situation and the instructional strategies that are incorporated into the instruction (Dick et al., 2005; Smith & Ragan, 2005). They review the assignments, exercises, and assessments for educational soundness and congruence with stated goals and objectives. They check materials for completeness, interactivity, clarity, and feedback. They review the WBI and its website for graphic and message design and for effectiveness and appeal.

Technical Expert Reviews

Technical experts review the WBI for its capabilities and its accessibility to the Web. They provide the technical specifications needed for the WBI project and information to identify the common denominator of the equipment end users need to access the WBI (Savenye, 2004). Technical experts not only provide input during design as to how to best set up the website, they also review the website for its ease of use, compatibility with the various hardware and software applications, use of plug-ins, and the download speeds of individual Web pages. Technical experts check for errors and weaknesses with connectivity and provide suggestions and solutions on how to correct those technical problems.

End-User Reviews

End-user reviewers typically are selected from the prospective learners or from the actual target group. In some analysis or evaluation situations, the online instructor or trainer is included in end-user reviews. End users provide information about their needs, abilities, and interests to the analyst to define the learner characteristics and entry-level skills. End users review the WBI design plan and prototypes in their preliminary states to provide input on the WBI applicability and appeal. They offer information on whether directions are clear, examples relevant, and exercises useful. They, too, identify errors in information presented or the functionality of the website, sharing perceptions on ease of use and completeness.

Benefits of Using Reviews

Use of expert and end-user reviews of WBI design plans and prototypes has been a traditional way for instructional designers to determine the quality of instruction and to improve that instruction. All of these experts provide different perspectives of the WBI—content, instructional strategies, and technical aspects of the course. End-user reviews may provide a fresh pair of eyes and may find things overlooked by the designer due to familiarity with the WBI and its website.

Drawbacks of Using Reviews

Using reviewers can be expensive because many experts require remuneration for their time and efforts. End users may need to be compensated in some manner for their time and effort as well. Such reviews take time to complete and to analyze the findings. Reviewers, either expert or end user, must be reliable and dependable so that they provide useful information in a timely fashion; otherwise, the WBI design and development may be stalled.

WBI Data Gathering through Evaluative Studies

Another method for gathering data is to set up evaluative studies using an empirical approach. Conducting evaluative studies usually occurs in summative evaluation rather than in analysis or formative evaluation. Several types of studies can be used to evaluate WBI.

Benchmarking

The Institute for Higher Education Policy (2000) has identified 45 benchmarks in seven categories such as institutional support, course development, the teaching and learning process, and so on that can be used to ensure the success or quality of distance education or any type of technology-mediated education. Benchmarking (gathering information) from instructors and learners periodically throughout the course identifies any changes in performance, attitudes, frustration level, and experiences with Web-based learning as participants become more familiar with the WBI's technology and flow. Several methods and tools can be used for benchmarking (questionnaires, interviews, etc.), all of which yield data that evaluators can later compare (Boulmetis & Dutwin, 2000; Institute for Higher Education Policy, 2000).

Self-Study

In the literature, self-reports are "the most frequently occurring studies" (Phipps & Meriostis, as cited in Sherry, 2003, p. 443) and may be subject to anecdotal bias. Self-studies are often used by accrediting agencies to evaluate organizational performance. According to Sherry (2003), their purpose is to examine the operational and administrative aspects of course and program design. With course design, self-study is a way to examine the effectiveness and appeal of the WBI. The purpose is for participants to report on the goals, activities, resources, accomplishments, problems, and impacts of the WBI. Observations may be necessary to triangulate the data and to verify that the self-study reports are accurate and unbiased. Observation might be conducted through site visits, where an evaluation team reviews and verifies an organization's self-study.

Case Studies

Case studies are similar to self-study in that they are detailed studies and descriptions of a single WBI project, program, or instructional material in its setting (Joint Committee, 1994). The difference between the two is that case studies are specifically focused on identified evaluation and research questions. Multiple tools are used to gather and analyze data, and the result is a detailed report of specific information about a particular situation. With case studies, care must be taken to not overinterpret the data or generalize to dissimilar situations.

Experimental–Control Group Studies

Another empirical approach is the experimental–control group methodology. A detailed discussion of this methodology is beyond the scope of this book, but we note here that evaluators need to follow proper research guidelines, such as controlling the effects of intervening factors that may affect the validity of the study (Creswell, 1994; Gall et al., 2003). An experimental–control group study could be used to investigate the effects of variables, such as chat versus no chat treatments on learner performance and preferences.

Planning an experimental–control group study may be difficult within a WBI situation because of small class sizes or the inability to randomly assign participants to experimental and control groups. Instead, it may be preferable to use comparison groups in which participants are assigned to one of two or more types of treatments. In this manner, all participants are receiving some type of treatment and their scores are then compared to each other rather than comparing treatment to no treatment groups. The caveat is that in this case evaluators must not overinterpret the data in terms of the effectiveness of one type of treatment over another.

Pre- and Posttest Design

Another approach that can be used in WBI evaluation is a pre- and posttest design, which examines how scores change as a result of an intervention such as WBI (Creswell, 1994; Gall et al., 2003). It could be used, for example, to investigate learner attitudes or performance. This type of evaluation allows for the total group of participants to be included in the study. Through statistical procedures the difference (gain scores) can be determined between the pretest and posttest data. Evaluators should be aware that threats to validity may be encountered, such as pretests cuing participants to the important topics in the WBI, which may influence the actual gain.

Benefits of Evaluative Studies

Evaluative studies provide an empirical approach to evaluation. They can provide meaningful, as well as statistical significance to the effects of the WBI on learning performance and to the opinions of its participants.

Drawback of Evaluative Studies

It can be difficult to set up a well-designed, valid study. With WBI projects, a lack of both participants and a controlled environment can limit the power of the evaluative investigation.

WBI Data Gathering with Cost-Effectiveness Studies

A final data source is determining the cost effectiveness of using WBI by an organization. According to Jung (2003), many educators or stakeholders assume that operating costs of education or training can be reduced through implementing online instruction. Cost savings occur when the cost of delivery and maintenance have been reduced, when content that otherwise might not have been delivered is, or when there is a savings due to efficiency in time spent learning the information. Cost savings can be associated and derived from reduction in travel and lost time on the job, and shortened training time, as well as from improved performance on the job and improved customer relations (Davidove, 2002). Return on investments (ROI) and cost savings are usually reserved for business-oriented environments and are not documented within educational settings; however, that may be changing.

Jung (2003) suggests that through "costs distributed over a large number of students, resulting in an economics of scale for educational institutions . . . it is assumed that large student enrollment would increase revenue and lower the cost per [fixed costs] of student and operating expenses [in an on-campus environment]" (p. 718). Several approaches for examining costs of online education have been employed at these types of institutions. Cukier (as cited in Jung) identifies four approaches, a value-based approach, mathematical modeling approach, a comparative approach, and an ROI approach. Jung proposes an integrated approach for cost-benefit analysis of WBI, which incorporates all of the four approaches identified by Cukier. This integrated approach also includes looking at the value added in terms of improving the quality of students' learning and increasing access in addition to costs.

Some of the data associated with costs and benefits may be difficult to identify or gather (Phillips, 2002; Rumble, 2003). However, algorithms do exist and can be extrapolated into a variety of situations.

Benefits of Cost-Effectiveness Studies

Many organizations are concerned with identifying effective learning performance while providing a savings in time (efficiency) or in cost (effectiveness). Conducting cost-benefit analysis, using various approaches, provides this data.

Drawbacks of Cost-Effectiveness Studies

It can be difficult to document whether costs savings are a direct result of implementing WBI. Up-to-date records may not be kept and changes in learning performance and attitudes may be too subtle to detect, which make analyzing costs and benefits of online instruction difficult. Other factors, in addition to the WBI intervention, may contribute to the gains and/or losses.

Summary

In this appendix, we have provided an overview of the methods and tools for use in the analysis and evaluation stages of WBID. However, this general discussion does not provide enough detail to actually plan, develop, and conduct these approaches. We suggest that readers consult additional resources on research and evaluation design and methodology, some suggestions are as follows:

Creswell, J. W. (2003). Research Design: Qualitative, Quantitative, and Mixed Methods Approaches (2nd ed.). Thousand Oaks, CA: Sage Publishers.

Denzin, N. K. & Lincoln, Y. S. (Eds.). (1994). *Handbook of qualitative research.* Thousand Oaks, CA: Sage.

Eggen, P. D., & Kauchak, D. (2003) *Educational psychology: Windows on classrooms* (6th ed.). Upper Saddle River, New Jersey: Prentice Hall.

Fitzpatrick, J. L., Sanders, J. R., & Worthen, B. R. (2004) *Program Evaluation* (3rd ed.). New York: Pearson.

Guba, E. G. & Lincoln, Y. S. (1989). *Fourth generation evaluation.* Newbury Park, CA: Sage Publications.

Johnson, B., & Christenson, L. B. (2003). *Educational research quantitative, qualitative, and mixed approaches, Research Edition* (2nd ed.). Boston, MA: Pearson Allyn & Bacon.

Kirkpatrick, D. L. (1998) *Evaluating training programs: The four levels* (2nd ed.). San Francisco: Berrett-Koehler Publishers.

Leedy, P. D., & Ormrod, J. E. (2005). Practical Research: Planning and Design (8th ed.). Upper Saddle River, NJ: Prentice Hall/Pearson Education.

Patton, M. C. (1990). *How to use qualitative methods in evaluation.* Newbury Park, CA: Sage Publishers.

Popham, W. J. (2002). *Classroom assessment: What teachers need to know* (3rd ed.). Boston, MA: Allyn & Bacon.

Shrock, S., & Coscarelli, W. (2000). *Criterion-referenced test development.* Washington, D.C.: ISPI.

Appendix B

Further Design Considerations for WBI

How learners will interact with the instruction is of utmost concern when designing WBI. If learners are unable to find and understand the instructional information, it will be quite difficult for them to succeed in learning. Appendix B provides additional information on navigation and learner control (refer to Chapter 7). It provides further information on message design, flowcharts, storyboards, and style guides (refer to Chapter 8). This information is presented to help the designer through some of the complexities involved in designing WBI. Appendix B also provides additional considerations for implementing on-line instruction (refer to Chapter 9). Additional resources on Web page development should be consulted, as necessary, for WBI design and development as well as implementation.

Navigation and Learner Control Design

In Chapter 7, we briefly identified navigation and learner control as important factors to consider when developing the WBI design plan or completing the WBI Strategy Worksheet and referred readers to Appendix B for further discussion. Because navigation and control are intertwined, we will here discuss each concurrently. Navigation facilitates learner control and, in turn, learner control dictates navigational techniques. Selecting the most appropriate navigational strategy depends on the type of learner, content, outcome(s), and environment. Designers, as they reflect on the navigational and learner control requirements of the instruction, will define general strategies to guide developers as they create the WBI.

The examples displayed in Figures B.1 and B.2 present two basic navigational approaches (Lin & Davidson, 1996). In Figure B.1, learners are able to access all parts of the website from any point. This *random* navigation design provides learners with a high level of control: they may visit the relevant parts of the site as they structure their learning to fit their individual needs (Becker & Dwyer, 1994; Jonassen & Grabinger, 1993; Kinzie & Berdel, 1990).

Figure B.1 Random access design.

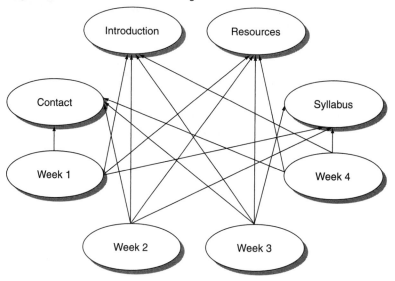

Figure B.2 Structured access design.

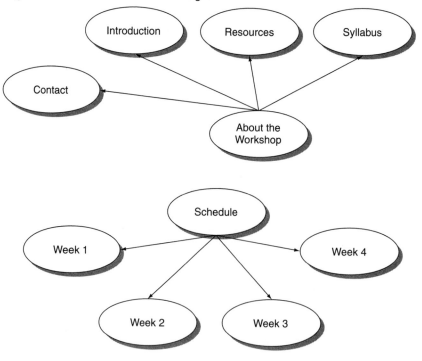

In Figure B.2, the navigational system offers learners only a few choices. In this *structured* navigation, learners are restricted to following the path established by the designer. In the following sections we first discuss random navigational design followed by three types of structured design—linear, hierarchical, and hierarchical with association.

Random Design

In random design (Figure B.3), learners have complete control over how they navigate the website's pages. They can move through the instruction in any manner that they choose. This navigation is a good strategy if learners need the freedom to explore the instructional topic at their own discretion. When using random design, it is important that navigation elements such as *return to main page, back,* and so on be included and emphasized so that learners do not get lost in the website.

Structured Designs

Linear Design.   A linear design requires that learners navigate through the instruction in a specified sequential order, one concept or Web page after another. Learners do not view, or access, all of the instruction at one time but must complete one Web page before advancing to the next. A linear design is best used when the instruction requires step-by-step performances or when an established process or procedure is followed. Figure B.4 shows two examples of linear-design instruction. There is very little learner control with this design of instruction.

Hierarchical Design.   The hierarchical design format allows learners to begin with any topic or section after an introduction or start page, but they then must progress through that particular concept completely before moving to another page or section of instruction. Generally speaking, this design path moves learners from simple to complex concepts. Learners must then return to the introduction page to go to the next concept, topic of instruction, or Web page. This design lends itself to ideas, concepts, or topics that are related to each other but not necessarily dependent on a specific ordering of the major concepts or sections. Figure B.5 presents examples of this type of design.

Hierarchical with Association Design.   The hierarchical with association design allows learners to view an introduction and then move to any main topic of their choosing. Learners can move between topics or pages and then continue to subtopics. In the examples in Figure B.6, practice, feedback, and new subtopic pages are linked to each other as well as to the instructional pages. Learners do not return to the main page to go to other topics. If topics are closely related to each other and learners can access any of them in any order to assist understanding, then this type of design is a good choice.

Selecting an Appropriate Design

When determining which approach to use in the navigational design of WBI, the designer must evaluate both the needs and skills of the learners and the type of content. There is no one best navigational structure for WBI and designers should carefully consider the implications of each navigational choice that is made.

Figure B.3 Random designs.

Example 1

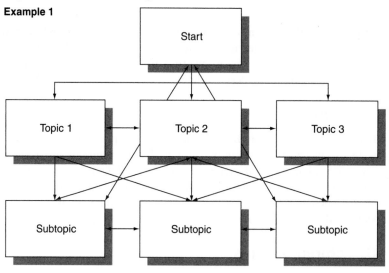

Random Design

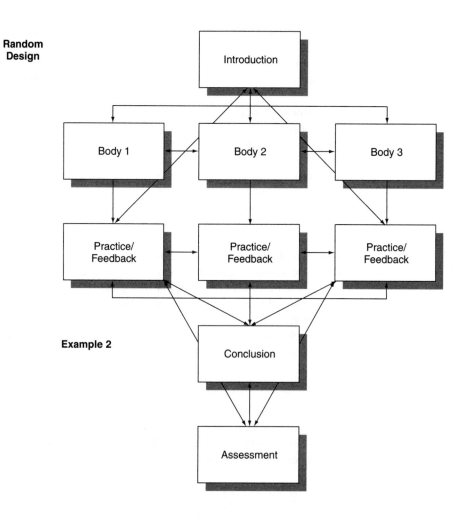

Example 2

Figure B.4 Linear designs.

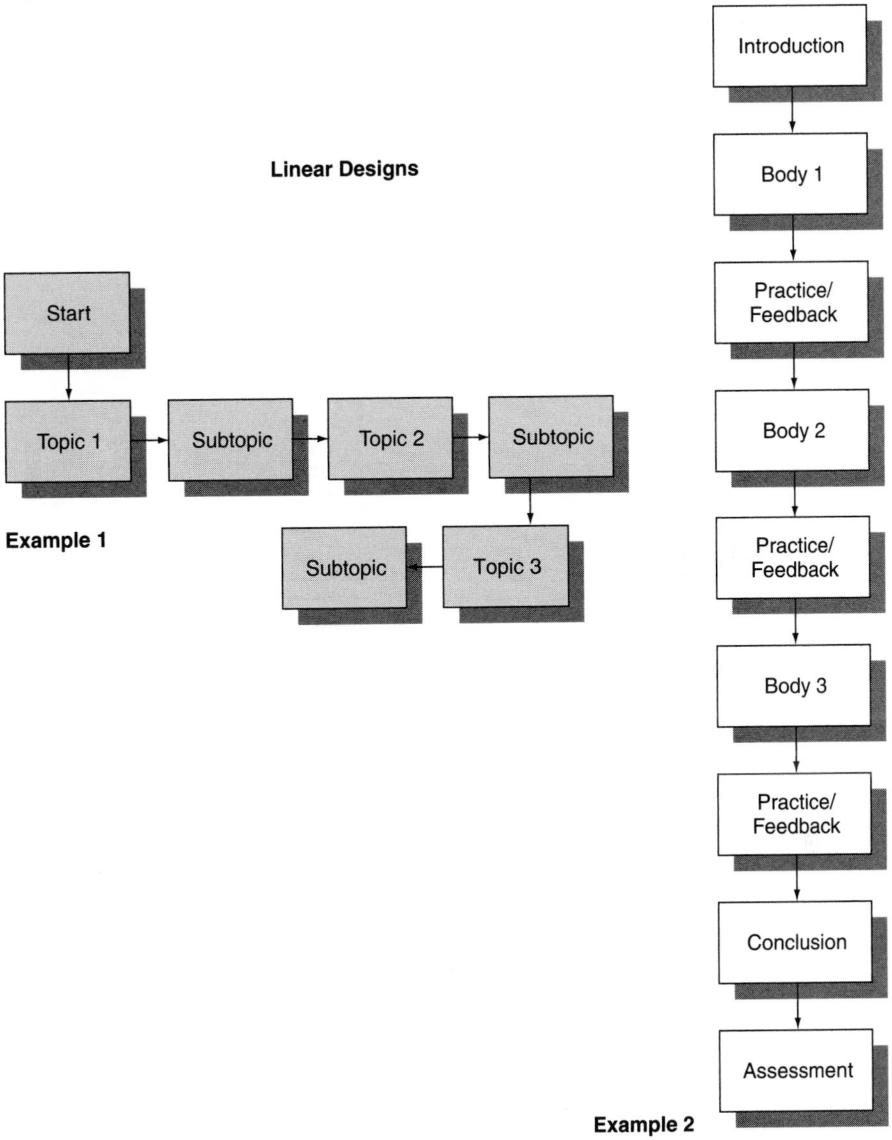

Linear Designs

Example 1

Example 2

Figure B.5 Hierarchical designs.

Example 1

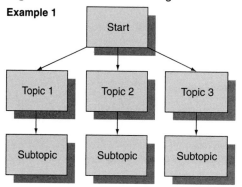

Hierarchical Design

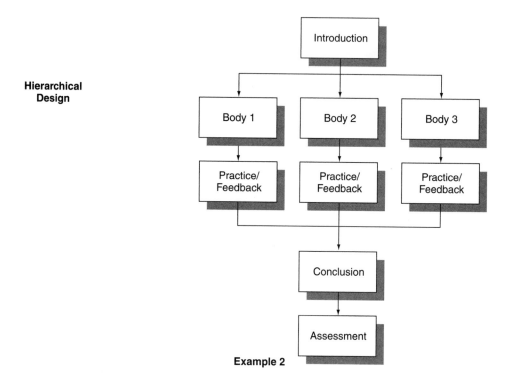

Example 2

Figure B.6 Hierarchical with association designs.

Example 1

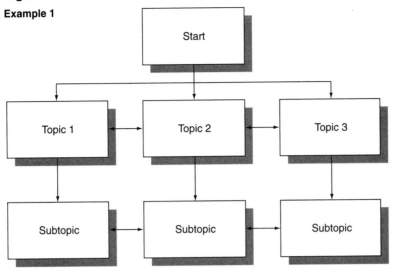

Hierarchical with Association Design

Example 2

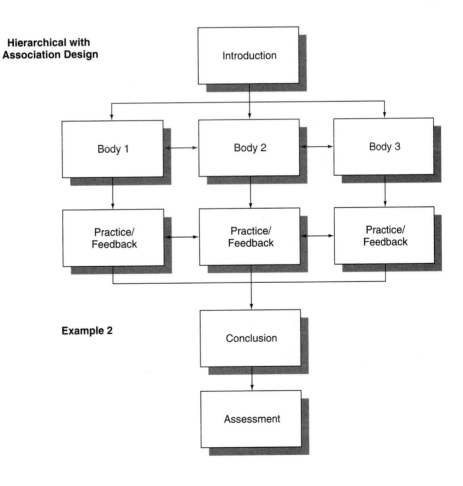

Message Design

As stated in Chapter 8, the designer uses both text (printed words) and graphics (photos, stills, maps, charts, etc.) to convey messages. Due to space restrictions we could not include examples of visual design elements in Chapter 8, but we offer a brief overview here. The examples relate to the four main principles of simplicity, balance, emphasis, and harmony (or unity).

The principle of **simplicity** can be described in terms of how the elements (whether text or graphics) appear on the Web page. The page and its elements should be easy to follow or read visually, elements should not be overcrowded, and the design should not use too many fonts or colors. Figure B.7 provides a graphical representation of the principle of simplicity. The "KISS" adage ("Keep It Simple, Stupid") is applicable with this principle.

Keeping other elements in mind, the designer must consider how the text and graphics are balanced. **Balance** can be characterized in terms of a formal or an informal sense of balance. Formal balance relates to elements (text or graphics) that are symmetrical; informal balance relates to elements asymmetrically arranged. Although formal balance is easier to create, asymmetrical visuals are more interesting; however, it is best to avoid anything actually off balance. An example of the principle of balance is shown in Figure B.8.

The third principle, **emphasis,** relates to making sure that the most important feature of the information is the focal point of the Web page. Visual emphasis occurs through contrast in size, change in color, and cues of arrows, highlights, and so on. Although emphasis is often thought of as a visual representation, information presented through text can be emphasized by embedding highlighting features, using redundancy of information, and stating that the information is important, significant, or key, such as by explicitly directing online learners to remember this point, key term, or concept. Figure B.9 presents an example of emphasis.

Figure B.7   The principle of simplicity—white space, simple lettering and drawings, or limited colors keep an image, figure, or Web page uncluttered.

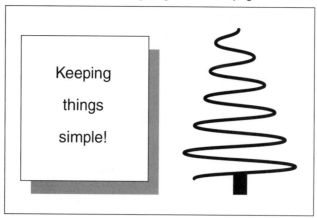

Figure B.8 The principle of balance—a symmetrical graphic on the left and an asymmetrical figure on the right.

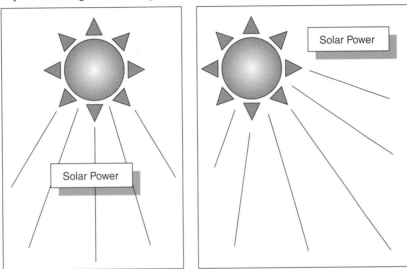

Figure B.9 The principle of emphasis—strong colors, high contrast, large sizes, or dominant shapes add emphasis, which helps learners focus on important instructional elements.

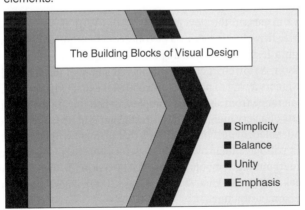

The last visual design principle is that of **harmony,** or unity (Figure B.10). Text and graphic elements on the Web page must be coordinated and must display a relationship. Other terms used in relation to this principle are *contiguous* and *connected* (Clark & Mayer, 2003; Gagné, 1985). The use of colors or text size may represent unity of items. As in this textbook, heading levels signify the levels of information in the discussion.

Figure B.10   The principle of harmony (or unity)—similarity of shapes, lines, colors, or text and use of arrows unify the information.

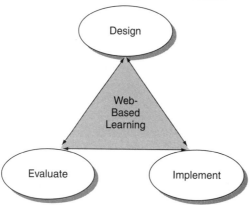

There is no single manner in which to apply these principles of visual design; designers need to carefully consider them in combination with each other. Refer to Chapter 8 for a discussion on message design guidelines for Web page elements.

Flowcharts

In Chapter 8, we discussed the development of the WBI flowchart. Hannafin and Peck (1988) characterize flowcharting as a way to observe consequences that may result as learners move through a lesson. A flowchart permits designers to articulate the sequence and structure of a lesson. A flowchart can be considered a map of the lesson (Hannafin & Peck) and provides designers a way to plan the instructional event (Maddux & Cummings, 2000).

Flowcharts can range from simple to complex, depending on the requirements of the situation. Flowcharts of a very high level describe the general structure of a lesson. Flowcharts also can be very detailed, identifying each step that learners will take during the instruction.

Organizations will have their own protocols for flowcharting. Some organizations will use computer programming symbols (Figure B.11) to provide visual meaning for designers (Hannafin & Peck, 1988; Maddux & Cummings, 2000). These symbols are combined to show how the lesson is structured.

Figure B.12 is an example of a high-level flowchart, depicting the structure of a lesson that contains four topics and a series of decision points. In this example, learners begin the lesson by entering their name and viewing information about their class. They then select a topic. If they have not completed the entire lesson, they are routed back to another concept. After completion, they view a summary. Another decision point is displayed to ensure they have completed the lesson. If the lesson has actually been completed, it ends; if learners need to complete other topics, they are routed back to the concepts.

Figure B.11 Sample flowcharting symbols.

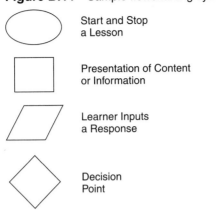

Start and Stop
a Lesson

Presentation of Content
or Information

Learner Inputs
a Response

Decision
Point

Figure B.12 Sample high-level flowchart.

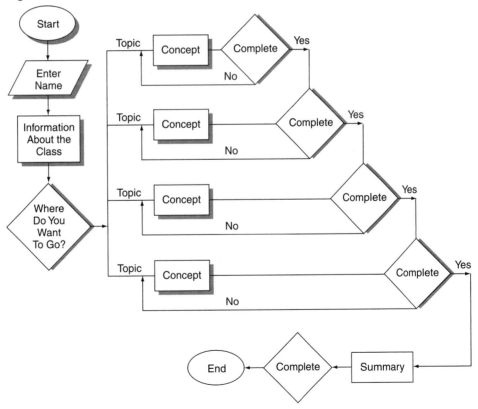

Figure B.13   Sample detailed storyboard (not full scale).

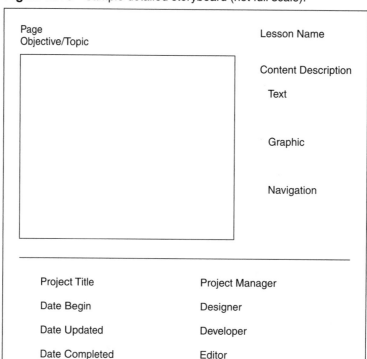

Regardless of the system used for flowcharting, designers should be consistent in their structure (Hannafin & Peck, 1988). Flowcharting permits planning of the instructional event (Maddux & Cummings, 2000) and facilitates a common framework that can be used throughout WBI development.

Storyboards

In Chapter 8, we presented an overview of two types of storyboards, detailed and streamlined. Hillman (1998) explains that storyboarding is the process of "building a story on paper that details the message or story of a product" (p. 165). Storyboarding has been described as a visualization of how the story will flow and a system that ensures that no information is left out of the instruction (Hannafin & Peck, 1988). In an environment such as the Web, storyboarding is a way to link messages to content (Hillman) and organize those messages (Hannafin & Peck).

There is no one way to structure a storyboard. The elements on a storyboard should reflect the requirements of the sponsoring organization. Before designing WBI, establishing a form for the storyboards contributes to the success of the project. Figures B.13 and B.14 are two additional examples of detailed storyboards that can be used as models

Figure B.14   Sample detailed storyboard (not full scale).

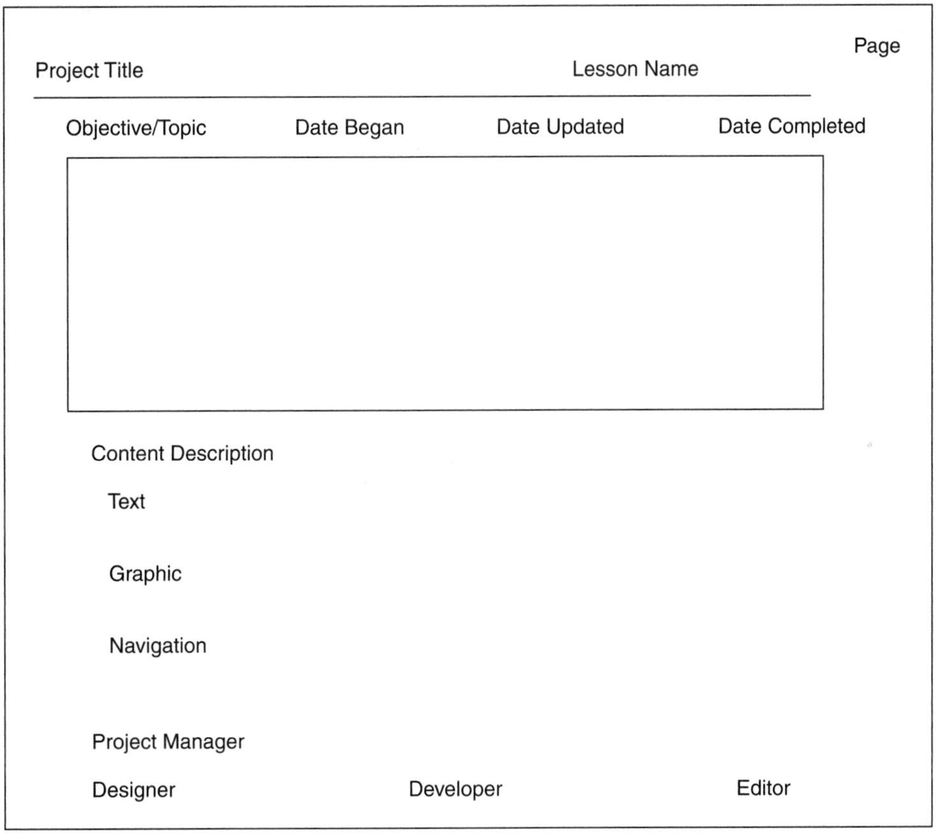

			Page
Project Title		Lesson Name	

Objective/Topic	Date Began	Date Updated	Date Completed

Content Description

Text

Graphic

Navigation

Project Manager

Designer	Developer	Editor

in the design of WBI (the first example was shown in Chapter 8). These examples can be revised as needed to meet designers' needs.

Style Guides

In conjunction to using storyboards, style guides can be designed to direct designers through storyboarding. Developing a comprehensive style guide ensures that there is a high level of internal consistency in a website. Used as reference documents, style guides outline the type of fonts, size of text, use of colors, preferred screen layouts, and navigation and linking structures (Goto & Cotler, 2004). Style guides may describe any element that might influence the development of the WBI project's Web pages, and are especially useful when teams of designers work together on projects. Style guides provide designers with a way to agree on Web page elements before design and development begins.

There are style guides provided in the literature on Web-based instructional design. One of the best known for college and university faculty is Lynch and Horton's *Web Style Guide,* first published in 1999 and also known as the Yale Style Guide; it can be found at http://www.webstyleguide.com. Other style guides may be found by searching the library or the Web. Several resources specifically for Web development, such as style guides and HTML guides, can be found at the International Webmasters Association/HTML Writers Guild (2004) website at http://www.hwg.org/resources.

System Management During Implementation

The complexity of website management depends on both the website and the network infrastructure. At a minimum, a system will have a server and access to the Web. Even small WBI systems require coordinating technology and networking systems so that they function smoothly. As the number of individuals and integrated networks increase, system complexity naturally increases.

A complex system might consist of a learning management system residing on a set of servers, connected together, for example, in a server farm directly attached to an Internet backbone (Connor, 2000; Khan, 1997).

Quality control is a continual process in WBI due to the Web's fluidity. That is, the nature of the information, resources, and websites changes frequently and demands that websites and systems be monitored and managed during the life cycle of the instruction (Nielsen, 2000). Staff members in the organization's information technology services or computer service centers usually perform system management duties. In general, the tasks in managing the system include the following (Microsoft Corporation, 2001; Weiss, 2001):

- Scheduling system outages and notifying learning community of such events, including dates and times of the outage
- Supporting a second server that mirrors (copies) the primary production server in the event of technology problems
- Networking with other technology support personnel to ensure that upgrades, backups, software enhancements, and system supports do not interfere with the course progression
- Linking learners with unusual requests to the correct individual in the support network or staff

System management to maintain the WBI and its website requires an ongoing commitment, lasting throughout the lifespan of the WBI (Welsh & Anderson, 2001). The online instructor or mentor may perform some of these activities, including maintaining the links to outside websites. The links to outside resources may change; server addresses and URLs may be active one day and inactive the next (Brooks, 1997). Making sure that these links to outside URLs are still active can be time intensive for the instructor or mentor.

To reduce the time, some development software, such as Microsoft *FrontPage,* can automatically review links and identify broken or inactive ones. In the event that an outside resource is inactive, the link identifier is removed and the search to find its replacement begins. Links to URLs that are no longer needed are simply removed.

Table B.1 Activities and Strategies for Managing the WBI and Its Website

Management Activities	Strategies
Maintain website	• Keep documentation and design specifications, including flowcharts and storyboards, up to date. • Follow naming conventions and document those conventions.
Maintain server(s)	• Back up servers and other storage devices. • Create new multimedia for new versions of browsers or plug-ins, when new versions are released. • Keep only most current versions of files on server for space. • Work closely with network administrators to ascertain how server upgrades will influence site. • Schedule server maintenance and upgrades when WBI is not active.
Maintain software	• Test site with new browsers and state minimum browser requirements. • Upgrade browsers and test WBI between course offerings.
Maintain content changes	• Correct links, remove links, and find new appropriate resources. • Keep files in central location for easy access. • Name files appropriately to make them easy to find. • Appoint an individual to be responsible for monitoring content changes.

Another task, maintaining the WBI content (Welsh & Anderson, 2001), may be performed by the instructor or mentor. When designing WBI, one advantage is that its content can be easily updated (Schank, 2002). Keeping the instructional content up to date is a high priority in online learning organizations. Table B.1 identifies various activities and strategies for managing the WBI and its website.

Learning Content Management Systems

Organizations are moving toward developing learning using reusable learning objects (RLO) in the design and development of Web-based instruction. *RLOs* are discrete pieces of instructional information (such as a concept, lesson, chapter, section of a chapter, quiz, etc.) (Cognitivity Intelligent Learning Systems, 2003) and comprise the underlying principles on which learning content management systems (LCMS) are founded (Chapman, 2003). LCMSs use database structures that permit easy modification of data so that information can be dynamically updated (Hamel, Ryan-Jones, & Joint Advanced Distributed Co-Laboratory, 2001). An LCMS is not the same thing as a learning management system (LMS) even though there may be overlaps with their characteristics (Chapman; Hall, 2002). According to Hall, "an LMS focus is to manage learners and track their progress and performance through the training or instructional activities. A LCMS manages the content, or learning objects, that are provided to the right learner at the right time" (n.p.). An LCMS permits a multiple designer (or developer) environment where, using a style guide, an instructional design plan, and RLOs, learning content can be efficiently created, stored, reused, managed, and delivered to the learner from a content repository (Chapman; Hall; Hamel et al.).

Implementation Considerations: Communicating in Writing

In addition to the information presented in Chapter 9, there are other guidelines to consider when communicating online. For instance, Lewis (2000) suggests that there is a "WRITE" way to communicate in a WBI setting; *WRITE* is an acronym for w*armth,* r*esponsiveness,* i*nquisitiveness,* t*entativeness,* and e*mpathy.* With each component, Lewis provides suggestions for communicating with students. The following is a synopsis of his suggestions.

Because miscommunication can readily occur in online messages, *warmth* is explained as decreasing the psychological distance between sender and receiver without getting "touchy feely." He suggests that the online instructor consider using the telephone to clarify a point or negotiate sensitive issues, and sending sensitive messages, such as constructive feedback, privately. In additions, warmth can be shared through humor, using examples and metaphors that are unique but relevant to the content, or sharing information based on personal interests or experiences. Online instructors might personalize their setting by letting students know about the weather conditions, music playing in the background, and so on.

Lewis's component, *responsiveness,* includes setting deadlines or being consistent when giving feedback. Responsiveness reduces the sender's anxiety and negative feelings. A second way to be responsive is to provide occasional reminders.

The *inquisitiveness* component serves two purposes—to provide useful information and to reduce defensiveness. Not making assumptions and asking questions rather than stating perceptions accomplishes this component.

According to Lewis, *tentativeness* helps reduce defensiveness. One suggestion he offers is to use tentative language such as "it seems that" or "it might be" rather than absolute statements, unless the situation dictates otherwise. He further suggests that "I-messages" rather than "you-messages" are better received.

His last component, *empathy,* suggests that the online instructor consider the other person's position and perspective and perhaps, when warranted, give them some latitude or flexibility. Missed deadlines may not necessarily be because of procrastination; the student may have had technology problems.

A second consideration for WBI implementation is that of moderating discussions. Although in Chapter 9 we presented information on facilitating online synchronous and asynchronous discussion, more information can be provided from the perspective of instructor, mentor, and student. Interested readers may wish to consult the following resources:

Collison, G., Elbaum, B., Haavind, S., & Tinker, R. (2000). *Facilitating online learning: Effective strategies for moderators.* Madison, WI: Atwood.

Gilbert, S. D. (2001). *How to be a successful online student.* New York: McGraw-Hill.

Ko, S., & Rossen, S. (2001). *Teaching online: A practical guide.* Boston: Houghton Mifflin.

Palloff, R. M., & Pratt, K. (2003). *The virtual student: A profile and guide to working with online learners.* San Francisco: Jossey-Bass/John Wiley & Sons.

Salmon, G. (2000). *E-moderating: The key to teaching and learning online.* London: Kogan Page.

Wood, A. F., & Smith M. J. (2001). *Online communication: Linking technology, identity, & culture.* Mahwah, NJ: Lawrence Erlbaum Associates.

Much has been published (and will continue to be published) about Web-based instruction; this list is by no means exhaustive. They are just a few of the references used in our own discussion of designing, developing, and implementing Web-based instruction.

Summary

The discussion on navigation and learner control, message design, flowcharting, storyboarding, and style guides is naturally limited by space. We suggest that readers consult additional resources on Web page and website development, as well as implementation and online teaching and learning for further information. Many such resources appear in the References to this text.

Glossary

Actuals   The current conditions and happenings within an organization that are identified in gap analysis.

Alternative Assessment   The process by which performance is evaluated in nontraditional fashion, through artifacts such as portfolios.

Appeal   Gaining and maintaining learner attention and interest. Usability (i.e., ease of access and use) of the WBI may add to its appeal.

Assessment   The process of gathering information used to measure learners' progress toward achieving instructional goals, which permits designers and instructors to determine learners' success and, ultimately, the success of the WBI. Assessment also can diagnose learners' difficulties and monitor their progress in surmounting them.

Asynchronous   Online interactions that do not occur simultaneously between or among participants and included processes such as emails, threaded discussions, etc.

Baseline Data   Information gathered on existing instructional situation or program that is then compared with data gathered about new interventions or innovations.

Behavioral Theories of Learning   Suggest that learning is a permanent change in behavior due to experiences other than maturation, fatigue, hunger, etc. Learning is considered an action, and is studied through observable measures of overt behaviors.

Benchmark   A preestablished criterion for quality or success that guides evaluation. Provides *Baseline Data* for statistical analysis of questionnaire or other instrument responses.

Browser   Software program installed onto a computer that permits access to the Web as long as the computer is connected to the Internet. Browsers include Internet *Explorer,* Apple *Safari,* and Netscape *Navigator.* Other browsers are *Amaya, Internet in a*

Box, Emissary, Lynx [text browser], *OmniWeb, Firefox, Mosaic, NeoPlanet, Opera, I-View, I-Comm, UdiWWW,* and *SlipKnot.* Also called *Web Browser.*

Causes   Relate to why problems exist.

Closed-Ended Question   Items in questionnaires, surveys, examinations, or other instruments that restrict respondents' range of choices to those within a scale or set of answers.

Closed Systems   Those entities that are self-reliant and excluded from external elements, including the environment.

Cognitive Theories of Learning   Suggest that learning is a permanent change in an individual's mental associations. Learning is considered a mental operation, and is studied by inferring processes from observable measures of overt behaviors.

Condition   The part of a three-component objective that sets the framework for the objective; the situation in which the learning will occur or be assessed.

Congruence   The degree to which instructional goals and objectives, content, instructional activities, and learning assessment are consistently matched, or aligned, to each other.

Constructivist Theories of Learning   Suggest that learning is acquired knowledge, which has been constructed by the learner to make sense of the surrounding environment and is founded on shared experiences with others.

Criteria   The part of a three-component objective comprised of the standard(s) by which performance is judged. Without this part of the objective, the student's mastery of learning, or performance, cannot be determined.

Delivery System   The means by which instruction is brought to and from learners, sometimes known as the delivery medium.

Design Document   Written report that documents the WBID process, beginning with the analysis stage. Design Documents describe the procedures used, report findings, and state decisions made. Also included rationales and justifications as to why decisions were made and by whom.

Detailed Storyboard   Full-page, comprehensive storyboard that includes all the details about the page including all graphics, font style, color, size, background color or image name, and navigational buttons. This storyboard should look very similar to the resulting Web page.

Diagnostic Assessment   Determines the learner readiness to participate in the new instructional activity; it is not used to assign value to student work (assigning grades per se). Typically these types of assessments are taken prior to or at the beginning of the instruction.

Distance Education   Instruction where instructors and learners are separated by time and/or location.

Distributed Learning   "The use of a wide range of computing and communications technologies to provide learning opportunities beyond time and place constraints of traditional classrooms" (Center for Distributed Learning, 2004, n.p.). It is related to *Distance Education,* and the terms are often interchanged. Examples of distributed learning include learning situations where the student and an instructor are at a distance, use computer mediated communications or CMC, and communicate synchronously or asynchronously.

Effectiveness   Measured by determining whether learners achieved the instructional goals.

Efficiency   The degree to which instruction is delivered in a timely or cost-saving manner; whether instruction adds to the learner's productivity.

e-learning   The use of electronic applications and processes for instruction, including CBT (computer-based training), WBI, CDs (compact disks), etc. Contrast with *Online Learning* and *Web-Based Instruction (WBI).*

Evaluation   Determining the value, or worth, of an instructional product or program. It is the process of gathering information to decide whether the WBI needs revision or whether it should be continued as is.

External Evaluator   An individual who has not taken part in the design or implementation of the project and does not work at the organization. This individual is independent of the sponsoring organization.

Facilitation   An aspect of implementation, the execution of the WBI and the establishment of the learning community.

Feedback   The process by which learners receive a response to their questions, comments, and assignments in a Web-based environment.

Field Trial   Formative evaluation activity, occurs after major revisions to the prototype are made. The evaluator monitors the field trial, distributes evaluation instruments (or may have the instructor distribute them), and identifies revisions to the instruction. Once these revisions are completed, the instruction usually goes into final production and is then implemented.

Formative Assessment   Gauges learner progress towards meeting the instructional goal and is used to provide feedback. The feedback allows learners and instructors to increase students' likelihood of mastering the stated goal. This type of assessment usually occurs throughout the WBI up until the final assessment.

Formative Evaluation   Reviewing the WBI during its design and development for weaknesses and strengths so that designers may revise to correct errors and enhance effectiveness prior to implementation.

Gantt Chart   Illustrates sequences of project tasks.

Gap   The difference between the *Actuals* that are occurring and *Optimals* that should be occurring in an organization.

Gap Analysis   Examining the environment to find *Actuals* and *Optimals* to determine the difference between what is actually occurring in the environment and what is desired.

Groupthink   When individuals respond in complete agreement with one another and accept discussed information and decisions without asking questions or providing any contradictory opinions.

High-Gain Question   Items in questionnaires, surveys, examinations, or other instruments that allow the designer to move beyond the original response to an *Open-Ended Question* and probe for further details.

Instructional Designer   The primary architect of Web-based instruction, analyzing and creating the strategies for the instruction and its learning environment.

Instructor   Individual who works with students and learners in the online environment; roles and responsibilities depend on the design of the Web-based instruction.

Integrated, Multitheoretical Approach to Learning   Combines as needed elements of behaviorist, cognitive, and constructivist learning theories, suggesting that learning is a permanent change in an individual's cognitive processes, skills, and behaviors brought about by active, meaningful engagement with knowledge- or skill-based information and with the environment, and by purposeful interaction with others.

Interaction   The transaction between and among participants of learning communities and with the WBI. There is a continuum of interaction: at one end of the continuum, WBI can be highly interactive where a strong learning community is developed; at the other, individuals participate in the learning environment in a highly individualized fashion, depending on the structure and focus of the interaction. Also called interactivity.

Interface   What the user sees when viewing a Web page—the pieces of information displayed and the arrangement of that information. It is the "look" of the WBI and includes the navigational and structural features of the website, and is made up of text, graphical elements, and other media.

Internal Evaluator   Individual who is involved in the design and development of an instructional project or who is a member of the sponsoring organization. The internal evaluator could be the instructional designer, the facilitator of the course, or in-house administrator.

Internet   Computer hardware and software aggregate that allows data to be transmitted and displayed through interconnected computer networks.

LAN   See *Local Area Network*.

Learner Control   Defined by variables such as sequence, pace, display mode, content, instructional strategy, completion time, amount of practice, and level of difficulty.

Learning Community   Any group of individuals who share a common language, value system, or interest. The group pursues shared or similar learning interests or goals and provides its members with tools and processes required to develop each individual member's potential.

Learning Environments   Interrelated and integrated components that interact with each other and that are focused on meeting needs of individuals within a system or organization. They include any subsystems that are part of their overarching organization. For Web-based learning environments, the major systems are individuals who and technologies that help to create the environment.

Local Area Network (LAN)   Interconnected computer network which permits interactions among participants within a single organization or entity and serves as an inter-networking communication system.

Macro-Level Design   Focuses on planning or developing entire training or educational programs or curricula rather than on course or lesson design.

Management   A second aspect of implementation, refers to the administration and operation of a learning environment.

Mentor   Individual who supports the learning environment by working with the instructor, facilitator, or trainer, and the participants in the Web-based instruction. May take a variety of roles, depending on the organization's support abilities, including those of technical or content support. Also called a *Tutor*.

Micro-Level Design   Focuses on planning and developing at the lesson, unit, or course level, using any form of delivery (e.g., print-based, multimedia, etc.).

Milestones   Indicate the deadlines when significant tasks must be completed to keep the project on schedule, used to determine if the timeframe needs to be adjusted. Milestones are used to gauge the success of the project in terms of being on time and within budget.

Motivation   A state that arouses individuals to action, which also pushes them in a particular direction and keeps them occupied in activities (Ormrod, 2004). Motivation can be characterized as intrinsic (internal to the individual) or extrinsic (external to the individual).

Navigation   The path that learners take to move around the instructional website. Navigational paths should be easy for learners to understand and locate so that they do not have an additional task of determining how to get to various activities.

Noise   Anything that prevents the sender from correctly sending the message or the receiver from correctly receiving or interpreting a message.

One-to-One Tryout   Evaluation in which the evaluator and a learner review the materials together. Dick et al. (2005) suggest that three one-to-ones be conducted to gain different student perspectives about the instruction.

Online Learning   (or instruction) The process of learning at a distance where learners are separated from the instructor but all are connected via the Internet and Web. For purposes of this textbook, WBI and online learning (or instruction) are considered to be synonymous. Contrast with *e-learning,* and see *Web-Based Instruction (WBI).*

Open-Ended Question   Items in questionnaires, surveys, examinations, etc. that allow respondents to reply in their own words with no or minimal restrictions.

Open Systems   Systems influenced by the environment, in addition to the other parts of the entity, in terms of the processes, inputs, and outputs involved within the system.

Optimals   The desired conditions of what should be occurring within an organization that are identified in a gap analysis.

Performance   The part of a three-component objective that stems from a learning task item and outcome level; it is written as an action verb to identify an observable or measurable behavior that the learner is to do or achieve.

Portal   A specialized website that organizes information and resources for easy user access. Portals are designed to provide access to different Web services much the same as search engines do, but provide a wealth of other services, including expanded search capabilities and other types of information.

Reinforcement   Strengthens or weakens a behavior or response, depending on whether it is a positive or negative reinforcer.

Search Engine   Software that facilitates locating information on the Internet and the Web and that assists online users in connecting to databases of Web addresses (uniform resource locators, or URLs).

Small-group Tryout   Formative evaluation technique that uses a small sample of the targeted audience (typically 4–10 students) who work through the prototype instruction in a fashion that is more or less as intended, but usually not in the actual setting.

Stakeholder   Individual directly or indirectly involved in WBI design and delivery. Primary stakeholders are individuals or groups directly involved in WBI production and delivery or who have decision-making authority. Secondary stakeholders are individuals or groups indirectly affected or tangentially responsible or interested in the WBI situation.

Storyboard   Visual aid for WBI designers that organizes all website elements into a meaningful structure, defining what each Web page will look like and how the instructional elements will function together. See *Detailed Storyboard* and *Streamlined Storyboard.*

Streamlined Storyboard   A way to present the information, text, graphics, animations, URLs, etc. that will be contained on a Web page; used to facilitate website development. It is formatted as a table and contains the instructional content for every Web page that is developed, and ensures that the lesson objectives, instructional text, and media (graphics, animations, videos, etc.) are aligned on the Web page.

Summative Assessment   Final assessment that permits an instructor to judge the quality of learner work and determine whether learners have achieved the instructional goal. Allows assigning value to levels of achievement to facilitate grading.

Summative Evaluation   Examines the effects of the WBI to determine the overall value, or worth, of the product after it has been fully implemented. The evaluator provides summative evaluation results and makes recommendations to stakeholders for decision making. Summative evaluation is conducted after formative evaluation, after the WBI is no longer undergoing major revisions, and after a large number of learners have used the WBI.

Symptoms   The effects of problems.

Synchronous   Any online interactions that occur simultaneously (at the same time) between or among participants, such as chats, emails, net conferencing, etc.

Systematic   An organized approach to developing instructional innovation (product or process).

Systemic   Relates to the idea that the innovation, whether it is a product, policy, or process, is disseminated and diffused throughout the organization. The impact of the innovation is felt by the entire organization.

Triangulation   Qualitative data analysis process whereby data from different sources are considered to ensure the validity of findings.

Tutor   See *Mentor.*

Usability   The ease of access and use of the WBI for the instructor and learners; the intuitiveness of navigation through the WBI and its website.

Value Added   Something positive happened that would not have otherwise been accomplished without the intervention (in this case, WBI) being implemented.

Verbal Reports   Communication mechanism between individuals and among groups to share information quickly and informally.

WAN   See *Wide Area Network.*

WBI   See *Web-Based Instruction.*

Web   See *World Wide Web.*

Web-Based Instruction (WBI)   A form of distance education where the instruction is delivered entirely online (i.e., via Internet, Intranet, and Web). In this text, WBI and *online learning* are used interchangeably, and are considered to be synonymous. Contrast with *e-learning.*

Web-Based Learning Community   A Web-based group of individuals who share common goals, interests, and experiences and have the opportunity to integrate concepts, acquire deep learning, and develop their potential through group

communication and interaction. The community can vary from one with minimal interaction among learners and instructor to one that is highly collaborative.

Web Browser   See *Browser.*

Web-Enhanced Instruction (WEI)   Courses where some class sessions or lessons are delivered entirely on the Web and others are delivered face to face. The key distinction from WBI is that some class sessions require that the learners and instructor meet in person, whereas others do not.

Web-Supported Instruction (WSI)   When learners regularly attend classes (i.e., with face-to-face meetings), but are assigned Web assignments and activities to support classroom activities.

WEI   See *Web-Enhanced Instruction.*

Wide Area Network (WAN)   Large-scale communication network that permits synchronous interaction among participants by connecting computers and smaller networks (LANs) together.

World Wide Web (WWW or Web)   A graphical information environment that allows users to find data, communicate, and use software over the Internet.

Written Reports   Formal documents that record decisions related to the design and development of WBI.

WSI   See *Web-Supported Instruction.*

WWW   See *World Wide Web.*

References

Abbey, B. (Ed.). (2000). *Instructional and cognitive impacts of Web-based education.* Hershey, PA: Idea Group.

Aggarwal, A. (2000). *Web-based learning and teaching technologies: Opportunities and challenges.* Hershey, PA: Idea Group.

Airasian, P. W., & Walsh, M. E. (2000). 8 constructivist cautions. In D. Podell (Ed.), *Stand! Contending ideas and opinions.* Madison, WI: Coursewise.

Alagumalai, S., Toh, K. A., & Wong, J. Y. Y. (2000). Web-based assessment: Techniques and issues. In A. Aggarwal (Ed.), *Web-based learning and teaching technologies: Opportunities and challenges* (pp. 246–256). Hershey, PA: Idea Group.

Albion.com. (1999). *Netiquette.* Retrieved August 24, 2003, from http://www.albion.com/netiquette/

Alderman, M. K. (1999). *Motivation for achievement: Possibilities for teaching and learning.* New Jersey: Lawrence Erlbaum Associates.

Alexander, J. E., & Tate, M. A. (1999). *Web wisdom.* Mahwah, NJ: Lawrence Erlbaum Associates.

Amazon.com. (2004). *Financial reports.* Retrieved March 8, 2005, from http://amazon.com

American Association of Retired Persons. (2002). *Home page.* Retrieved December 10, 2002, from http://www.aarp.com

American Educational Research Association. (2005). *Special interest group directory.* Retrieved March 8, 2005, from http://www.acra/net/Default.aspx?id=274

Andrews, D. H., & Goodson, L. A. (1980). A comparative analysis of models of instructional design. *Journal of Instructional Development, 3*(4), 2–16.

Andrews, D. H., Moses, F. L., & Duke, D. (2002). Current trends in military instructional design and technology. In R. A. Reiser & J. V. Dempsey (Eds.), *Trends and issues in instructional design and technology* (pp. 211–224). Upper Saddle River, NJ: Merrill/ Prentice Hall.

Banathy, B. B. (1987). Instructional systems design. In R. M. Gagné (Ed.), *Educational technology foundations* (pp. 85–112). Hillsdale, NJ: Lawrence Erlbaum Associates.

Barker, P. (1999). Electronic course delivery, virtual universities, and lifelong learning. *Educational Technology Review, 10*(Spring/Summer), 14–18.

Barrington, M., & Kimani, L. (2003). ID in the military. Class presentation in ISD 610, Trends and Issues in Instructional Design and Development. Unpublished manuscript. Mobile, AL: University of South Alabama, Spring term.

Barron, A. E., & Lyskawa, C. (2001). Course management tools. In B. H. Kahn (Ed.), *Web-based training* (pp. 303–310). Englewood Cliffs, NJ: Educational Technology Publications.

Becker, D. A., & Dwyer, M. M. (1994). Using hypermedia to provide learning control. *Journal of Educational Multimedia and Hypermedia, 3*(2), 155–172.

Beer, V. (2000). *The Web learning fieldbook: Using the World Wide Web to build workplace learning environments.* San Francisco: Jossey-Bass/Pfeiffer.

Berge, Z. L., Collins, M., & Dougherty, K. (2000). Design guidelines for Web-based courses. In B. Abbey (Ed.), *Instructional and cognitive impacts of Web-based education* (pp. 32–40). Hershey, PA: Idea Group.

Berge, Z. L., Collins, M., & Fitzsimmons, T. (2001). Web-based training: Benefits and obstacles to success. In B. H. Khan (Ed.), *Web-based training* (pp. 21–16). Englewood Cliffs, NJ: Educational Technology Publications.

Berry, L. H. (2000). Cognitive effects of Web page design. In B. Abbey (Ed.), *Instructional and cognitive impacts of Web-based education* (pp. 41–55). Hershey, PA: Idea Group.

Bigge, M. L., & Shermis, S. S. (2000). *Learning theories for teachers* (6th ed.). New York: Longman.

Blackboard, Inc. (2000). *Home page.* Retrieved December 5, 2000, from http://www.blackboard.com

Bloom, B. S., Engelhart, M. D., Furst, F. J., Hill, W. H., & Krathwohl, D. R. (1956). *Taxonomy of educational objectives: Cognitive domain.* New York: McKay.

Boling, E., & Frick, T. W. (1997). Holistic rapid prototyping for Web design: Early usability testing is essential. In B. H. Khan (Ed.), *Web-based instruction* (pp. 319–328). Englewood Cliffs, NJ: Educational Technology Publications.

Bonk, C. J. (2004). Navigating the myths and monsoons of online learning strategies and technologies. In P. Formica & T. Kamali (Eds.), *e-ducation without borders: Building transnational learning communities.* (n.p.). Tartu, Estonia: Tartu University Press.

Bonk, C. J., Daytner, K., Daytner, G., Dennen, V., & Malikowski, S. (2001). Using Web-based cases to enhance, extend, and transform pre-service teacher training: Two years in review. In C. D. Maddux & D. L. Johnson (Eds.), *The Web in higher education: Assessing the impact and fulfilling the potential* (pp. 189–212). New York: Haworth.

Bork, A. (2000). Highly interactive tutorial distance learning. *Information, Communication and Society, 3*(4), 639–644.

Boulmetis, J., & Dutwin, P. (2000). *The ABCs of evaluation: Timeless techniques for program and project managers.* San Francisco: Jossey-Bass.

Bourdeau, J., & Bates, A. (1997). Instructional design for distance learning. *Journal of Science Education and Technology, 5*(4), 267–283.

Bowman, M. (1999). What is distributed learning? *Tech Sheet, 2*(1). Retrieved August 24, 2004, from http://techcollab.csumb.edu/techsheet2.1/distributed.html

Brennan, M., Funke, S., & Anderson, C. (2001). *The learning content management system: A new elearning market segment emerges.* IDC White Paper: Framingham, MA. Retrieved April 22, 2004, from http://www.lcmscouncil.org/idcwhitepaper.pdf

Brooks, D. W. (1997). *Web-teaching: A guide to designing interactive teaching for the World Wide Web.* New York: Plenum.

Brooks, J. G., & Brooks, M. G. (1999). *In search of understanding: The case for constructivist classrooms.* Upper Saddle River, NJ: Merrill/Prentice Hall.

Bunker, E. L. (2003). The history of distance education through the eyes of the International Council for Distance Education. In M. G. Moore & W. G. Anderson (Eds.), *Handbook of distance education* (pp. 49–66). Mahwah, NJ: Lawrence Erlbaum Associates.

Burgess, J. V. (2002, March). *Once you have them, how do you keep them?* Paper presented at the annual meeting of the Florida Educational Technology Conference.

Burgstahler, S. (2002). *Distance learning: Universal design, universal Access.* Retrieved June 11, 2002, from http://www.aace.org/pubs/etr/burgstahler.efm

Cable in the Classroom. (2002). *About CIC.* Retrieved December 10, 2002, from http://www.ciconline.com/

Candiotti, A., & Clarke, N. (1998). Combining universal access with faculty development and academic facilities. *Communications of the ACM, 41*(1), 36–41.

Carr-Chellman, A. A. (2001). Long distance collaborative authentic learning (CAL): Recommendations for problem-based training on the Web. In B. H. Khan (Ed.), *Web-based training* (pp. 435–444). Englewood Cliffs, NJ: Educational Technology Publications.

Cecez-Kecmanovic, D., & Webb, C. (2000). A critical inquiry into Web-mediated collaborative learning. In A. Aggarwal (Ed.), *Web-based learning and teaching technologies: Opportunities and challenges* (pp. 327–346). Hershey, PA: Idea Group.

Center for Technology in Education at Johns Hopkins University. (2003). *CTE home page.* Retrieved April 10, 2004, from shttp://www.cte.jhu.edu/

Chapman, B., & the staff of Brandon-Hall.com. (2003). *LCMS report: Comparative analysis of enterprise learning content management systems.* Retrieved May 5, 2004, from http://www.brandon-hall.com/public/execsums/execsum_LCMS2003.pdf

Cheney, C. O., Warner, M. M., & Laing, D. N. (2001). Developing a Web-enhanced, televised distance education course: Practices, problems, and potential. In C. D. Maddux & D. L. Johnson (Eds.), *The Web in higher education: Assessing the impact and fulfilling the potential* (pp. 171–188). New York: Haworth.

Chi-Yung, L., & Shing-Chi, C. (2000). Modeling and analysis of Web-based courseware systems. In A. Aggarwal (Ed.), *Web-based learning and teaching technologies: Opportunities and challenges* (pp. 155–173). Hershey, PA: Idea Group.

Ciavarelli, A. P. (2003). Assessing the quality of online instruction: Integrating instructional quality and Web usability assessments. In J. E. Wall & G. R.

Walz (Eds.), *Measuring up: Assessment issues for teachers, counselors and administrators (n.p.).* Washington, DC: ERIC.

Clark, R. C., & Mayer, R. E. (2003). *E-learning and the science of instruction: Proven guidelines for consumers and designers of multimedia learning.* San Francisco: Jossey-Bass/Pfeiffer.

CNN News (2004). *Cheating.* Retrieved December 10, 2004, from: http://www.turnitin.com/static/resource_files/cnn1.wmv

Cognitivity Intelligent Learning Systems. (2003). *Reusable learning objects (RLOs).* Retrieved March 24, 2003, from http://www.cognitivity.com/resources/rlos.html

Collins, M., & Berge, Z. (1996). Components of the on-line classroom. In R. E. Weiss, D. S. Knowlton, & B. W. Speck (Eds.), *Principles of effective teaching in online classrooms.* San Francisco: Jossey-Bass.

Collis, B. (2001). Web-based rapid prototyping as a strategy of training university faculty to teach Web-based courses. In B. H. Khan (Ed.), *Web-based training* (pp. 459–468). Englewood Cliffs, NJ: Educational Technology Publications.

Collison, G., Elbaum, B., Haavind, S., & Tinker, R. (2000). *Facilitating online learning: Effective strategies for moderators.* Madison, WI: Atwood.

ComputerUser.com, Inc. (2000). *ComputerUser high-tech dictionary! Emoticons.* Retrieved August 31, 2003, from http://www.computeruser.com/resources/dictionary/emoticons.html

Connor, D. (2000). *Server farm focus.* Retrieved May 9, 2004, from http://www.nwfusion.com/newsletters/servers/2000/0619serv1.html

Cornell, R., & Martin, B. L. (1997). The role of motivation in Web-based instruction. In B. H. Khan (Ed.), *Web-based instruction* (pp. 93–100). Englewood Cliffs, NJ: Educational Technology Publications.

Correspondence Courses and Schools (2003). *Home page.* Retrieved April 1, 2003, from http://www.correspondence-courses-schools.com/

Creswell, J. W. (1994). *Research design: Qualitative and quantitative approaches.* Thousand Oaks, CA: Sage.

Creswell, J. W. (2005). *Educational research: Planning, conducting, and evaluating quantitative and qualitative research* (2nd ed.). Upper Saddle River, NJ: Merrill/Prentice Hall.

Cross, K. P. (1981). *Adults as learners.* San Francisco: Sage.

Crumlish, C. (1998). *The Internet,* San Francisco: Sybex.

CSU Center for Distributed Learning. (2004). *Home page.* Retrieved August 24, 2004, from http://www.cdl.edu/index.html

Cucchiarelli, A., Panti, M., & Vanenti, S. (2000). Web-based assessment in student learning. In A. Aggarwal (Ed.), *Web-based learning and teaching technologies: Opportunities and challenges* (pp. 175–197). Hershey, PA: Idea Group.

Cyrs, T. (1997). *Teaching and learning at a distance: What it takes to effectively design, deliver, and evaluate programs.* San Francisco: Jossey-Bass.

Dabbagh, N. H. (2000). Multiple assessment in an online graduate course: An effectiveness evaluation. In B. L. Mann (Ed.), *Perspectives in Web course management* (pp. 179–197). Toronto: Canadian Scholars Press.

Dabbagh, N. H., Bannan-Ritland, B., & Silc, K. F. (2001). Current and ideal practices in designing, developing, and delivering Web-based training. In B. H. Kahn (Ed.), *Web-based training* (pp. 343–354). Englewood Cliffs, NJ: Educational Technology Publications.

Danielson, J., Lockee, B., & Burton, J. (2000). ID and HCI: A marriage of necessity. In B. Abbey (Ed.), *Instructional and cognitive impacts of Web-based education* (pp. 118–128). Hershey, PA: Idea Group.

Darbyshire, P. (2000). Distributed Web-based assignment management. In A. Aggarwal (Ed.), *Web-based learning and teaching technologies: Opportunities and challenges* (pp. 198–215). Hershey, PA: Idea Group.

Dashti, A., Kim, S. H., Shahabi, C., & Zimmerman, R. (2003). *Streaming media server design.* New York: Prentice Hall PTR.

Davidove, E. (2002). Maximizing training investments by measuring human performance. In R. A. Reiser & J. V. Dempsey (Eds.), *Trends and issues in instructional design and technology* (pp. 154–167). Upper Saddle River, NJ: Merrill-Prentice Hall.

Davidson, G. V. (1988, October). The role of educational theory in computer mediated instruction. *The CTISS File, 7,* 33–38.

Davidson, G. V. (1990). Matching learning styles with teaching styles: Is it a useful concept in instruction? *Performance and Instruction, 29*(4), 36–38.

Davidson, G. V. (1992). EDC 384P, CAI Design and Languages. Unpublished course materials. Austin, TX: University of Texas at Austin, Spring 1990–Summer 1992.

Davidson-Shivers, G. V. (1998). ISD 622, Advanced Instructional Design. Unpublished course materials. Mobile, AL: University of South Alabama, Spring, 1998 & ongoing.

Davidson-Shivers, G. V. (2001). IDE 640, Instructional Development. Unpublished course materials. Mobile, AL: University of South Alabama, Fall, 2001 & ongoing.

Davidson-Shivers, G. V. (2002). Instructional technology in higher education. In R. A. Reiser & J. V. Dempsey (Eds.), *Trends and issues in instructional design and technology* (pp. 239–255). Upper Saddle River, NJ: Merrill-Prentice Hall.

Davidson-Shivers, G. V., Morris, S. B., & Sriwongkol, T. (2003). Gender differences: Are they diminished in online discussions? *International Journal on E-Learning, 2*(1), 29–36.

Davidson-Shivers, G. V., Muilenburg, L. Y., & Tanner, E. J. (2001). How do students participate in synchronous and asynchronous online discussions? *Journal of Educational Computing Research, 25*(4), 351–366.

Davidson-Shivers, G. V., & Rasmussen, K. L. (1998, November). *Collaborative instruction on the Web: Students learning together.* Paper presented at the meeting of WebNet '98, Orlando, FL.

Davidson-Shivers, G. V., & Rasmussen, K. L. (1999, June). *Designing instruction for the WWW: A model.* Paper presented at the meeting of Ed-Media '99, Seattle, WA.

Davidson-Shivers, G. V., & Rasmussen, K. L. (in press). Competencies for instructional design and technology professionals. In R. A. Reiser & J. V. Dempsey (Eds.). *Trends and issues in instructional design and technology* (2nd ed.) (n.p.). Upper Saddle River, NJ: Merrill/Prentice Hall.

Davidson-Shivers, G. V., Salazar, J., & Hamilton, K. (2002). *Design of faculty development workshops: Attempting to practice what we preach.* Proceedings of Selected Research and Development Paper Presentations for the 2002 National Convention for the Association for Educational Communications and Technology, Dallas, TX.

Davidson-Shivers, G. V., Salazar, J., & Hamilton, K. (in press). Design of faculty development workshops: Attempting to practice what we preach. *College Student Journal.*

de Boer, W., & Collis, B. (2001). Implementation and adaptation experiences with a WWW-based course management system. In C. D. Maddux & D. L. Johnson (Eds.), *The Web in higher education: Assessing the impact and fulfilling the potential* (pp. 127–146). New York: Haworth.

Dean, P. J. (1999). Designing better organizations with human performance technology and organization development. In H. D. Stolovitch & E. J. Keeps (Eds.), *Handbook of human performance technology: Improving individual and organizational performance worldwide* (2nd ed., pp. 321–334). San Francisco: Jossey-Bass/Pfeiffer.

Dede, C. J. (1990). The evolution of distance learning: Technology-mediated interactive learning. *Journal of Research on Computing in Education, 22*(3), 247–264.

Dempsey, J. V. (2002, January). *Integrating instructional technology into training.* Presentation at the Mobile Area Training and Education Symposium, Mobile, AL.

Denzin, N. K., & Lincoln, Y. S. (Eds.). (1994). *Handbook of qualitative research.* Thousand Oaks, CA: Sage.

Department for Education and Skills (2002). *Home page.* Retrieved December 15, 2004, from http://www.dfes.gov.uk/

Dick, W., Carey, L., & Carey, J. O. (2005). *The systematic design of instruction* (6th ed.). New York: Addison-Wesley/Longman.

Dodge, B. (1997). *Some thoughts about WebQuests.* Retrieved April 20, 2000, from http://edweb.sdsu.edu/courses/edtec596/about_webquests.html

Driscoll, M. P. (2005). *Psychology of learning for instruction* (3rd ed.). Boston: Pearson/Allyn & Bacon.

Duffy, T. M., & Jonassen, D. H. (1992). Constructivism: New implications for instructional technology. In T. M. Duffy & D. H. Jonassen (Eds.), *Constructivism and the technology of instruction* (pp. 1–16). Hillsdale. NJ: Lawrence Erlbaum Associates.

eBay Inc. (2005). *Company overview.* Retrieved March 8, 2005, from http://pages.ebay.com/community/aboutebay/overview/index.html

eCollege.com. (1999). *How to design, develop, and teach an online course.* Denver, CO: Author.

Eggen, P. D., & Kauchak, D. (2003). *Educational psychology: Windows on classrooms* (6th ed.). Upper Saddle River, New Jersey: Merrill/Prentice Hall.

Ertmer, P. A., & Newby, T. J. (1993). Behaviorism, cognitivism, constructivism: Comparing critical features from a design perspective. *Performance Improvement Quarterly, 6*(4), 50–72.

Esque, T. J. (2001). *Making an impact: Building a top-performing organization from the bottom up.* Silver Spring, MD: ISPI.

Esser, J. K. (1998). Alive and well after 25 years: A review of groupthink research. *Organizational Behavior and Human Decision Processes, 73,* 116–141.

Fisher, M. M. (2000). Implementation considerations for instructional design of Web-based learning environments. In B. Abbey (Ed.), *Instructional and cognitive impacts of Web-based education* (pp. 78–101). Hershey, PA: Idea Group.

Fisher, S. G., & Peratino, W. S. (2001). Designing Web-based learning environments at the Department of Defense: New solutions. In B. H. Khan (Ed.), *Web-based training* (pp. 405–414). Englewood Cliffs, NJ: Educational Technology Publications.

Fitzpatrick, J. L. Sanders, J. R., & Worthen, B. R. (2004). *Program evaluation* (3rd ed.). New York: Pearson.

Fleming, M. L. (1987). Displays and communication. In R. M. Gagné (Ed.), *Instructional technology: Foundations* (pp. 233–260). Hillsdale, NJ: Lawrence Erlbaum Associates.

Florida Information Resource Network. (2003). *Welcome.* Retrieved May 8, 2004, from http://www.firn.edu/

Flynn, E. (2003). *NKO gives sailors single point access to the future.* Retrieved May 12, 2004, from www.news.navy.mil

4Teachers.org. (2004). *QuizStar.* Retrieved December 1, 2004, from http://www.4teachers.org

Fox News. (2004). *Turnitin.* Retrieved December 10, 2004, from http://www.turnitin.com/static/resource_files/foxNews.wmv

French, D., & Valdes, L. (2002). Electronic accessibility practices: United States and international perspectives. *Educational Technology Review, 10*(1), Retrieved April 1, 2004, from http://www.aace.org/pubs/etr/issue2/french-a.cfm

Frick, T. W., Corry, M., & Bray, M. (1997). Preparing and managing a course Web site: Understanding systemic change in education. In B. H. Khan (Ed.), *Web-based instruction* (pp. 431–436). Englewood Cliffs, NJ: Educational Technology Publications.

Fullan, M. (1990). Staff development, innovation, and institutional development. In B. Joyce (Ed.), *Changing school culture through staff development: The 1990 ASCD Yearbook* (pp. 3–25). Alexandria, VA: ASCD.

Fullan, M., & Pomfret, A. (1977). Research on curriculum and instruction implementation. *Review of Educational Research, 47*(2), 335–397.

Gagné, R. M. (1985). *The conditions of learning and theory of instruction.* New York: Holt, Rinehart & Winston.

Gagné, R. M. (Ed.). (1987). *Instructional technology: Foundations.* Hillsdale, NJ: Lawrence Erlbaum Associates.

Gagné, R. M., Briggs, L. J., & Wager, W. W. (1992). *Principles of instructional design* (4th ed.). Orlando, FL: Harcourt, Brace, Jovanovich.

Gagné, R. M., & Medsker, K. L. (1996). *The conditions of learning: Training applications.* Fort Worth, TX: Harcourt Brace & Co.

Gagné, R. M., Wager, W., Golas, K. C., & Keller, J. M. (2005). *Principles of instructional design* (5th ed.). Belmont, CA: Wadsworth/Thomson.

Gall, M. D., Gall, J. P., & Borg, W. R. (2003). *Educational research: An introduction* (7th ed.). New York: Allyn & Bacon.

Gibbons, A. S., Lawless, K. A., Anderson, T. A., & Duffin, J. (2001). The Web and model-centered instruction. In B. H. Khan (Ed.), *Web-based training* (pp. 137–146). Englewood Cliffs, NJ: Educational Technology Publications.

Gilbert, S. D. (2001). *How to be a successful online student.* New York: McGraw-Hill.

Goto, K., & Cotler, E. (2004). *Web redesign 2.0: Workflow that works* (2nd ed.). Indianapolis, IN: New Riders.

Grabowski, B. L. (1995). Message design: Issues and trends. In G. J. Anglin (Ed.), *Instructional technology: Past, present and future* (2nd ed., pp. 222–232). Englewood, CO: Libraries Unlimited.

Greer, M. (1992). *ID project management: Tools and techniques for instructional designers and developers.* Englewood Cliffs, NJ: Educational Technology Publications.

Greer, M. (1999). Planning and managing human performance technology projects. In H. D. Stolovitch & E. J. Keeps (Eds.), *Handbook of human performance technology: Improving individual and organizational performance worldwide* (2nd ed., pp. 96–121). San Francisco: Jossey-Bass/Pfeiffer.

Gronlund, N. E. (2003). *Assessment of student achievement* (7th ed.). Boston: Pearson/Allyn & Bacon.

Gronlund, N. E. (2004). *Writing instructional objectives for teaching and assessment* (7th ed.). Upper Saddle River, NJ: Merrill/Prentice Hall.

Guba, E. G., & Lincoln, Y. S. (1989). *Fourth generation evaluation.* Newbury Park, CA: Sage.

Gunawardena, C., Plass, J., & Salisbury, M. (2001). Do we really need an online discussion group? In D. Murphy, R. Walker, & G. Webb (Eds.), *Online learning and teaching with technology: Case studies, experience and practice* (pp. 36–43). London: Kogan Page.

Gustafson, K. L. (2002). The future of instructional design. In R. A. Reiser & J. V. Dempsey (Eds.), *Trends and issues in instructional design and technology (n.p.).* Upper Saddle River, NJ: Merrill/Prentice Hall.

Gustafson, K. L., & Branch, R. M. (2003). *Survey of instructional development models* (4th ed.). Syracuse, NY: Syracuse University, ERIC Clearinghouse on Information & Technology.

Hale, J. (2002). *Performance-based evaluation.* San Francisco: Jossey-Bass/Pfeiffer.

Hall, B. (2002). *Learning management systems and learning content management systems demystified.* Retrieved March 15, 2004, from http://www.brandonhall.com/public/resources/lms_lcms/

Hall, J. P., & Gottfredson, C. A. (2001). Evaluating Web-based training: The quest for the information-age employee. In B. H. Khan (Ed.), *Web-based training* (pp. 507–514). Englewood Cliffs, NJ: Educational Technology Publications.

Hall, R. H. (2001). Web-based training site design principles: A literature review and synthesis. In B. H. Khan (Ed.), *Web-based training* (pp. 165–172). Englewood Cliffs, NJ: Educational Technology Publications.

Hall, R. H., Watkins, S. E., & Ercal, F. (2000, April). *The horse and the cart in Web-based instruction: Prevalence and efficacy.* Presentation at the annual meeting of the American Educational Research Association, New Orleans, LA.

Hallet, K., & Essex, C. (2002, June). *Evaluating online instruction: Adapting a training model to e-learning in higher education.* Paper presented at the Ed-Media 2002 World Conference on Educational Multimedia, Hypermedia & Telecommunications, Denver, CO. (ERIC Document Reproduction Service No. ED477023)

Hamel, C. J., Ryan-Jones, D. L., & Joint Advanced Distributed Co-Laboratory. (2001). *We're not designing courses anymore.* Retrieved March 29, 2003, from http://www.fcfu.ck/artikel/hamel.htm

Hannafin, M. J., & Peck, K. L. (1988). *The design, development, and evaluation of instructional software.* New York: Macmillan.

Hannum, W. H. (2001). Design and development issues in Web-based training. In B. H. Khan (Ed.), *Web-based training* (pp. 155–164). Englewood Cliffs, NJ: Educational Technology Publications.

Hannum, W. H., & Hansen, C. (1989). *Instructional systems development in large organizations.* Englewood Cliffs, NJ: Educational Technology Publications.

Harvard Business School. (2003). *Global 2000 companies rely on Harvard Business School publishing for online leadership and management training.* Retrieved April 19, 2004, from http://www.elearning.hbsp.org/news/may19.html

Haugen, B. (2003). *Learning management systems: LMS integrates with human resources.* Retrieved March 20, 2002, from http://www.entrepreneurstrategies.com/ILT_MD/LMS/lmstour2.htm

Hawkins, B. L. (1999). Distributed elearning and institutional restructuring. *Educom Review, 4*(34), n.p. Retrieved August 24, 2004, from http://www.educase.edu/ir/library/html/erm9943.html

Hawkridge, D. (2002). Distance learning and instructional design in international settings. In R. A. Reiser & J. V. Dempsey (Eds.), *Trends and issues in instructional design and technology* (pp. 269–278). Upper Saddle River, NJ: Merrill/Prentice Hall.

Hazari, S. (2001). Online testing methods in Web-based training courses. In B. H. Khan (Ed.), *Web-based training* (pp. 297–302). Englewood Cliffs, NJ: Educational Technology Publications.

Hedberg, J. C., Brown, C., Larkin, J. L., & Agostinho, S. (2001). Designing practical websites for interactive training. In B. H. Khan (Ed.), *Web-based training* (pp. 257–270). Englewood Cliffs, NJ: Educational Technology Publications.

Henke, H. (2001). *Electronic books and epublishing: A practical guide for authors.* NY: Springer.

Hill, T., & Chidambaram, L. (2000). Web-based collateral support for traditional learning: A field experience. In A. Aggarwal (Ed.), *Web-based learning and teaching technologies: Opportunities and challenges* (pp. 282–291). Hershey, PA: Idea Group.

Hillman, D. (1998). *Multimedia technology and applications.* Albany, NY: Delmar.

Hittleman, D. R., & Simon, A. J. (2002). *Interpreting educational research: An introduction for consumers of research* (3rd ed.). Upper Saddle River, NJ: Merrill/ Prentice Hall.

Horgan, B. (1998). *Faculty, instruction and information technology.* Retrieved January 18, 2001, from http://www.asia.microsoft.com/education/hed/articles/facsep98.htm

Horton, S. (2000). *Web teaching guide.* New Haven, CT: Yale University Press.

Hughes, M., & Burke, L. (2000). Usability testing of Web-based training. In B. H. Khan (Ed.), *Web-based training* (pp. 531–536). Englewood Cliffs, NJ: Educational Technology Publications.

Inspiration Software, Inc. (2005). *Inspiration® v. 7.6.* Retrieved March 4, 2005, from http://www.inspiration.com/index.cfm

Institute for Higher Education Policy. (2000). *Quality on the line: Benchmarks for success in internet-based distance education.* Washington, DC: Author.

Instructional Technology Research Center. (2004). *Storyboarding.* Morgantown, WV: West Virginia University. Retrieved November 10, 2004, from http://www.itrc.wvu.edu/coursedev/production/chapter06.html

International Webmasters Association/HTML Writers Guild. (2004). *WWW Development Resources.* Retrieved May 5, 2005, from http://www.hwg.org/resources

iParadigms, LLC. (2005a). *iThenticate.* Retrieved March 19, 2005, from http://ithenticate.com/

iParadigms, LLC. (2005b). *Turnitin.* Retrieved March 19, 2005, from http://turnitin.com/

Janis, R. (1973). *Victims of groupthink: A psychological study of foreign policy decisions and fiascos.* Boston: Houghton Mifflin.

Johnson, B., & Christenson, L. B. (2003). *Educational research quantitative, qualitative, and mixed approaches, research edition* (2nd ed.). Boston: Pearson Allyn & Bacon.

Johnson, D. W., & Johnson, R. T. (2002). *Meaningful assessment: A manageable and cooperative process.* Boston: Allyn & Bacon.

Johnson, R. B. (1997). Examining the validity structure of qualitative research. *Education, 118*(2), 282–292.

Joint ADL Co-Laboratory. (2001). *Guidelines for design and evaluation of Web-based instruction.* Orlando, FL: Institute for Simulation and Training. Retrieved January 23, 2002, from http://www.adlnet.org/adldocs/Document/guidelines.doc

Joint Committee on Standards for Educational Evaluation. (1994). *The program evaluation standards* (2nd ed.). Thousand Oaks, CA: Sage.

Joint Information Systems Committee. (2003). *E-learning and pedagogy programme.* Retrieved December 22, 2003, from http://www.jisc.ac.uk/index.cfm?name=elearning_pedagogy

Jonassen, D. H. (1992). Evaluating constructivist learning. In T. M. Duffy & D. H. Jonassen (Eds.), *Constructivism and the technology of instruction* (pp. 137–148). Mahwah, NJ: Lawrence Erlbaum Associates.

Jonassen, D. H. (1999). Designing constructivist learning environments. In C. Reigeluth (Ed.). *Instructional-design theories and models: A new paradigm of instructional theory.* (Vol. 2, pp. 215–239). Mahwah, NJ: Lawrence Erlbaum Associates.

Jonassen, D. H., & Grabinger, R. S. (1992). Applications of hypertext: Technologies for higher education. *Journal of Computing in Higher Education, 4*(2), 12–42.

Jonassen, D. H., & Grabowski, B. L. (1993). *Handbook of individual differences, learning, and instruction, Hillsdale,* NJ: Lawrence Erlbaum Associates.

Jonassen, D. H., & Hannum, W. H. (1995). Analysis of task analysis procedures. In G. J. Anglin (Ed.), *Instructional technology: Past, present, and future* (2nd ed., pp. 197–209). Englewood, CO: Libraries Unlimited.

Jonassen, D. H., Hannum, W. H., & Tessmer, M. (1989). *Handbook of task analysis procedures.* New York: Praeger.

Jones, M. G., & Farquhar, J. D. (1997). User interface design for Web-based instruction. In B. H. Khan (Ed.), *Web-based instruction* (pp. 239–244). Englewood Cliffs, NJ: Educational Technology Publications.

Jones, T. S., & Richey, R. C. (2000). Rapid prototyping methodology in action: A developmental study. *ETR&D, 48*(2), 63–80.

Jung, I. (2003). Cost-effectiveness of online education. In M. G. Moore & W. G. Anderson (Eds.), *Handbook of distance education* (pp. 717–740). Mahwah, NJ: Lawrence Erlbaum Associates.

Jupitermedia Corp. (2003). *Browser evolution.* Retrieved May 1, 2004, from http://www.jupiterresearch.com

Keller, J. M. (1987). The systematic process of motivational design. *Performance and Instruction, 26*(9–10), 1–8.

Keller, J. M. (1999). Motivational systems. In H. D. Stolovitch & E. J. Keeps (Eds.), *Handbook of human performance technology: Improving individual and organizational performance worldwide* (2nd ed., pp. 373–394). San Francisco: Jossey-Bass.

Khan, B. H. (1997). Web-based instruction: What is it and why is it? In B. H. Khan (Ed.), *Web-based instruction* (pp. 5–18). Englewood Cliffs, NJ: Educational Technology Publications.

Khan, B. H. (2001). A framework for Web-based learning. In B. H. Khan (Ed.), *Web-based training* (pp. 75–98). Englewood Cliffs, NJ: Educational Technology Publications.

Khan, B. H., & Vega, R. (1997). Factors to consider when evaluating a Web-based instruction course: A survey. In B. H. Khan (Ed.), *Web-based instruction* (pp. 375–380). Englewood Cliffs, NJ: Educational Technology Publications.

Kinshuk, & Patel, A. (2001). Implementation issues in Web-based training. In B. H. Khan (Ed.), *Web-based training* (pp. 375–380). Englewood Cliffs, NJ: Educational Technology Publications.

Kinzie, M. B., & Berdel, R. L. (1990). Effective design and utilization of hypermedia. *Educational Technology Research & Development, 38*(3), 61–68.

Kirkpatrick, D. L. (1998). *Evaluating training programs: The four levels* (2nd ed.). San Francisco: Berrett-Koehler.

Knowles, M. S., Holton, E. F., & Swanson, R. A. (1998). *The adult learner* (5th ed.). Woburn, MA: Butterworth-Heinemann.

Ko, S., & Rossen, S. (2001). *Teaching online: A practical guide.* Boston: Houghton Mifflin.

Kozulin, A. (2003). Psychological tools and mediated learning. In A. Kozulin, B. Gindis, V. Ageyev, & S. M. Miller (Eds.), *Vygotsky's educational theory in cultural context* (pp. 15–38). New York: Cambridge University Press.

Krathwohl, D. R. (2002). A revision of Bloom's taxonomy: An overview. *Theory into Practice, 41*(4), 213–218.

Krathwohl, D. R., Bloom, B. S., & Masia, B. B. (1964). *Taxonomy of educational objectives: Book 2—Affective domain.* New York: Longman.

Kraushaar, J. M., & Shirland, L. E. (1985). A prototyping method for application development by end users and information systems specialists. *MIS Quaterly,* (November), 189–197.

Kubin, L. (2002, April). *Understanding faculty productivity.* Paper presented at the Special Interest Group–Instructional Technology meeting at the Annual Meeting of the American Educational Research Association, New Orleans, LA.

Kubiszyn, T., & Borich, G. (1987). *Educational testing and measurement: Classroom application and practice* (2nd ed.). Glenview, IL: Scott, Foresman.

Lefrançois, G. R. (2000). *Theories of human learning: Kro's report* (4th ed.). Pacific Grove, CA: Brooks/Cole.

Lee, J. R., & Johnson, C. (1998). Helping higher education faculty clear instructional technology hurdles. *Educational Technology Review, 10*(Autumn/Winter), 15–17.

Leedy, P. D., & Ormrod, J. E. (2005). *Practical research: Planning and design* (8th ed.). Upper Saddle River, NJ: Merrill/Prentice Hall.

Lewis, C. (2000). Taming the lions and tigers and bears: The WRITE WAY to communicate online. In K. W. White & B. H. Weight (Eds.), *The online teaching guide: A handbook of attitudes, strategies, and techniques for the virtual classroom* (pp. 13–23). Needham Heights, MA: Allyn & Bacon.

Lin, C. H., & Davidson, G. V. (1996). Effects of linking structure and cognitive style on students' performance and attitude in a computer-based hypertext environment. *Journal of Educational Computing Research, 15*(4), 317–29.

Linn, R. O., & Gronlund, N. E. (2002). *Measurement and assessment in teaching* (8th ed.) Englewood Cliffs, NJ: Merrill/Prentice Hall.

Lohr, L. L. (2003). *Creating graphics for learning and performance: Lessons in visual literacy.* Upper Saddle River, NJ: Merrill/Prentice Hall.

Lynch, P. J., & Horton, S. (1999). *Web style guide: Basic design principles for creating Web sites.* New Haven, CT: Yale University Press.

MacKnight, C. B. (2001). Supporting critical thinking in interactive learning environments. In C. D. Maddux & D. L. Johnson (Eds.), *The Web in higher education: Assessing the impact and fulfilling the potential* (pp. 17–32). New York: Haworth.

Maddux, C. D., & Cummings, R. C. (2000). Developing Web pages as supplements to traditional courses. In B. Abbey (Ed.), *Instructional and cognitive impacts of Web-based instruction* (pp. 147–155). Hershey, PA: Idea Group.

Mager, R. F. (1997). *Preparing objectives for effective instruction* (3rd ed.). Atlanta, GA: CEP.

Malaga, R. A. (2000). Using a course Web site to enhance traditional lecture style courses: A case study and approach for site development. In A. Aggarwal (Ed.), *Web-based learning and teaching technologies: Opportunities and challenges* (pp. 293–306). Hershey, PA: Idea Group.

Marable, T. D. (1999). The role of student mentors in a precollege engineering program. In M. J. Haring & K. Freeman (Eds.), Mentoring underrepresented students in higher education [Special issue]. *Peabody Journal of Education, 74*(2), 44–54.

Maslow, A. H. (1987). *Motivation and personality* (3rd ed.). New York: Harper & Row.

Maxwell, W. E., & Kazlauskas, E. J. (1992). Which faculty development methods really work in community colleges? A review of the research. *Community/Junior College Quarterly, 16*(1), 351–360.

Mayer, R. E. (2003). *Learning and instruction.* Upper Saddle River, NJ: Merrill/Prentice Hall.

McClelland, D., Eisman, K., & Stone, T. (2000). *Web design studio secrets.* New York: John Wiley & Sons.

McLagan, P. (2002). *Change is everybody's business.* San Francisco: Berrett-Koehler.

McLellan, H. (1997). Creating virtual communities via the Web. In B. H. Khan (Ed.), *Web-based instruction* (pp. 185–212). Englewood Cliffs, NJ: Educational Technology Publications.

McMillan, J. H., & Schumacher, S. (1997). *Research in education: A conceptual introduction* (4th ed.). New York: Addison-Wesley.

Merriam, S. B., & Caffarella, R. S. (1999). *Learning in adulthood: A comprehensive guide* (2nd ed.). San Francisco: Jossey-Bass.

Merrill, M. D., Tennyson, R. D., & Posey, L. O. (1992). *Teaching concepts: An instructional design guide* (2nd ed.). Englewood Cliffs, NJ: Educational Technology Publications.

Merrill, P. F. (1987). Job and task analysis. In R. M. Gagné (Ed.), *Instructional technology: Foundations* (pp. 143–173). Hillsdale, NJ: Lawrence Erlbaum Associates.

Microsoft Corporation. (1999). *Building and using intranets and the Internet for your college or university.* Retrieved January 3, 2003, from http://www.asia.microsoft.com/education/hed/admin/solutions.intranet/

Microsoft Corporation. (2001). *Small business server 2000 getting started guide.* Retrieved May 9, 2004, from http://www.microsoft.com/technet/prodtechnol/sbs/2000/plan/guide/sbspni5k.mspx

Milheim, W. D., & Bannan-Ritland, B. (2001). Web-based training: Current status of this instructional tool. In B. H. Khan (Ed.), *Web-based training* (pp. 279–286). Englewood Cliffs, NJ: Educational Technology Publications.

Miller, G. A. (1956). The magical number seven, plus or minus two: Some limits on our capacity for processing information. *Psychological Review, 63,* 81–97.

Miller, S. M., & Miller, K. L. (2000). Theoretical and practical considerations in the design of Web-based instruction. In B. Abbey (Ed.), *Instructional and cognitive impacts of Web-based instruction* (pp. 156–177). Hershey, PA: Idea Group.

Mills, G. E. (2003). *Action research: A guide for the teacher researcher* (2nd ed.). Upper Saddle River, NJ: Merrill/Prentice Hall.

Ministry of Education. (2003). *Digital horizons: Learning through ICT* (rev. ed.). Retrieved May 1, 2004, from http://www.minedu.govt.nz/index.cfm?layout=document&documentid=9359&indexid=9320&indexparentid=1024

Moore, M. G. (1989). Three types of transaction. In M. G. Moore & C. G. Clark (Eds.), *Readings in principles of distance education* (pp. 100–105). University Park, PA: Pennsylvania State University.

Moore, M. G., & Kearsley, G. (1996). *Distance education: A system view.* New York: Wadsworth.

Morrison, G. R., Ross, S. M., & Kemp, J. E. (2004). *Designing effective instruction* (4th ed.). Hoboken, NJ: John Wiley & Sons.

Morrison, J. L. (1996). Anticipating the future. *On the Horizon, 4*(3), 2–3.

Mosley, D. C., Pietri, P. H., & Megginson, L. C. (1996). *Management: Leadership in action.* New York: Harper Collins.

Mourier, P., & Smith, M. (2001). *Conquering organizational change.* Atlanta, GA: CEP.

Neely, M. (2000). *Writing objectives for precision teaching.* Retrieved December 4, 2004, from http://www.cerleration.org/articles/writing_objectives.htm

Nicenet. (2003). Home page. Retrieved March 23, 2005, from http://nicenet.org/

Nichols, G. W. (1997). Formative evaluation of Web-based instruction. In B. H. Khan (Ed.), *Web-based instruction* (pp. 369–374). Englewood Cliffs, NJ: Educational Technology Publications.

Nielsen, J. (2000). *Designing Web usability.* Indianapolis, IN: New Riders.

Nike, Inc. (2004). *Nike time line.* Retrieved May 9, 2004, from http://www.nike.com/nikebiz/media/nike_timeline/nike_timeline.pdf

Nix, B. (2003, September). *Using technology to get more bang for your training buck!* Paper presented at the meeting of the Mobile Area for Training and Education Symposium. Summerdale, AL.

Nixon, E. K., & Lee, D. (2001). Rapid prototyping in the instructional design process. *Performance Improvement Quarterly, 14*(3), 95–116.

Norman, K. L. (2000). Desktop distance education: Personal hosting of Web courses. In A. Aggarwal (Ed.), *Web-based learning and teaching technologies: Opportunities and challenges* (pp. 117–134). Hershey, PA: Idea Group.

Northrup, P. T. (2001). A framework for designing interactivity into Web-based instruction. *Educational Technology, 41*(2), 31–39.

Northrup, P. T. (2002). Online learners' preferences for interaction. *Quarterly Review of Distance Education, 3*(2), 219–226.

Northrup, P. T., & Rasmussen, K. L. (2001). Considerations for designing Web-based programs. *Computers in the Schools, 17*(3–4), 33–46.

Northrup, P. T., Rasmussen, K. L., & Burgess, V. (2001, October). *Online learning: A survivor's guide.* Paper presented at the CNET CISO Conference, Pensacola, FL.

Northrup, P. T., Rasmussen, K. L., & Dawson, D. B. (2004). Designing and reusing learning objects to streamline Web-based instructional development. In A-M. Armstrong (Ed.), *Instructional design in the real world: A view from the trenches (n.p.).* Hershey, PA: Idea Group.

Oblinger, D. G., Barone, C. A., & Hawkins, B. L. (2001). *Distributed education and its challenges: An overview.* Retrieved September 30, 2004, from http://www.acenet.edu/bookstore/pdf/distributed-learning/distributed-learning-01.pdf

Opera Software. (2003). *Home page.* Retrieved May 4, 2004, from http://www.opera.com/

Ormrod, J. E. (2004). *Human learning* (4th ed.). Upper Saddle River, NJ: Merrill/Prentice Hall.

OTT/HPC Spider. (2003). *Office of training technology.* Retrieved March 24, 2003, from http://www.ott.navy.mil (currently http://www.spider.hpc.navy.mil/)

Palloff, R. M., & Pratt, K. (1999). *Building learning communities in cyberspace.* San Francisco: Jossey-Bass.

Palloff, R. M., & Pratt, K. (2003). *The virtual student: A profile and guide to working with online learners.* San Francisco: Jossey-Bass/John Wiley & Sons.

Parks, E. (2001). *E-tales of instructional design: Principles of effective elearning design.* Retrieved February 28, 2002, from http://www.linezine.com/3.1/features/epetid.htm

Patton, M. Q. (1990). *How to use qualitative methods in evaluation.* Newbury Park, CA: Sage.

Patton, M. Q. (2002). *Qualitative research and evaluation methods.* Thousand Oaks, CA: Sage.

Peal, D., & Wilson, B. G. (2001). Activity theory and Web-based training. In B. H. Khan (Ed.), *Web-based training* (pp. 147–154). Englewood Cliffs, NJ: Educational Technology Publications.

Persichitte, K. A. (2000). A case study of lessons learned for the Web-based educator. In B. Abbey (Ed.), *Instructional and cognitive impacts of Web-based instruction* (pp. 192–199). Hershey, PA: Idea Group.

Peters, O. (2003). Learning with new media in distance education. In M. G. Moore & W. G. Anderson (Eds.), *Handbook of distance education* (pp. 87–112). Mahwah, NJ: Lawrence Erlbaum Associates.

Phillips, P. P. (2002). *The bottomline on ROI.* Atlanta, GA: CEP.

Pintrich, P. R., & Schunk, D. H. (2002). *Motivation in education: Theory, research, and applications* (2nd ed.). Upper Saddle River, NJ: Merrill/Prentice Hall.

Pittman, V. V. (2003). Correspondence study in the American university: A second historiographic perspective. In M. G. Moore & W. G. Anderson (Eds.), *Handbook of distance education* (pp. 27–35). Mahwah, NJ: Lawrence Erlbaum Associates.

Popham, W. J. (2002). *Classroom assessment: What teachers need to know* (3rd ed.). Boston: Allyn & Bacon.

Powers, S. M., & Guan, S. (2000). Examining the range of student needs in the design and development of a Web-based course. In B. Abbey (Ed.), *Instructional and cognitive impacts of Web-based education* (pp. 200–226). Hershey, PA: Idea Group.

Ragan, T. J., & Smith, P. L. (2004). Conditions theory and models for designing instruction. In D. H. Jonasser, (ed.). *Handbook of research on educational communications and technology.* (pp. 623–649). Mahwah, NJ: Lawrence Erlbaum Associates.

Rasmussen, K. L. (2002, June). *Online mentoring: A model for supporting distant learners.* Paper presented at the annual meeting of Ed-Media 2002, Denver, CO.

Rasmussen, K. L., & Davidson, G. V. (1996, June). *Dimensions of learning styles and their influence on performance in hypermedia lessons.* Paper presented at the meetings of Ed-Media & Ed-Telecom, '96, Boston, MA.

Rasumssen, K. L., & Northrup, P. T. (2000, February). *Interaction on the Web: A framework for building learning communities.* Paper presented at the annual meeting of Association for Educational and Communications Technology, Long Beach, CA.

Rasmussen, K. L., Northrup, P. T., & Lee, R. (1997). Issues in implementation of Web-based instruction courses. In B. H. Khan (Ed.), *Web-based instruction: Development, application, and evaluation* (pp. 341–346). Englewood Cliffs, NJ: Educational Technology Publications.

Rasmussen, K. L., Northrup, P. T., & Lombardo, C. (2002, December). *Seven years of online learning.* Paper presented at the annual meeting of IITSEC, Orlando, FL.

Ravitz, J. (1997). Evaluating learning networks: A special challenge in Web-based instruction. In B. H. Khan (Ed.), *Web-based instruction* (pp. 361–368). Englewood Cliffs, NJ: Educational Technology Publications.

Real Media. (2004). *Meeting your unique streaming needs.* Retrieved April 15, 2004, from http://www.realnetworks.com/industries/index.html

Reddick, R., & King, E. (1996). *The online student: Making the grade on the Internet.* Orlando, FL: Harcourt Brace.

Reigeluth, C. M. (1987). *Instructional theories in action: Lessons illustrating selected theories and models.* Hillsdale, NJ: Lawrence Erlbaum Associates.

Reigeluth, C. M. (Ed.). (1999). *Instructional-design theories and models: A new paradigm of instructional theory* (Vol. 2). Mahwah, NJ: Lawrence Erlbaum Associates.

Reigeluth, C. M., & Garfinkle, R. J. (Eds.). (1994). *Systemic change in education.* Englewood Cliffs, NJ: Educational Technology Publications.

Riesbeck, C. K. (1996). Case-based teaching and constructivism: Carpenters and tools. In B. G. Wilson (Ed.). *Constructivist learning environments: Case studies in instructional design* (pp. 49–64). Englewood Cliffs, NJ: Educational Technology Publications.

Reiser, R. A. (2002). A history of instructional design and technology. In R. A. Reiser & J. V. Dempsey (Eds.), *Trends and issues in instructional design and technology* (pp. 26–54). Upper Saddle River, NJ: Merrill/Prentice Hall.

Reiser, R. A., & Dempsey, J. V. (Eds.). (2002). *Trends and issues in instructional design and technology.* Upper Saddle River, NJ: Merrill/Prentice Hall.

Reiser, R. A., & Dick, W. (1996). *Instructional planning: A guide for teachers* (2nd ed.), Boston: Allyn & Bacon.

Rice, J. C., Coleman, M. D., Shrader, V. E., Hall, J. P., Gibb, S. A., & McBride, R. H. (2001). Developing Web-based training for a global corporate community. In B. H. Khan (Ed.), *Web-based training* (pp. 191–202). Englewood Cliffs, NJ: Educational Technology Publications.

Richey, R. (1986). *The theoretical and conceptual bases of instructional design.* New York: Nichols.

Richey, R., & Morrison, G. (2002). Instructional design in business and industry. In R. A. Reiser & J. V. Dempsey (Eds.), *Trends and issues in instructional design and technology* (pp. 197–210). Upper Saddle River, NJ: Merrill/Prentice Hall.

Ritchie, D. C., & Hoffman, B. (1997). *Using instructional design principles to amplify learning on the World Wide Web.* Syracuse, NY: ERIC. (ERIC Document Reproduction Service No. ED415835)

Robinson, M. T. (2000). *The career planning process explained in 60 seconds.* Retrieved May 1, 2004, from http://www.careerplanner.com/Career-Articles/Career_Planning_Process.htm

Robinson, P., & Borkowski, E. Y. (2000). Faculty development for Web-based teaching: Weaving pedagogy with skills training. In A. Aggarwal (Ed.), *Web-based learning and teaching technologies: Opportunities and challenges* (pp. 216–226). Hershey, PA: Idea Group.

Romiszowski, A. J. (1981). *Designing instructional systems: Decision making in course planning and curriculum design.* London: Kogan Page.

Romiszowski, A. J. & Chang, E. (2001). A practical model for conversational Web-based training: A response from the past to the needs of the future. In B. H. Khan (Ed.), *Web-based training* (pp. 107–128). Englewood Cliffs, NJ: Educational Technology Publications.

Rosenberg, M. (2001). *E-learning: Strategies for delivering knowledge in the digital age.* New York: McGraw-Hill.

Rossett, A. (1987). *Training needs assessment*. Englewood Cliffs, NJ: Educational Technology Publications.

Rossett, A. (1999). Analysis for human performance technology. In H. D. Stolovitch & E. J. Keeps (Eds.), *Handbook of human performance technology: Improving individual and organizational performance worldwide* (2nd ed., pp. 139–162). San Francisco: Jossey-Bass/Pfeiffer.

Rossett, A. (Ed.). (2002a). *The ASTD e-learning handbook*. New York: McGraw-Hill.

Rossett, A. (2002b). From training to training and performance. In R. A. Reiser & J. V. Dempsey (Eds.), *Trends and issues in instructional design and technology* (pp. 123–132). Upper Saddle River, NJ: Merrill/Prentice Hall.

Rossi, P. H., Freeman, H. E., & Lipsey, M. W. (1999). *Evaluation: A systematic approach*. Newbury Park, CA: Sage.

Rothwell, W. J., & Kazanas, H. C. (1998). *Mastering the instructional design process: A systemic approach*. San Francisco, CA: Jossey-Bass.

Rothwell, W. J., & Kazanas, H. C. (2004). *Mastering the instructional design process: A systematic approach* (3rd ed.). San Francisco: John Wiley & Sons/Pfeiffer.

Rudd, J., Stern, K. R., & Isensee, S. (1996, January). Low vs. high fidelity prototyping debate. *Interactions*, 76–85.

Rumble, G. (2003). Modeling the costs and economics of distance education. In M. G. Moore & W. G. Anderson (Eds.), *Handbook of distance education* (pp. 703–716). Mahwah, NJ: Lawrence Erlbaum Associates.

Ryder, R. J., & Hughes, T. (1998). *Internet for educators* (2nd ed.). Upper Saddle River, NJ: Merrill.

Saettler, P. (1990). *The evolution of American educational technology*. Englewood, CO: Libraries Unlimited.

Salmon, G. (2000). *E-moderating: The key to teaching and learning online*. London: Kogan Page.

Salomon, G., & Gardner, H. (1986). The computer as educator: Lessons from television research. *Educational Researcher, 15*(10), 13–19.

Santrock, J. W. (2001). *Educational psychology*. Boston: McGraw-Hill.

Saunders, L. (1997). The multimedia learning curve can be steep. *Internet Librarian* (April), 43.

Savenye, W. C. (2004). Evaluating Web-based learning systems and software. In N. M. Seel & S. Dijkstra (Eds.), *Curriculum, plans, and processes in instructional design: International perspectives* (pp. 309–330). Mahwah, NJ: Lawrence Erlbaum Associates.

Savenye, W. C., Smith, P. L., & Davidson, G. V. (1989, October). *Teaching with technology*. Paper presented at the Conference for Experienced Faculty. Austin, TX: University of Texas at Austin.

Secretary's Commission on Achieving Necessary Skills. (1999). *Learning a living: A blueprint for high performance: A SCANS report for America 2000*. United States Department of Labor. Retrieved July 12, 2000, from http://www.ttrc.doleta.gov/SCANS/lal/LAL.HTM

Schank, R. (2002). *Designing world-class e-learning*. New York: McGraw-Hill.

Schermerhorn, J. R. (1999). *Management* (6th ed). New York: John Wiley & Sons.

Scheurman, G. (2000). From behaviorist to constructivist teaching. In D. Podell (Ed.), *Stand! Contending ideas and opinions*. Madison, WI: Coursewise.

Schouten, F. (2004). *Webcams keep suspended students on track*. Retrieved December 10, 2004, from http://www.usatoday.com/tech/webguide/internetlife/2004-01-05-class-webcams_x.htm

Schwier, R. A., & Misanchuk, E. R. (1993). *Interactive multimedia instruction*. Englewood Cliffs, NJ: Educational Technology Publications.

Seels, B. B., & Glasgow, Z. (1990). *Exercises in instructional design*. Columbus, OH: Merrill.

Seels, B. B., & Glasgow, Z. (1998). *Making instructional design decisions* (2nd ed.). Upper Saddle River, NJ: Merrill/Prentice Hall.

Seels, B. B., & Richey, R. C. (1994). *Instructional technology: The definitions and domains of the field*. Washington, DC: Association for Educational and Communications Technology.

Seufert, S., Lechner, U., & Stanoevska, K. (2002). A reference model for online learning communities. *International Journal on E-Learning, 1*(1), 43–54.

Shapiro, N. S., & Levine, J. (1999). *Creating learning communities*. San Francisco: Jossey-Bass.

Shepard, C. (2000). *Objects of interest*. Retrieved January 16, 2004, from http://www.fastract-consulting.uk/tactix/features/objects/objects.htm

Sherry, L. (1996). Issues in distance learning. *International Journal of Educational Telecommunications, 1*(4), 337–365.

Sherry, L. (2003). From literacy to mediacy: If it's on the Internet, it must be true. *Texas Study of Secondary Education, 12*(2), 19–22.

Shrock, S. A., & Coscarelli, W. (2000). *Criterion-referenced test development*. Washington, DC: ISPI.

Shrock, S. A., & Geis, L. (1999). Evaluation. In H. D. Stolovitch & E. J. Keeps (Eds.). *Handbook of human performance technology: Improving individual and organizational performance worldwide* (2nd ed., pp. 185–209). San Francisco: Jossey-Bass/Pfeiffer.

Simonson, M., Smaldino, S., Albright, M., & Zvaek, S. (2003). *Teaching and learning at a distance: Foundations of distance education* (2nd ed.). Upper Saddle River, NJ: Merrill/Prentice Hall.

Simpson, E. (1972). *The classification of educational objectives in the psychomotor domain: The psychomotor domain* (Vol. 3). Washington, DC: Gryphon House.

Singer, R. N. (1982). *The learning of motor skills.* New York: Macmillan.

Skinner, B. F. (1986). Programmed instruction revisited. *Phi Delta Kappan, 68*(2), 103–110.

Slavin, R. (1991). *Educational psychology: Theory into practice* (3rd ed.). Englewood Cliffs, NJ: Prentice Hall.

Smaldino, S., Russell, J. D., Heinich, R., & Molenda, M. (2005). *Instructional technology and media for learning* (8th ed.). Upper Saddle River, NJ: Merrill/Prentice Hall.

Smith, P. L. (1990). Beginning instructional design. Packet for course handouts, unpublished manuscript. Austin, TX: University of Texas at Austin, Fall, 1900 & Fall, 1991.

Smith, P. L., & Ragan, T. J. (1999). *Instructional design* (2nd ed.). New York: Merrill.

Smith, P. L., & Ragan, T. J. (2005). *Instructional design* (3rd ed.). Hoboken, NJ: John Wiley & Sons.

Southard, A. (2001). *Student satisfaction with the assessment of online collaborative work.* Unpublished doctoral dissertation. Pensacola, FL: University of West Florida.

Spector, J. M., & Davidsen, P. I. (2000). Designing technology enhanced learning environments. In B. Abbey (Ed.), *Instructional and cognitive impacts of Web-based instruction* (pp. 241–261). Hershey, PA: Idea Group.

Spector, J. M., & de la Teja, I. (2001). *Competencies for online teaching.* ERIC Digest, ED-99-CO-0005. Syracuse, NY: ERIC Clearinghouse on Information & Technology. Retrieved March 18, 2004, from http://www.ibstpi.org

Spitzer, D. R. (2001). Don't forget the high-touch with the high-tech in distance learning. *Educational Technology, 51*(2), 51–55.

Sprinthall, N. A., Sprinthall, R. C., & Oja, S. N. (1994). *Educational psychology: A development approach* (6th ed.). New York: McGraw Hill.

Sriwongkol, T. (2002). *Online learning: A model of factors predictive of course completion rate as viewed by online instructors.* Unpublished dissertation, University of South Alabama, Mobile, AL.

Stiggins, R. J. (2005). *Student-involved assessment FOR learning,* 4th ed. Upper Saddle River, NJ: Merrill/Prentice Hall.

Stockley, D. (2003). *E-learning definition and explanation (E-learning, online training, online learning).* Retrieved December 22, 2003, from http://derekstockley.com.au/elearning-definition.html

Stolovitch, H. D., & Keeps, E. J. (1999). What is human performance technology? In H. D. Stolovitch & E. J. Keeps, (Eds.), *Handbook of human performance technology: Improving individual and organizational performance worldwide* (2nd ed., pp. 3–24). San Francisco: Jossey-Bass/Pfeiffer.

Stringer, E. (2004). *Action research in education.* Upper Saddle River, NJ: Merrill/Prentice Hall.

Teaching and Learning in an Information Environment. (2004). *Distributed learning.* Retrieved August 24, 2004, from http://www.educ.sfu.ca/fp/title/pte/applunits/dist_learning.html

Technology, Education, and Copyright Harmonization Act. (2002). Retrieved May 8, 2004, from http://www.lib.ncsu.edu/scc/legislative/teachkit/act_text.html

Throne, D. (2001). Copyright issues in Web-based training. In B. H. Khan (Ed.), *Web-based training* (pp. 381–390). Englewood Cliffs, NJ: Educational Technology Publications.

Trentin, G. (2001). Designing online education courses. In C. D. Maddux & D. L. Johnson (Eds.), *The Web in higher education: Assessing the impact and fulfilling the potential* (pp. 47–66). New York: Haworth.

Tripp, S., & Bicklemyer, B. (1990). Rapid prototyping: An alternative instructional design strategy. *ETR&D, 38*(1), 31–44.

Tsunoda, J. S. (1992). Expertise and values: How relevant is preservice training? *New Directions for Community Colleges, 79*(Fall), 11–20.

Tweedle, S., Avis, P., Wright, J., & Waller, T. (1998). Towards criteria for evaluating Web sites. *British Journal of Educational Technology, 29*(3), 267–270.

20/20. (2004, November 19). *Plagiarism.* New York: American Broadcasting Corporation.

U.S. Army. (2003). *e.Army.U.* Retrieved March 23, 2003, from http://eArmyU.com

U.S. Coast Guard Institute. (2003). *Home page.* Retrieved December 20, 2004, from http://www.uscg.mil/hq/cgi/

U.S. Department of Commerce. (2003). *Measuring the electronic economy: 2001 E-commerce multi-sector report.* Retrieved May 8, 2004, from http://www.census.gov/eos/www/archives.html

U.S. Department of Justice. (1990). *Americans with Disabilities Act home page.* Retrieved April 10, 2004, from http://www.usdoj.gov/crt/ada/adahom1.htm

U.S. Navy. (2003). *The U.S. Navy's reusable learning objects strategy.* Retrieved March 23, 2003, from http://www.cnet.navy.mil

University of Florida. (2002). *UF computer and software requirement.* Retrieved May 8, 2004, from http://www.circa.ufl.edu/computers/

University of Illinois. (n.d.) Teaching at the Internet distance: The pedagogy of online teaching and learning. Report of a 1998–1999 University of Illinois faculty seminar. Retrieved December 18, 2003, from http://www.vpaa.uillinois.edu/reports_retreats/tid_report.asp

Van Tiem, D. M., Moseley, J. L., & Dessinger, J. C. (2001). *Performance improvement interventions: Enhancing people, processes, and organizations through performance technology.* Washington, DC: International Society for Performance Improvement.

Verduin, J. R. (1991). *Distance education: The foundations of effective practice.* San Francisco: Jossey-Bass.

Villalba, C., & Romiszowski, A. J. (2001). Current and ideal practices in designing, developing, and delivering Web-based training. In B. H. Khan (Ed.), *Web-based training* (pp. 325–342). Englewood Cliffs, NJ: Educational Technology.

Wager, W., & McKay, J. (2002). EPSS: Visions and viewpoints. In R. A. Reiser & J. V. Dempsey (Eds.), *Trends and issues in instructional design and technology* (pp. 133–144). Upper Saddle River, NJ: Merrill/Prentice Hall.

Wagner, E. D. (2001). Emerging technology trends in elearning. Retrieved February 28, 2002, from http://www.linezine.com/2.1/features/ewette.htm

Wakefield, M. A., Frasciello, M., Tatnall, L. & Conover, V. (2001). *Concurrent instructional design: How to produce online courses using a lean team approach.* ITFORUM Paper No. 56. Posted on the ITFORUM on December 1, 2001, http://it.coe.uga.edu/itforum/paper56/paper56.htm

Weiner, B. (1992). *Human motivation: Metaphors, theories, and research.* Newbury Park, CA: Sage.

Weinstein, C. E., & Mayer, R. (1986). The teaching of learning strategies. In C. Wittrock (Ed.). *Handbook of research on teaching* (3rd ed., pp. 315–327). New York: Macmillan.

Weiss, A. (2001). *The truth about servers.* Retrieved May 9, 2004, from http://www.serverwatch.com/tutorials/article.php/1354991

Welsh, T. M., & Anderson, B. L. (2001). Managing the development and evolution of Web-based training: A service bureau concept. In B. H. Khan (Ed.), *Web-based training* (pp. 251–256). Englewood Cliffs, NJ: Educational Technology Publications.

Weston, T. J., & Barker, L. (2001). Designing, implementing, and evaluating Web-based learning modules for university students. *Educational Technology, 41*(4), 15–22.

Whatis?com. (2001). *Definitions.* Retrieved April 10, 2002, from http://whatis.techtarget.com/

Whatis?com. (2005). *Definitions.* Retrieved February–April 2005, from http://whatis.techtarget.com/

Wheeler, P., Haertel, G. D., & Scriven, M. (1992). *Teacher evaluation glossary.* Kalamazoo, MI: Western Michigan University, CREATE Project, the Evaluation Center. Retrieved May 18, 2004, from http://ec.wmich.edu/glossary/glossaryList.htm

White, K. W., & Weight, B. H. (Eds.), (2000). *The online teaching guide.* Boston: Allyn & Bacon.

Willis, B. (1994). *Distance education: Strategies and tools.* Englewood Cliffs, NJ: Educational Technology Publications.

Wlodkowski, R. J. (1997). Motivation with a mission: Understanding motivation and culture in workshop design. *New Directions for Adult and Continuing Education, 76*(Winter), 19–31.

Wlodowski, R. J. (1999). *Enhancing adult motivation to learn: A comprehensive guide for teaching all adults.* San Francisco: Jossey-Bass/John Wiley & Sons.

Wlodkowski, R. J., & Ginsberg, M. B. (1995). *Diversity & motivation: Culturally responsive teaching.* San Francisco: Jossey-Bass/John Wiley & Sons.

Wood, A. F., & Smith, M. J. (2001). *Online communication: Linking technology, identify, & culture.* Mahwah, NJ: Lawrence Erlbaum Associates.

World Wide Web Consortium. (1999). *Recommendations.* Retrieved January 23, 2002, from http://www.w3.org/TR/WCAG10/

World Wide Web Consortium. (2000). *Techniques for Web content accessibility guidelines W3C note, 6 November 2000.* Retrieved January 23, 2002, from http://www.w3.org/TR/WCAG10-TECHS/

World Wide Web Consortium. (2001). *Web Accessibility Initiative (WAI).* Retrieved March 25, 2001, from http://www.w3.org/WAI/

Yoon, G. S. (1993–1994). The effects of instructional control, cognitive style, and prior knowledge on learning of computer-assisted instruction. *Journal of Educational Technology Systems, 22*(4), 357–370.

Young, J. (1997). Rethinking the role of the professor in an age of high-tech tools. *Chronicle of Higher Education* (October 3), A26–A28.

Zacbary, L. J. (2000). *The mentor's guide: Facilitating learning relationships.* San Francisco: Jossey-Bass/John Wiley & Sons.

Zastrow, J. (1997). Going the distance: Academic librarians in the virtual university. *Proceedings of the twelfth Computers in Libraries Conference.* Arlington, VA. March 10–12, n.p. Retrieved from http://library.kcc.hawaii.edu/~illdoc/de/DEpaper.htm

Zemke, R., & Kramlinger, T. (1982). *Figuring things out: A trainer's guide to needs and task analysis.* Reading, MA: Addison-Wesley.

Zhang, J., Khan, B. H., Gibbons, A. S., & Ni. Y. (2001). Review of Web-based assessment tools. In B. H. Khan (Ed.), *Web-based training* (pp. 287–296). Englewood Cliffs, NJ: Educational Technology Publications.

Zillman, M. P. (2003). *Searching the Internet using brains and bots.* Retrieved May 4, 2004, from http://internet-101.com/Zillman-Internet-Columns/february2003_newsletter.htm

Zobel, S. (1997). Legal implications of intellectual property and the World Wide Web. In B. H. Khan (Ed.), *Web-based instruction* (pp. 337–340). Englewood Cliffs, NJ: Educational Technology Publications.

Zwaga, H. J. G., Boersema, T., & Hoonhout, H. C. M. (1999). *Visual information for everyday use.* London: Taylor & Francis.

Index